INTRODUCTION TO COMPARATIVE COGNITION

A Series of Books in Psychology

Editors

Richard C. Atkinson
Gardner Lindzey
Richard F. Thompson

Introduction to Comparative Cognition

Herbert L. Roitblat

University of Hawaii at Manoa

W. H. Freeman and Company
New York

FRONT COVER: A Yerkish computer keyboard used by two chimpanzees at the Yerkes Primate Center. Each key corresponds to one lexical item. Courtesy of E. S. Savage-Rumbaugh.

Library of Congress Cataloging-in-Publication Data

Roitblat, Herbert L.
      Introduction to comparative cognition.

      Bibliography: p.
      Includes index.
      1. Cognition in animals. I. Title.
QL785.R68   1985   156'.34   86-2135
ISBN 0-7167-1778-6
ISBN 0-7167-1777-8 (pbk.)

Printed in the United States of America

1 2 3 4 5 6 7 8 9 0   MP   5 4 3 2 1 0 8 9 8 7

To my wife, Debra

Contents

x   Contents

Preface

Over the last several years there has been growing interest in a field that can be called "comparative cognition." For example, a 1976 conference held at Dalhousie University brought together many psychologists interested in a cognitive approach to explaining animal behavior. A more recent conference at Columbia University attracted a substantially larger audience. The organizers of the Columbia conference (including me) felt that the Dalhousie conference marked the birth of the field and that the Columbia conference marked its "coming of age." Many of the chapters in the volume resulting from the Dalhousie conference[1] were concerned with justifying a cognitive approach to animal behavior as useful and effective. In contrast, the chapters in the book resulting from the Columbia conference[2] were less concerned with justifying a

---

[1]Hulse, S. H., Fowler, H. S., & Honig, W. K. (1978) *Cognitive processes in animal behavior.* Hillsdale, N.J.: Erlbaum.
[2]Roitblat, H. L., Bever, T. G., & Terrace, H. S. (1984) *Animal Cognition.* Hillsdale, N.J.: Erlbaum.

cognitive approach than in using that approach to understand behavior. Although the Columbia conference appeared to show that comparative cognition was a fairly mature field, it lacked a textbook. There was no straightforward means to introduce new students to this area. This textbook was born out of a desire to meet that need.

Comparative cognition is the study of the minds of organisms and the ways in which those minds produce adaptive behaviors. It is an approach to understanding behavior that emphasizes what animals know and how they use that information in guiding their behavior. Comparative cognition seeks to understand how animals acquire, process, store, and use knowledge about their world. The material I have chosen for this book is intended to illustrate many of these processes and the representations on which they operate.

In preparing this book I have tried to choose material that demonstrates the approaches, methods, and goals of comparative cognition—the questions that workers in the field are asking, the methods they are using to answer those questions, and the range of possible answers they may find. My intention in selecting this material has been to introduce students to the tools they need to have in order to ask the important questions. As a result, the book emphasizes competing hypotheses over finished stories and solid facts. This goal has also forced me to be selective. Despite the fact that comparative cognition is a new field, more relevant material has already accumulated than can be treated comfortably in a book of moderate size. As a result, some areas of research have been left out, not because they are unimportant but simply because I could not make the book any longer than it is.

It may be useful to comment at this point on some of the things that this book is not. For example, it is not a book on the comparative intelligence of different species. I do not address questions such as "Is a dog smarter than a pig?" Psychologists have found questions like this one to be very problematical. When tested on tasks that are relevant to the animal's ecological niche, most animals appear intelligent, yet when tested on other tasks, these same animals may appear quite stupid. In addition, there seems not to be any simple dimension along which to compare animals' intelligence. The relative intelligence of animals depends very strongly on the methods one uses in studying intelligence.

Second, this is not a book about animal consciousness or animal awareness. I do not address questions like "What is it like experientially to be a bat?" "What does my dog think about when it dreams?" "Does a mouse have self-awareness?" Questions such as these have their place in the complete development of an animal psychology, but they are not the main interest of the investigations I report. With respect to issues such as consciousness and self-awareness, the approach taken in this book is similar to that ordinarily found in the study of human cognition. We can describe many of the characteristics of cognitive processes without becoming bogged down in whether these processes are conscious or unconscious.

I have assumed that the typical reader of this book is an advanced undergraduate who has had at least one course in what has traditionally been called animal learning. For example, I expect the reader to be familiar with the general facts of classical and instrumental conditioning and the standard methods for studying discriminations. Students lacking this background would benefit from a quick examination of one of the textbooks listed below.

Davey, G. (1981) *Animal learning and conditioning.* Baltimore: University Park Press.

Domjan, M., & Burkhard, B. (1986) *The principles of learning and behavior.* Monterey, Calif.: Brooks/Cole.

Flaherty, C. (1985) *Animal learning and cognition.* New York: Knopf.

Schwartz, B. (1984) *The psychology of learning and behavior.* New York: Norton.

Tarpy, R. M. (1982) *Principles of animal learning and motivation.* Glenview, Ill.: Scott, Foresman.

AN OVERVIEW OF THE BOOK

Chapter 1 defines comparative cognition and describes many of its basic assumptions and concepts, its relation to other fields of enquiry, and its methods. Briefly, comparative cognition is characterized as a subfield of cognitive science with ties to other approaches to the study of behavior, such as ethology and neuroscience.

Chapter 2 presents an overview of the historical roots of comparative cognition. I trace its development from early conceptualizations of the evolution of mind and the continuity of mental life among species through the experimental analysis of behavior and into behaviorism. Also described are important conceptual and methodological differences between the cognitive and the behaviorist approaches to understanding behavior.

In Chapter 3, I discuss attention and related processes. Many of the topics appearing in Chapter 3 are traditionally covered under the heading of stimulus control. Here I discuss the cognitive mechanisms—their nature and their operation—that appear to underlie stimulus control. Animals show selectivity in the stimuli to which they respond. In some cases, this selectivity seems to be the result of learning that some stimuli are relevant and others are irrelevant. When time to process information is limited, however, animals also seem to show selectivity that derives from limits on the speed with which they can process information.

Chapters 4 and 5 discuss memory. Chapter 4 begins by considering some of the many different kinds of systems animals could use when they remember information. It then proceeds to a cognitive analysis of classical conditioning in terms of an expectancy model. Instrumental learning is also considered in this chapter in terms of a hierarchical control system.

Chapter 5 discusses working memory, the kind of memory an organism uses to remember information about ongoing events. Work with a radial arm maze and with the delayed matching-to-sample procedure are described. The chapter presents detailed models of both tasks and compares those models with alternative views.

Chapter 6 discusses work on timing and serial order. Animals time the duration of events using an internal clock that shares many properties with a stopwatch. They are also capable of coherent sequence representations involving the simultaneous representation of events and information about their order.

Chapter 7 concerns the role of cognition in "natural" behavior. Its primary focus is on foraging. I discuss the cognitive processes by which animals find food and some of the processes by which certain animals avoid becoming food. The chapter concludes with a consideration of the vocal communication of vervet monkeys and its implications for comparative cognition.

Finally, Chapter 8 considers the attempts to teach apes and other animals a form of human language. It also examines some of the effects that this type of training has on the other cognitive capacities of the trained apes, especially on their ability to acquire conceptual categories.

ACKNOWLEDGMENTS

Many people helped in the preparation of this book. Among the colleagues who read part or all of the manuscript are Thomas Bever, William Gordon, Werner Honig, Edward Manier, David Olton, Duane Rumbaugh, Robert Scopatz, and John Staddon. I also wish to thank the students who encouraged me to write cogently. While preparing this book I was supported by grants from the National Science Foundation and the National Institutes of Mental Health. I thank them for their assistance. Finally, I thank my wife and son for their support during this long project.

INTRODUCTION TO COMPARATIVE COGNITION

CHAPTER 1

Introduction

Science is essentially a puzzle-solving activity. Surrounded by bits and pieces of information in the world around us, we struggle to find all of the pieces, struggle to make sense of them, and struggle to fit them together. As with a jigsaw puzzle, the way in which we try the pieces against one another depends largely on the picture we expect the finished puzzle to resemble. A new picture of animals and their behavior has begun to emerge over the last couple of decades. Instead of thinking about animals as if they were simple reflexive automata or response emitters, many psychologists have begun to think of them as active processors of information. This new picture is the basis for the growing field of comparative cognition. This book is an introduction to that field, its methods, and some of its findings.

WHAT IS COMPARATIVE COGNITION?

Comparative cognition is the study of the minds of organisms. Mind is the set of cognitive structures, processes, skills, and representations that intervene between experience and behavior. Comparative cognition views animals as intelligent processors of information capable of adapting to their environments through expression of varied cognitive skills. These skills include learning, remembering, problem solving, rule and concept formation, perception, recognition, and others. Comparative cognition seeks to explain behavior in terms of the skills, representations, and processes that organisms use as they interact with their environment.

Comparative cognition in relation to other fields

Comparative cognition is the product of the convergence of four fields of enquiry. Table 1.1 lists each of them along with some of its characteristic questions.

Comparative psychology. As part of comparative psychology, comparative cognition is concerned with comparing the cognitive processes and capacities of multiple species. By examining species side by side we can learn about the features of cognition that are unique to the particular species versus those features that are shared by all species performing similar tasks. By examining the correlations across species of various cognitive skills, we can learn whether these skills are produced in different species by one common mechanism, or whether they are produced by separate, independent mechanisms. The variety we see among species also helps in developing alternative competing explanations. Species may differ not only in what they are capable of doing, but also in the

TABLE 1.1 Parent fields of comparative cognition

Parent field	Characteristic questions
Comparative psychology	How does the behavior of one species compare with that of another, particularly when the other is human? How does behavior relate to the evolution, development, and ecology, of the species? How does the behavior contribute to the organism's survival and reproduction?
Ethology and behavioral ecology	How does behavior evolve? What are the functions fulfilled by behavior? What are the immediate causes of behavior? How is the animal's behavior a specific adaptation to its ecological niche?
Neuroscience	What is the structure of the brain? How does it relate to mental function? What is the relationship between brain structure and mental function? What is the function of parts of the animal brain? How does the brain control behavior?
Cognitive science	What are the structures and processes of the mind? How does an organism represent experience and process the information in those representations? What processes do organisms have for creating, storing, maintaining, retrieving, and using the information contained in representations?

mechanisms they use to implement those capacities. By examining different species, we can begin to understand the implications of possibly different cognitive mechanisms and capacities.

Although comparative cognition is interested in studying many species, the relationship between human and animal cognition is especially important.[1] By analyzing the similarities and differences in the cognitive processes of humans and nonhumans, we gain perspective and insight into both. For example, in discussing the scientific analysis of human language, Miller suggests:

> One way is to look at human language as a particular form of communication, among many alternative varieties. If we can see it side by side with other forms of communication, we will have taken the first step toward putting it in scientific perspective. (Miller, 1981, p. 11)

A similar approach may be useful in analyzing other cognitive systems. We are all so intimately familiar with the processes of our own cognition that it is difficult to examine it objectively. Studying cognitive processes in other, less intimately familiar animals helps to put those processes in perspective and promotes the objective analysis of our own process as a particular form of cognition among many alternative varieties. Seeing two systems (e.g., two species) side by side helps to understand both.

Ethology and behavioral ecology.   As part of ethology and behavioral ecology, comparative cognition is concerned with the relationship between evolution and ecology on the one hand and animals' cognitive capacities on the other. Each species' cognitive capacities presumably contribute to its survival and reproduction. Comparative cognition is concerned with identifying exactly how the capacities observed in a species function to promote its survival. Similarly, we should expect evolution to favor the development in a species of capacities that are appropriate to the species' ecological niche. Knowledge of a species' evolutionary history and ecology, then, can help us to predict and identify its cognitive capacities. Understanding the interplay between cognitive capacities and ecology makes it easier to analyze the functions of an organism's cognitive capacities and helps us to understand how the organism makes its living.

Neuroscience.   As part of neuroscience, comparative cognition is concerned with the brain mechanisms that are responsible for cognitive processes. Neuroscience seeks to understand the neurophysiological mechanisms that underlie behavior. Understanding the relation between brain mechanisms and behavior requires that we understand both the brain mechanisms and the behavior they presumably produce. Inadequate knowledge about either mechanisms or behavior puts in jeopardy the entire attempt to explain their relationship. Since cognitive processes are brain functions,[2] comparative cognition can increase our understanding of brain mechanisms by contributing to their functional analysis.

Until recently, many neuroscientists concentrated on restricted sets of behavioral tasks and on a simplistic view of animal behavior derived largely from the behaviorist tradition (see Chapter 2). By accepting such a view, these neuroscientists limited themselves to searching for simplistic, and perhaps fundamentally inappropriate, brain mechanisms. More important, acceptance of this view also led to doubts about the relevance of a neuroscience of nonhumans to understanding the brain mechanisms of human behavior (Norman, 1973). More recently, however, some investigators have begun to take note of the advances in the cognitive analysis of animal behavior and to use these advances as a guide in brain research. The continued development of neuroscience, because it relies so heavily on animal "models," depends on the continued development of adequate functional analyses of animal cognition. Similarly, studies of animal behavior have been inadequately informed by neuroscientific investigations. The behavior of neurons, as much as the behavior of whole organisms, is an important source of data for developing cognitive theories.

Cognitive science.   As part of cognitive science, comparative cognition serves the broader field as a bridge between neuroscience and human cognition, as a source of alternative viewpoints, and as an independent and distinctly biological approach to the study of the representation of knowledge. One of the central notions in cognitive science, and in comparative cognition, is the idea of representation. External events and objects do not enter the mind directly, but are represented there according to certain types of codes (see Roitblat, 1982). Another central notion is that processes intervene between experience and behavior and are modified by them. Each process takes time and operates on the outputs of previous processes. Cognitive theorists use the process concept in various ways to conceptualize the sequence of mental activities that intervene between events and behavior.

In the late 1960s and early 1970s, many cognitive psychologists accepted a general "stages-of-processing" view of cognition (Atkinson & Shiffrin, 1968; Broadbent, 1958). In this view, processing proceeds in discrete stages from sensory input to long-term memory or response production. Environmental information enters through a sensory buffer. It then is processed in short-term memory and eventually stored in long-term memory. In recent years this discrete stages view has been recognized as too simplistic (e.g., Craik & Lockhart, 1972). Cognitive functioning is often difficult to divide into discrete stages; it is difficult to discriminate where one stage ends and another stage begins, and it is difficult to determine a strictly linear ordering of stages. As a result, cognitive science has evolved a more interactive view of cognitive processing, including both sensory-driven and concept-driven processes. *Sensory-driven* processes, also called bottom-up processes, begin with the input of raw sensory information and allow this raw information to determine the nature of subsequent processing. *Concept-driven* processes, also called top-down processes, analyze the information presented in the raw sensory array in a manner directed by the organism's knowledge and expectancies. Current theories of cognition include many types of interactions between top-down and bottom-up processing.

Cognitive scientists seek to study the representation of knowledge, the nature of the processes that operate on those representations, and the causal order among those processes. The goal is to learn how these cognitive processes and representations mediate between experience and behavior.

Thinking and consciousness

Thinking and consciousness have long been problematic terms for psychology, and for comparative psychology in particular. Neither term has a universally acceptable definition. For present purposes it is sufficient to define thinking as the processing of information or the employment of cognitive skills. Similarly, for present purposes it may be adequate to define consciousness as a cognitive process that refers to other cognitive processes (a kind of metaprocess). By this definition, consciousness is simply one cognitive process among many. It need have no special status, except that, instead of referring to behaviors or external events, as other cognitive processes do, its content (defined below) is simply the organism's other cognitive processes. Similarly, by these definitions, thinking does not imply consciousness, but consciousness implies thinking. Specifically, it implies thinking about thinking. (See Griffin, 1984, and Walker, 1983, for different, though related views of thinking and consciousness in animals.)

Neither of these definitions is entirely satisfactory, but however thinking and consciousness are defined, something is clearly going on within the heads of behaving organisms. The task for comparative cognition, and for cognitive science in general, is to describe that something, whatever it might be.

Comparative cognition does not seek to prove or disprove the existence of minds in animals. An animal that behaves in a certain way is not doing so because it has a mind. It behaves as it does because of the particular representations and the particular processes it has for dealing with them. The question is not: Does this animal have a mind?; it is: Why does this animal have this particular mind and not others? How has the animal's mind come to function as it does?

Information and information processing

A main focus of comparative cognition is the analysis of organisms and their behavior in terms of information processing. For example, Estes has argued that

> Just as the physical sciences can be conceived as the study of energy in its many
> aspects, the behavioral and social sciences can be characterized in terms of their
> concern with the processing and transformation of information. The scientific study of
> the processing of information on a short time scale [as opposed to the scale used to
> measure evolutionary changes] defines the field of learning and cognitive psychology.
> (Estes, 1975, p. 1)

The conceptualization of psychology as an information science rather than a physical science has important implications.[3] When psychology is conceptualized as a physical science (analogous to biology or physics), the goal is to analyze the physical properties of situations and behaviors and thereby to induce general principles that relate physically defined changes in the environment to physically defined changes in behavior. For example, a question appropriate to psychology when viewed as a physical science might be: What properties must a stimulus have to be a reinforcer? When psychology is conceptualized as an information science, the goal is to analyze the informational properties of situations and behaviors and to infer the information-processing mechanisms and structures that underlie the relationship between environmental and behavioral factors. For example, a question appropriate to psychology when viewed as an information science might be: What does an organism have to know to solve a problem?

The information-processing view depends on the assumption that physically distinct behaviors nevertheless share something important when they both serve to accomplish the same goal or when they are similarly affected by a certain experience. For example, the movements used in typewriting are very different from those used in writing with a pen and ink, yet the message, in this case the text being written, can be identical in the two forms of writing. The two forms of writing are distinctly different in terms of their physical properties—the movements used to produce them—but are substantially identical in their informational properties—the message being written. Psychology as a physical science emphasizes the physical properties of the behavior and seeks to develop general principles relating the writing situation to the movements used in writing. Psychology as an information science emphasizes the message being written and seeks to explain the content of the text as a function of the writing situation.

The concept of information derives from a theory developed in the 1940s (Shannon, 1948). Information theory provides an abstract mathematical system for discussing stimuli, messages, and knowledge that is independent of their physical characteristics. The basic idea in information theory is the concept of a communication channel. A communication channel transmits information from a source to a destination. The source is the sender and the destination is the receiver. For example, if you were trying to transmit over a telephone line the spelling of some word, you, the sender, would "choose" one of the 26 letters in the alphabet and transmit this letter over the phone line to your friend, the receiver. Information would be transmitted to the extent that your friend chose the same letter that you chose to send. In fact, the theory is much more general than this and can be applied to any conceivable kind of communication system. Informally, information is knowledge. When you receive or obtain information, you know more than you knew before; you are less uncertain about the world.

Information theory also specifies a way to measure the commodity being transmitted over the communication channel. The receiver was initially uncertain as to which letter would be sent over the communication channel. After the message was received, however, your friend was no longer uncertain. The letter was now known; therefore, uncertainty was reduced. The amount of information in a message is the extent to which that message reduces uncertainty when it is received. This amount is measured in *bits* (binary digits). A bit is exactly the amount of information needed to decide between two equally probable events. It is the information necessary to answer a yes/no question when the yes answer is just as likely to be correct as the no answer. For example, if I toss a coin, it could have either its head or its tail on top. Because heads and tails are equally probable outcomes, there is exactly one bit of uncertainty regarding the current status of the coin. Therefore, finding out whether the head or the tail side was showing after the flip would provide you with exactly one bit of information. Similarly, if there were eight possible alternatives, finding out which of those alternatives was correct would provide 3 bits of information. For example, if I were thinking of a number between 1 and 8, the most efficient questioning strategy would take three yes/no questions to guess the number. Each successive question would divide the alternatives in half (i.e., each answer would provide one bit of information). The first question might be: Is the number less than 5? If the answer to that question is yes (then $x = 1$, 2, 3, or 4), then the next question could be: Is the number less than 3? If the answer to that question is no (then $x = 3$ or 4), then the next question could be: Is the number 4? If the answer to this question is yes, then the number has been guessed. If the answer is no, the answer is still known: the number is 3.

One advantage of using the approach suggested by information theory is that it highlights the fact that the information in a message remains the same when the message changes from one medium to another. The amount of information in a message depends on the way in which it reduces uncertainty, not on its physical characteristics. The information in a message would be the same whether it was handwritten, typed, telegraphed, or radioed. Information is abstract. Although it is always represented in one physical medium or another, the information is independent of the medium. For example, the information in a message remains the same, even if the medium changes from writing to speaking.

The concept of information had an important impact when it was introduced to psychology because it provided a way to talk about knowledge in an abstract, but mathematically precise form, which is independent of the physical properties of its storage and expression. It suggested that knowledge could be studied scientifically, even if we did not yet know the physical mechanisms responsible.

By emphasizing the informational aspects of cognitive phenomena, cognitive scientists do not seek to deny that the information is contained within the physical medium of the nervous activity of the brain. Cognitive scientists recognize that different combinations of physical activity can result in identical cognitive effects. Mental activity is not supernatural or mystical; it is a property derived from the organization, structure, and operation of the brain. If experience at one time is to affect behavior at another, then information from the experience must endure as a temporal bridge between the event and the behavior. That information must be contained in some medium. When the information is maintained within the organism's nervous system, we say that the organism has learned or remembered the information.

Broadbent's model.   The development of information theory also led to the idea that cognition, and especially memory, could be considered as a communication channel between the inputs of experience and the outputs of behavior. Donald Broadbent was one of the first to bring this insight to bear on cognitive psychology. Broadbent (1958) proposed that information flows through a number of general memory systems. Information from the environment is received in a preattentive store called the *s-system*. Information is then filtered and some of it is then passed into the *p-system*, which has a limited capacity; the rest is lost. The combination of the p- and the s-systems make up immediate, primary, or short-term memory. Rehearsal maintains information in immediate memory by circulating it from the p-system back to the s-system and back into the p-system. Without rehearsal, information begins to decay. Information from the s- and the p-systems can also be transferred into secondary, or long-term, memory, which has unlimited capacity.

Broadbent's model influenced virtually every approach to cognition that followed it. Four of its assumptions remain particularly influential (though not universally accepted). These are that (1) primary and secondary memory involve different memory systems, (2) primary memory is of limited capacity and secondary, or long-term, memory is of unlimited capacity, (3) there is a selective channel, of limited capacity, controlling the information that is allowed into primary and secondary memory, and (4) information in primary memory must be rehearsed or it is lost.

Limited information-processing capacity.   Miller (1956) compiled evidence that primary memory did actually have a limited capacity that was consistent, and more or less independent of the type of stimuli that were being remembered.

He noticed that discriminations involving a wide variety of stimuli and a wide variety of measurement methods all showed a common limitation. If the stimuli to be discriminated vary along only a single dimension, then people are capable of discriminating without error only about seven alternatives, plus or minus two. If more categories are provided, people can convey no more information about the stimuli being discriminated than they can if only seven categories are used (i.e., there is more uncertainty within each category and more confusions between categories). Similarly, people are generally capable of maintaining only about seven unrelated digits in memory at one time (that is why a local phone number has exactly seven digits). This "magical number 7" was observed in many different types of tasks and appeared to reflect a fundamental limit on the capacity of primary memory. This finding greatly encouraged psychologists to think in terms of information processing.

Contribution from computer science and mathematical logic. The importance of information as a means to talk about knowledge was further encouraged by developments within computer science. Computers had begun to be available both as computational tools and as a potential metaphor for the mind. Computer scientists were developing programs that allowed computers to function as general symbol-manipulating devices capable of simulating some functions of the mind. (See Hodges, 1983, for an interesting, if biased, history of this development.) Recognizing the potential in the computer metaphor, Newell, Simon, and Shaw (1958) proposed that the mind is an example of a general symbol-manipulation system just as the computer can be an example of a general symbol-manipulation system.[4]

The use of a computer as a metaphor for the mind has often been misunderstood. The argument is not that the mind and computer are equivalent, rather it is that they are both instances of the same kind of general device. In order to understand this point, it is necessary to consider some of the history of the concept of a general symbol-manipulation system. This notion is derived, in part, from developments within the mathematical logic of abstract automata. For example, in a seminal paper, Turing (1936) proposed a notion of a "universal machine." A universal machine is a mathematical system (or set of rules) containing only a limited (though perhaps large) number of possible operations, such as read a symbol, write a symbol, scan over a list of symbols; a limited number of types of symbols; and a limited number of internal states. Turing conceived of the machine as having an external memory, such as a tape, with symbols marked on it. The machine can either read or write a symbol, or it can move from one location on the tape to another. Later conceptualizations of the universal machine included more complex external memories. The nature of the external memory affects only the speed, not the principle of operation of the machine. In addition to its external memory, Turing also proposed that the machine has an internal memory, which can be in any one of a limited, though perhaps large, number of possible states at a time. The sequence of the machine's operation is determined completely by its rules for operation, the symbol it is currently reading, and its current internal state. Turing showed that any definite (computable) process can be described in an instruction table of finite length and implemented on a universal machine in a finite amount of time.

A universal machine is concrete in that its rules of operation are specific and the machine can be built. It is also abstract in the following sense: (1) It is described in terms of its mathematical and logical functions, not in terms of the electronics and mechanics used to build it. (2) Machines with equivalent sets of operations are equivalent machines, even though they may be built with very different components. The rules of their operation, not their mechanics, define the equivalence of machines. (3) Machines operate on symbols, not on objects in the world. Different objects, if represented by the same symbols, can be processed equivalently, so the machines are very general. The machines emphasize the processing of information, not of objects.

Modern digital computers qualify as universal machines.[5] They operate on symbols (e.g., magnetic fluxes on a tape or disk, holes punched into cards, ones and zeroes); in practice, these symbols represent objects in the real world. Computers physically exist, but they are defined by their operations (e.g., IBM-compatible personal computers), not by the particular patterns of wires and so forth from which they are constructed. Depending on its programming (i.e., its list of instructions), a computer is able to deal with an unspecified variety of different types of objects in an indefinite variety of situations and tasks.

The mind also qualifies as a universal machine. It operates on symbols, has access to a limited number of fundamental operations, and so forth. The mind is physically built out of neurons, but defined (at least within cognitive science) by its operations. The mind is also able to deal with an indefinite variety of objects in an indefinite variety of situations and tasks. No computer is yet equivalent to the mind. Current digital computers tend to operate serially on one element at a time, whereas the mind seems to operate extensively in parallel, performing many operations simultaneously (e.g., Hinton & Anderson, 1981). Nevertheless, they both qualify in interesting ways as examples of the kind of machine Turing envisioned.

The analogy between the mind and universal machines revolutionized the way many psychologists think about their field. Among its more important results was that they began to use the language of mathematical logic. Mathematical logic developed as an objective, formal system with explicit standards for validity and consistency. It could be applied to any number of different kinds of problems, and it was unquestionably scientific. Mathematical logic held the promise of allowing an information-based approach to psychology that could, in principle at least, be as abstract as mathematics and as rigorous as any of the physical sciences. The earliest computers made it clear that the abstract functions of mathematical logic could be applied to actual machines. Real machines could be built that would perform the functions of mathematical logic. These same machines could also be described in the language of mathematical logic. Most important for psychology, the same kind of language used to describe machines of known design could also be used to develop theoretical descriptions of machines whose physical design was unknown. The computational analogy between computers and minds as examples of symbol-manipulating machines could then be used to test these theories. If a computer programmed with all of the relevant assumptions of the theory did not mimic the behavior of the organism, then the theory was either wrong or incomplete. In either case it would have to be changed.

Finally, the analogy between minds and universal machines led to the notion that the mind is not static but rather consists of computations and operations that are changeable, sometimes even under the control of the machine itself.

REPRESENTATION

The operations of a symbol-manipulating machine, such as a computer or a mind, are defined relative to the symbols used by the machine, not relative to the objects that those symbols represent. (For example, addition is defined relative to numbers, not relative to the apples or oranges those numbers symbolize.) In principle, a given symbol can stand for any number of different objects, events, or features in the world. How the machine treats the symbols depends on the nature of its processes and the nature of the symbols, not on what the symbols represent. The relationship between the symbols and the objects is the problem of representation.

For example, a computer might be used to calculate the orbital track of the space shuttle. The shuttle itself is not, of course, entered into the computer; rather, a set of numbers representing various features of the shuttle, such as its mass, is entered. The number 692 (in its binary form) might represent the number of seconds of thrust available, the number of orbits the shuttle will make, or the number of calories in the apple pie the astronauts will have for their second dinner. Similarly, the computer does not perform operations on the space shuttle itself, such as increasing its speed. Instead, it performs symbolic operations such as addition, subtraction, logical-and, and so forth. These operations are organized into a process, usually called a program, that specifies certain relationships between sets of numbers in the form of equations and the operations that are to be performed on those numbers. Parameters of the equations stand for properties of the space shuttle, the laws of gravitation, and so forth. By allowing the computer to perform the operations for which it is programmed, we can have it symbolically report the orbital track of the space shuttle.

The same numbers in the computer could just as well stand for the list of supplies needed by the shuttle crew. The number 692 could stand for the 692d item in the list of space-shuttle supplies. A different program would provide different sets of operations, which could then treat these same numbers as representations of supplies, rather than as representations of the shuttle's mass, and so forth. The relations between the numbers in the computer's memory and the objects of the world are determined by the processes that enter those numbers into the computer's memory and the processes that operate on them.

Representation is one of the central concepts of cognitive science, so understanding the concept is important. A symbol is a representation of an object if it provides information about that object. A symbol can "stand for" an object in many ways. Some of these are very simple. For example, a system might have a code (e.g., a number, a pattern, a set of neurons firing at a specific rate) for the color of an object, another for its height, another for its shape, and so forth. The representation of the object in the system is the list of codes corresponding to its features. In this system there is a one-to-one correspondence between features of the representation (the codes for its color, shape, etc.) and its features (its color, shape, etc.). Each feature of the object is represented by a single value of the corresponding code in the representation. Other representations involve more complex coding relationships, in which one feature of the representation stands for many features of the object. For example, your name represents you in some sense; among other things, it provides information that we are talking about you and not someone else. A certain pattern of letters and spaces represents all of your features, eye color, height, bank balance, and so forth, provided that an appropriate process is available to interpret this representation (e.g., by giving an index into other lists). No clear relationship exists between the features of the representation (the letters in your name) and the features of the object they represent (you). Similarly, most of the items sold in the supermarket are marked with a special bar code called the "Universal Product Code." The bars of this code can be translated into a number that stands for the manufacturer and for the specific product. The bars do not directly reflect the ingredients of the product. Figure 1.1 shows the code from two different cans of tuna. Although both cans contain exactly the same ingredients, the codes representing those cans are distinctly different from one another. Many supermarkets have scanners at their checkout counters that can read the bars and transmit the number to the store's computer. The pattern of bars represents the product you are buying.

Figure 1.1. Two Universal Product Code labels from two different brands of tuna. Although both cans have identical ingredients, they are represented by very different codes.

The features of representations

Because of the potential complexity of representations, a complete specification of a representational system requires the specification of five different types of features: its domain, content, code, medium, and dynamics. A theory of the representations used by an animal must specify each of these features.

The *domain* of a representation is the limited class of situations or tasks in which the representation is used and to which it applies. A representation can be useful in only one situation, or it may have general use over a wide range of situations. The range of situations in which it is useful is the domain of the representational system. For example, the kind of representation that might be useful in a multiple-choice exam, in which you must simply recognize the correct answer, may be different from that which would be useful for an essay exam, in which you must know topics to a greater "depth" and organization in order to produce a coherent essay. The point is that some representations may be useful in some tasks because they encode the information in a convenient manner (e.g., for a multiple-choice versus for an essay exam), or because they preserve distinctions that are uniquely important to those tasks.[6] That same representation, however, may not be useful in other tasks because the coding scheme is not adapted to the task, perhaps because distinctions are preserved that are irrelevant to the performance of the task. We must specify the domain of a representational system because organisms may have different representational systems that are specifically adapted to different tasks.

The *content* of a representation consists of the particular features of the represented experience that are preserved in the representation and the information that can be derived from it. Organisms have only a limited capacity to process information. Not every feature of every object is represented. Consider, for example, the eye color of the last person who served you in a restaurant. Unless that waiter or waitress had particularly striking eyes or you had some other reason for attending to his or her eye color, you probably cannot say what that color was. Most likely it was not relevant to your needs. In general, representations are limited in the number and kinds of features they preserve.

The *code* of a representation specifies the relationship between features of the representation and features of the experience. The book you are reading consists primarily of paper on which certain patterns of ink-spots have been deposited. The pattern of ink-spots represents words that could also be spoken, taped, or recorded in some other form. Writing and reading are processes of translation. Writing encodes ideas or speech sounds into a representation consisting of ink on paper. Reading reverses this translation process, encoding the pattern of ink into speech sounds or ideas. A code is useless without a coding process.[7] Part of the assumption of the information-processing approach to cognition is that the symbols of the system can stand for an undetermined number of different objects in the world. The particular objects, or features of objects, for which they do stand is the product of their coding relationship. For example, during visual perception the pattern of light falling on the retina is *transduced* into a pattern of neural signals. These neural signals are the code for the pattern of light. They are subsequently translated in various ways, for example, into codes for the object that reflected that pattern of light and dark onto the eye.

The *medium* of a representation is the physical stuff of which a representation is made. For example, information identifying a can of tuna can be in the form of magnetic fluxes on a revolving disk, of voltage states in a microchip, or of printed bars on the side of the can. The content of a message does not change when the medium of its transmission changes, nor does the content of a representation change when its medium changes. All messages must be in some kind of medium at all times, but the medium does not itself provide information about the message or the experience being represented. It merely supports, the way paper supports ink, the information-carrying aspect of the representation. A text would have the same meaning if it were written by hand on a piece of notebook paper, typewritten on typing paper, recorded on a cassette recorder, or photographed on microfilm. To be sure, some features of the information change or are lost when the medium changes: tape recordings of music often do not record the high frequencies of live music; translation processes are not always perfect. Nevertheless, the information about features in which we are interested, such as the meaning of a text, is maintained or the representation becomes useless.

Cognitive representations are in the neural medium of the organism's nervous system. Experience changes the organism's nervous system in specific, if still unknown ways. Representational systems also exist, however, in other media such as magnetic tape, photographs, electrical impulses, marks on paper. These other media are sometimes used as external representations by information-processing systems.

The *dynamics* of a representation pertain to its changes over time. Representations cannot be considered in isolation of the processes that interpret and modify them. Of particular interest are the means by which representations come into being (are encoded), change, and in some systems, cease to exist (e.g., are forgotten).

THE METHODS OF COMPARATIVE COGNITION

When we seek to develop a theory of the cognitive system used by an animal, we cannot examine directly the representations and processes that make up that system. Rather, we infer their structure and function from the effects they have on behavior. Quite powerful inferences are possible by carefully combining effective tasks with sophisticated analysis of the resulting behavior. For example, in a series of experiments by Shepard and Metzler (1971), people were shown pairs of line drawings depicting three-dimensional objects made from connected cubes. An example of some of these figures is shown in Figure 1.2. Subjects were asked to judge whether two figures depicted different objects or the same object at different orientations. They were asked to respond as quickly as possible.

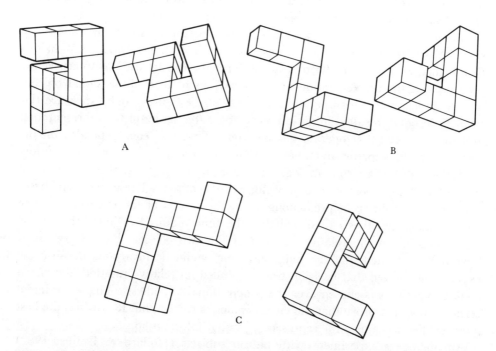

Figure 1.2. Stimuli used by Shepard and Metzler (1971). (A) Two "same" stimuli: one is rotated 80 degrees in the picture plane relative to the other. (B) Two "same" stimuli: one is rotated 80 degrees in depth relative to the other. (C) Two "different" stimuli that cannot be matched by any rotation. [From Shepard & Metzler, 1981.]

Shepard and Metzler found that the speed with which the subjects responded "same" depended on the angular rotation of the two objects relative to one another. Figures could be rotated up to 180 degrees, and the latency to respond was proportional to the amount of rotation. Shepard and Metzler concluded from this that the subjects were "mentally rotating" an image of one of the figures to match the orientation of the other. This mental rotation took more time the further the figure had to be rotated. They argued, in other words, that within the domain tested by their experiment, the people were representing the objects depicted by the line drawings in a representation coded as an image. The dynamics of this representation system included a process that could "rotate the image."

The finding that the time necessary to respond was a function of the difference in the orientation of the two stimuli limited the kinds of codes that the people could plausibly be using to represent the figures. It is difficult to think of a representation system that does not involve images, but whose decision time depends on the degree of rotation of the two objects relative to one another. Rather, the most plausible interpretation is that proposed by Shepard and Metzler: the representation used by humans in this task is coded as an analog of the appearance of the stimuli, and the process used to judge whether the figures are the same or different is an analog of physical rotation.

Although the conclusion drawn from this experiment is currently subject to some debate, the method it illustrates is clear. Processing components—in this case mental rotation and the time to perform it—can be used to interpret the code used in the representation of line drawings of three-dimensional objects. The conjunction of a manipulation (rotation of the figures) and a measure (latency to respond) resulted in an inference about the nature of the representation and the processes that operate on that code. That inference depended on the comparison of competing hypotheses. According to one hypothesis, visual information is coded as a visual analog; according to the other hypothesis, it is coded in the form of propositional descriptions of the objects. These two hypotheses made distinctly different predictions about the results of the experiment. The visual analog hypothesis predicted that the time required to judge the objects would depend on the relative rotation of the two objects. The propositional hypothesis predicted that the judgment time would be invariant. Because the experiment showed that decision time depended on relative rotation, the visual analog hypothesis is chosen over the propositional hypothesis. This experiment certainly does not prove that the visual analog is correct, but it provides the best guess of the mechanism for representing visual information.

An analogous experiment with pigeon subjects (Hollard & Delius, 1982) came to a different conclusion. Pigeons were trained to perform matching-to-sample with two-dimensional forms as the sample and comparison stimuli. During early training the matching comparison stimulus was identical to the sample, and the incorrect comparison stimulus was a mirror image of the sample. The birds were then trained with the comparison stimuli rotated between 0 and 180 degrees relative to the sample. During the final test phase of the experiment, the piegons were tested with novel stimuli to which they responded with above-chance accuracy on the first presentation. Accurate performance on the first trial involving a novel configuration suggests that the pigeons were not learning the correct response to configurations of samples and comparison stimuli but were learning to perform the rotation task. Unlike humans, however, the latency to choose the matching alternative did not depend on the angular difference between the sample and the correct choice. Humans tested with the same apparatus, task, and stimuli performed in the same way as the subjects tested by Shepard and Metzler. Their latency to respond increased with increasing amounts of rotation. Furthermore, the response latencies of the humans were consistently longer than the pigeons' at all angular rotations. These two facts imply that the failure of the birds to respond with a speed proportional to the angular rotation was probably not due to some difference in the task (Hollard and Delius used matching-to-sample; Shepard and Metzler used same/different judgments) or to the different stimuli used in the two experiments. Rather, the difference seems to be due to different representational systems used by the two species. Pigeons and humans apparently used different "methods" to solve the problem of judging the similarity between rotated figures. Hollard and Delius speculate that the difference between humans and pigeons in this task may be the result of pigeons' difficulty in detecting the similarity in mirror images. The pigeons probably treated these stimuli as radically different from one another. As a result they discriminated easily without any necessity for rotation, perhaps by attending to specific features of the figures. By this argument, pigeons and people both represent the objects in the same way, but the pigeons can solve the discrimination problem without rotation because the objects being represented are sufficiently different from one another to allow the pigeons to use different processes than humans use. Alternatively, Hollard and Delius suggest that because pigeons fly, they have evolved special representational systems that are adept at recognizing two-dimensional objects at all orientations (e.g., when flying northward, westward, etc.). In contrast, humans deal more frequently with objects that have a characteristic, gravity-governed orientation. By this argument pigeons and people have different systems for representing and processing two-dimensional figures. Both of these suggestions are interesting, but further experiments are necessary to converge on the appropriate explanation.

The difference in the speed with which pigeons and humans judge objects to be the same is interesting. Both species performed the same task with the same kinds of stimuli, yet they performed differently. Thus, the pattern of results cannot be a product simply of the task being performed. For example, some models of perception (e.g., Gibson, 1966) argue that it is controlled directly by the pattern of stimulation in the environment. Any system perceiving the same information from the environment, therefore, ought to perceive it in exactly the same way. In the case of mental rotation, rotating objects in the world takes longer the greater the required rotation, so any organism that rotated mental objects should also take longer. Pigeons did not behave as this sort of view would predict. These results are too new for us to be able to say very convincingly why pigeons were found to be different from humans, but the mere fact of the difference raises interesting possibilities for investigation.

Another example of the way in which we infer the code used is seen in some experiments on memory for letters. These experiments also show how the same experience can be coded in different ways in different situations. In one experiment (Conrad, 1964), people were asked to remember visually presented consonants. When the subjects produced memory errors, their errors tended to be acoustically similar—the erroneously produced letters sounded like the correct letter—but not visually similar—the erroneously produced letters did not look like the correct letter. Many have taken this result as an indication that Conrad's subjects coded the visually presented items in an acoustic code.

Another experiment (Parks, Kroll, Salzburg, & Parkinson, 1972) found that people could control the code they used. Subjects in this experiment were asked to perform two tasks at once. One task was auditory shadowing. A continuous string of words was presented through earphones while the subject tried to repeat each word as it was heard. While they were performing this shadowing task, the subjects were also required to perform a letter-matching task. Pairs of letters were presented one at a time, separated by a short interval. Subjects were required to respond "same" if two successively presented letters either looked identical (e.g., A and A) or if they had the same name (e.g., A and a). Ordinarily, people respond "same" faster when the two letters both have the same name and appear identical than when they share the same name but do not look identical (e.g., A and A are judged "same" more quickly than are A and a). This difference usually disappears, however, when the interval between letters is longer than about 2 s. In a visual code "A" and "a" are represented differently, but "A" and "A" are represented identically. People apparently find it easier to judge two stimuli to be the same when they are represented similarly than when they only share the same name. A 2-s interval between the presentation of the two letters apparently allows the subject to translate the first letter into an acoustic code in which "A" and "a" are represented identically, thereby allowing rapid letter matching.

When the subjects were asked to perform both the shadowing and the letter-matching task, the difference between identity-letter matching and name-letter matching did not disappear, even after 8 s. Subjects were still slower to respond when the two letters appeared different than when they appeared the same.

Apparently the shadowing task produced a high level of auditory interference, which caused the subjects to maintain the letters in a visual code.[8]

Similar experiments with pigeons, employing the same conceptual methods, are described in Chapter 5. Those experiments found that pigeons also recode information about the stimuli they observe.

Experimental complexity

The experimental techniques used in comparative cognition are often more complex than those typical of behavioral investigations of a few years ago. This has led some investigators to infer that it might be fruitful to divide behaviors into those that are cognitively produced and those that are not. For these investigators, some behaviors are explained by principles of reinforcement or reflex organization, whereas more complex behaviors, which are not easily explained in such terms, are to be explained "cognitively." These complex behaviors are taken as evidence that animals do, after all, think (Terrace, 1981, 1984).

Attempting to divide behavior into cognitive and noncognitive components is a mistake. Cognition is not that portion of behavior that is left over when reflex-based and reinforcement-based explanations have been exhausted (see Bever, 1984). Even simple behaviors, those that have traditionally been viewed as paradigm examples of noncognitive behaviors, are rich for cognitive analysis (e.g., see Dickinson, 1980; Mackintosh, 1983; Roitblat, 1986; Wagner, 1981). Furthermore, unless one wants to argue for direct action across temporal gaps (i.e., that events at one time affect events at another time without affecting any intervening events), experience at one time must produce some change in the organism in order for that experience to affect later behavior. That change is a representation that transmits information from one time to another. Reflex- and reinforcement-based explanations suggest one kind of representation an organism might use. They are not alternatives to the concept of representation.

On close examination, even the "basic" phenomena of animal learning have sufficient complexity to warrant the effort necessary for a cognitive analysis of these behaviors. However, exclusive concentration on phenomena such as classical and instrumental conditioning is simply too narrow a base on which to build a discipline.

Complex behaviors are more typical of comparative cognition because (1) many investigators are dubious that complex behaviors can be reduced meaningfully to simple processes, (2) complex behaviors are more informative in differentiating among competing cognitive hypotheses, and (3) because an animal's ecology is thought to play an important role in determining its cognitive and behavioral capacities, the investigation of those capacities is often best done through tasks that have similar forms and complexities.

Although comparative cognition emphasizes the study of complex behaviors and cognitive explanations of them, it has not abandoned the experimental rigor associated with earlier attempts to understand animal behavior, such as those found in behaviorism or ethology. Careful demonstrations of the lawfulness and predictability of behavior must necessarily accompany any serious attempt to explain it. Students of comparative cognition are not content simply to outline those regularities without also attempting to understand their mechanism.

SUMMARY

Comparative cognition is an approach to understanding the behavior of organisms. Some of the main characteristics of this approach are shown in Table 1.2.

Comparative cognition is the study of how organisms gain and use information about the world. It is the product of the convergence of four fields of enquiry: comparative psychology, ethology and behavioral ecology, neuroscience, and cognitive science. It shares questions and approaches with each of its parents.

Comparative cognition emphasizes the informational aspects of experience and behavior. A central concept in comparative cognition and in cognitive science generally is that of representation. The minds of organisms are general symbol-manipulating devices that operate on the representations the organism has, not directly on the objects themselves.

TABLE 1.2 Cardinal features of comparative cognition

---

1. Subject matter is the behavior of organisms explained in terms of environmental and mental variables.

2. Theory emphasizes information processing.

3. Mind is the set of structures, processes, skills, and representations that intervene between experience and behavior. Mind is conceived as an example of a symbol-manipulating universal machine.

4. Monism—cognitive theories are theories of brain function.

5. The concept of representation is essential to understanding cognition. Representations "stand for" environmental events.

6. Representations are characterized by their domain, content, code, medium, and dynamics.

7. Cognitive processes are inferred from experiments that vary environmental features and measure resulting behaviors. The methods of inference involve the comparison of competing hypotheses.

8. Complete analysis of "simple" phenomena (e.g., classical conditioning), while important, may not be adequate to understanding complex phenomena, because complex phenomena may rely on mechanisms that are not apparent in simple phenomena.

9. Typical tasks studied in comparative cognition include radial arm maze, delayed matching-to-sample, sequence learning, concept learning, and others.

Theories of cognition are developed from observations of the effects that experiences of various types have on the organism's behavior. Effective theory development requires precise, well-designed experiments that compare alternative hypotheses. Although the experimental methods of comparative cognition are often more complex than those of other approaches to animal behavior (e.g., behaviorism), the complexity does not imply that only complex behaviors are cognitive whereas simple behaviors are noncognitive. Even the paradigm examples of simple behaviors such as classical conditioning, have enough cognitive complexity to merit a cognitive analysis, and there is no clear basis for deciding that some behaviors are cognitively based and others are not.

RECOMMENDED READINGS

Estes, W. K. (Ed.) (1975–1979) *Handbook of learning and cognitive processes.* Six volumes. Hillsdale, N.J.: Erlbaum.

Glass, A. L., & Holyoak, K. J. (1986) *Cognition.* New York: Random House.

Griffin, D. R. (1984) *Animal Thinking.* Cambridge, Mass.: Harvard University Press.

Lachman, R., Lachman, J. L., & Butterfield, E. R. (1979) *Cognitive psychology and information processing: An introduction.* Hillsdale, N.J.: Erlbaum.

Lakatos, I., & Musgrave, A. (1970) *Criticism and the growth of knowledge.* Cambridge, U.K.: Cambridge University Press.

Walker, S. (1983) *Animal thought.* London: Routledge & Kegan Paul.

CHAPTER 2

History and Tactics of Comparative Cognition

Comparative psychology has existed as a field for more than 100 years. During that time the tactics people have used—the questions they have asked and the ways they sought answers for them—have changed dramatically. This chapter outlines some of the history of investigation into the mental and behavioral processes of animals that led to what we now call comparative cognition.

EVOLUTION OF MIND

Ancient Greek philosophers, such as Anaximander, thought that there was no clear separation between people and the rest of nature. Humans were considered to be a continuous part of nature. During the Middle Ages, the doctrine of special creation replaced that of continuity. Humans were seen as the result of special, enlightened creation. They were not part of nature, but created separately. In this approach, the most notable difference between humans and beasts was that humans were thought to have souls and free will, but animals did not. Human behavior, because it is free, is subject only to the will of the individual and the will of God. Both of these were thought to be the proper subject matter of theology, not of science or natural philosophy, as it was called. This view of humans as separate from nature and inappropriate to scientific investigation prevailed into the seventeenth century, when humans began again to be seen as a continuous part of nature (Fearing, 1930).

Descartes

Dualism.   René Descartes (1596–1650) promoted the scientific study of human behavior by distinguishing between two sources: voluntary behavior and involuntary behavior.[1] He attributed voluntary behavior to the action of the soul and involuntary behavior to mechanical actions of the body (Descartes, 1662). The outcome was a dualistic view of human behavior based on a separation of mind or soul from body. Voluntary behavior, because it was the product of the soul, was still inappropriate to scientific study. On the other hand, involuntary behavior, because it was the mere product of the mechanics of the bodily machine, was acceptable to scientific study. The mechanics of the body were already being studied by physiologists and other natural philosophers, so it was only a small step to extend this kind of study to the behavioral product of this mechanism. It was a step, nevertheless, that required insight before it could occur.

The assumption of dualism solved many philosophical problems for Descartes. It promoted the scientific study of behavior, it allowed him to come to grips with the problem of identifying the source of action, and it reconciled the existence of the soul with the mechanical action of the body. All but the most mundane aspects of human behavior were still thought to be controlled by the will of the soul.

Descartes argued that the mechanical action of the limbs was produced by the motion of windlike "animal spirits." These animal spirits flowed through the nerves and caused the muscles to swell and contract. Descartes derived his concept of the machinelike body from his experiences with hydraulically controlled statues in the royal gardens of Europe, such as that at St. Germain:

> You may have seen in the grottoes and fountains which are in our royal gardens that the simple force with which the water moves in issuing from its source is sufficient to put into motion various machines and even to set various instruments playing or to make them pronounce words according to the varied disposition of the tubes which convey the water.
>
> And, indeed, one may very well compare the nerves of the machine [of the body] which I am describing with the tubes of the machines of these fountains, the muscles and tendons of the machine with the other various engines and springs which serve

to move these machines and the animal spirits, the source of which is the heart and
of which the ventricles are the reservoirs, with the water which puts them into
motion. . . .

External objects, which by their mere presence act upon the organs of sense of the
machine and which by this means determine it to move in several different ways
according as the parts of the machine's brain are disposed, may be compared to
strangers, who entering into one of the grottoes containing many fountains, themselves cause, without knowing it, the movements which they witness. For in entering
they necessarily tread on certain tiles or plates, which are so disposed that if they
approach a bathing Diana, they cause her to hide in the rosebushes, and if they try to
follow her, they cause a Neptune to come forward to meet them threatening them
with his trident. (Descartes, 1662, translated and quoted by Fearing, 1930, pp. 20–21)

Descartes reasoned that the movement of human limbs was caused by the
same kind of device that caused the mechanical Neptune to behave like a real,
jealous human. On entering the grotto, the visitor stepped on a pedal. The effect
of this stimulus was then transferred hydraulically to the mechanical Neptune,
causing it to behave in a certain predetermined manner. Human action, insofar
as it was involuntary, was caused by a similar mechanism. External stimuli
striking the human open certain pores in the brain and allow animal spirits to
flow into the relevant muscles where they activate behavior.

For Descartes, the mechanical behavior observed in St. Germain not only
mimicked the behavior of real humans, it was produced by essentially similar
mechanisms. The human machine is built of flesh and bones, not metal and
wood, but, except for the action of the human soul, both machines are controlled
by the same principles. It follows, then, that animal behavior is also controlled by
exactly the same kind of mechanism that controls involuntary human behavior.
Animals, who lack souls, are merely "machines of flesh." (See Jaynes, 1973.)

If there were any machines which had the organs and appearance of a monkey or of
some other unreasoning animal, we would have no way of telling that it was not of
the same nature as these animals. But if there were a machine which had such a
resemblance to our bodies, and imitated our actions as far as is morally possible, there
would always be two absolutely certain methods of recognizing that it was still not
truly a man. The first is that it could never use words or other signs for the purpose of
communicating its thoughts to others as we do. . . . The second method of recognition
is that, although such machines could do many things as well as, or perhaps even
better than, men, they would infallibly fail in certain others, by which we would discover that they did not act by understanding or reason, but only by the disposition of
their organs. (Descartes, 1637/1960, pp. 41–42)

Thought provides evidence for the action of a soul, and thereby distinguishes
animals from humans. Although a machine could be constructed that would
imitate any particular behavior of a human (including individual speech acts, for
example), the complexity and reasoned nature of human behavior would always
serve to distinguish it from the behavior of machines and animals. Automata can

behave only in the limited ways for which they are prepared by virtue of their construction. Intelligent action, on the other hand, requires a soul.

The separation between the soul and the body restored part of human behavior to continuity with animals. Both humans and animals had machinelike components to their behavior, which could be studied scientifically. Descartes's dualism also implied that, to the extent that human behavior is involuntary, it can be studied equally well in either humans or in animals. The same processes will be found in both humans and animals, because both are produced by essentially the same kind of machine. Any differences between human and animal behavior would simply be attributed to the presence of souls in humans and their absence in animals. Descartes's dualism opened the way for the development of modern physiology and eventually of comparative psychology.

The reflex arc.   The reflex arc was the major mechanism Descartes proposed for the explanation of involuntary behavior. The basic notion of a reflex arc is a stimulus-response connection. An environmental stimulus elicits some reflexive action from the organism. Descartes illustrated the idea of a reflex arc by "explaining" how a foot placed in a fire is rapidly withdrawn. According to him, the flame tickles a nerve in the foot. This nerve is connected to the brain by a cord. The movement imparted by the flame at one end of the nerve cord is transmitted to the other end in the brain in the same way that pulling a bell cord causes an attached bell to ring. Instead of ringing a bell, however, the movement of the nerve opens the pores in the brain, which allow animal spirits to flow back through the nerve and swell the muscles of the foot. Swelling of the muscles, he thought, causes them to move. At the same time that the animal spirits are flowing into the foot and removing it from the flame, they are also flowing into other muscles, such as those in the head and neck. These cause the eyes to turn toward the flame, and via the eyes, the soul becomes aware of what has happened.

Although Descartes was mostly wrong about the mechanisms involved (e.g., sensory nerves do not pull open doors in the brain, there are no animal spirits, and muscles do not swell when contracted), his notion of the reflex arc was still quite insightful and remains influential. One reason for its success lies in its suggestion that apparently complex behavior—such as the approach of Neptune, shaking his trident; or turning to face a flame—can be explained in terms of simple stimuli mechanically eliciting simple responses. Another reason for its success was that it was the first attempt to formulate a wholly physical explanation for at least some behavior without recourse to nonmaterialist causes such as souls.

In addition to admitting at least some human behavior to scientific investigation and encouraging the study of behavior in animals, Descartes's mind/body dualism also suggested a tactic for developing theories of behavior. At the lowest level of behavioral mechanisms were the "mechanical" animal functions. At the highest level, separate from the others, were the actions governed by the soul or mind. Because only involuntary behavior was considered to be acceptable subject matter for scientific investigation, a scientific study of behavior would have to consist of attempts to find the limits of the involuntary behavioral mechanisms and, hence, the limits of the scientific analysis of behavior. In other words, the goal of the research program inaugurated by Descartes was to account for as much of behavior as possible using only mechanical principles such as the reflex arc. Only when such explanatory mechanisms were exhausted would it be necessary to propose a role for the mind, and thus remove the phenomenon from the realm of scientific investigation. We shall see shortly how a similar research tactic was used in the development of behaviorism in the twentieth century.

Darwin

Charles Darwin (1809–1882) completed the job, begun by Descartes, of reassimilating humans into nature and into the territory of science. Darwin went further than Descartes in rejecting not only Descartes's strict demarcation between the mind and the body but also that between humans and animals. In Darwin's view people are not the product of special creation. Humans are, instead, a part of nature and the product of the same natural evolutionary laws that produced other species.

In 1831, at the age of 22, Darwin sailed on the HMS Beagle as a gentleman naturalist and captain's companion. The primary purpose of the 5-year voyage was to chart the coastline of South America. In Argentina, Darwin saw how the native vegetation of the pampas was being replaced with newly introduced European plants. In Patagonia, at the southern tip of South America, Darwin saw rich fossil beds showing that the animals of the past were different from modern day forms, but clearly related to them. In the Galapagos Islands, he found peculiar species of finches, tortoises, and lizards; while obviously related to mainland species, they were also distinctly different from them and from each other. From these observations Darwin developed the ideas of variation and continuity. Animals, both within and between species, differ from one another along many dimensions, but are clearly related along many others.

Following his return to England in 1838, Darwin read a book by Malthus (1798) called *An Essay on the Principle of Population*. In this book, Malthus argued that, unless limited by disease, famine, or by conscious efforts at birth control, the population of the world would soon increase until everyone would be standing shoulder to shoulder. The same factors apply to limit population growth in other species as well. Life is a constant struggle for existence.

As a naturalist, Darwin knew that animals are adapted to their specific environments, often through bizarre and elaborate structures and activities, and that even within a species, two individuals are seldom identical. From Malthus's book Darwin got the idea of a universal struggle for existence. Darwin's insight was to add to this idea the realization that the factors that limit populations would act more strongly on some varieties within a population than on others. Those varieties of organism that were better able to find food, for example, would be more resistant to destruction by famine and would survive in preference to their relatives who were less able to find scarce food. The result is that favorable variations would be preserved and unfavorable variations destroyed.

Darwin was also a pigeon breeder. He had studied the ways in which fancy breeds had been produced and the anatomical characteristics that distinguished the breeds. All of the fancy breeds of pigeon were derived through artificial selection from a single, well-known species of wild pigeon. The differences between fancy breeds of the single species of pigeon, however, are often greater than are the differences between many distinct species. This convinced Darwin that selection, if continued long enough, could produce the kinds of differences that distinguish one wild species from another.

Although it was not recognized until the 1930s, Mendel's work on genetics provided the mechanism for heredity necessary to Darwin's theory, and the so-called synthetic theory of evolution was developed. The centerpiece of this theory is the concept of adaptation. Simplifying somewhat, a trait is adaptive to the extent that it helps an individual reproduce (see Dawkins, 1976).

An organism's structure and behavior (its phenotype) are controlled by an interaction between the genes carried on its chromosomes and the environment in which it develops. As a result of differing combinations of genes (its genotype) and of differences in the environment and its experience, each individual differs from the next in numerous systematic and random ways. Some of these variations influence the individual's ability to survive and reproduce. Those phenotypic traits that contribute to the bearer's ability to reproduce its genes are adaptive relative to less beneficial traits.

Darwin recognized that not only static, morphological features of the organism's form, but also its behaviors, could be adaptive and contribute to its ability to reproduce. Favorable variations in behavior, to the extent that they are heritable (i.e., can be genetically transmitted from one generation to the next), will be preserved and unfavorable variations destroyed.

Comparative psychology: A search for minds

By arguing that people were not the product of special creation, Darwin restored continuity between humans and animals and, in the process, made all behavior accessible to scientific study.[2] Darwin recognized that his theory demanded continuity of mental characteristics as well as of physical characteristics:

> It is, therefore, highly probable that with mankind the intellectual faculties have been
> mainly and gradually perfected through natural selection. . . . Undoubtedly it would
> be interesting to trace the development of each separate faculty from the state in
> which it exists in lower animals to that which exists in man. . . . (Darwin, 1874,
> pp. 128–129)

Comparative psychologists following Darwin took up this challenge and tried
to trace the development of the human mind from its precursors in nonhuman animals. Their goal was partly to show that mental continuity exists, and
partly to discover the fundamental elements of mental evolution and thereby, of
the mind. Although evolutionary theory demands continuity between species, it
does not specify the nature of that continuity. In place of Descartes's demarcation
(separation) between mind and body and its associated separation between humans and animals, Darwin and his followers entertained the hypothesis of a
demarcation between those species with minds and those species that had so few
of the mental precursors that it no longer made sense to say that they had minds.
The tactic underlying their investigation became one of discovering where to
place the dividing line between animals that did have minds and those that did
not and then trying to characterize the development of mind in evolution.[3]

Two different views developed regarding the "location" of this demarcation.
Romanes and other "vitalists" argued for a separation "far down the evolutionary scale," arguing, in essence, that practically all animals have minds. Alternatively Loeb, Sechenov, and other "mechanists" argued for a separation at a
higher level, suggesting that few if any animals (including humans) had any
cognitive functioning. Some, such as Sechenov, took the mechanist position to the
extreme, arguing that human cognition is itself basically a mistake, not causally
related to the true causes of behavior.

Romanes and the vitalists.   George John Romanes (1848–1894) was a friend
and student of Darwin and continued Darwin's work on behavior. According to
Romanes, the aim of comparative psychology was the classification of psychological traits that reveal "phyletic affinities" and allow one to trace the course of
mental evolution. He characterized mental evolution as a progressive development of discriminative capacity and an enhanced capacity for adapted response.
Consciousness was a property that developed gradually in phylogeny. It did not
develop suddenly at some point in evolution, but is present to greater or lesser
degrees in most species.

Romanes supposed that the presence of consciousness can be known "ejectively" through inference of another's mental state:

> That is to say, starting from what I know subjectively of the operations of my own
> individual mind, and of the activities which in my own organism they prompt, I

proceed by analogy to infer from the observable activities displayed by other organisms what are the mental operations that underlie them. (Romanes, 1883/1977,
pp. 1–2)

The basis of ejective inference is the comparison of the observed behavior of
some organism with one's own behavior. The logic of ejective inference is the
same as that used to infer that people other than ourselves have minds like our
own. Our only evidence that other people have consciousness is that they behave
in the same way we would in particular situations. We are intimately familiar
with our own mental states, so it is an easy matter to infer that other people
would have similar mental states when they behave in similar ways.

We can ejectively infer the behavior of animals in the same way. Similar behavior is as indicative of similar mental states in animals as it is in humans. In
essence, one observes the behavior of some animal and imagines what one would
be thinking if performing the same behavior under the same circumstances. Most
modern conceptualizations of cognition in animals take Romanes's ejective inferences to be unwarranted anthropomorphism (casting animals in human form).
Animals may indeed have mental states, but reasoning by analogy, as the ejective
method proposes, is not considered adequate to understanding those states.

Romanes saw evidence for mind everywhere he looked. He argued that the
ability to form new discriminations was sufficient objective evidence for the presence of mind. "The distinctive element of mind," he argued, "is consciousness,
the test of consciousness is the presence of choice, and the evidence of choice
is antecedent uncertainty of adjustive action between two or more alternatives"
(Romanes, 1884/1969, p. 18). If the animal learns to modify its behavior as the
result of its own experience, then these modifications cannot be the result of mere
automatic reflexes because "it is impossible that heredity can have provided in
advance for innovations upon, or alterations of, its machinery during the lifetime
of a particular individual" (Romanes, 1883/1977, p. 5).

In Romanes's view the mind is organized into faculties (a notion probably
borrowed from Darwin's cousin Francis Galton). These faculties (e.g., reflexes,
instincts, emotions, reasoning, judgment, and volition) are hierarchically organized, each level developing gradually in evolution from its predecessor.

Romanes's main method for investigating animal minds was to analyze carefully collected anecdotes. He recognized the limitations of this sort of data collection, but nevertheless felt that carefully collected anecdotes would at least provide
a rich source of hypotheses that could be investigated in a more controlled manner later. His methods seem strange by modern standards, yet they were not un-
reasonable for his times. The "New Experimental Psychology" was just beginning. The main method of this new psychology, as distinguished from the old
philosophical kind, was introspection. Individuals would attempt to observe the
functioning of their own minds in the same way that a chemist observes the

functioning of a mixture of chemicals. Many psychologists thought that introspection was the only way to gain access to the workings of the mind. In this
light it is hardly surprising that Romanes combined the then current introspective methodology of psychology with his commitment to the continuity of mental
life in developing his ejective method.

Based on a somewhat different methodology, Herbert Spencer Jennings
(1868–1947) also argued for the widespread presence of mind. He argued that
the behavior of even the simplest organism was too variable and modifiable to
be explained solely on the basis of blind responses of body tissue to stimulation.
Modifiability of behavior causes us to suspect the presence of consciousness, not
because modifiable behavior is free or indeterminate (cf. Descartes), but because
its variety makes possible many kinds of adaptive responses and consciousness is
the organ of adaptation.[4]

Loeb and the mechanists.   In contrast to the so-called vitalist position of
Romanes and Jennings, Jacques Loeb (1859–1924) argued for a mechanistic
interpretation of behavior in which the concept of mind was restricted to humans
and perhaps a few other species. Loeb started his investigations with plants.
These organisms are able to orient appropriately (e.g., toward the sun, away
from gravity) without any obvious organs of sensation or mind. Although the
movement of the plants could be described as purposive, light seeking, Loeb
showed how it could be explained by differential growth rates occurring when
two sides of a plant do not receive equal light. He called these adaptive movements "tropisms" and attributed them to the direct action of stimuli on
protoplasm.

Loeb applied tropistic concepts to explain the behavior of animals as well as
plants (e.g., Loeb, 1900). For example, certain caterpillars such as the gypsy
moth caterpillar, climb upward on hatching toward the top of trees where the
most tender leaves and shoots are located. Before Loeb, such behavior was attributed to intelligence or instinct, but Loeb showed that it was due to the caterpillar's reaction to light. The insect orients itself so that equal amounts of light fall
on its right and left eyes. If the light is brighter on the right side, for example,
then the caterpillar turns toward its right. If the light is brighter on the left side,
then it crawls to its left. On average, the brightest part of the sky will be directly
overhead (or most nearly so), so the path of the caterpillar tends to be upward. If
one eye is blinded, then the caterpillar crawls around in circles constantly turning in the direction of the good eye. If bright lights are placed below the insect, it
crawls downward. Loeb showed that instead of being purposeful, caterpillars'
climbing behavior is controlled by a negative feedback mechanism. Brighter light
on one eye than the other causes the animal to turn in such a way as to reduce

the discrepancy between the two eyes. This is a negative feedback mechanism because the behavior that results from a discrepancy (in this case between the brightness at each eye) operates to decrease rather than increase the discrepancy.

The tropism concept was later modified. Instead of referring to the direct action of stimuli on protoplasm, the idea later referred to the orientation of animals within a "field of force." Given a sufficient supply of tropisms, therefore, one could explain virtually any behavior that involved either approach or withdrawal from something. This generalization proved to be a major embarrassment for the tropistic view. For example, even learned behavior was attributed to tropisms. These tropisms responded to memory images, which were described as physical traces in a specific region of the brain (Loeb, 1918). In fact, the tropism concept was able to "explain" any behavior, because every behavior that appeared to present a challenge to a tropistic explanation was explained by creating a new tropism.

Despite its difficulties, the mechanistic approach represented by Loeb had a powerful impact on the study of animal behavior. Beer, Bethe, and von Uexkull (1899) proposed to discard all psychological terms, because they thought these terms were inextricably linked with introspection. Instead, they argued for the adoption of a more neutral language such as that used in physiology. They proposed, for example, that the terms *reception, antiklise,* and *resonance* be substituted for inherently mental terms like *sensation, modifiable movement,* and *learning/memory* respectively.

Ivan Michailovich Sechenov (1829–1905) combined a strong commitment to mechanism with a development of the reflex concept. He attempted to show how apparently voluntary behavior could be due to the operation of reflexes. Just as the violent behavior of a sneeze can be elicited by minute stimuli, such as a particle of dust or a small feather in the nose, so too could large-scale, apparently voluntary behavior be elicited by stimuli so small that the individual might not notice them. These small, unnoticed stimuli release or activate gross motor behavior and initiate activities in the brain that we call thought. By this view, consciousness, or our awareness of our own thoughts, is nothing more than coincident activity elicited by minute stimuli. All of these stimuli are either in the environment or the product of responses to the environment. Thought does not intervene between stimulus and response as part of the cause of behavior, it is simply another response.

Morgan's canon as compromise.   Romanes and Jennings both recognized that there might be some animals without minds, but these animals were thought to be very simple indeed. For example, Jennings attributed the presence of mind even to protozoa:

> Is the behavior of lower organisms of the character which we should "naturally" expect and appreciate if they did have conscious states, of undifferentiated character, and acted under similar conscious states in a parallel to man? Or is their behavior of such a character that it does not suggest to the observer the existence of consciousness?
>
> If one thinks these questions through for such an organism as Paramecium, with all its limitations of sensitiveness and movement, it appears to the writer that an affirmative answer must be given to the first of the above questions, and a negative one to the second. (Jennings, 1906/1923, p. 336)

Hence, Jennings and Romanes sought to solve the "continuity problem" by asserting that mind, or at least its precursors, was present in all animal species. On the other hand, Sechenov eliminated the demarcation between those organisms that do and those that do not have minds by arguing that no species had a mind, at least no mind that had any real function. This, then, was the ultimate mechanistic position.

Conwy Lloyd Morgan (1852–1936) presented a compromise between the mechanists and the vitalists. (Actually, Morgan's work intervened, in time, between Romanes and Jennings, and preceded the more radical mechanistic proposals). In his *Introduction to Comparative Psychology* (1894), Morgan proposed what has become known as Morgan's canon:

> In no case may we interpret an action as the outcome of the exercise of a higher psychical faculty if it can be interpreted as the outcome of the exercise of one which stands lower in the psychological scale. (Morgan, 1894, p. 53)

Morgan's canon is commonly interpreted as an argument in favor of the mechanistic position. This interpretation goes far beyond Morgan's intentions, however. When considered in the context of the rest of his work, his canon can be seen to be a compromise between the mechanistic and vitalistic positions. For example, like Romanes, Morgan argued that

> When we say that conduct is modified in the light of experience, we mean that the consciousness of what happened, say yesterday, helps us to avoid similar consequences to-day. If the happenings of yesterday were unconscious, they could afford no data for to-day's behaviour. If, then, the first peck is unconscious, it is as such completely outside the experience of the chick, and can therefore afford no data for subsequent guidance control. Similarly, the second, third, and succeeding pecks, so far as automatic and unconscious, afford no data to experience. But observation shows that the activities concerned in pecking are not only guided to further perfection, but play a part in that active life of the little bird which cannot without extravagance be interpreted as unconscious; for only by appealing to consciousness can they be thus guided. (Morgan, 1896, p. 130)

Passages such as this make it clear that Morgan was less strongly committed to mechanistic explanations than is commonly believed. Morgan emphasized the importance, however, of systematic and sustained investigation in order to understand the true nature of apparently intelligent behavior. This was the start of the experimental movement.

THE EXPERIMENTAL APPROACH TO BEHAVIOR

Morgan's impact on comparative psychology extends far beyond any interpretation attached to his canon. His most important contribution was his proposal that comparative psychology should be based on carefully controlled observations. Morgan advocated an experimental method consisting primarily of careful observation of behavior in the animal's natural environment, which was often modified to create special and, hence, revealing situations.

Thorndike

Edward Lee Thorndike (1874–1949) further developed Morgan's method by bringing the study of animal behavior into the laboratory where he could even more closely control conditions and more precisely measure behavior.

Thorndike began his dissertation research on "mind reading" in children. He wanted to investigate the subtle cues (e.g., facial expressions, unconscious movements) to which children might actually be attending when they appeared to be mind reading. Although the study concerned the perception of subtle cues and not mind reading, Thorndike had difficulty gaining support for his research. As a result, he changed to a more acceptable subject—the study of intelligence in chicks. In doing so, he brought not only a new methodology, but also a new perspective to the study of animal behavior.

By the time that Thorndike's work was becoming known, Darwin's theory of evolution was already well established in the scientific if not the popular community. As a result, research in animal behavior could turn from "testing" evolutionary theory to using it. Thorndike characterized the differences among the mental capacities of animals not in terms of the presence or absence of mind, but rather in terms of their intelligence as determined by the "delicacy, complexity, permanence, and speed of formation of ... associations" (Thorndike, 1901, p. 65). Hence, Thorndike led a shift in the tactics of comparative psychology from the investigation of animal consciousness in the service of supporting evolutionary theory to the investigation of animal intelligence. To some extent this shift represented an accommodation to the arguments of the mechanists and a rejection of introspective methods, but it also reflected the influence of functionalism.

Functionalism was then a developing view of psychology that emphasized the functions performed by mental processes rather than the study of the structure of those processes (see Boring, 1950). Functional psychology studied mental func-

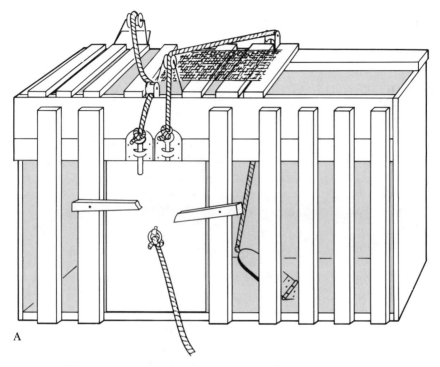

A

Figure 2.1. (A) One of the puzzle boxes in which Thorndike tested cats. In order to escape from the box, the cat had to depress a platform in the back of the box. Depressing the platform pulled a string running from the floor of the box near the back up through a pulley near the corner of the box and then over another pulley down the front of the box above the door. (B) (*opposite page*) The time it took cat 2 (top graph) and cat 4 (bottom graph) to escape on successive trials. Although the curves are not smooth, there is a noticeable trend for escapes to be faster on successive trials. [From Thorndike, 1911.]

tion, not mental contents. Whether or not animals have what we would call consciousness, they certainly do modify their behavior through experience. Therefore, even if we do not know the nature of the mental structure of consciousness, we can still study mental function through observations of the ways in which animals' behavior is modified by experience. The modifiability of behavior was to be Thorndike's main subject matter.

Thorndike's method was truly experimental, beginning with his now famous puzzle boxes. He constructed 15 puzzle boxes for cats. Each puzzle box required a different response in order for the cat to escape. For example, the cat might have to claw on a rope, push up on a bobbin, or push against a pole. Thorndike also had 9 puzzle boxes for dogs and a large number of mazes made of books on edge for the testing of chicks. One example of a puzzle box is shown in Figure

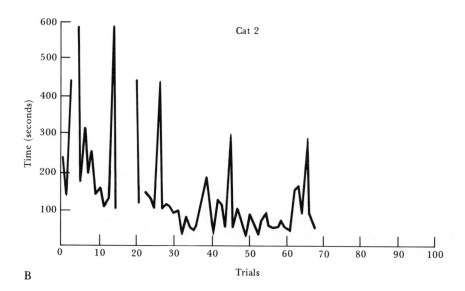

B

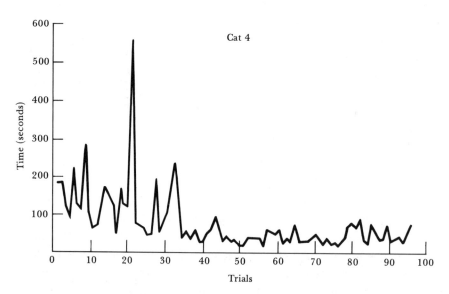

2.1. Thorndike placed an animal in the puzzle box, recorded how long it took the animal to get out on each trial, and plotted each latency in the form of a learning curve, also seen in Figure 2.1.

Thorndike felt that this rigorous experimental method was necessary if any progress was to be made in the study of animal intelligence because

> In the first place, most of the books [on comparative psychology] do not give us a psychology, but rather an *eulogy*, of animals. They have all been about animal *intelli-*

> *gence,* never animal *stupidity.* . . . Human folk are as a matter of fact eager to find
> intelligence in animals. Dogs get lost hundreds of times and no one ever notices it or
> sends an account of it to a scientific magazine. But let one find his way from Brooklyn
> to Yonkers and the fact immediately becomes a circulating anecdote. (Thorndike,
> 1898, pp. 3–4)

Thorndike's work with the puzzle boxes led him to formulate the law of
effect:

> Of several responses made to the same situation, those which are accompanied or
> closely followed by satisfaction to the animal will . . . be more firmly connected to the
> situation, so that, when it recurs, they will be more likely recur. (Thorndike, 1911,
> p. 244)
>   Perhaps the entire fact of association in animals is the presence of sense-impres-
> sions with which are associated, by resultant pleasure, with certain impulses, and that
> therefore, and therefore only, a certain situation brings forth a certain act. (Thorn-
> dike, 1911, pp. 108–109)

The law of effect is a reinforcement principle by which an animal learns to
perform a response in a situation when that response is followed by a reward.
Thorndike argued that the nature of the learning process is the formation of a
connection between sense impressions and unconscious impulses to action "without the intervention of any representations of the taste of the food, or the experience of being outside, or the sight of oneself doing the act" (Thorndike, 1911,
p. 109). In other words Thorndike was arguing for an associationism consisting
of the direct connection between stimuli (S) and responses (R). The function of
the reward was to stamp in this S-R connection.

Small

Other experimenters were also undertaking research programs to investigate
animal intelligence. For example, W. S. Small (1870–1943) published a study on
the mental processes of the rat in 1901 in which he used a miniature replica of
the Hampton Court maze. Small chose the maze because of its apparent similarity to the natural environment of rats. He felt that the closer one came to the
natural environment in testing an animal, the more accurate would be the assessment of the animal's intelligence. Although Small's objectives were to infer the
nature of the rat's conscious states on the basis of its behavior, the primary
impact of this research was to introduce to the comparative psychology community the use of the maze and the white rat.

Pavlov

Ivan Petrovich Pavlov (1839–1936) became a student of animal behavior more
or less by accident. He had already done work on digestive secretions and the

innervation of the pancreas which would win him the Nobel Prize in 1904. While he was studying salivary secretions in response to food, Pavlov noticed that the animal would sometimes salivate before the food was presented. The entrance of the laboratory assistant was often sufficient. Pavlov recognized in this accident the possibility of studying "psychic secretions" and the means by which new reflexes could be acquired by an animal. He then vigorously pursued this line of research.

The essential feature of Pavlovian or classical conditioning is the pairing of a "neutral" or conditional stimulus (CS) with an unconditional stimulus (US). Prior to training, the US has been found to "automatically" elicit a particular response. This response is called the unconditional response (UR), because it is unconditionally elicited by the US. After several pairings of the CS and US the subject comes to perform a conditional response (CR) in the presence of the formerly neutral CS. This response is typically similar or identical to the unconditional response. It is called a conditional response because its occurrence, in the presence of the CS, is conditional on training.

Pavlov was fundamentally a physiologist. He was determined to avoid using psychological terms (such as *consciousness, thoughts,* and *images* to describe the phenomena of conditioning. Instead, he intended to describe conditioning in the same objective manner he used in the study of other physiological phenomena. Pavlov was encouraged in his pursuit of the conditioned reflex by his acquaintance with Thorndike's work (Boring, 1950).

Kohler

While Thorndike and Pavlov were advocating a wholly mechanical approach to the explanation of animal behavior, based on the formation of reflexlike connections between stimuli and responses, Wolfgang Kohler (1887–1967) was arguing for a more cognitive approach. Kohler argued that animals did not learn by dumb trial and error, the way that Thorndike's research and law of effect would suggest, but by sudden insight. Animals are capable of learning about the relations among stimuli, not just connections between stimuli and responses. Kohler (1927/1976) argued that Thorndike came to the conclusion of blind trial and error only because he tested animals in situations that allowed no other kind of solution. Thorndike's puzzle box was designed so that his animals could do nothing but appear stupid. Its complex mechanism for opening the door prevented animals from observing the relationships among the parts of the apparatus and thus gain insight into its function. When such observations were possible, Kohler argued, an animal could modify its behavior merely by perceiving a situation in a new and appropriate way.

During World War I, Kohler was interned on the island of Teneriffe, where he had access to a colony of chimpanzees. He studied the animals' ability to use

tools to reach otherwise inaccessible objects, to stack cartons together, and to join two sticks together to make a longer stick. Each of these examples, and others, appeared to be the product of insight. The animal would manipulate various objects in its environment, perhaps "playing" with them. Eventually, it would suddenly change its behavior and deal with the objects in a new way that would solve the animal's problem.[5]

Hunter

Walter S. Hunter (1889–1954) introduced the delayed response task to the study of animal intelligence. He trained animals to observe a light over one of three doors. The subject was then confined in a start box until some time after the light went off. Hunter then released the animal and allowed it to open one door. Delays of different lengths intervened between the termination of the light and the opening of the restraint chamber. The delay required the animal subjects to maintain information about the correct door for some time after the cue had disappeared. Hunter argued that "if a selective response has been initiated and controlled by a certain stimulus, and if the response can still be made successfully in the absence of that stimulus, then the subject must be using something that functions for the stimulus in initiating and finding the correct response" (Hunter, 1913, p. 2). Hunter's notion of "something" that functions in place of an absent stimulus is a forerunner of our modern conceptions of representations (see Chapters 1 and 5). Hunter was reluctant to assume that these representations were ordinarily the result of so-called higher mental faculties. Therefore, he distinguished three categories of "representative facts" that animals could use in performing on his delayed response task.

The most obvious alternative Hunter considered was that of "overt orienting attitudes," in which the animal identified the correct compartment by posing in a particular manner, usually oriented toward the correct door. The use of orientation as the cue that stands for the correct door could be seen as a fairly low-level kind of representation because it involves the functioning of, say, an orienting reflex and little more. Restraint in the start box would be sufficient to inhibit the further approach that would ordinarily accompany such an orientation. In principle, then, any organism capable of an orienting reflex could perform the delayed response task on the basis of an overt orientation mediator.

Hunter also proposed that some organisms, such as children and raccoons, were capable of utilizing "intra-organic cues, or sensory thought." These intra-organic cues were presumably internal stimuli such as those arising from kinesthetic feedback (i.e., sensations derived from movement of one's limbs). This feedback may be the result of orienting responses that were so subtly made that they were undetected by the experimenter. Similarly, sensory thought might in-

volve simple perseveration of sensory information of the sort seen in afterimages or the like, or they might be as sophisticated as the processes underlying recognition. In Hunter's day, distinctions were made between "true memory," of the sort necessary to recall or recollect in the absence of the stimulus to be remembered, and the more elementary kind of memory that permits recognition (i.e., comparing the available sensory input with the presumed physical trace of an earlier sensory experience). It was widely argued that animals were capable of recognition, but not of recall.

Hunter considered thought that included the use of imagery to be the highest level. He argued that only adult humans were capable of this sophisticated form of representation.

Hunter (1920) also investigated animal memory in an apparatus he called a temporal maze, which consisted of two rectangular pathways in the form of a figure 8. The subject was required to make a sequence of responses, such as two loops from the central common path around the left block, followed by two loops around the right block. The correct choice after any given loop depends on the direction of turn made on the two previous loops. Following the first left loop another left loop is correct, but following the second left loop a right loop is correct. In Hunter's view, correct performance on this task is analogous to human counting. Because nothing in the maze changed between the animal's first left turn and its second left turn, whatever cues were guiding the animal's choice had to come from inside the animal. Hunter called these internally generated cues *representations*. Rats were rather poor at performing in the double alternation task (two right turns followed by two left turns, followed by two right turns, etc.). Raccoons succeeded at double alternation, but failed at triple alternation (three turns of each sort). Monkeys were able to perform both double and triple alternation in the temporal maze.

THE BIRTH OF BEHAVIORISM: JOHN BROADUS WATSON

In contrast to Hunter's cognitive approach to animal behavior, John Broadus Watson (1878–1958) advocated a strictly behaviorist approach:

> Psychology as the behaviorist views it is a purely objective experimental branch of natural science. Its theoretical goal is the prediction and control of behavior. Introspection forms no essential part of its methods, nor is the scientific value of its data dependent upon the readiness with which they lend themselves to interpretation in terms of consciousness. (Watson, 1914, p. 1)

Watson's position was a reaction to the introspective method that had previously characterized experimental psychology and that had apparently failed as an experimental discipline. Introspectionism had become enmeshed in a "series of speculative questions [e.g., whether all thought involved images] which, while fundamental to its present tenets, are not open to experimental treatment" (Watson, 1914, pp. 26–27). Watson blamed this failure partly on the subjective methods used in introspective observation. If one psychologist fails to replicate the introspective evidence of another, this is not due to some lack in the experimental setting as it would be in physics or chemistry, rather it is attributed by introspectionists to the observer and his lack of training. Freud's influence on psychological thought was also growing at this time. He had convinced many psychologists that people do not always know why they act and that many psychological processes were simply inaccessible to conscious examination and, therefore, inaccessible to introspectionist psychology.

The ideas of Freud and the mechanists, the apparent failures of introspection, and certain other factors meant that conditions were right in experimental psychology for Watson's arguments that a scientific psychology required them to abandon all "unanswerable questions regarding the structure of the mind" and concentrate instead on the observation of behavior in relation to the nervous system.

Watson's objective behaviorism removed consciousness from the subject matter of psychology, focusing it instead on the assumption that all organisms adjust themselves to their environments by means of stimulus-induced responses (stimulus-response or S-R connections). Some of these S-R connections are innate products of the organism's heredity, others are learned as habits. A fully developed psychology would be able to predict the stimuli that had been present on the basis of the response the organism made and to predict the response on the basis of the stimuli present.

Following Sechenov, Watson denied the existence of any mentally initiated processes. Stimuli are the true source of behavior. These stimuli are usually external to the organism, but Watson also included a role for stimuli arising from within the organism, especially those arising from the movement of the organism's limbs—kinesthetic feedback. In support for the importance of kinesthetic feedback as a factor in behavior, Watson tested the ability of rats to learn a maze under conditions of varying sensory deprivation. One group of rats was blinded, another deafened, another made anosmic (i.e., they could not smell), and another was tested intact. Watson found that each group showed essentially the same facility in learning the maze and concluded that none of these senses was necessary. The appropriateness of this experiment to his conclusions is dubious, but Watson (1907) concluded on this basis that the single sense common to all groups, their ability to sense their own movements, was the only sense that was necessary.

Following these experiments kinesthetic sensations became increasingly important in Watson's explanations of behavior. They were used in attempts to account for practically all so-called mental phenomena. For example, Watson argued that most mental phenomena in humans, such as images and thought, could be explained as the illusory result of feedback from incomplete muscle movements, especially of the larynx and tongue (Watson called these movements implicit behavior). If we could adequately record these movements, they would produce a record of what we mistakenly call mental activity. This record would be as objective as records of larger muscular movements and just as much behavioral. "*Saying* is doing—that is, *behaving*. Speaking overtly or to ourselves (thinking) is just as objective a type of behavior as baseball" (Watson, 1925, p. 6). By this attribution Watson removed mental phenomena from some separate realm requiring consciousness and attributed them, instead, to behavior. The same principles that were used to explain the behavior of rats in a maze could be used to explain mental phenomena without any recourse to consciousness. This was a bold departure for psychological thought.

As Watson's behaviorism developed, it placed increasing emphasis on conditioning as the source of stimulus-response connections and less emphasis on innate connections. Watson was familiar with the work of Pavlov and attached to it great significance as the means by which new S-R connections were formed. In later years, in fact, Watson turned more and more toward a radical environmentalism. This environmentalism is perhaps best illustrated in a famous quotation (see also Logue, 1978):

> Give me a dozen healthy infants, well-formed, and my own specified world to bring them up in, and I'll guarantee to take any one at random and train him to become any type of specialist I might select—doctor, lawyer, artist, merchant-chief and, yes, even beggar-man and thief, regardless of his talents, penchants, tendencies, abilities, vocations and race of his ancestors. (Watson, 1925, p. 82)

Watson's environmentalism[6] is one of the reasons that behaviorism caught on so well. It fit very well with the individualism and democratic spirit found in America of the 1920s, a time characterized by mass immigrations from Europe (see Watson, 1965; Logue, 1978).

ADVANCES OF BEHAVIORISM

Although Thorndike never considered himself a behaviorist and Watson initially criticized Thorndike's law of effect as essentially mentalistic, the behaviorists after Watson recognized in Thorndike's methods and theories the essentials of a science of behavior that reinforced the program proposed by Watson and allowed it to grow in influence until it virtually dominated experimental psychology.

> The psychology of animal learning ... has been and still is primarily a matter of agreeing or disagreeing with Thorndike, or trying in minor ways to improve upon

him. . . . All of us here in America have taken Thorndike overtly or covertly as our starting point. (Tolman, 1938, p. 11)

Thorndike's law of effect asserted that learning consists of the gradually strengthening connection of a stimulus with a response as controlled by the outcome of the response. Behaviorist analyses of learning after Thorndike either explored the possibility that other combinations of the three events in a learning situation (stimulus situation, response, outcome) were associated together, or attempted to formalize the relationships among these variables in ways that would account for more complex behaviors and situations.

Guthrie

Edwin Guthrie (1886–1959) proposed a theory of learning (Guthrie, 1935) that depended on contiguity of the stimulus and response. In opposition to Thorndike's proposal that learning occurred gradually, Guthrie assumed that a single contiguous occurrence of a stimulus and a response was necessary and sufficient for the formation of a learned connection. Guthrie explained the apparent gradualness of typical learning (e.g., that seen in Figure 2.1) by distinguishing between the nominal stimulus as the experimenter specifies it and the functional stimulus as it functions in learning. The stimulus that accompanies a response has some duration during which multiple responses can become associated with it. Each successive response displaces the previous responses that were earlier associated with that same stimulus. The animal learns the response that leads to reinforcement because the presentation of the reinforcer introduces a new stimulus environment. For example, when food is delivered to a hungry rat it will begin eating. The stimuli that were present when the reinforced behavior was performed are no longer present for the animal. As a result, no more behaviors can occur in their presence and the reinforced response remains the response associated with those stimuli. On the next trial, the stimuli that were present before the reinforcer appeared will now elicit the learned response. In Guthrie's view, reinforcers work simply because they change the stimulus environment.

Another part of Guthrie's explanation for the apparent gradualness of learning is his proposal that each nominal stimulus actually consists of many "stimulus components" and is accompanied by other "incidental" stimuli consisting of the training context, response produced stimuli, and so forth. Each of these stimulus components may initially be associated with a different response, but, during training, they eventually co-occur with the response being measured and thereby become associated with it. They then cease eliciting incompatible responses.

Guthrie's view of learning is thus based on a simple set of fundamental assumptions. Voeks (1950) described it in terms of four postulates. The *principle of association* says that a single co-occurrence of a stimulus and a response provides the necessary and sufficient conditions for the formation of an association. Once an association has formed, the reoccurrence of that stimulus will produce the reoccurrence of that response. According to the *principle of postremity*, only the last response occurring together with a stimulus is associated with that stimulus. This principle is Guthrie's explanation of reinforcement. According to the third postulate, the *principle of response probability*, the probability of observing any given response, depends on the number of stimulus components associated with that response. Finally, the *principle of dynamic situations* asserts that the effective stimulus consists of a bundle of stimulus components. Responses occur in the context of an ever-changing set of these stimulus components, and no two situations are ever exactly identical.

Guthrie's direct impact on learning theory was limited primarily because of his proposal that as many as a million unspecified and unspecifiable stimulus elements might impinge on the organism at any one time and play a role in learning. For Guthrie's behaviorist colleagues, this multitude of stimulus elements and their resistance to observation were problematical, smacking of mentalism. His influence has been more indirect, highlighting the importance of response competition and substitution and of contiguity. Finally, Guthrie's influence led Estes and his associates (e.g., Neimark & Estes, 1967) to develop a mathematical theory of learning that does attempt to quantitatively analyze the stimulus elements that enter into a learning situation.

Tolman

Edward Chase Tolman (1886–1959) also considered himself a behaviorist, though his behaviorism was somewhat different from that advocated by Watson. In contrast to Watson's reflex-based behaviorism, Tolman argued for a purposive behaviorism, emphasizing the adaptiveness, creativity, and intelligence of behavior. He argued that behavior is goal directed, controlled by its outcome. When the hungry rat seeks food, it is behaving as if it has a purpose or a goal.[7] According to Tolman, behavior is best understood when it is analyzed at the level of whole actions, rather than at the level of movements or muscle twitches. Because of its adaptiveness and variability, purposive behavior can be made of many alternative kinds of basic units such as movements, varying even from episode to episode. Analysis of behavior in terms of whole actions emphasizes the features of behavior that are constant from one episode to another and deemphasizes variations in behavior that may be physically substantial but are irrelevant. The important feature of a behavior is how it serves the animal to meet the goal, not the particular pattern of movements that mechanically produce it. Behavior has "emergent" properties that are related to its goal-directed nature and are lost when that behavior is analyzed into its physiological parts.

> In short, our conclusion must be that Watson has in reality dallied with two different notions of behavior, though he himself has not seen how different they are. On the one hand, he has defined behaviorism in terms of its strict underlying physical and physiological details . . . . We shall designate this as the *molecular* definition of behavior. And, on the other hand, he has come to recognize . . . that behavior, as such, is an "emergent" phenomenon that has descriptive and defining properties of its own. And we shall designate this latter as the molar definition of behavior. (Tolman, 1932, pp. 6–7)

As a result of his focus on whole behaviors and his claim that whole behaviors have emergent properties, derived from their organization, that cannot be meaningfully analyzed into more atomistic components, Tolman's psychology is often called a Gestalt theory.[8]

The essential feature of Tolman's learning theory is the assertion that animals gain knowledge about their environment and use this knowledge to control their behavior. Simple exposure to the environment is sufficient for an animal to acquire knowledge; no explicit reinforcers are necessary. Knowledge is the relationship between two or more stimuli (a stimulus-stimulus or S-S association) or among two stimuli and a response (an S-R-S* association). These relationships, especially the latter, were called expectancies, meaning that in a certain situation (S), the organism expects that some response (R) will bring about some outcome (S*). Of course, the R in Tolman's formulation is a whole purposive behavior whose function in the situation is to bring about the occurrence of S*. These expectancies are organized into families called cognitive maps to which we will return in Chapter 4.

Tolman was one of the first psychologists to distinguish between learning and performance. He noted that knowledge is not always expressed. Under certain conditions it may be behaviorally silent. For example, you may know how to ride a bicycle, but you are probably not expressing this knowledge at the present moment; yet it would be silly to claim that now you do not know how to ride. Strict S-R views equate learning with behavior change, so this distinction turned out to be very important in challenging these strict views.

Latent learning experiments demonstrated one of the phenomena that challenged the strict S-R interpretation and the importance of the distinction between learning and performance. These experiments showed that a rat could acquire useful knowledge simply by exploring a maze in the absence of any explicit reward. When the appropriate motivation conditions are later presented (thereby providing the animal with a goal), animals that were exposed to the maze without reinforcement perform as accurately as animals that have been rewarded from the start. For example, Tolman and Honzik (1930a) tested three groups of rats in a maze. The experimental group was initially allowed to explore the maze without any food reward. One control group was given standard maze-learning trials on which they were fed in the goal box. The other control group was never rewarded. After 10 latent learning trials without reward, members of the experimental group were rewarded with food when they reached the goal box.

During the exploration phase of the experiment, prior to the introduction of explicit reward, the animals in the experimental group explored the maze more or less haphazardly, entering many more blind alleys than did the control group that was fed in the goal box at the end of each trial. As is typical in experiments on maze learning, the rewarded control group showed a gradual decrease in their frequency of errors (i.e., entries into blind alleys) during the entire course of the experiment. The experimental, latent learning group, however, did not show a similar decline in their frequency of "errors" until they began receiving food in the goal box, when they immediately stopped making errors. Once they began receiving rewards for correctly moving through the maze, the animals in the experimental group became indistinguishable from the animals that had received reward from the start (see Figure 2.2). The never-rewarded control group continued to make "errors."

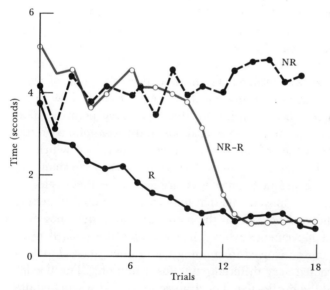

Figure 2.2. Learning curves from a latent learning experiment. Rats in the experimental group were not reinforced during the first 10 trials. When reinforcement was begun on trial 11, the frequency of entries into blind alleys dropped dramatically to a level comparable to that shown by the control group that was reinforced on every trial. A second control group that was never reinforced showed a relatively small decline in the number of entries into blind alleys. Group NR was never reinforced; Group NR-R was not reinforced for the first 10 trials and was then reinforced; group R was reinforced from the beginning. [From Tolman & Honzik, 1930.]

Tolman argued that the animals in each group learned equally about the maze during the first 10 trials. The rats in the latent learning group, however, did not activate or use this knowledge until the reward was presented on trial 11. The never-rewarded group never used this knowledge. The rats in both groups had knowledge of the maze, but this knowledge was latent. They did not express their knowledge of the maze until the goal became "positively valenced" or attractive. Food is attractive to a hungry rat, so when the food was presented to the rats in the latent learning group on trial 11, they formed an S-S* association or expectancy between the goal box and the food. The positive valence associated with the food in the goal box spread to activate the set of S-R-S expectancies leading to the goal box. The rats then behaved according to these activated expectancies and ran through the maze without error. The responses leading to blind alleys were not performed because their expectancies were not positively valenced. They did not lead to expectancies of reward in the goal box.

Tolman's molar analysis of behavior also asserts that animals learn more global properties of behavior, rather than simple motor movements. If Tolman's analysis is correct, then it should be possible to show that learning is not hindered when the experimenter requires the animal to use different motor movements to solve the same problem. Tolman and his associates conducted "place-learning" experiments to investigate this hypothesis. MacFarlane (1930) trained rats to swim through a maze filled with several inches of water. Once in the goal box, they could climb out of the water and receive some food. After learning to reach the goal box, the maze was drained. From the expectancy point of view, the flooded and the drained mazes both presented the same problem: how to get to the goal box. Furthermore, also according to the expectancy point of view, they had the necessary knowledge to reach the goal box in the form of a cognitive map of the maze; they knew which of the arms were blind alleys and which led eventually to the goal box. The only relevant difference between performance in the flooded maze and in the drained maze was argued to be the irrelevant features of the particular muscle movements that happened to be used in getting the rat from the start to the goal box. From the more molecular view, however, the rats' actual patterns of movement involved in swimming the flooded maze were quite different from those involved in running the drained maze. Furthermore, the two mazes presented very different stimulus conditions. The flooded maze was wet and cold and the rat floated. The drained maze was warm and dry and the rat felt the solid floor beneath its paws. Therefore, the molecular view predicts little transfer between the flooded maze and the drained maze because both the stimuli and the molecular responses were different in the two mazes. MacFarlane, however, found almost complete transfer from swimming to running. The animals were immediately able to run the maze without error. He argued that the rats could not be learning about which muscles to move, rather they appeared to be learning about locations in the maze.

Another group of place-learning experiments was arranged so that the molar and molecular analyses predicted opposite results. In one of these experiments (Tolman, Ritchie, & Kalish, 1946), rats were trained to run in a + maze, like that shown in Figure 2.3, with one of the arms (e.g., the north one) blocked off. The rat was always started in the south arm and rewarded for going, for example, to the east arm, that is, making a right turn. Under these circumstances, the molecular view predicts that the rats learn a pattern of right-turning movements. They learn to turn to the right to get food. On the other hand, the molar view predicts that the rats learn to expect food in a particular place. They learn to go into the east arm to get food. Both analyses predict the same results during the initial training phase of the experiment. They make different predictions, however, when the south arm is blocked off and the rat starts from the north arm of the maze during the second phase of the experiment. The molecular analysis predicts that the rat will continue to turn right, but now, because it is starting from the opposite end of the maze, it will enter the west arm. The molar view predicts that the rat will continue to expect food in the same place, and so will

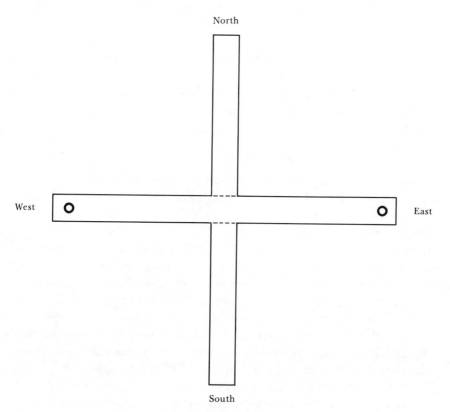

Figure 2.3. A "plus" maze of the sort used by Tolman, Ritchie, and Kalish (1946).

continue to go to the east arm. The rats in this experiment generally went to the east arm, whether they were started from the south arm in phase 1, or from the north arm in phase 2. They thus made opposite responses in the two phases of the experiment and, therefore, showed evidence of having learned about place, rather than about the specific response they performed in getting to that place. Other experiments involving adapation to blocks and detours showed compatible evidence for place learning (e.g., Tolman & Honzik, 1930b).

These experiments argue strongly for a molar rather than molecular level of analysis of animal behavior. Animals learn about properties of their experience that are more general than specific muscular response patterns. Although their behavior can always be described at the molecular level, the molar analysis captures more of the regularities in behavior—regularities that would be cumbersome to describe at the molecular level.

Despite the evidence on phenomena like place learning, however, Tolman's viewpoint was not widely shared by other behaviorists, who were unwilling to accept his emphasis on a molar point of view and on purposiveness of behavior. For example, Guthrie (1935) accused Tolman of being vague and of leaving his animals buried in thought, because he was not willing to specify the exact behavior of his animals. Nevertheless, Tolman did influence the direction of theorizing of other behaviorists, who had to account for his findings using more mechanistic reflexlike terms. His theory provided the main alternative to Hull's need-reduction theory, which argued that a reduction in the animal's need state is necessary for learning to occur. In more recent years Tolman's influence has once again increased with the rise of comparative cognition.

Hull

Clark L. Hull (1884–1952) developed a theory of behavior that is extensive, behavioristic, mechanistic, and deductive. Hull argued that learning is primarily habit formation. By this equation he sought to highlight the unconscious, impulsive nature of learned behavior.

Like Tolman, Hull recognized the importance of motivation in attempts to explain behavior. While Tolman argued that motivation was primarily a factor in performance and not in learning, Hull included motivation in the learning process itself. A state of need such as hunger or thirst produces motivation which Hull called drive. Drive activates behavior, and reinforcement occurs whenever drive is reduced. Reinforcement serves two functions: it selects the behavior that happens to be generated by the drive state, and it strengthens the connection between the stimuli present at the time and the behavior (the habit).

In addition to habit strength and drive level, Hull postulated a number of other intervening variables. Intervening variables are hypothetical factors that occur between the observable properties of the environment and the observable properties of the behavior (cf. Tolman, 1936). In Hull's system they were mainly summaries of S-R relationships. For example, a number of events or operations—such as eating salt, water deprivation, or eating dry food—all result in an increase in the likelihood of a number of behaviors, such as drinking, water seeking, or working to obtain water. Thirst is a label summarizing these operations and observations. Because any operation is interchangeable with any of the others, and because all operations influence each of the behaviors in the same way, it makes sense to label this general relationship (e.g., thirst). We can then use one term to summarize what would otherwise be a large number of operation-observation relations. Although Hull typically used intervening variables to refer to hypothetical (e.g., need) states internal to the organism, for most purposes it makes no difference whether intervening variables are taken to be actual internal physiological states or are taken simply as summary statements. Either way they help to organize Hull's behavior system.

The general tactic of Hull's system is to derive a relatively small set of behavioral postulates and use these postulates to predict behavior. If these postulates are sufficiently specific, then anyone who cared to do so could test them and either confirm them or find where they required modification. Hull spent a major part of his career seeking those postulates and specifying them in a form that was probably more precise than was merited. The result was a cumbersome hypothetico-deductive system based on the formation of association between stimuli and responses.

Hull eventually modified his system in response to Tolman's research. In addition to observable stimuli and responses, Hull also included internally generated responses and stimuli. Among these were "fractional anticipatory goal responses (r_g)" and the internal stimuli they produced (s_g). Through principles of Pavlovian conditioning, drive and other stimuli come to elicit conditional responses that are related to the consummatory response. The fractional anticipatory responses produce kinesthetic feedback stimuli which can then become associated with other responses, and so forth. Hull asserted that these internal stimuli serve as the equivalents of directing ideas, purposes, or intentions. Through the use of fractional anticipatory responses and internally generated stimuli, Hull sought to replace cognitive concepts with apparently more objective stimulus-response connections.

Hull's system had profound effects on the rest of behaviorism, not all of them positive. Nevertheless, his mathematical, hypothetico-deductive style of theorizing is precise (some say too precise) and thus, extremely testable. His ideas, directly and indirectly, generated a great deal of research (see Amsel & Rashotte, 1984; Estes, Koch, McCorquodale, Meehl, Mueller, Schoenfeld, & Verplank, 1954).

Skinner

Burrhus Frederick Skinner (1904–) developed a methodology, an apparatus, a single dependent variable, and a philosophical perspective that has come to be known as radical behaviorism. Skinner (1931, 1935) argued that the word *reflex* has two meanings. One definition is derived from physiology and refers to a connection between sense organs and patterns of muscular response. The other definition, used in psychology, refers to the correlation between a stimulus and a response. Although these two definitions are clearly related, Skinner argued that the science of behavior should concern itself with devising experiments that make observations more lawful and orderly, not with attempts to determine or to postulate internal mechanisms. Psychologists should, therefore, concentrate on the functional relations between stimuli and responses (the second sense of the word *reflex*) and not on the analysis of potential physiological connections from the sense organs to muscle systems. He further developed this theme into an argument against all kinds of theorizing about behavior in which the theory refers to events or objects at any level of analysis other than that of observable stimuli and behavior. A behavioral science needs to be developed in terms of behavior. It cannot be reduced to any other level of analysis or to events occurring at some other place or time. Reductionist theories only interfere with the progress of a science of behavior; they do not advance it.

> This does not exclude the possibility of theory in another sense. Beyond the collection of uniform relationships lies the need for a formal representation of the data reduced to a minimal number of terms. A theoretical construction may yield greater generality than any assemblage of facts. But such a construction will not refer to another dimensional system and will not, therefore, fall within our present definition. It will not stand in the way of our search for functional relations because it will arise only after relevant variables have been found and studied. Though it may be difficult to understand, it will not be easily misunderstood, and it will have none of the objectionable effects of the theories here considered. (Skinner, 1950, pp. 215–216)

Skinner (1938) elaborated his conceptualization of psychological (as opposed to physiological) reflexes. He identified two types of psychological reflexes (respondents and operants) and described two types of conditioning of those reflexes (respondent conditioning and operant conditioning).

Respondents are behaviors that are elicited by easily identifiable stimuli. They are learned through respondent conditioning, or *conditioning type S*, because the S or stimulus of the reflex could be identified. We now refer to this type of conditioning as Pavlovian or classical conditioning. Operants are behaviors that appear to be spontaneous, because it is difficult to identify the stimuli that are responsible for their performance. The behavior in this type of reflex is said to be emitted (as opposed to elicited) because it appears to occur in the absence of causal stimulation. It is not that operant behaviors are uncaused, their cause is simply difficult to identify. Operants are acquired through operant conditioning (also called *conditioning type R* or instrumental conditioning). Skinner concentrated his study on the analysis of operants.

Operants are defined in terms of the work they perform. A typical operant is bar pressing. A rat could press the bar with its nose, its right paw, its left paw, and so forth. Each of these responses, although of different form, is an equivalent operant because it has the same consequence. Each depresses the bar and produces a reinforcer. In many situations, such as discrimination learning (see Chapter 3), the observed response has a relationship to prior stimuli, but this relation is not one of causation. For example, an animal may be trained to discriminate between when a light is on and when it is off. The light is the discriminative stimulus, and the animal eventually comes to respond when the light is on and not when the light is off. The discriminative stimulus does not cuase the behavior, however; it merely sets the occasion on which it occurs. Because operant behaviors are not elicited by known stimuli, they cannot be described, as are other reflexes, in relation to properties of their eliciting stimulus. As a result, Skinner argued that response rate was the appropriate measure for operants.

To study operants, Skinner developed an operant chamber (which has since come to be called, despite Skinner's objections, a "Skinner box"). The chamber consists of a small compartment that was made to contain a rat, a lever, and a device for delivering food pellets. External equipment controls the delivery of food pellets (the reinforcer) and records the responses made and the reinforcers delivered on a cumulative record. This record contains a cumulative count of the responses made over time. One advantage of the cumulative record is that response rate, the primary datum in an operant experiment, can be read directly as the slope of the line relating responses to time.

Skinner rejected mentalistic or cognitive explanations of all sorts along with physiological mechanisms. The former are, he argued, nonphysical and so outside the realm of science; the latter are the subject matter of another science, and a science of behavior need have no recourse to them. We fully understand a behavior, he asserted, when we can predict and control it. Mentalistic explanations can neither tell us how to manipulate variables to control behavior, nor, since they are not themselves observable, help predict behavior (Skinner, 1974).

Skinner also argued that our analysis should focus on the behavior of a single individual. Generalizations that apply only to mythical average individuals obviously do not meet his criterion for understanding. Prediction and the control of an average animal is not the same as prediction and control of a real animal. He advocated an experimental method based on the performance of a single individual, tested first under one condition, then under another, then under the first again.

The main parameter varied between conditions in an operant experiment is the schedule with which the reinforcer is delivered. The study of these schedules and their combinations reached their culmination in a massive tome by Ferster and Skinner (1957) that presents hundreds of cumulative records for individual animals responding on practically every conceivable schedule and combination of schedule.

For Skinner, learning is a relatively simple process. In a certain situation a behavior is followed by a reinforcer. As a result of that reinforcement, the next time the situation occurs, the behavior is more likely to occur. For example, in a so-called superstition experiment (Skinner, 1948), a pigeon was presented with a filled food hopper every 15 s, regardless of what it was doing. Under these conditions nearly every bird developed stereotyped behavior patterns that differed between individuals but tended to recur from one trial to the next. One bird turned circles, another flapped its wings, and so forth. Skinner explained these results by saying

> The conditioning process is usually obvious. The bird happens to be executing some response as the hopper appears; as a result it tends to repeat this response. If the interval before the next presentation is not so great that extinction takes place, a second "contingency" is probable. This strengthens the response still further and subsequent reinforcement becomes more probable. (Skinner, 1961, p. 405)

Perhaps following only Freud, Skinner has been the most influential modern psychologist. His influence stems partly from his tremendous productivity and partly from his development of a coherent system, but mostly from the behavior technology to which his system has led and from his attempts to apply his system to social problems and other aspects of human behavior.

SUMMARY OF THE BEHAVIORIST PARADIGM

It would not be exaggerating too greatly to say that from the 1920s until the 1960s or 1970s, American experimental psychology was virtually synonymous with behaviorism. As a result, behaviorism had an exquisitely powerful influence on the development of all aspects of comparative psychology, an influence that continues. Many of the problems that confront comparative cognition arose either within the context of the behavioristic approach or in reaction to it. Therefore, an understanding of the basics of behaviorism is important to an understanding of comparative cognition. Summarizing the characteristics of behaviorism is difficult, however, because behaviorism has not been static during its long life but has continued to evolve in response to empirical challenges. Furthermore,

TABLE 2.1 Cardinal features of the behaviorist paradigm

1. Theory restricted to observable stimuli and behaviors.

2. Strict correspondence between internal variables and external variables. Internal variables, whether cognitive or physiological, may exist, but their analysis is outside psychology.

3. Ubiquity—all behaviors are describable as S-R associations or correlations.

4. Association is the mechanism of relationship between stimulus and response. Reinforcers control the formation or expression of associations.

5. The laws of behavior are those relating variations in stimulus input to variations in response output.

6. Equipotentiality—All behavior follows the same principles of learning, basically indifferent with regard to species or to task. Apparently complex behaviors are simply combinations of simpler behaviors.

7. Complete analysis of these simple phenomena is necessary before there can be meaningful analysis of complex behaviors.

8. Learning is the main means by which behavior is controlled and the main subject matter of psychology.

9. The main research tools are the maze, the operant chamber, classical conditioning, and, for human subjects, the memory drum.

many behaviorists, following Skinner, attempted to avoid explicit theorizing about behavior. As a result, there are few explicit descriptions of the basic assumptions of Skinnerian behaviorism, and one is left to infer the nature of the underlying theory from examples of its use. One should recognize, therefore, that there is ample room for disagreement.[9] The following is intended as a kind of composite of behaviorism, highlighting those features that particularly influenced the development of comparative cognition. Table 2.1 provides an outline of the basic assumptions of the behaviorist paradigm.

Assumptions of behaviorism

The correspondence assumption.   The most obvious feature of behaviorism is its commitment to accounts of behavior strictly in terms of observable stimuli and behaviors. "For the behaviorist all things are open and above-board" (Tolman, 1932, p. 3). In explaining behavior, we can go directly to the "prior physical causes while bypassing feelings or states of mind. . . . If all linkages are lawful, nothing is lost by neglecting the supposed nonphysical link" (Skinner, 1974, p. 13). This argument assumes that intervening mental events, if they exist at all, are uniquely determined by the prior stimulus events. If mental events intervene between stimulus and response, they are completely redundant. Therefore, knowledge of the stimulus events is sufficient to predict both the supposed mental events and the resulting behavior. The mental events are simply superfluous.

When observable events were found (e.g., by Tolman, see above) not to be sufficient to predict the resulting behavior, behaviorists turned to internal (e.g., kinesthetic) stimuli and responses to augment the more easily observed stimulus events as causal factors in their accounts. Internal events are conceptually identical to more conventional external events, except that they occur within the skin of the behaving organism. Skinner called the internal stimuli and responses *private events*. He suggested that they may "occur on a scale so small that [they] cannot be detected by others" (Skinner, 1974, p. 103). Further, "behavior is internalized as mental life when it is too slight to be observed by others—when, as we say, it is covert" (Skinner, 1978, p. 100). Hull (1930, 1931) used r_g and s_g, and Watson described thought as subvocal speech. Private events are no more mentalistic than baseball throwing; they are simply more difficult to observe.

Both views of internal events, either as unnecessary or as internal stimuli, assume strict correspondence between the theoretical and the observational variables such as stimuli and responses. In typical learning experiments, the data show an increase in the strength of some response (operationally defined), and so the behaviorist infers an underlying (conceptual, not internal) increase in the strength of association. The change on a theoretical level is assumed to run parallel to or isomorphic with the observed data (Bolles, 1975).

Although neither Pavlov nor Thorndike were actually behaviorists, the theoretical accounts they gave of learning were paradigm examples of the kind of account later used by behaviorists. As described above, Thorndike argued that learning is the connection of sense impressions with unconscious impulses to action. Pavlov argued that the two stimuli involved in a conditioning trial each excited particular neural elements (or areas on the cortex) and that the formation of a conditioned reflex was the formation of a connection between the two sets of elements. Hull described learning as the formation of stimulus-response (S-R) connections. Skinner avoided explicit description of anything we would call an internal theoretical event (but see Scharff, 1982; Wessells, 1982). For him the operational definition of strength was sufficient. An operational definition is one in which a concept is defined by the operations used to measure the concept. It is an explicit statement of the correspondence between the theoretical concept and the observable operations used to measure the concept. For example, "the concept of length [as operationally defined] involves as much as and nothing more than a set of operations; the concept is synonymous with the corresponding set of operations" (Bridgman, 1927, p. 5). According to Bolles (1975), the correspondence assumption is the defining feature of the behaviorist paradigm.

The ubiquity assumption.   A corollary of the correspondence assumption is the ubiquity assumption that S-R associations (or correlations; see Scharff, 1982) are sufficient to describe all kinds of learning. For example, Hull said,

> Perhaps no theorists have been more naive in their attempts at system construction
> than those who seek in the principles of stimulus-response the main explanation of
> those forms of behavior called mental. . . . Even so, the author has considerable confi-
> dence in the possibilities of this point of view. (Hull, 1930, pp. 242–243)

Because learning can be described in terms of a change in response tendencies
in the face of certain stimulus situations, following the correspondence assumption, the theoretical explanation of learning should be statable in similar terms.

The equipotentiality assumption.   A third assumption of the paradigm is the
notion of equipotentiality: the S-R (stimulus-response) framework applies uniformly in all cases, indifferent to species, stimulus, or response particulars.
Learning studied in one situation—such as the rat lab—should apply without
major modification to all other situations. This assumption is a version of radical
empiricism, according to which organisms are fundamentally blank slates written upon by experience (cf. Locke, 1690). Though organisms may differ in the
means by which they make contact with their environments, the same rules of
behavior change are assumed to apply to all organisms in all situations. Given a
common experience, they will all come to behave in essentially the same way.
This assumption is also often called the general process view. The title of
Skinner's first book, *The behavior of organisms* (1938), highlights his belief in
the uniform application of the laws of learning. Further, he argued

> Pigeon, rat, monkey, which is which? It doesn't matter. Of course, these three species
> have different behavioral repertoires which are as different as their anatomies. But
> once you have allowed for differences in the ways they make contact with the environ-
> ment, and in the ways in which they act on the environment, what remains of their
> behavior shows astonishingly similar properties. (Skinner, 1956, pp. 230–231)

The only difference between apparently simple behavior of the sort observed
in animals running through mazes or pressing bars in an operant chamber and
the apparently complex behavior that constitutes much of human activity is one
of degree.[10] Analysis of simple phenomena will directly yield the basic principles
necessary to account for complex as well as simple behavior (e.g., see Skinner,
1957).

Radical environmentalism.   It follows from the equipotentiality assumption
that if all organisms start as essentially equivalent blank slates, then only differences in their experience can account for differences in their behavior. By properly structuring the experience of the organism, we can control its behavior.

Radical peripheralism.   Behaviorism is also characterized by a radical peripheralism. Behavior is thought to be controlled primarily or exclusively by envi-

ronmental events. The source of action is in the immediate environment, not the individual. For example, "The appeal to cognitive states and processes is a diversion which could well be responsible for much of our failure to solve our problems. We need to change our behavior and we can do so only by changing our physical and social environments" (Skinner, 1978, p. 112). In fact, some behaviorists have extended this radial peripheralism into an "empty black box" approach, in which, "'causes' produce their effects across a temporal gap, and in many cases that gap can be large. Thus to be comfortable with a behavioristic position one must be comfortable with the notion of 'action at a temporal distance'" (Branch, 1982, p. 372). A complete description of the functional relationships between environmental variables and behavior is the task of behaviorist investigations and theory. Understanding is indexed solely by the ability to predict and control behavior.

DIFFICULTIES WITH THE BEHAVIORIST PARADIGM

Scientific progress is typically not a simple process of building up of fact upon fact. Rather, it seems to proceed by alternating periods of so-called normal science, in which scientists solve the problems dictated by their paradigms, and periods of so-called revolutionary science, in which the difficulties and anomalies that have emerged during normal science precipitate a change in the paradigm, in the way the science is done, and in the way in which its foundations are conceived (Kuhn, 1970). One of the premises of the present book is that the normal science of behaviorism, as described above, has resulted in the accumulation of a sufficient number of anomalies to prompt a reappraisal of the basics of comparative psychology, leading to the development of comparative cognition.

The misbehavior of organisms

Although there had always been some puzzles that presented difficulties for behaviorism (e.g., motivation, the partial reinforcement in extinction effect, behavioral contrast, and avoidance conditioning), a number of findings in the early 1960s challenged the equipotentiality assumption and greatly decreased the perceived usefulness of behaviorism as a way to conceptualize behavior. For example, Breland and Breland (1961) noted that some animals tended toward "instinctive drift" during extended training with food rewards. Early in training the animals behaved as the usual rules of reinforcement would predict, but later in training they began to show patterns that were more appropriate to consuming the food than to obtaining it.

   The Brelands were students of Skinner. After receiving their doctorates, they formed a business involved with the training of animals according to Skinnerian, behaviorist principles, for store displays and the like. In 1961 they reported a summary of some interesting outcomes of that work. At the time they wrote the report they had trained over 6000 individual animals from 38 different species, including reindeer, cockatoos, raccoons, porpoises, and whales. They reported their experience with a raccoon as follows:

> The response concerned the manipulation of money by the raccoon (who has "hands" rather similar to those of the primates). The contingency for reinforcement was picking up the coins and depositing them in a 5-inch metal box.
>
> Raccoons condition readily, have good appetites, and this one was quite tame and an eager subject. We anticipated no trouble. Conditioning him to pick up the first coin was simple. We started out by reinforcing him for picking up a single coin. Then the metal container was introduced, with the requirement that he drop the coin into the container. Here we ran into the first bit of difficulty: he seemed to have a great deal of trouble letting go of the coin. He would rub it up against the inside of the container, pull it back out, and clutch it firmly for several seconds. However, he would finally turn it loose and receive his food reinforcement. Then the final contingency: we put him on a ratio of 2, requiring that he pick up both coins and put them into the container.
>
> Now the raccoon really had problems (and so did we). Not only could he not let go of the coins, but he spent seconds, even minutes, rubbing them together (in a most miserly fashion), and dipping them into the container. . . . The rubbing behavior became worse as time went on, in spite of nonreinforcement. (Breland & Breland, 1961, p. 682)

The Brelands reported several other instances of similar "instinctive drift." In each example, an animal being trained with food reward initially responds according to the contingencies of the task. After some amount of experience with the task and the reward, however, it starts responding to the props or other stimulus attributes of the situation in a way reminiscent of the behaviors it uses when handling food. The response that is reinforced is replaced by another response which is resistant to control by the reinforcer.

Whereas one might argue that the so-called instinctive drift is simply a curious result of using a strange species in an even stranger task, the same kind of results have also been seen with pigeons performing in an operant chamber. Staddon and Simmelhag (1971) replicated Skinner's (1948) superstition experiment described above. They presented food to hungry pigeons every 12 s, independent of the behavior being performed at the time. During the initial stages of conditioning on this schedule, they observed the kinds of idiosyncratic behaviors Skinner described. With extended training, however, this behavior became more fixed in form and tended to occur only early in the interfood interval. Staddon and Simmelhag called these stereotyped behaviors interim behaviors. As the interim behaviors became restricted to earlier parts of the interfood interval, nearly every bird began to show the same form of terminal behavior just prior to the food delivery. Nearly every bird pecked! Some pecked at the opening to the food hopper, others pecked at the wall, still others at screw heads in the chamber, but pecking was clearly the dominant behavior. In short, whatever behavior was initially followed by reinforcement—and so should have been strengthened according to theories of reinforcement—was replaced with a behavior that was clearly related to the behavior the bird uses in response to food. In fact, so powerful is the pigeon's tendency to peck when expecting food that pecking is maintained even if it prevents food delivery (Williams & Williams, 1969).

These experiments challenged two of the central behaviorist assumptions. They appeared to show a failure of the equipotentiality assumption in that the principles of reinforcement that operated with other kinds of responses seemed to have failed. They appeared to show a failure of the ubiquity assumption in that learning was apparently occurring that could not easily be described as the formation of stimulus-response connections. At the start of training all of the animals behaved in the way the behaviorist assumptions would predict: reinforcement strengthened some arbitrary behavior. Following extended training, however, instead of further strengthening the response, continued reinforcement caused it to be replaced by some food-related behavior. This "instinctive drift" from the reinforced arbitrary behavior to one related to food clearly depended on learning of some sort, but it was obviously different from the strengthening of stimulus-response associations—the responses that had been associated with the stimuli were replaced. Thus, these experiments made it clear that learning involves some change in the internal state of the organism that is independent of the behavior the animal happens to be performing.

Long-delay taste aversion learning

A second line of experiments showed that animals were selective in their learning. Garcia and Koelling (1966) found that the stimuli used by rats in an avoidance situation depended on the particular reinforcer used. When shock was the reinforcer, rats readily learned to avoid on the basis of specific audiovisual cues. When illness was the reinforcer, however, rats learned to avoid on the basis of taste or flavor cues, and not on the basis of audiovisual cues.

Garcia and Koelling (1966) trained rats to drink tasty water from a spout. For one group, the water was sweetened with saccharin. For the other group, the water was made tasty by the addition of a small amount of lithium chloride. Each time the rat licked, a light flashed and a clicker clicked. Drinking was punished either by making the animals ill or by presenting electric shock. Both punishers were effective in reducing the amount of bright-noisy-tasty water the animals drank relative to the amount drunk in alternating control sessions in which plain water was given. When the animals who were made ill during training were later tested with the bright-noisy water alone (i.e., without the taste), they showed no sign of avoiding the audiovisual cues. When they were tested with the taste alone, however, they showed a strong aversion for the taste used in training. The animals who were shocked during training showed the opposite pattern of results: they avoided the bright noisy water, but not the tasty water. Only one combination of stimulus and consequent was learned.

When both audiovisual and taste cues are present, the type of punisher determines the cues about which animals will learn. These findings challenged the basic behaviorist models of learning. The stimuli used in the experiment (the light, the noise, and the taste) were each demonstrated to be sufficiently salient (noticeable) to produce learning with the appropriate reinforcer. Lack of salience could not, therefore, explain the selectivity. Furthermore, other experiments demonstrated that learning was still obtained if the illness was delayed for several hours after the presentation of the novel taste (Smith & Roll, 1967). It is unclear how a reflexlike mechanism could connect a stimulus with another event that occurred 6 hours later. While behaviorist theories were modified in response to such findings, many researchers found these accommodations to be less than adequate.

Challenges from other fields

While these challenges were developing from within comparative psychology, a large number of events were occurring in other fields. For example, behavioral ecology was developing theories of optimal foraging (e.g., Schoener, 1971; Pyke, Pulliam, & Charnov, 1977; Kamil & Sargent, 1981; Kamil & Roitblat, 1985; see Chapter 7). These theories view animals as active (though not necessarily conscious) decision makers. Ethologists in both the field and laboratory were finding evidence that implied the existence of selective attention mechanisms (e.g., Dawkins, 1971; Pietrewicz & Kamil, 1978; Tinbergen, 1960), and of particularly well-developed cognitive capacities in certain insects. For example, the digger wasps are able to quickly learn about an area and navigate within it (e.g., van Iersel and van dem Assem, 1965). Finally, cognitive psychology, with its emphasis on information processing, took over the study of human behavior (see Lachman, Lachman, & Butterfield, 1979, for a discussion of this process). In response to these challenges and to changes both within and outside of comparative psychology, comparative cognition began to take shape.

BEHAVIORISM AND COMPARATIVE COGNITION

Comparative cognition arose in part out of a sense that the basic assumptions of behaviorism were inappropriate. Many investigators felt that there were too many examples of behavior, such as those reviewed above, that were difficult to accommodate within the behaviorist framework. These "anomalies" did not prove that behaviorism was inappropriate; but they did induce some investigators to reexamine the foundational assumptions of behaviorism and to reject its longstanding objections to considering cognitive processes as part of an explanation of behavior. Comparative cognition was the outcome of that reexamination.

Comparative cognition shares with behaviorism a commitment to observation and experimentation. Within comparative cognition, sound inferences still depend as much on solid behavioral observations as they do within behaviorism. Careful demonstration of the lawfulness and regularity of behavior must necessarily accompany any serious attempt to explain it.

In all areas of science the best one can do is to manipulate the circumstances under which observations are made (inputs) and then measure the results (outputs). This is especially true when trying to understand the causes of behavior. The only data available are the records of inputs to the behaving system and the record of outputs from that system. (These records include physiological interventions and measures.) A main difference between comparative cognition and behaviorism is the interpretation placed on those observations. Most behaviorists attempt to limit the interpretation to the functional relationship between observable stimulus variables and observable behavioral variables. The word *functional* in this context has two meanings. On the one hand, it refers to the kind of function used in mathematics in which the stimuli allow the prediction of the response (i.e., analogous to the algebraic statement: $y = f(x)$). On the other hand, it refers to the function of the stimulus-response system, that is, to how the behavior serves the organism. Functional relations have the appearance of being straightforward and not particularly subject to differences in interpretation; that is, they appear reliable. Nevertheless, even this simple level of analysis has not been entirely successful. For example, there is still considerable debate within behaviorism whether animals who are reinforced for making either of two responses distribute their responses so as to match the rate of reinforcement available for each response or whether they distribute their responses so as to maximize the overall rate of reinforcement (Baum, 1981; Herrnstein, 1970; Hinson & Staddon, 1981). The functional analysis within behaviorism emphasizes the task being performed, whereas the analysis within comparative cognition emphasizes the organism performing the task.

Comparative cognition rejects behaviorism's assertion that mental events are nonphysical. Comparative cognition is firmly committed to the physical, specifically biological, nature of mental events. Cognitive processes and structures are physical entities analogous to the biological processes and structures forming the explanatory basis of modern genetics. The relation between mental events and biological-neural events may not be simple or straightforward, but neither is it mysterious. Cognitive descriptions are simply one possible level for describing biological-neural events. A psychology that ignores cognition is as irrelevant as one that ignores the brain or as a biology that ignores the gene.

The behaviorist claim that mental events are irrelevant is also unsatisfactory. A functionalist analysis is always limited. As long as the behaviors being analyzed were relatively simple and performed in relatively limited environments, a functional analysis relating stimuli and responses could appear adequate. As many of the behaviors described above indicate, however, it was often difficult to extend similar analyses to more complex behaviors in different environments. The isomorphism between stimulus and mental events that behaviorism must assume is simply inadequate. If mental events can be related to stimulus events in more than one way, then the resulting behavior may not depend so strongly on the observed stimulus conditions, as the organism's representation of those stimulus conditions (e.g., see Roitblat, 1980, 1982).

The available evidence from comparative cognition indicates that the representations used by animals are more complex than the simple stimulus-response relations proposed by behaviorism. Obviously, mental events are lawfully related to experience, but they are not limited by strict isomorphism with either stimuli or responses (see Bolles, 1975; Dickinson, 1980; Roitblat, 1982). Even if this were not known, there seems no reason to limit the kinds of relations between mental and stimulus events to the strict parallelism inherent in behaviorism's implicit theory of mind. The correspondence assumption provides a false sense of parsimony because the assumed parallel between stimulus events and mental events implicitly allows us to describe cognitive events when describing stimulus events. This hidden assumption seems to put an unnecessary and far-reaching constraint on the potential complexity of an animal's cognitive processes.

The behaviorist position has led animal psychologists to an obsession with simple learning processes such as operant and classical conditioning in the hope that an understanding of these would lead automatically to an understanding of complex processes (e.g., Skinner's, 1957, attempt to extend the principles of operant conditioning to the explanation of verbal behavior). Even the apparently simple systems, however, have been resistant to purely behavioristic explanations and have proved to be rich domains for cognitive analysis (e.g., Dickinson, 1980; Wagner, 1981; see Chapter 4). Furthermore, one does not need to deny the importance of classical and instrumental conditioning to insist that it is a serious error to ignore the rich variety of behavior exhibited by a variety of organisms. Behaviorism must remain silent on how, for example, birds such as nutcrackers find their buried caches of pine nuts, often months after they have made those caches (see Chapter 7). If we wish to understand the complexity of an animal's mind, we must confront that complexity, not simplify it out of existence.

SUMMARY

In ancient times, humans and animals were thought to be continuous with each other, part of nature. In the Middle Ages, this view changed in favor of special creation and a separation between humans and animals. Descartes redressed part of this separation through his proposal of mind-body dualism, but it was left to Darwin to reanimate continuity. Two different approaches followed from Darwin's resumption of continuity. The vitalists proposed that consciousness existed in all creatures. The mechanists proposed that consciousness was, at best, an epiphenomenon, and all behavior could be explained on mechanistic principles. Eventually behaviorism developed out of this mechanistic approach and dominated experimental psychology for half a century. Although comparative cognition argues for a rejection of a universally mechanistic position in favor of one that includes mental phenomena, it is not a return to the vitalist position of Romanes and his associates. Because we have generally accepted the notion of evolution by natural selection, the question of which animals have and which do not have consciousness has lost its importance for most investigators of comparative cognition. Rather, comparative cognition pursues the study of cognitive processes in organisms in a rich, but, we hope, methodologically rigorous manner. The goal is to understand and explain behavior on the basis of both external and internal factors.

RECOMMENDED READINGS

Boring, E. G. (1950) *A history of experimental psychology.* New York: Appleton.

Bolles, R. C. (1979) *Learning theory* (2d ed.). New York: Holt, Rinehart, & Winston.

Bower, G. H., & Hilgard, E. R. (1981) *Theories of learning* (5th ed.). Englewood Cliffs, N.J.: Prentice-Hall.

Dennis, W. (1948) *Readings in the history of psychology.* New York: Appleton.

Henle, M., Jaynes, J., & Sullivan, J. (1973) *Historical conceptions of psychology.* New York: Springer.

Herrnstein, R. J., & Boring, E. G. (1965) *A source book in the history of psychology.* Cambridge, Mass.: Harvard University Press.

Marx, M. H., & Hillix, W. A. (1973) *Systems and theories in psychology* (2d ed.). New York: McGraw-Hill.

Rachlin, H. (1970) *About behaviorism.* San Francisco: Freeman.

Reynolds, G. S. (1975) *A primer of operant conditioning.* Glenveiw, Ill.: Scott-Foresman.

Tolman, E. C. (1959) Principles of purposive behavior. In S. Koch (Ed.), *Psychology: A study of a science,* vol. 2. New York: McGraw-Hill, 92–157.

Turing, A. M. (1950) Computing machinery and intelligence. *Mind, 59,* 433–460.

Walker, S. (1983) *Animal thought.* London: Routledge & Kegan Paul.

CHAPTER 3

Attention and Related
Cognitive Processes

*One of the most extraordinary facts of our life is that, although we are besieged
at every moment by impressions from our whole sensory surface, we notice so
very small a part of them ... Yet the physical impressions which do not count
are* there *as much as those which do, and affect our sense organs just as
energetically. Why they fail to pierce the mind is a mystery.*

(*JAMES, 1892, p. 217*)

STIMULUS CONTROL AND ATTENTION

One premise of this book is that animals are active processors of information,
who behave according to their representations of their experience. To form a
representation of an event, an animal must be able to sense the event with its
sensory apparatus—for example, its eyes, ears, and skin. It must then transduce
the event's features into neural information for its brain to process and translate
into the representations that guide its later behavior. Investigators have studied
the means by which animals take in information from the environment at many
different levels, including sensory (e.g., Devalois & Jacobs, 1968) as well as
psychophysical processes (e.g., Blough, 1958). In this chapter we are concerned
with the processes that control the formation of representations, specifically with
the question of whether there are, as William James noted regarding humans,
limits to the number of stimuli to which an animal can attend.

The concept of attention

Experimental psychologists have used the concept of attention to refer to two separable, but related processes. First, they have used it to describe a *selective mechanism* that determines which stimuli will control an animal's behavior and which will not. In many experiments a number of stimuli are equally available and valid, but the organism comes to respond to some of these and not to others. Researchers have identified a number of factors that are important in determining whether an animal will attend to a stimulus, including its past validity as a predictor of reinforcement and its salience or noticeability (e.g., brightness). Those stimuli to which the animal attends are those that control its performance.

Second, experimental psychologists have used the concept of attention to describe a *limited capacity for processing information*. In this sense of attention, animals are presumed to have a limited cognitive capacity. They must allocate some of this capacity to learn about or respond to a stimulus, and, to the extent that they allocate attention to one stimulus, they have less capacity available to allocate to the processing of others. For example, you may find it difficult to both read a text book and watch television at the same time. The effort expended in performing one task—such as reading the book—presumably uses up a considerable amount of your information-processing capacity and, consequently, you have little left for watching television.[1] Although these two uses of the concept of attention are clearly related, they are not identical. An organism may selectively respond to some stimuli and not to others even if the stimuli do not tax its information-processing capacity. Work with both human and animal subjects has found evidence for selectivity. Organisms respond to some of the stimuli around them, and not to others. Work with human subjects has generally found that this selectivity results from a limited information-processing capacity (Kahneman, 1973). Discrimination-learning experiments with animals, on the other hand, have generally failed to find any evidence that their selectivity results from any particular limits on their information-processing capacity. However, this failure apparently results from the tasks that have been used to study attention in animals, because when researchers use tasks other than simple discrimination learning, they do find evidence for limits. First we will consider the evidence regarding selectivity in animal learning, then we will consider limits on information-processing capacity.

SELECTIVITY IN DISCRIMINATION LEARNING

Many experiments on discrimination learning use complex stimuli, varying along a number of dimensions, such as hue, loudness, brightness, and position.[2]

In fact, one might argue, discrimination-learning experiments always involve the presentation of a multitude of different stimuli, such as the sound of the ventilating fan in the operant chamber, the smell of food, the brightness of the light, and so forth. The subject must determine which stimuli or stimulus dimensions are important to the discrimination task, and the "value" or response appropriate to each. For example, an animal may be required to learn that brightness is the dimension to be discriminated and that the correct response is to perform behavior A when the light is on and behavior B when it is off.

If one stimulus is associated with reinforcement and the other with nonreinforcement, we would expect an animal to respond only to the reinforced stimulus and not to the nonreinforced stimulus. Even when two stimuli are equally associated with reinforcement, however, they may still differ in the degree to which they control behavior. For example, Reynolds (1961) tested pigeons on a *successive discrimination*. From time to time, the pigeons saw either a white triangle on a red surround or a white circle on a green surround, both projected onto a pecking key. If the triangle/red appeared, then the pigeons' pecks were reinforced, if the circle/green appeared, pecks were not reinforced. The birds easily learned this discrimination. They were then tested separately on each element—either red alone, green alone, circle alone, or triangle alone—without reinforcement. During the test, one pigeon pecked to the triangle, but did not peck at red, circle, or green. The other pigeon pecked at red, but did not peck at circle, triangle, or green.

Reynolds's experiment clearly demonstrates that the association between an element and a reinforcer is not sufficient to ensure that the feature will control an animal's response. Furthermore, because the two birds chose different dimensions to control their responding, this selective effect cannot plausibly be an artifact resulting from such factors as a difference in the salience of the stimuli. For example, if color were simply more salient than form, then both birds should have attended to color and not to form. Also, because the birds were pecking at the stimuli, it would have been difficult for them to selectively orient to one feature of the stimulus without also orienting to the other. Therefore, selective orientation is also implausible as an account of the selectivity. Reynolds's experiment demonstrates that animals selectively use certain features of a situation to control their performance, even when other factors, such as salience selective orientation and correlation with reinforcement are controlled.

CONTINUITY VERSUS NONCONTINUITY

Two general theories have been introduced to account for results such as those obtained by Reynolds. They differ in the claims they make about how learning takes place and in the role they attribute to perceptual attention. Based on early experiments that are conceptually related to that of Reynolds, Lashley (1929) and Krechevsky (1932) proposed an attentional explanation, which has come to be called the "noncontinuity position":

> When any complex of stimuli arouses nervous activity, that activity is immediately organized and certain elements or components become dominant for reaction while others become ineffective . . . In any trial of the training series, only those components of the stimulating situation which are dominant in the organization are associated. Other stimuli which excite the receptors are not associated because the animal is not set to react to them. (Lashley, 1942, p. 242)

In its strongest form the hypothesis says that, in learning a discrimination, an animal attends to only a single stimulus or dimension—for example, color, shape, position—at a time. While the animal is responding to one stimulus, it "learns (wrongly perhaps) something about the significance of this particular stimulus . . . but does not learn about the 'correctness' or 'wrongness' of the to-be-finally-learned set of [stimuli]" (Krechevsky, 1938, p. 111). Krechevsky called the selective attention to a dimension a "hypothesis" because, in the course of learning a discrimination, rats and other animals change "from one systematic, generalized, purposive way of behaving to another and another until the problem is solved" (Krechevsky, 1932, p. 532). Each systematic way of responding is analogous to a hypothesis for the correct solution to the discrimination problem—for example, that the shape of the stimulus is the relevant factor. Krechevsky did not necessarily mean that the rat consciously formed these hypotheses. Rather, he used the concept of hypothesis as a metaphor reflecting the facts that (1) the rat behaves regularly according to a single dimension as if that dimension were the correct or relevant dimension, and (2) the rat changes from one dimension to another when the current dimension is not consistently correlated with reinforcement.

According to the noncontinuity hypothesis, an animal learning a discrimination is always responding systematically to one dimension or another. Therefore, it is either responding to the correct dimension or it is responding to some other uncorrelated dimension. When the animal changes from one dimension to another, the pattern of its behavior also changes. Until it chooses the correct dimension, however, its behavior is still unrelated to the *correct* response pattern. Only when the animal does begin testing the correct dimension, does its behavior suddenly switch from errorful to correct responding.

This theoretical account of discrimination learning is called the "noncontinuity position" because it proposes that learning is a noncontinuous, all-or-none process, analogous to hypothesis testing. It seeks to explain selectivity in stimulus control as the result of a severe limit on the number of stimuli to which the animal can attend at one time. According to this view, animals can only attend to a single dimension at a time. They learn about the selected dimension, but not about any others. Once an animal begins attending to the correct dimension, it switches immediately from errorful to correct responding.

The noncontinuity position described by Lashley and Krechevsky stands in contrast to a "continuity position" proposed by Spence (1936, 1937) and Hull (1943). According to the continuity theory, animals have no attentional limits. They learn simultaneously about every stimulus they can perceive. Spence and Hull argued that learning is the gradual acquisition of excitatory and inhibitory potentials. Each stimulus or feature that is present receives these potentials independently of every other stimulus or feature. All stimuli present when a response is reinforced gain "excitatory potential"; all stimuli present when a response is not reinforced gain "inhibitory potential." The response an animal makes in the presence of a set of stimuli depends on the sum of the excitatory potentials minus the sum of the inhibitory potentials. The stimuli associated with reinforcement come to excite the appropriate response, whereas those associated with nonreinforcement come to inhibit the response. Stimuli that are not differentially associated with reinforcement—those present during both reinforcement and nonreinforcement—receive both excitatory and inhibitory potential. As a result they neither excite nor inhibit the correct response. Continuity theory explains selectivity of the sort observed by Reynolds by suggesting that stimuli differ in the rate at which they accumulate excitatory or inhibitory potential.

The continuity and noncontinuity theories are polar opposites. They make fundamentally different assertions about the way animals learn. According to the noncontinuity theory, learning is limited, controlled by attention, and sudden. Animals learn about the dimensions that characterize stimuli as well as about the individual stimuli themselves. According to the continuity theory, learning is unlimited in scope and gradual. As animals learn, they attach excitatory potential to stimuli that predict reinforcement and attach inhibitory potential to stimuli that signal nonreinforcement. They learn about individual stimuli, not about dimensions of those stimuli.

Comparisons between the continuity and the noncontinuity positions revolve mainly around two questions: (1) Do animals learn about all the stimuli that are present and can be sensed (continuity), or do they learn only about some (noncontinuity)? (2) Do they learn about stimuli exclusively (continuity), or do they also learn about dimensions (noncontinuity)? If animals can be shown to learn about dimensions—for example, that one dimension is valid, another irrelevant—it would show that they can learn about higher-order properties of stimuli, which cannot be attributed to learning about individual stimuli. What the animal learns about the validity of one dimension, from experience with some of the stimuli along it, could affect its performance in the presence of other stimuli along that dimension, even when these stimuli are novel. In the history of research on attention in animals, the continuity position has been viewed as the simpler, and hence, the preferred explanation, because it did not assume the presence of attention. The "burden of proof," so to speak, has been on supporters of the noncontinuity position to demonstrate that animals are selective in their learning. The evidence indicates, however, that both views require modification and that attention does play a role in animal learning.

Some early experiments

Systematic error responses.   Consistent with the assumptions of noncontinuity theory, Krechevsky (1932) found that rats did behave systematically relative to some identifiable stimulus dimension even when they were not responding systematically relative to the correct stimulus dimension. He trained rats in a discrimination in which the S+ was a small hurdle placed at the entrance to the rewarded arm of a Y maze. The presence versus absence of the hurdle was the correct dimension. Wherever the hurdle was, that was where food would be available. Brightness and location were the incorrect dimensions. Sometimes the food would be on the right, sometimes on the left. Sometimes it would be in the brighter arm, sometimes in the darker arm. Krechevsky found that every choice a rat made was correlated with one of these dimensions. For example, for some number of trials in a row, a rat might respond systematically to position, perhaps going consistently to the left arm. Then it might respond systematically to brightness, perhaps always going to the brighter arm. Finally, if it solved the discrimination problem, the rat would eventually adopt the correct strategy of going to the arm with the hurdle, wherever it was located.

In another experiment Krechevsky presented the rats with an insoluble discrimination problem, in which responses were reinforced at random; no stimulus or position was uniquely associated with reinforcement. Even under these conditions, the rats behaved in a systematic manner, first according to one stimulus, then according to another. The results of both of these experiments are consistent with the prediction of noncontinuity theory that animals learn discriminations by testing alternative hypotheses regarding the relevant stimulus dimension. The systematic error response patterns are inconsistent with the prediction of continuity theory that learning occurs gradually and simultaneously to all available stimuli.

Presolution reversal.   According to the noncontinuity hypothesis, animals learn about only a single stimulus dimension at a time. Furthermore, it assumes that they always respond according to the dimension they are currently testing. It follows, then, that while they are still making errors by responding to one of the incorrect dimensions, they have not yet learned anything about the correct dimension. If they had learned about the correct dimension, they would be responding to it and not making errors. Therefore, noncontinuity theory predicts that reversing the discrimination—reinforcing responses to the formerly negative stimulus and extinguishing responses to the formerly positive stimulus—will have no effect as long as the reversal occurs before the animal has solved the discrimination problem. This is called a "presolution reversal" because the reinforcement contingencies are reversed before the animal has solved the discrimination problem.

A typical presolution reversal experiment works as follows: Rats are trained with a multidimensional discrimination, in which the two alternatives vary in brightness (e.g., black versus white), position (e.g., left versus right), and shape (e.g., triangular versus circular). The stimuli are located on cards at the choice point of a T maze. One stimulus—for example, black—is positive and is associated with reinforcement; the rat must turn into the arm indicated by the black card (S+) in order to receive the food reward. Shape and location are irrelevant. After some training with these stimuli, but before the rat begins responding systematically to black and white, the values of black and white are reversed. Black becomes the negative stimulus (S−), and white becomes the positive stimulus (S+); after the reversal white indicates where food is, and black indicates where it is not.

Continuity and noncontinuity theories predict different outcomes in this kind of experiment. Noncontinuity theory predicts that presolution reversal will have no effect because the rat is not yet attending to the correct dimension and so has learned nothing about it. Continuity theory predicts that presolution reversal will hinder acquisition because the rat must "unlearn" the excitatory and inhibitory associations it formed during the presolution period.

A few experiments (e.g., Krechevsky, 1938; Ehrenfreund, 1948) found that presolution reversal had no effect on the total number of trials necessary for an animal to learn the discrimination. Other experiments, however, especially if they involved a larger number of presolution trials than did Krechevsky's, found that presolution reversal did retard acquisition (e.g., McCulloch & Pratt, 1934; Spence, 1945; Ritchie, Ebeling, & Roth, 1950).

The appropriate conclusion from these and other experiments appears to be that animals do learn about dimensions or stimuli while responding systematically to other stimuli. This could mean either that animals can learn about more than one stimulus dimension at a time or that they may continue responding to one dimension while learning about another. Either way, the strong version of noncontinuity theory proposed by Lashley and Krechevsky requires modification.

Evidence for control by stimulus dimensions

Subsequent experiments indicate that the continuity position also requires modification. Continuity theory asserts that learning consists exclusively of attaching
excitatory or inhibitory potential to individual *stimuli,* not dimensions or any
other "abstraction."

Contrary to this assumption, many experimental phenomena indicate that
animals learn about stimulus dimensions as well as about individual stimuli.
Among these phenomena are (1) overtraining reversal learning, (2) serial reversal learning, (3) acquired distinctiveness of cues, and (4) intradimensional versus
extradimensional shifts. (See Riley, 1968; and Sutherland & Mackintosh, 1971,
for more complete reviews.)

Overtraining reversal.   Overtraining reversal is the operational reverse of
presolution reversal. Instead of reversing the values of the relevant stimulus dimension before the animal has solved the problem, they are reversed after solution. For example, Reid (1953), trained three groups of rats in a brightness
(black versus white) discrimination in a Y maze. All rats were trained until they
chose the correct brightness on 18 out of 20 trials. One group continued to
receive training for 50 more trials; another continued training for 150 more
trials. Then the brightness discrimination was reversed for all groups. If the
brighter stimulus had been associated with reinforcement during training, it was
now associated with nonreinforcement and vice versa. The group overtrained for
150 trials showed faster acquisition of the reversed discrimination (70.0 trials)
than did the group that was trained only to criterion (138.3 trials) or the group
that was overtrained for 50 trials (129.0).

At first glance, the facilitation of discrimination reversal by overtraining is
puzzling. The more an animal is trained to select one stimulus and not the other,
the faster it learns to reverse its preference. According to continuity theory every
time a stimulus is paired with reinforcement its excitatory potential is increased,
and every time it is paired with nonreinforcement, its inhibitory potential is
increased. Continuity theory tried to explain the interfering effects of presolution
reversal by claiming that these potentials were growing even before the animal
showed any evidence of learning. It is puzzling, therefore, why continued training should not also have increased these potentials. From this point of view,
overtraining should interfere with reversal, not make it easier.

Reid explained the effects of overtraining on discrimination reversal by pro-
posing that animals learn to attend to stimulus dimensions—for example, brightness—while they are learning about the stimuli along those dimensions—for
example, black versus white. The initial discrimination and its reversal both

involve a brightness discrimination. Consequently, the animals could learn about the relevance of the brightness dimension as well as about the individual stimuli. This learning would then promote reversal learning because the same dimension remains relevant. Reid also argued that learning about dimensions proceeds more slowly than learning about the individual stimuli. Those animals who were merely trained until they discriminated the relevant stimuli did not have sufficient time to learn about the dimension of the discrimination. As a result they were slow to learn the reversed discrimination. In contrast, the animals who were overtrained did have time to learn about the relevant dimension. Therefore, they quickly learned the reversed discrimination.

Reid's hypothesis is a weaker version of noncontinuity theory (cf. Sutherland & Mackintosh, 1971). As in noncontinuity theory, Reid proposed that animals learn about dimensions while they are learning about individual stimuli. Noncontinuity theory assumed that attention to a dimension is required before animals can learn about the stimuli on the dimension. In contrast, Reid's hypothesis assumes that they learn about dimensions and about stimuli at the same time. Once an animal does learn to attend to a dimension, however, this attention makes further learning about stimuli easier along that dimension. Also in contrast to noncontinuity theory, Reid included the possibility that animals attend to more than one stimulus at a time and that they learn gradually about those dimensions and stimuli.

Overtraining apparently causes both an increase in attention to the relevant dimension and a decrease in attention to irrelevant dimensions. The addition of novel, but irrelevant, stimulus dimensions at the start of reversal training disrupts acquisition for animals trained only to criterion, but not for animals that were overtrained (Mackintosh, 1963). Overtraining reversal also facilitates subsequent reversal of a discrimination on another dimension (Hall, 1974), again presumably because it causes the animals to decrease their attention to irrelevant dimensions. Rats in this experiment who were overtrained on a line-orientation discrimination were no faster in learning a black-white discrimination than rats who were trained only to criterion, but they were faster at learning to reverse the black-white discrimination. Overtraining in this experiment caused the rats to attend less to the irrelevant dimensions. This tendency apparently persisted during later parts of the experiment. Reduced attention to irrelevant dimensions did not facilitate the original black-white discrimination because brightness had been irrelevant in the original problem, and the subject had learned to ignore it. It did facilitate the reversal, however, because no new dimensions had to be selected for attention, only the values of the stimuli along the already attended dimension. These experiments suggest that animals are capable of controling the attention they pay to various stimulus dimensions, depending on the relevance of that

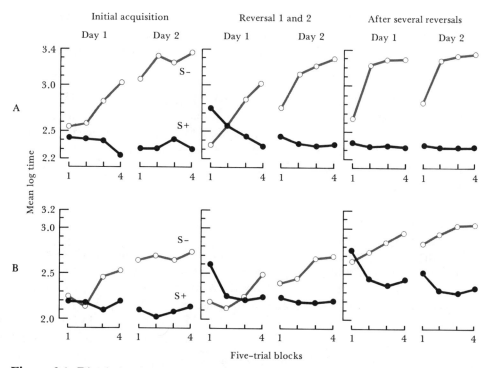

Figure 3.1. Discrimination-reversal performance of (A) pigeons and (B) goldfish. The latency of response to the stimulus associated with reinforcement (S+) and the stimulus associated with extinction (S−) is shown. [From Woodard, Schoel, & Bitterman, 1971.]

dimension to reinforcement.[3] Animals can learn to ignore some dimensions and attend to others.

Serial reversal learning.   Serial reversal learning experiments also show that animals can control the degree to which they attend or ignore dimensions. Subjects in these experiments are trained on a discrimination until they reach a criterion of accuracy. The values of the stimuli are then reversed: the formerly positive stimulus is made negative and the formerly negative stimulus is made positive. When the animal again reaches criterion, the values are again reversed, followed by another reversal, retraining, and so forth. As Figure 3.1 shows, each successive reversal requires fewer and fewer trials to reach criterion (Gatling, 1952; Schusterman, 1962; Woodard, Schoel & Bitterman, 1971). Presumably, serial reversal learning is similar to overtraining in causing the animal to increase attention to the relevant dimension and decrease attention to the irrelevant dimension. Contrary to the predictions of continuity theory, the increasing speed with which subjects learn each successive reversal indicates that they are learning about more than the association between the discrimination stimuli and reinforcement.

Acquired distinctiveness of cues.   Lawrence (e.g., 1949, 1950, 1952) found that rats who were trained to perform a simultaneous discrimination transferred their performance to a successive discrimination, for example, between black and white. In a simultaneous discrimination the S+ and S− are both present at the same time. Continuity theory (e.g., Spence, 1952) explains performance on this type of discrimination as the result of learning to approach the excitatory S+ and avoid the inhibitory S−. In a successive discrimination, on the other hand, the two alternatives are presented on separate trials. The animal's task is to make one response, such as a left turn in a T maze, when, for example, two white stimuli are presented and then to make another response, such as a right turn when two black stimuli are presented. The approach and avoidance tendencies presumably acquired during the simultaneous discrimination cannot help in the successive discrimination because both arms are signaled by the same stimulus on each trial. Both alternatives should then be equally attractive or equally abhorrent. Training on the simultaneous discrimination should thus be of no help in learning the successive discrimination if the continuity theory is correct.

Contrary to the predictions of continuity theory, a number of experiments have found positive transfer (Lawrence, 1949, 1950; Mumma & Warren, 1968; Winefield & Jeeves, 1971). Because these results cannot be explained by particular approach and avoidance tendencies, they must be based on some feature of the task that was common to the simultaneous and successive discriminations. Lawrence (1949, 1940, 1952) argued that the distinctiveness of the cues increased for the animal, or, in other words, the results were due to an increase in the attention the animal paid to the relevant stimulus dimension.

Intradimensional versus extradimensional shift.   Many experiments have found that training in a discrimination with one set of stimuli makes it easier for an animal to learn another discrimination problem involving novel stimuli from the same dimension (intradimensional shift) than one involving novel stimuli from a different dimension (extradimensional shift). A typical example of this type of experiment appears in Table 3.1. Humans (Wolff, 1967), rats (Shepp & Eimas, 1964; Schwartz, Schwartz, & Tees, 1971), pigeons (Mackintosh & Little, 1969) and monkeys (Rothblat & Wilson, 1968; Shepp & Schrier, 1969) have all shown better transfer with an intradimensional than with an extradimensional shift. Different stimuli are used in the two parts of the experiment, so learning about the values of the specific stimuli is not sufficient to account for the findings. Instead, it appears that the first stage of training increases the animal's

TABLE 3.1 Intradimensional versus extradimensional shifts

Dimension	Stimuli
Initial training	
Color relevant	red versus yellow
Shape irrelevant	circle versus square
Intradimensional shift	
Color relevant	blue versus green
Shape irrelevant	triangle versus star
Extradimensional shift	
Shape relevant	triangle versus star
Color irrelevant	blue versus green

attention to one dimension and decreases its attention to others (Mackintosh, 1983; Turrisi, Shepp, & Eimas, 1969).

The evidence is clear; attention plays a role in animal discrimination learning. Contrary to the predictions of continuity theory, animals are capable of learning about aspects of a discrimination task in a way that cannot be attributed to learning about the values of individual stimuli. They are also capable of learning to attend to some stimuli or dimensions and to ignore others. Similarly, contrary to the predictions of noncontinuity theory, animals are capable of learning about one dimension at the same time that their performance is controlled by another. Thus, both theories of discrimination learning require modification.

Hypothesis testing by humans

Although the noncontinuity theory appears to require modification to account for animal discrimination learning, under some conditions human discrimination learning appears to be consistent with Krechevsky's hypothesis. For example, Levine (1970) tested human subjects on a complex multidimensional-discrimination problem. The difficulty of this problem lay not in differentiating the stimuli from one another, but in identifying which of the available dimensions was correct, that is, relevant. Figure 3.2 shows a typical set of stimuli. Each stimulus consists of four binary dimensions: large versus small, left versus right, black versus white, and X versus T. The subject's task is to learn the correct stimulus by choosing one of the two alternatives appearing on each trial. For example, the first trial, described in the top row, presents a large black X on the left versus a small white T on the right. The subject, by pointing either at the left—and on this trial, large, black, and X—or the right—and on this trial, small, white, and T—stimulus.

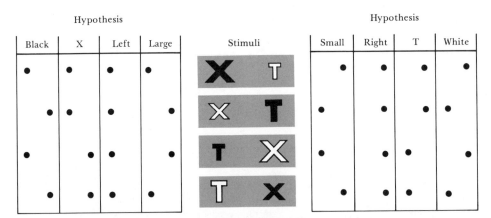

Figure 3.2. Eight possible choice patterns, each corresponding to one hypothesis for discriminating the stimuli shown in the middle of the figure. The dots in the columns labeled Black, X, Left, etc., indicate the side that would be chosen by a subject using the strategy indicated by the column heading. [From Levine, 1970.]

Levine presented blocks of trials, consisting of feedback trials on which the subjects were told whether their choice was correct or incorrect, and nonfeedback trials on which the subjects were not told whether they chose correctly or incorrectly. Levine assumed that people select hypotheses at random and maintain them until they are told that a choice is incorrect. Hence, they would maintain the same hypothesis through a block of nonfeedback trials because they could not receive feedback that their hypothesis was wrong.

These assumptions allowed Levine to use the sequence of responses made on a block of nonfeedback trials as an indication of the hypothesis the subject was using. Notice in Figure 3.2 that each of the eight simple hypotheses is represented by a unique pattern of choices. For example, if the subject is using the hypothesis that large stimuli are correct, then the first choice should be left, the second right, the third right, and the fourth left. On the other hand if the hypothesis is that black is positive then the sequence should be left, right, left, right. Response patterns different from those shown in Figure 3.2 have one of two explanations: (1) The hypothesis the subject is testing is more complex. For example, it may consist of a conjunctive concept, such as big and black is positive, all others are negative. (2) Alternatively, the person could be responding randomly.

Levine found that the behavior of adult humans conforms almost exactly to the pattern predicted by the hypothesis-testing view. Subjects tend to adopt a win-stay/lose-shift strategy for selecting hypotheses to test. If a hypothesis leads to a correct choice (win), subjects stay with it. If it leads to a choice producing negative feedback (loss), they shift to a new hypothesis.

TABLE 3.2 The experimental design and results obtained by Kamin (1968)

Group	16 reinforced trials	8 reinforced trials	4 nonreinforced trials	Suppression ratio
NL	—	NL	L	0.05
N→NL	N	NL	L	0.45
N only	N	N	L	0.44
NL	—	NL	N	0.25
L→NL	L	NL	N	0.50
L only	L	L	N	0.49

Note: N refers to noise, L to light. On NL trials the two stimuli were presented simultaneously. Suppression ratio is the degree to which presentation of the stimulus depressed bar pressing. Smaller suppression ratios (i.e., closer to 0) indicate more learning about the stimulus.
Source: Table after Mackintosh, 1974.

Attention to redundant stimuli and the role of surprise

Except for the experiment by Reynolds (1961), all of the work we have considered so far has presented compound stimuli, in which one dimension was relevant and the others were irrelevant and unrelated to the reinforcement contingencies. Under these circumstances animals were found to selectively attend to some dimensions and ignore others. We shall now consider what happens when two stimuli or dimensions are redundant, that is, when they are both equally valid predictors of reinforcement. In Reynolds's experiment the color and the form were equally good predictors of reinforcement, but the pigeons were selective in the dimension to which they responded.

Blocking.   Blocking demonstrates clearly that animals are capable of attending selectively. In the typical blocking experiment (Kamin, 1968, 1969) reinforced pretraining with one conditional stimulus (CS) interferes with subsequent acquisition of a novel CS presented in compound with it. The design of the basic blocking experiment appears in Table 3.2. Although other procedures have been used, the experiment described in Table 3.2 uses *conditioned suppression* to measure learning about the CS.

Conditioned suppression is the decrease in the rate at which an animal performs an appetitive response when presented with a stimulus previously associated with an aversive outcome. Before the start of the experiment Kamin trained his rats to bar press for food on a variable interval schedule. At various points during a session, independent of the rat's behavior, the CS indicated in Table 3.2 was presented for 3 minutes, then followed by a brief electric shock as the US. To the extent that the rat has learned about the relationship between the CS and the shock, presentation of the CS depresses the rate at which it presses the bar.

(The CS is said to produce a conditioned emotional response which interferes with bar pressing.) The amount of suppression is indexed by a *suppression ratio.* It is the ratio of rate of responding during the CS relative to that before and during the CS:

$$R = \frac{D}{B + D}$$

where R = the suppression ratio
D = the rate of responding during the aversive CS
B = the rate of responding during the period before the CS

A value of 0.5 indicates no suppression; the rate of responding during the CS is the same as that before the CS presentation. Thus, a ratio of 0.5 is the value one would expect if the animal has learned nothing about the shock-signaling properties of the CS. Conversely, a suppression ratio of 0.0 indicates complete suppression; the animal responded before, but not during the CS presentation. Therefore, a ratio of 0.0 is the value one would expect if the animal has learned a lot about the shock-signaling properties of the CS. In brief, the lower the suppression ratio, the greater the learning about the relationship between the CS and shock.

As Table 3.2 shows, group NL was trained from the start with a compound CS consisting of both a noise and a light. When the animals in this group were tested with the light alone (no shock was presented during the test trials) a great deal of suppression was observed. Hence, animals in this group learned about the relationship between the light and shock, even though the light was never presented without the noise. Apparently, they learned about both elements of the light/noise compound.

Group N→NL was pretrained with the noise for 16 trials and was then trained with the noise/light compound for 8 more trials. When tested with the light alone, the animals in this group showed virtually no suppression, as if they had not learned anything about the light. In fact, their suppression ratio during the test was about equal to the animals in group N-only, who had not been trained with the light at all. The rats in the N→NL group and in the NL group both received exactly the same number of pairings of the light with the shock. Therefore, both groups experienced the same correlation between the light and the shock, yet one group responded to the light as a predictor of shock, whereas the other did not. Pretraining with the noise alone *blocked* acquisition to the light. In general, blocking occurs when a pretrained stimulus prevents a new stimulus with which it is presented from acquiring conditioned suppression properties.

There are three ways in which attention might be used to explain the blocking phenomenon. The strong version of noncontinuity theory argues that during the initial 16 N trials, the rats in group N→NL learned to attend to the noise. Because it was consistently associated with the presentation of the US, they had no reason to reject the noise dimension and consider another. Therefore, the rats in this group continued to attend to the noise and learned nothing about any other dimension. Similarly, a limited-capacity attention hypothesis argues that training with the noise CS caused the animals to allocate all of their attention to the noise. Then, when the NL compound was presented, the rats had no attentional capacity left, and so could not attend to the light. As a result they neither noticed the light nor learned about it. Finally, it is possible that training with the noise CS taught them to attend to the noise stimulus. Because the added light stimulus was redundant with the noise, they then learned to ignore the redundant stimulus.

The first two attentional explanations assert that blocking occurs because the animals do not notice the added stimulus. The third hypothesis says that blocking occurs because they do notice it but they also notice that it is redundant. In order to discriminate between these explanations, it would be helpful to know whether animals respond differently to the first compound trial than they did to the previous single-stimulus trial. They could not respond differently to the first compound trial unless they noticed the added stimulus.

Two findings lead to the conclusion that animals do notice the added stimulus, at least the first time it is presented. The first is an experiment, shown in Table 3.3, which found that rats change their behavior in response to the added stimulus. Kamin (1968) trained two groups of rats for 16 trials, with noise as the CS and shock as the US. By the end of this training, both groups showed near complete suppression. On the 17th trial, one group was presented with a compound of noise and light, and the other group continued to receive noise alone. Those rats that received the added light significantly increased their suppression

TABLE 3.3 Suppression ratio observed on the first compound trial

CS during 16 training trials	Suppression ratio at end of training	CS on test trial	Suppression ratio on test trial
Noise	0.02	Noise + light	0.18
Noise	0.02	Noise	0.02

Note: The test occurred on trial 17. The suppression ratio measures the amount of suppression obtained during the CS, before the presentation of the shock US.
Source: From Kamin, 1968.

ratio on that trial. The other animals, still tested with the noise alone, did not increase their suppression ratio. For the animals to respond differently to the first noise/light trial relative to the last noise-only trial, they must have been able to detect the difference between the two, namely, the addition of the light. Therefore, blocking cannot be due to a failure to notice the blocked stimulus.

The second finding is that changing the US when the second stimulus is added interferes with blocking. This is called *unblocking*. For example, Dickinson, Hall, and Mackintosh (1976) trained rats in a three-part experiment, outlined in Table 3.4. Group L+ was originally trained with a light signaling one shock, then was switched to a light/clicker compound CS, signaling two shocks, presented 8 s apart. Group L+4 was originally trained with a light, signaling two shocks, presented 4 s apart. These animals were then switched to a compound CS, signaling two shocks but presented 8 s apart. Both groups, for whom the US changed when the clicker CS was added, showed significantly more suppression than did the L+8 group, which was trained throughout with two shocks, separated by 8 s. Thus, changing the US when the clicker was added, decreased the extent to which the light blocked acquisition to the clicker.

Blocking is controlled by the reinforcer that follows the compound CS. When the added CS element signals a changed US, then animals show some evidence of learning about the added element. When the added CS element does not signal a changed US (relative to that predicted by the initially trained CS element), then blocking is observed: the animal appears not to learn about the added element and its relation to shock. By the time the reinforcer is presented, however, the

TABLE 3.4 Experimental procedure and results of the unblocking experiment of Dickinson, Hall, & Mackintosh, 1976

Group	Stage 1 12 reinforced trials		Stage 2 10 reinforced trials		Stage 3 2 nonreinforced trials	Suppression ratio
	CS	US	CS	US	CS	
L+	L	S	L/C	S-S	C	0.40
L+4	L	S-S	L/C	S-S	C	0.38
L+8	L	S-S	L/C	S-S	C	0.50
N	—	—	L/C	S-S	C	0.15

Note: L = light, C = clicker, S = one shock, S-S = two shocks. For group L+4 the two shocks were separated by a 4-s interval during stage 1. For group L+8 the two shocks were separated by an 8-s interval during stage 1. For all groups the two shocks presented during stage 2 were separated by an 8-s interval. Groups L+ and L+4 showed some suppression to the clicker trained in stage 2. Changing the reinforcer (US), either by adding a second shock or by delaying the second shock, interfered with blocking.

added stimulus element has already disappeared and is no longer available. Hence the animal neither attends to nor ignores it. Consequently, blocking cannot be the result of a failure to detect the added stimulus when it is first presented.

Kamin interpreted the results of his blocking experiment in terms of *surprise:* conditioning happens only if the occurrence of the US is surprising. Because the noise in his blocking experiment already predicted the shock, the light was not surprising and the rats learned nothing about it. If the US does not change, then the added member of the compound CS is redundant and not surprising. Blocking occurs. If the US does change, then the added member of the compound signals the changed US. It is not redundant and the new US is surprising. No blocking occurs.

Rescorla and Wagner (1972) described the surprise hypothesis more formally in a mathematical model of conditioning. They argued that any given reinforcer can support only a fixed level of conditioning. When a US is surprising, it is because the animal has not learned to predict it. As the animal learns about the relationship between a CS and a US, the CS gains associative strength, and the US becomes expected—that is, not surprising. As the associative strength of the pretrained element in the blocking experiment approaches the limit for that reinforcer, no more strength is available for the blocked stimulus and the animal fails to learn about the added element. In the unblocking experiment, an increase in the magnitude of the US also increases the pool of available associative strength. Therefore, even though pretraining with one CS uses up all the associative capacity of the original US, the increase in the magnitude of the US simply provides a greater pool of associative strength, which can then be obtained by the added CS element.

Rescorla and Wagner's model is sometimes called a neocontinuity model because, like the continuity model, it assumes that learning is a gradual process and that the animal learns about all available stimuli simultaneously. Where Hull and Spence assumed that each stimulus gains or loses strength independently of every other stimulus, Rescorla and Wagner assumed that the strength gained by a given stimulus depends on the current strengths of other simultaneously present stimuli and on the contiguity between stimulus and reinforcer. As one member of a compound gains excitatory (or inhibitory) potential, it uses up the available pool of potential strength associated with each reinforcer, and so less is left for the other member of the compound.

In summary, the Rescorla-Wagner model explains the apparent attentional effects observed in blocking as the result of a limited associational capacity. When the animal has learned that one stimulus predicts a reinforcer, that stimulus absorbs the available associative capacity, leaving little, if any, available for the added stimulus. Changing the reinforcer during training with the compound, however, changes the pool of available associative capacity. Therefore, blocking does not occur when the reinforcer associated with the compound is different from the reinforcer used during single-stimulus training.

Overshadowing.   Overshadowing is a phenomenon like blocking that occurs when a more salient stimulus of a compound prevents a less salient stimulus from controlling the animal's responding. The Rescorla-Wagner model recognizes that stimuli differ in their salience: animals learn faster about more intense than about less intense stimuli. For example, we would expect an animal to learn more quickly about the relationship between a loud noise and a reinforcer than about a dim light paired with the same reinforcer. When two stimuli that differ in salience are both simultaneously and redundantly associated with some reinforcer, the faster learning about the more salient stimulus interferes with learning about the less salient stimulus. Presumably, this occurs because the stronger stimulus takes up the animal's available associative capacity first and then "blocks" acquisition by the weaker (D'Amato & Fazzaro, 1966; Lovejoy & Russell, 1967; Miles & Jenkins, 1973).

Although the Rescorla-Wagner model has been very influential, it is inadequate to explain all of the results of compound conditioning or the results of dimensional selectivity just described. For example, Table 3.2 shows two groups that were trained from the beginning with a compound CS, consisting of noise and light. One group was tested for the suppressive effects of the noise, the other for the suppressive effects of the light. The animals tested on noise showed less suppression than did those tested on light, even though the training experience of the two groups had been identical. Apparently, the subjects learned more slowly about the noise than about the light when the two were presented in compound. Because of the apparent difference in the animal's speed of acquisition to the two stimuli, there should be more associative capacity remaining after 16 noise trials than there is after 16 light trials. The noise should then be a less effective blocker than the light. As a result, we should expect less suppression to the noise in the L→NL group than suppression to the light in the N→NL group, because the light will have taken up relatively more of the available associative strength than the noise after the same number of trials. In fact, this was not observed. Pretraining with either element blocked acquisition of suppression to the added element. Therefore, the weaker noise interfered with the animal's acquisition to the light just as effectively as the stronger light interfered with its acquisition to noise. This indicates that the amount of associative strength available and the amount taken up are not sufficient to predict whether blocking will or will not occur. Although there was clearly associative strength remaining after the noise trials, apparently, this strength was unavailable to the light during the noise-light compound trials (cf. D'Amato & Fazzaro, 1966; Lovejoy & Russell, 1967; Miles & Jenkins, 1973).

Finally, Mackintosh and Turner (1971) have found that blocking of a stimulus interferes with the subsequent training of that stimulus, even if the magnitude of the reinforcer is later changed. Contrary to the Rescorla-Wagner model, this indicates that animals do learn something about the blocked stimulus and that this learning then interferes with later learning.

A two-stage attention model

A two-stage discrimination learning mechanism is necessary to explain blocking and the other phenomena described above. The animal learns (1) to attend to the relevant dimension and ignore those that are irrelevant and (2) to attach the correct responses to the stimuli along that dimension.

An example of a two-stage model containing separate processes for learning about dimensions and learning about stimuli appears in Figure 3.3 (Sutherland & Mackintosh, 1971; also see Zeaman & House, 1963). Stimuli enter the organism from the outside environment and are processed by various analyzers. Each analyzer classifies the stimulus input according to one dimension. For example, analyzer 1 in Figure 3.3 classifies stimuli according to the dimension of brightness; its output is the stimulus value on that dimension—its brightness. Analyzer 2 classifies the stimuli according to orientation; its output is the value of the

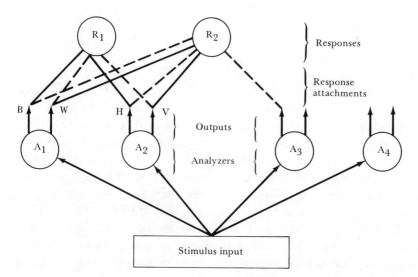

Figure 3.3. Diagram of the two-stage attentional model described by Sutherland and Mackintosh. Stimuli are shown entering at the bottom. These are then "analyzed" by the analyzers. Each analyzer gives a value along a single dimension. The analyzers then lead to response mechanisms. Learned responses are shown by solid lines; other possible connections are shown by dashed lines. B = black, W = white, H = horizontal, V = vertical. [From Sutherland & Mackintosh, 1971.]

stimulus on the orientation dimension. Only two possible outputs are shown for each analyzer, but more outputs are also possible, corresponding, for example, to shades of gray or to orientations between vertical and horizontal.

For simplicity, the model described in Figure 3.3 says that an animal can only effectively employ one analyzer at a time. The full model described by Sutherland and Mackintosh allows more analyzers to be active to varying extents, but supposes a limit on the number. Animals learn to switch in certain analyzers, and attend to their outputs, or to switch out certain analyzers and ignore their outputs. Learning to solve a discrimination problem consists of switching in the appropriate analyzer detecting the relevant cue and attaching the correct response to its output.

The Sutherland-Mackintosh model in Figure 3.3 could be used to solve a discrimination problem in a T-maze as follows: The discrimination is between a horizontal black bar and a vertical white bar. The animal must enter the arm indicated by the horizontal black bar in preference to the arm indicated by the vertical white bar. In addition to the color and the orientation of the bar, the discriminative stimuli also differ along other dimensions, such as position (left arm versus right arm), size (large versus small), and so forth, but these dimensions are irrevelant. The arm with the reward is just as likely to have a large as a small stimulus at its entrance and is as likely to be on the right as on the left.

In this model animals learn by switching in the correct analyzers (i.e., either analyzer 1 for color, or analyzer 2 for orientation), switching off those that are irrelevant (analyzer 3 for position, analyzer 4 for size), and learning which response (response 1 for approach, response 2 for avoid) to attach to the outputs of the relevant analyzers.

At the beginning of the trial, the animal is released from the start box and allowed to run down the alley. At the end of the alley, it looks at one of the two stimulus cards and then either enters the arm indicated by that card or examines the other card. Whether the rat enters an arm is controlled by the combination of its analyzer output and its response output. The animal initially selects analyzers and responses roughly at random. If the response is reinforced, then both the analyzer and the response attached to it are strengthened. If, however, the response is not reinforced, then the strength of the response and of the analyzer are both decreased. Both the probability of a response and the probability that a given analyzer will be switched in are proportional to their strength. The appropriate analyzers and the appropriate analyzer-response connections are strengthened through acquisition, and the inappropriate analyzers and connections are weakened. According to the model illustrated in Figure 3.3, the animal will enter the arm indicated by the black stimulus if analyzer 1 is switched in or the arm indicated by the horizontal stimulus if analyzer 2 is switched in. Alternatively, the animal will avoid the arm if the stimulus is white and analyzer

1 is switched in, or if the stimulus is vertical and analyzer 2 is switched in. When analyzer 1 is switched in—and analyzer 2 is not—the orientation of the stimulus is irrelevant, and when analyzer 2 is switched in—and analyzer 1 is not—the brightness of the stimulus is irrelevant.

The assumption that animals use separate processes to attend to dimensions and to attend to stimuli allows the model to account for the data described above. It argues that animals learn about dimensions while they learn about stimuli along those dimensions.

Conclusion

The most reasonable conclusion from the data concerning discrimination learning is that animals can selectively attend to certain stimuli, but there is no evidence that the observed selectivity is an automatic outcome of an attentional capacity that is limited to a single stimulus or to a small number of stimuli (i.e., of a limited processing capacity). Instead, attention appears to be a "voluntary" result of the relationship between stimulus dimensions and reinforcement. An animal ignores noninformative stimuli or dimensions, not because it *cannot* attend to them, but because they are uninformative. It has to learn which stimuli are informative and which are not. In short, discrimination learning appears to involve two processes. One process controls the dimensions to which the animal attends, and the other controls the values assigned to stimuli along those dimensions.

LIMITED-CAPACITY SELECTIVE ATTENTION

The experiments reviewed in the previous section provide evidence for mechanisms that control the dimensions and the stimuli to which animals attend. They require a revision of both the continuity and the noncontinuity positions, but they do not argue that animals have limited attentional capacities. When an animal in a discrimination-learning experiment fails to attend to an otherwise salient dimension, it is not because it *cannot* attend to the dimension, but because it has learned to ignore it. In contrast, much of the work on attention in humans is concerned with the analysis of limits of attention, when subjects *cannot* obtain all of the information that is present.

As the term is typically used in work with human subjects, attention involves an inverse relation: attention to some stimuli precludes simultaneous attention to other stimuli. Organisms are assumed to have only a limited capacity to process information. Attention in this sense refers to the fact that performance of one information-processing task—such as reading this book—reduces our ability to simultaneously perform other information-processing tasks—such as watching television. If we do try to perform both tasks at once, our performance on one or both is degraded. We may have to read the same passage again, or we may miss the crucial clue in the televised murder mystery.

Alternatively, if we do want to perform two demanding activities, we can do so if we have sufficient time to switch our attention, first to one task and then to another. If we have all night to study, we can take time out from studying to watch some television and take time out from television watching to do some studying. If we switch rapidly enough, it may appear that we are actually attending to two tasks simultaneously when, in fact, we are attending to only a single task at a time. By the end of the evening we would have both watched television and read. Because the stimuli in discrimination learning experiments are present for relatively long times, an animal can switch its attention from one to another. Under these conditions, even if it could attend to only a single dimension at a time, it would still have sufficient time to attend first to one dimension, then to another, and so forth. Because we only assess the extent to which the animals had processed both dimensions at the end of the stimulus presentation, we cannot know whether they switched their attention or divided it in some other way. In short, discrimination learning experiments have generally proved inadequate to discover information-processing limits, even if such limits exist. These experiments have used stimuli that are too simple and that are presented for too long a time to tax the limits of the organism's information-processing system.

An example

As an example of the type of research used to study attention in the sense of limited-processing capacity, Lindsay, Taylor, and Forbes (1968) required human subjects to perform a difficult multidimensional discrimination involving briefly presented stimuli. A compound stimulus was presented on each trial. It consisted of two visual dimensions—vertical and horizontal displacements of a small dot on a television screen—and two auditory dimensions—loudness and pitch of a tone. For example, the stimulus on one trial might be a dot in the upper right corner of the screen, accompanied by a soft, high-pitched tone. On another trial, it might be a dot in the lower left portion of the screen, accompanied by a loud, low-pitched tone. The experimenters used all combinations of horizontal and vertical displacement and loudness and pitch of the tone.

The compound stimulus was presented briefly. Subjects were then signaled to report the stimulus's value along one dimension. One signal indicated that subjects were to report the pitch, another that they were to report the horizontal position of the dot, and so forth. On every trial they had to report exactly one dimension, but they could not know until the signal was presented which of the four dimensions to report. As a result, they had to attend to all dimensions on every trial.

Divided attention.   In order to investigate the attentional capacity that subjects had available to process each dimension, Lindsay and his associates held some of the dimensions constant from trial to trial. For example, they presented a set of trials in which the dot always appeared in the lower part of the screen. Subjects were told that they would not be tested on the dimensions that were held constant. As a result they could presumably ignore these constant stimulus dimensions and focus their attention on the remaining dimensions. In some sessions the stimuli varied on only one of the available dimensions (e.g., pitch). During these sessions subjects were certain about which dimension they would have to report. The compound stimuli would differ from one another only on that single dimension. Some trials would present the high pitch, others the low pitch, but all the other stimulus dimensions would be held constant. Subjects could then focus their attention on that single dimension. During other sessions the stimuli could vary along two dimensions and subjects would have to report the stimulus's value on either dimension, but never on both. During these sessions, subjects had to divide their attention between the two varying dimensions, so they had less capacity available for processing each. During the remaining sessions, the stimuli varied along all four dimensions and subjects had to divide their attention among all four of them. Thus performance could be measured when subjects focused attention on a single dimension and when they had to divide it among either two or four dimensions. If humans do have a limited attentional capacity, then their discriminative performance on each dimension should decline as they have to process more dimensions. More and more of their available information-processing capacity is consumed in processing the other dimensions, and less and less is available for processing the to-be-reported dimension.

Consistent with the limited-capacity hypothesis, Lindsay and his associates found that the subjects' accuracy improved as duration of the stimuli increased from 67 to 200 ms. This indicates that the stimuli did actually tax the subjects' information-processing capacities. When they were allowed more time to process the stimuli, they performed better. Furthermore, subjects' discriminative accuracy for a given stimulus duration was highest when only a single dimension was varied and lowest when all four dimensions varied on every trial. Each additional dimension required additional processing capacity. Figure 3.4 shows both these results. This study argues that human subjects have a limited attentional capacity, which they can allocate to discriminate stimuli. Attention to one stimulus or dimension decreases the amount they have available for processing other stimuli. Once their capacity is reached, people can only process additional information if they take more time.

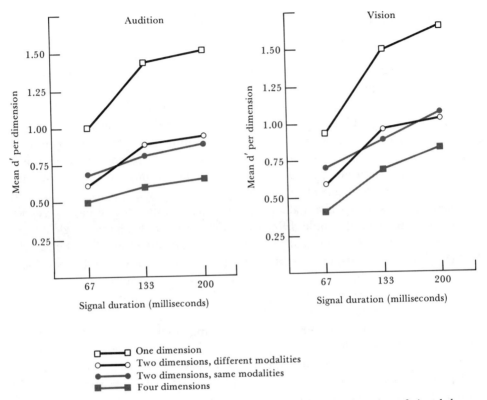

Figure 3.4. Mean discriminability per stimulus dimension as a function of signal duration, modality (audition or vision), and number of concurrently varying dimensions. Each curve is the average of two dimensions along the indicated modality. The measure d' is an indication of the discriminability between the two values along the dimension. Larger values indicate greater discriminability. [From Lindsay, Taylor, & Forbes, 1968.]

Directed attention.   If the limitation is in the perception and initial processing of the multidimensional stimuli, then, telling the subjects ahead of time which dimension would be tested, should improve their performance. Signaling the to-be-tested dimension allows subjects to focus their attention only on the relevant dimension and neglect the irrelevant dimensions. Alternatively, the lower performance observed when more dimensions are varied could be due to increased complexity of the display, unrelated to any limited cognitive capacity. For example, the dots might be more difficult to see when they are presented briefly in an uncertain location than when they are presented in a fixed location. In order to investigate this hypothesis, Forbes, Taylor, and Lindsay (1967) precued the subjects regarding which of the four dimensions they should report. When the cue appeared at least 40 ms before the stimulus, subjects' performance was near that obtained when only one dimension was varied. Their choice accuracy was slightly lower when the cue appeared 20 ms before the stimulus, and lower still if it followed it. With 40 ms between the precue and the stimulus, the subjects had enough time to process the cue and focus their attention specifically on the signaled dimension. They could not complete this allocation in time when the precue came 20 ms before the stimulus, or when it came after it. The difference between the effects of a preceding and a following cue indicate that the limitation is in the perception and identification of the stimulus dimensions. It is not caused by any artifact of the stimulus display itself.

These two experiments argue that the number of dimensions that a human can perceive and identify in a short period of time is limited. If subjects are told which dimension will be tested, they can allocate more of their processing capacity to this dimension and so improve their discrimination performance. Although it was not tested in these experiments, the selective attention hypothesis also predicts that attention to one dimension decreases the amount of information that can be obtained on other dimensions. In other words, subjects who perform more accurately on the selected dimension should perform less accurately on the neglected dimensions. Improved performance on the selected dimension is at the expense of poorer performance on the neglected dimension.

The important difference between the kind of experiment conducted by Lindsay and his associates and the experiments in discrimination learning previously described is the presence of a time limitation. Lindsay et al. tested their subjects with brief stimuli, which were less than 200 ms in duration. They found that longer stimulus durations improved choice accuracy, presumably by providing more time for processing each changing dimension. Because choice accuracy improved throughout the range of stimulus durations tested, it is reasonably certain that the complex stimuli and brief durations did actually tax the subjects' capacity. Even with the longest stimulus duration tested, however, the subjects were less than perfect. Still, it is reasonable to assume that given enough time— for instance, several seconds—they could perform with perfect or near perfect accuracy by first processing one dimension, then another, and so forth.

Animal discrimination-learning experiments seldom place any time constraints on the subjects' performance. Therefore, there is no reason to believe that it is limited by the animals' ability to distribute their attention among the various dimensions. Limited attentional capacities can only be observed if animals are tested under conditions comparable to those that reveal the limitation in humans. The task must overload the animal's ability to take in all of the required information in the available time.

Time-limited discrimination learning

At least one discrimination experiment with pigeons has found evidence for selective attention of the type described by Lindsay and his associates. Blough

(1969) trained the birds on a difficult discrimination of compound stimuli varying along two dimensions: the frequency of a tone and the hue of a light. Forty-
nine hue/tone compounds were made up from all possible pairs of seven similar
tones and seven similar hues (see Figure 3.5). The stimulus compound, consisting of one extreme value—for example, the highest tone or the reddest hue—was
chosen as the positive stimulus (S+). Pecks in the presence of this compound
were occasionally reinforced. Those in the presence of any other compound were
not reinforced. There were 48 S— compounds and 1 S+ compound. Stimuli
were presented for 1.5 s. This duration was brief enough so that, coupled with
the difficulty of the discrimination, the pigeons' information-processing capacities were apparently taxed.[4]

Choice accuracy on this task is indexed by the relative frequency with which
the birds pecked at each compound stimulus. Perfect discrimination would result
in pecking at the positive compound and not pecking at the 48 other compounds.
Discrimination was imperfect, however. Pecking was most frequent to the positive pair, declining as the difference between it and the test pair increased.

During the second phase of the experiment, the birds were tested on only one
dimension at a time. The other dimension was held constant at the S+ value.
During this phase, only seven compounds were presented, the S+ combination

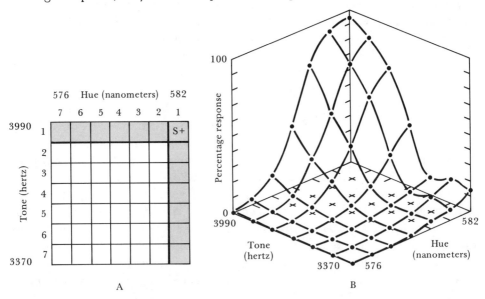

Figure 3.5. A diagram of the stimuli used by Blough (1969). All 49 stimulus compounds
were employed during initial training. Single-dimension training used either the stimuli
in the top row or in the right-most column. S+ indicates the positive stimulus compound, pecks to which were reinforced. (B) shows the response pattern for Bird 476 at
the end of phase 1 of training. [After Blough, 1969.]

used during the first phase and the other six values along the selected dimension in compound with the S+ stimulus from the neglected dimension. During single-dimension training, either the seven hues were presented in combination with tone 1 (hue-1/tone-1, hue-2/tone-1, . . . hue-7/tone-1), or the seven tones were presented in combination with hue 1 (hue-1/tone-1, hue-1/tone-2, . . . hue-1/tone-7).

Single-dimension training improved the birds' discriminability along the trained dimension. Their rate of pecking to the compounds was more sharply differentiated after single-dimension training than after bidimensional training. This finding is analogous to that observed by Lindsay and his associates. When one dimension was held constant, subjects were better able to discriminate the dimension that was varying.

After single-dimension training, the birds were returned to the two-dimensional discrimination task with all 49 compounds. Blough found that their ability to discriminate along the dimension that was held constant during single-dimension training was poorer than it had been at the end of the initial training with both dimensions. In other words, the improvement in discriminability observed during single-dimension training was at the expense of discriminability along the neglected dimension. This finding suggests that the change in performance was due to a reallocation of the birds' attentional capacity as a result of single-dimension training.

As further support for the hypothesis that single-dimension training resulted in a reallocation of attention, Blough observed that further training on the two-dimensional problem resulted in improved discrimination along the formerly neglected dimension, and poorer discrimination along the formerly attended dimension. As the birds were retrained on the two-dimensional problem, they again reallocated their attention, dividing it between the two dimensions, instead of attending selectively only to one. The result of this reallocation was a drop in the attentional capacity that the birds allocated to the formerly selected dimension and an increase in the attentional capacity that they allocated to the formerly neglected dimension, until both returned to the level observed during initial training.

Selective attention in delayed matching-to-sample

The attentional capacities of animals have also been studied, using the delayed matching-to-sample (DMTS; see Chapter 5) with limited sample durations. Figure 3.6 shows an outline of this procedure. Each trial begins with the presentation of a warning signal on the center key of a three-key operant chamber. A response to this signal produces the sample on the same key. Immediately following the termination of the sample—that is, after 0 s delay—two comparison

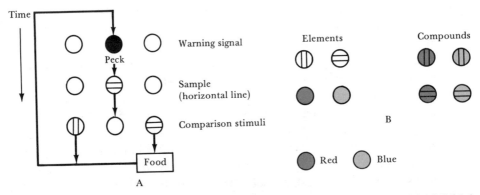

Figure 3.6. (A) shows the procedure and (B) shows stimuli of the sort used by Maki & Leith (1973) in delayed matching-to-sample. Samples were either compounds of a line and a color or elements (a line or a color). All comparison stimuli were elements. A single peck to the comparison stimulus matching the sample was rewarded with food. Incorrect responses terminated the trial without food.

stimuli appear on the side keys. One matches the sample; the other does not. The subject is rewarded for responding to the comparison stimulus which matches the sample.

Divided and directed attention.   As in the experiments of Lindsay and his associates (Lindsay, Taylor, & Forbes, 1968), the information-processing load is varied by increasing or decreasing the duration of the sample stimulus and by changing the number of stimulus dimensions present in the sample. On some trials the sample is a color, on others it is a line orientation, and on still others, it is a bidimensional compound of a color and a line orientation. Colors are always presented as the comparison stimuli following color samples; lines are always presented as the comparison stimuli following line-orientation samples. Following compound samples, however, the subject could be tested either with two color comparison stimuli—and required to choose the color that matches the one present in the sample—or with two line orientations—and required to choose the orientation that matches the one present in the sample. Both decreasing the sample duration and increasing the number of dimensions in the sample increases the likelihood of an error by pigeon subjects. (For a review see Riley & Roitblat, 1978).

Maki and Leith (1973) tested pigeons in a DMTS task with element and compound samples. When the trial began with a color sample, the bird could know that it would be tested with two color comparison stimuli. Similarly, when the trial began with a line-orientation sample the bird could know that it would be tested for line orientation. When a trial began with a compound of a color and a line orientation, however, it could not know whether it would be tested for color or for line orientation and would, presumably, have to divide its attention between the two dimensions.

Figure 3.7 shows that the results of this experiment with pigeons were similar to those obtained with humans by Lindsay and his associates. Choice accuracy was markedly lower following compound samples than following element samples, and both kinds of accuracy improved with increasing sample duration (Maki & Leith, 1973). Hence, these experiments appear to produce time-limited information overload.

Leith and Maki (1975) conducted a further experiment, in which they "instructed" their pigeon subjects to attend to only one dimension. For a month at a time, they tested the birds with only a single dimension. During one month, for example, they presented only line-orientation samples on element trials and tested only the line orientation dimension on compound trials. After a month of

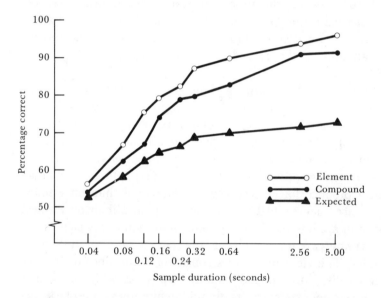

Figure 3.7. Delayed matching-to-sample choice accuracy observed by Maki & Leith, 1973. The stimuli are shown in (B) of Figure 3.6. The open circles represent performance on trials with single-element samples. The closed circles represent performance with compound samples. The triangles represent performance that would result on compound trials if the pigeons attended to only one sample dimension per trial. On half of the trials, it would attend to the correct dimension—that is, the one that will be tested—and so perform at the choice accuracy for element samples. On the other half of the trials it would attend to the incorrect dimension—that is, the one that will not be tested—and so choose between the comparison stimuli with chance accuracy. Obtained compound performance is significantly better than would be expected on the basis of this single-dimension hypothesis. [The data are taken from Maki & Leith, 1973. The figure is from Riley & Roitblat, 1978.]

this single-dimension training, the birds' choice accuracy on compound trials improved, but it was still below that obtained on element trials. When the subjects were returned to two-dimensional training, their choice accuracy on the neglected dimension was initially lower than it had been before training on a single dimension. Moreover, like Blough (1969), Leith and Maki found that during retraining accuracy on the selected dimension declined as accuracy on the formerly neglected dimension improved. The same pattern of results was observed when they tested only colors for a month.

Similar results were obtained by Leuin (1976), who used a procedure more closely analogous to that of Forbes, Taylor, and Lindsay (1967). Leuin cued the pigeons on half of the compound and on all of the element trials. He found that cueing a dimension improved their choice accuracy when that dimension was tested relative to uncued performance and lowered it when the noncued dimension was tested. This confirms that the improvement in choice accuracy observed when a dimension was cued is due to the animal's selective reallocation of attention to the cued dimension. Its attention to the cued dimension is at the expense of (i.e., reduced) its attention to the uncued dimension.

Alternative nonattentional explanations.   The lower choice accuracy displayed by animals on uncued compound trials relative to element trials appears to result from a division of attention on compound trials. When two dimensions can be tested, the pigeon has less attentional capacity to allocate to the processing of either. Consequently, its choice accuracy on both dimensions is lower. Although these results are consistent with this attentional explanation, other possible factors could also produce lower accuracy on compound than on element sample trials. Choice accuracy could be lower on compound than on element trials because the stimuli are less visible in the compound than in the element, or because the element samples are more similar to the comparison stimuli than are the compound samples. The element samples consist of white lines on a black surround or of colored disks. Compound samples appear as white lines on a colored surround. The element comparison stimuli—white lines on a black surround or colored disks—are more similar to the element samples than to the compound samples. If pigeons choose the correct comparison stimulus on the basis of its similarity to the sample (see Chapter 8), then this generalization decrement would explain why choice accuracy is lower following compound samples than following element samples. The two kinds of samples differ in their similarity to the element comparison stimuli.

Neither similarity between the samples and comparison stimuli nor degradation of the visibility of compound samples is sufficient to explain the difference in choice accuracy between tests using element samples and those using compound samples, because neither of these hypotheses can explain the improvement in performance observed following precueing and single-dimension training (cf. the discussion regarding Lindsay, Taylor, & Forbes's, 1968 experiment). On the other hand, neither single-dimension training nor precueing eliminated the difference between element- and compound-matching accuracy. The remaining difference could be a result of stimulus degradation or of the pigeon's inability to perfectly allocate its attention.

Further evidence against the generalization-decrement account of the element/compound difference is seen in the finding that pigeons are quite capable of performing "symbolic matching-to-sample," in which the sample and correct comparison stimulus are only arbitrarily related to one another (e.g., Roitblat, 1980). Similarity between sample and comparison stimuli cannot, by design, play a role in symbolic matching-to-sample.

Conclusion.   Under the appropriate circumstances, animals demonstrate the kind of selective attention that studies of human attention and performance show. In DMTS, the limited sample duration taxes the subject's information-processing capacities so that the attention it pays to one dimension of a compound appears to restrict the amount it can pay to the other. The result is a drop in performance on both dimensions. Although additional factors may help in determining performance following compound relative to element samples, limits on the subject's processing capacity are also clearly important.

The structure of the stimulus

An organism's ability to attend selectively to one dimension of a stimulus compound in preference to others implies that it can somehow decompose the compound into separate, independent dimensions. In some experiments this was undoubtedly straightforward. For example, Blough (1969) used stimulus compounds made from a tone of a particular pitch and a hue of a particular wavelength. Even these simple stimulus elements can themselves be characterized along a number of dimensions, however. For example, we can characterize a color as to its hue (corresponding to the wavelength of light), its saturation (corresponding to the extent to which it is mixed with other colors), and its brightness (corresponding to the amount of energy in the stimulus). However, although we can characterize it along these three dimensions, we would probably be unwilling to claim that a color is a compound of three stimulus elements. The question is partially one of determining what constitutes a single stimulus as opposed to a compound of several stimuli. Alternatively, we may ask the question in this form: What properties of a stimulus or dimension cause it to take up an organism's independent attentional capacity?

Garner (1974, 1976) has described some properties that control how humans process stimulus compounds. *Separable* compounds consist of two or more dimensions, which can each be added or removed independently of the others. The elimination of one dimension does not affect the presence of the others. A compound made of a colored light and a tone such as was used by Blough (1969) is a separable compound, because either the tone or the light may be presented without presenting the other. In contrast, an *integral* compound is one in which we cannot remove one dimension without also removing the other. A colored light that must be discriminated on the basis of its hue and its saturation is an integral compound. All colors must have a hue, a saturation, and a brightness. If we remove any one of these, the color is also removed. Roughly speaking, an integral compound is an *object* which differs along more than one dimension from other objects in the context. In contrast, a separable compound is usually judged to consist of more than one object, each of which varies along at least one dimension.

In the studies of pigeon DMTS performance described above, the compound samples were produced by simultaneously illuminating both a line orientation and a color. This method for producing compounds suggests that they were separable combinations of a line orientation and a hue. In support of this conclusion, Lamb and Riley (1981) found as Figure 3.8 shows that "unified compound" samples made from colored rectangles oriented either horizontally or vertically were matched almost as accurately as elements—colored squares or white rectangles—whereas "separable compound" samples, consisting of a patch of color and a separate rectangle, resulted in lower matching accuracy. This experiment suggests that the difference between element and compound samples in the standard matching-to-sample paradigm is the result of the number of separable stimulus elements that the pigeons must encode and remember. When the sample contains two separable elements, their choice accuracy is lower than when it consists of a single unit.

If unified compounds are treated as integral units, then the pigeon should find it relatively difficult to attend selectively to one dimension and ignore the other. To investigate this Lamb (1982) tested pigeons with unified and separated compounds and with elements. Each compound sample was either preceded (precue) or followed (postcue) by a cue. The cue consisted not only of an indicator of the correct dimension (cf. Leuin, 1976) but was actually the correct stimulus. For example, the precue might be a vertical line followed by a red/vertical compound sample and a choice between vertical and horizontal. The precue signaled the correct choice: vertical. On other trials, the same cue followed the sample.

As predicted the cueing procedure had no effect on the pigeon's performance with unified compounds. Its choice accuracy was equally high whether the cue occurred before or after the unified compound sample. With separated compounds, however, precueing improved the bird's choice accuracy relative to postcueing. This finding suggests that the cue functioned as a signal for the subject, telling it which stimulus to process and which to ignore. It functioned to

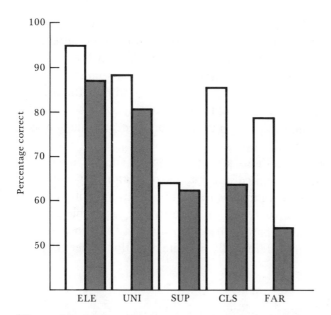

Figure 3.8. Mean percentage correct delayed matching-to-sample performance for element (ELE) and three different kinds of compound samples. The open bars represent choice accuracy with color tests, and the shaded bars represent choice accuracy with line-orientation tests. ELE = elements, UNI = unified compounds, SUP = superimposed compounds, CLS = close compounds, and FAR = far compounds. [From Lamb & Riley, 1981.]

control the input and processing of information from separated compounds, but could not control the input from unified compounds. This experiment is completely consistent with the hypothesis that the birds processed the two elements in the separated compound independently of one another, and, thus could selectively attend to one or another. In contrast they processed the two dimensions of the unified compound as an integral unit.

CONCLUSION: ATTENTION IN ANIMALS

The data reviewed in this chapter suggest that animals have attentional mechanisms that control the extent to which they process information about available stimuli. The selective processing of stimuli occurs both as a result of limitations on the animal's ability to process information and as a result of more "voluntary" allocation of its attentional capacity. Animals can learn to allocate selectively their information-processing capacity to informative stimuli and to ignore uninformative stimuli.

Traditional investigations of attention in animals have used discrimination learning. These experiments have demonstrated selective allocation of attention, but there is no evidence that this allocation is due to a limit on the animals' ability to process information. Under these conditions attention seems instead to function as a kind of control process. It determines which stimuli the animal processes—not because processing them would tax its capacity, but because the stimuli are uninformative. In these experiments attention seems to function as a process of selectively ignoring certain inputs.

In contrast, when temporal limitations are placed on an animal, it exhibits selective attention in the sense of a limited information-processing capacity. Under these conditions we can observe an inverse relation: Selective attention to one stimulus reduces the amount of capacity left to process other, separable stimuli. If, however, the organism cannot separate the dimensions of the stimulus into individual chunks, then it cannot differentially allocate attention. Selectivity depends on separability.

SUMMARY

The concept of attention has been used to refer to a limit on the organism's capacity to process information and to refer to selectivity in the stimuli that control its behavior. The first kind of limit would explain the second, but research on discrimination learning has found evidence for selectivity but not for a limit on the organism's attentional capacity. Presumably, they have failed to find such a limit because they used simple stimuli and provided the animal with sufficient time. Other experiments that restrict the time available for the animal to process information do show such limits. Thus, animals display both kinds of attentional mechanisms: they have limited information-processing capacities, and they learn to select some stimuli and to ignore others.

RECOMMENDED READINGS

Garner, W. R. (1970) The stimulus in information processing. *American Psychologist, 25,* 350–358.

Kahneman, D. (1973) *Attention and effort.* Englewood Cliffs, N.J.: Prentice Hall.

Mackintosh, N. J. (1975) A theory of attention: variations in associability of stimuli with reinforcement. *Psychological review, 82,* 276–279.

Riley, D. A., & Roitblat, H. L. (1978) Attention and related cognitive processes in pigeons. In S. H. Hulse, H. Fowler, & W. K. Honig (Eds.), *Cognitive processes in animal behavior*. Hillsdale, N.J.: Erlbaum, pp. 249–276.

Sutherland, N. S., & Mackintosh, N. J. (1971) *Mechanisms of animal discrimination learning*. New York: Academic Press.

CHAPTER 4

Learning and Reference Memory

MEMORY AND RETENTION

Memory is the retention of information from one time to another. It is a temporal bridge that allows an organism's past experience to affect its later behavior. It is a change in the organism that has resulted from some experience and that has the consequence of altering the organism's subsequent behavior in an indefinitely large number of ways (see Estes, 1975). Without memory, learning would be impossible because each experience would be as the first.

Consider a simple classical conditioning experiment: A tone CS is presented for 0.5 s, followed by a 0.5 s delay and the delivery of food into the animal's mouth. Over several trials, the animal begins to salivate at the sound of the tone, and, consequently, we say it has learned the relationship between the tone and the food. In order for the animal to learn this relationship, it must be able to perceive the stimuli involved, detect that they are related, and remember the relationship from one trial to the next. This procedure is called "trace conditioning" because Pavlov initially assumed that the connection formed during this kind of conditioning was between the US and a "trace," or remnant, of the neural activity produced by the CS. Pavlov invoked the idea of a trace in this kind of conditioning because he believed that temporal contiguity between elements was necessary for conditioning to occur. The CS ended before the US appeared, so the stimuli, themselves, could not be contiguous, but the US and a trace of the CS could be. Therefore, trace conditioning could be the formation of a connection between the trace of the CS and the US.

The trace interval (that is, the time between the end of the CS and the start of the US) is typically relatively brief in most classical conditioning experiments, on the order of seconds or less. Sometimes, however, it can be very long, measured in hours (e.g., long delay taste-aversion learning, Smith & Roll, 1967). Whether the interval is short or long, learning and performance both depend on the animal's remembrance of the relationship between the CS and US and of the fact that the CS had occurred.

Working and reference memory

Compare the kinds of memory necessary for classical conditioning—memory for the relation between the CS and US and memory that the CS has just occurred—with that involved in delayed matching-to-sample (DMTS). DMTS also requires the animal to maintain two kinds of memory. The animal must learn and remember the rules of the task—for example, that red is the correct choice after a horizontal sample—but it must also remember which sample occurred on the current trial. Differences of this sort have led a number of investigators (e.g., Honig, 1978, 1984; Olton, 1983; Roitblat, 1982a) to propose that memory can be usefully divided into at least two types: working memory and reference memory. Learning, as we usually use the term, produces changes in reference memory (also called long-term memory). The kind of information an animal gains by identifying a sample and maintaining information about its identity during the retention interval of a DMTS trial is usually thought to be stored in working memory.

I shall have more to say about the distinction between working and reference memory in Chapter 5. At this point it is sufficient to note that reference memory is the kind of memory an animal uses when it is learning to perform a task. The main questions of this chapter are: what does the animal learn, or what is the content of its representation, and how is this information coded? Partly because of space limitations, the processes by which learning occurs, or its dynamics, will concern us to a much lesser degree. The rest of this chapter describes investigations of reference memory as it is employed in classical and instrumental conditioning. The next chapter describes investigations of working memory.

MEMORY CODES

Learning organisms change as a result of their experience. Many proposals have been offered concerning the nature of that change—how organisms code information in reference memory. Each of these proposals makes different assumptions about the basic units of a memory code and how they should be combined to produce a theory of memory. A few of these proposals are described here.

Stimulus-response (S-R) associations

The oldest, most traditional way to conceptualize the storage of knowledge by animals is through a synthesis of the reflex and association traditions that led to the development of experimental psychology. Associationism holds that all learning is the formation of associations. The reflex view adds that these associations consist of the connection of stimuli and responses through the formation of new reflexes (see Chapter 2). The essence of this view is the assumption that all kinds of behaviors can be explained as the product of various combinations of reflexes.

The reflex is a convenient unit for the representation of knowledge because it specifies both knowledge, and the behavior that results from that knowledge, as a connection between a stimulus and a particular response.[1] Learning is equated with behavior change. Furthermore, a reflex approach has the appearance of providing objective mechanisms for the description and analysis of behavior (see Chapter 2).

In this S-R (stimulus-response) view, all knowledge is represented as the direct connection between stimuli or situations and behaviors.[2] Figure 4.1 shows the various ways in which reflexes can combine through potentiation, inhibition, and chaining to produce more complex forms of movement.

A reflex is said to fire or be activated when its releasing stimulus elicits the resultant behavior. When one reflex fires, some others are inhibited—they become less likely to fire—and still others are potentiated—they become more likely to fire. For example, walking involves the coordinated action of a number of muscle and limb systems. Certain muscles must operate to extend the leg and others to flex it. If both sets of muscles were to operate simultaneously, the leg would not move appropriately. When the reflexes resulting in leg flexion fire, they inhibit the complementary reflexes responsible for extension. Conversely, when the reflexes resulting in leg extension fire, they inhibit the complementary reflexes responsible for flexion. Each reflex is the movement of some muscles in response to a specific stimulus. Potentiation and inhibition simply make it more or less difficult for the stimulus to elicit the response.

Reflexes can also combine in chains. The firing of one reflex can provide the stimulus that elicits the next. For example, following a leg flexion, the leg is in a

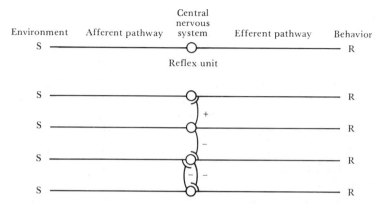

Figure 4.1. Reflex units and their interaction. Reflex units are direct connections between stimulus inputs and response outputs. They interact either by potentiating other reflex units (indicated by "+") or by inhibiting other units (indicated by "−"). Each reflex is activated by its sufficient stimulus and results in a behavioral product. Signals come in from the stimuli along the afferent pathway to the central nervous system. They then go out to the muscles along the efferent pathway.

flexed position. The leg's position can then serve as the eliciting stimulus for the extension reflex.

Complex behaviors involve more reflexes than do simple behaviors, but they are still organized according to the principles of potentiation, inhibition, and chaining. Every behavior is the direct and "automatic" product of environmental stimuli.[3] No internal factors are supposed, except for such internal stimuli as limb position, stomach contractions, and so forth. Learning is the formation of new reflexes through conditioning.

To summarize the S-R position for present purposes, the basic unit of representation is a connection between a stimulus and a response, mediated by the organism's nervous system. Some of these connections are formed through learning. The particular behavior that results from a given representation is specified by virtue of the assumed correspondence between internal elements and observable events. That is, some neural units correspond to the stimulus, and others correspond to the response. The connection between these units corresponds to the observable stimulus-response correlations in the environment. Activation of the neural response-producing units by presentation of the stimulus automatically leads to the production of the corresponding behavior by the organism. Although reflexes interact with one another, they are all at the same "level." They are all connections between stimuli and responses. In S-R theories there are no super reflexes that control subordinate reflexes, nor are there reflexes that consist of anything but the connection of a stimulus with a response.

Tolman's stimulus-stimulus associative system

Tolman also followed the associationist tradition. He did not, however, equate learning with behavior change; instead he argued for a distinction between knowledge and performance. In other words, animals do not always show what they know. For example, a rat that is satiated may not press a bar to receive food even though it would immediately do so if it were hungry. Hunger allows us to see evidence for knowledge that is otherwise "behaviorally silent." For example, although you may know how to ride a bicycle, your present behavior probably does not demonstrate that knowledge. Organisms' knowledge is not always reflected in their behavior.

Knowledge is stored primarily in the form of stimulus-stimulus (S-S) associations, or as stimulus-response-stimulus (S-R-S*) associations. Tolman called these relationships "expectancies" or "means-end readinesses."

> A means-end readiness, as I conceive it, is a condition in the organism which is equivalent to what in ordinary parlance we call a "belief" (a readiness or disposition) to the effect that an instance of this *sort* of stimulus situation, if reacted to by an instance of this *sort* of response, will lead to an instance of that *sort* of further stimulus situation, or else, simply by itself be accompanied, or followed, by an instance of that *sort* of stimulus situation. (Tolman, 1959, p. 113)

Families of these expectancies are organized into "cognitive maps," representing organism-environment interactions rather than unorganized collections of stimulus-response units.

> The stimuli ... are not connected by just simple one-to-one switches to outgoing responses. Rather the incoming impulses are usually worked over and elaborated ... into a tentative cognitivelike map of the environment. And it is this tentative map, indicating routes and paths and environmental relationships, which finally determines what responses, if any, the animal will finally release. (Tolman, 1948, p. 192)

In Tolman's system, knowledge is represented at two levels: the individual means-end expectancies and the cognitive map derived from and organizing them. Behavior emerges in a flexible manner from these representations, depending on the particular goal the organism is seeking. The goal-directed nature of behavior is a key feature of Tolman's system because it characterizes behavior, not as the automatic response to specific environmental stimuli, but as purposive action. Activation of a goal state potentiates related expectancies in the cognitive map and thereby guides the animal toward correct performance.

Neoassociationist theories

Modern "neoassociationist" (Anderson & Bower, 1973) conceptualizations also use association as the basis for knowledge representation. These theories, how-

ever, expand the relatively simple kind of associationism characteristic of Tolman's and of the reflex-based theories beyond expectancies and cognitive maps
into more abstract and complex hierarchical knowledge structures. They largely
abandon any direct connection between behaviors and representations.

S-R theories represent knowledge in a procedural form. They specify the
action to be performed in response to specific stimulus conditions. The organism's behavior is automatically specified when the stimulus is presented. In
contrast, Tolman's and neoassociationist theories use primarily declarative representations. According to these theories, animals store information in the form
of relationships among items and events. The behavior that is actually performed
is not specified, but is determined flexibly by the organism's goals and knowledge. Learning is the representation of knowledge.

Neoassociationist theories have been developed primarily in conjunction with
computer simulations and observations of human verbal behavior. Consequently,
they have tended to concentrate on modeling verbal memory using the kinds of
structures and processes that are easily programmed on a computer. There is no
reason, however, that similar kinds of models could not be built to account for
animal behavior. For example, Gallistel (1980) has developed a hierarchical
model of animal behavior, which includes many of the features of neoassociationist theory. This model is described later in the chapter.

Knowledge in a neoassociationist system consists of a network of connections
between *tokens* or *nodes* organized into hierarchical "databases." The connections between nodes each represent a particular kind—from a limited set—of
relationship between the connected tokens, such as "isa" in "dog—isa→domestic
pet." Figure 4.2 shows two examples of this type of associative network.

Nodes are fundamental memory units. They have no substructure and are not
analyzable into any smaller units. They are abstract units that stand for a concept, category, property, or stimulus. Two nodes, connected by an associative
link, such as "Muffin—isa→cat" or "shock—property→aversive," constitute a
proposition. Propositions can be translated into simple sentences in English or
some other language, but they are not, themselves, sentences. Rather, they are
representations of particular relationships.

All nodes have exactly the same complexity. Nodes that correspond to higher-
level concepts are exactly the same as nodes that correspond to lower-level concepts. Higher-level nodes correspond to higher-level concepts because they are
associatively connected to nodes representing lower-level concepts. For example,
in Figure 4.2, the node corresponding to the concept *chamber* is superordinate to
the concepts *tone* and *shock*. Tone and shock are part of the context of the
chamber. They are attributes of it. The superordinate/subordinate relationship
is determined by the pattern of the links between *chamber* and *tone* and between
chamber and *shock*. Otherwise, the superordinate node does not have any special
status or property not also held by lower-level nodes.

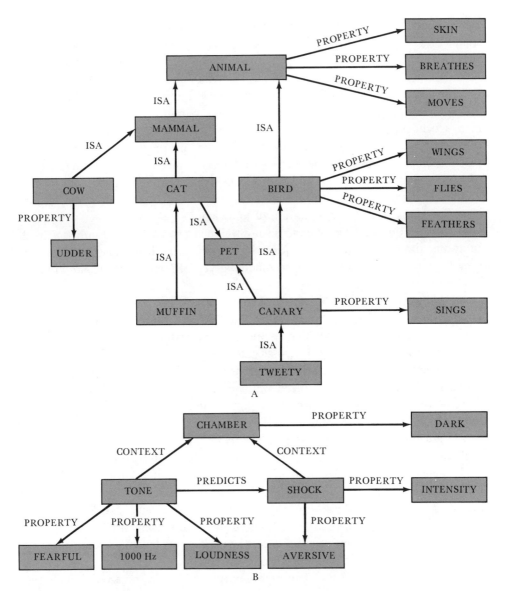

Figure 4.2. Two associative networks. (A) This network represents some knowledge about domestic and farm animals. The hierarchical property of such a network is the result of a higher order node (e.g., domestic pet) being connected to several lower level nodes (e.g., cat, canary, etc.). (B) This is the kind of associative network that might result from a conditioning experiment, in which a tone CS predicts a shock US.

Generally, the associative links are directional. *Fearful* is a property of the *tone; tone* is not a property of *fearful.* Similarly, *tone* predicts *shock,* not vice versa.

Learning is the formation of new connections among nodes in the database. A given experience activates certain nodes representing attributes of that experience (Spear, 1976; Underwood, 1969). Each node represents a feature of the experience. Nodes that are simultaneously activated become interconnected, and the set of interconnected nodes is a representation of that experience. The activation of the set of interconnected nodes is a recollection of the experience.

For example, when one node is activated by the presentation of a stimulus feature represented by that node, all of the nodes connected to the activated node are potentiated. Potentiated nodes are more easily activated than nodes that are not potentiated. Thus, presentation of one element of a situation facilitates recall of the rest of the situation. This is called cueing. For example, if a rat's body temperature is lowered significantly after a passive-avoidance training episode, then it shows much less retention of the effects of training than a control animal that is not chilled.[4] One hypothesis that might explain the amnestic effects of body cooling is that the animal includes sensations of being cooled as attributes of the training experience. If this hypothesis is correct, then cooling the animal prior to testing should activate those nodes corresponding to the sensations of being chilled. These, then, should potentiate the related nodes from the learning experience and facilitate its recall. Riccio and Ebner (1981) reported exactly this result. Animals who were cooled after training but not before testing showed little retention of the training experience, relative to rats who were cooled after training and just before testing.

Image and imagelike systems

Images provide another way in which animals may represent information. Images are difficult to implement on computer systems, and this difficulty has limited their exploration. Nevertheless, they are a commonly reported subjective experience, and the role of images in cognition is currently an important area of research (e.g., Anderson, 1978; Kosslyn, 1983).

The distinctive feature of an image is its apparent analog relationship to the objects being imaged. One system is an analog of another system when it simulates the structure of the other system and preserves a certain kind of parallelism between the two systems. The image represents features of objects and relationships among those features in a part-for-part and relation-for-relation correspondence. For example, consider the house in which you grew up. How many windows were in the front of that house? When asked questions such as this, most people report the experience of "visualizing" an image of the front of the house in their "mind's eye" and counting the windows. Another example of the apparent use of images during mental rotation was discussed in Chapter 1. Humans take longer to decide if two figures represent the same object the greater the angle between their orientations.

Images have an obvious appeal in animal research. For example, it seems intuitively reasonable that the presentation of the CS might elicit in the animal an image of the US. Pavlov's original explanation for conditioning involved the supposition that the area of the animal's brain activated by the perception of the US was also activated, after training, by perception of the CS.

The relationship between perception and image is currently one of the major concerns in the study of imagery (e.g., Finke, 1980). The evidence seems clear that images are not identical to pictures; that is, they are not arrays of points, each varying in intensity and perhaps in hue. Instead, they seem more "constructed" than a simple percept. The basic unit of an image seems to be related to the *objects* represented and to their distinctive features rather than to the points of light making up the scene. Furthermore, some, but not necessarily all of an object's features are represented. This difference between images and pictures has led a number of investigators (e.g., Pylyshyn, 1973) to propose that images are simply a byproduct of the use of a proposition-based representational system, such as associative networks. These investigators suggest that organisms do not store information in an image form, but rather that images are simply the result of a constructive translation from a proposition-based representation. Whether or not images are eventually found to be the actual code of a representation, at this point they do present a conceivable means of storing information.

The analysis of image-based representations will depend in part on a more complete understanding of the means by which the brain does direct visual processing. Brains do not "record" visual images in the same way as photographic emulsions record images, so the apparent differences between images and pictures may turn out to be as irrelevant to processes of imagery as they are to perception.

Pattern-directed inference systems

Another way to conceptualize representations also derives from computer simulations and is based on the idea of a pattern-directed inference system (Hayes-Roth, Waterman, & Lenat, 1978; Waterman & Hayes-Roth, 1978). A pattern-directed inference system is a kind of "production system" that responds flexibly to a wide variety of situations. Such a system consists of a loosely organized collection of mechanisms, instructions, or rules called "modules" or "productions." The modules are contained in a database, which also contains a sensory register and working and reference memory. The system also includes an "executive," which controls the scheduling and execution of the modules, and an "action system," which allows the system to act on external variables.

A module is a kind of stimulus-response rule. Each module specifies some set or pattern of conditions in the database and some action or "production" that

changes either the database or the outside environment. When the pattern specified by the module is present in the database, the module "fires," and its production occurs. This production necessarily changes the pattern presented to the
various modules. If the new pattern meets the criterion for another module, then
that module fires, again changing the database, and so on.

One of the differences between reflexlike stimulus-response units, of the sort
described earlier, and pattern-directed modules is that S-R units respond solely
to external or response-produced stimuli. In contrast, modules respond not only
to external stimuli, but also to changes in the system's database or memory. The
pattern of conditions resulting in the activation of a module may be wholly
cognitive, abstract, and internal, or it may include features of the external environment. Another difference between S-R and production systems is the presence
of an executive, or "interpreter," in the pattern-directed inference systems. The
executive is a higher-level system that controls the scheduling of the modules. If
the criteria for firing more than one incompatible module are met, the executive
resolves the conflict between the competing modules and allows one to proceed
while inhibiting the others.

Figure 4.3 shows one version of a pattern-directed inference system. The
executive communicates with the memories and detects patterns with the pattern
matcher. Each module has certain pattern criteria. The patterns consist of the
conditions of the sensory register, the working memory, and reference memory.
For example, the criterion pattern for a bar-pressing production might include
the representation of a discriminative stimulus in the sensory register, a food
motivation in working memory, and the knowledge in reference memory that bar
pressing leads to food. When these criteria are all met, then the production fires,
and the animal presses the bar. Other modules produce changes in the database, such as encoding a stimulus, retrieving associates, and so forth. When the
criterial patterns for more than one module are met, both modules are placed
in an "agenda" from which the scheduler selects the particular action(s) to be
performed.

The modules themselves are stored as part of the reference-memory database.
Hence, in this system, learning consists of the entry of new modules and their
criterial patterns into the database. Metaknowledge describes how the other
changes occurring in the system are to take place. Table 4.1 shows an example of
a more specific pattern-directed inference system. This system "explains" pigeons' performance on a delayed matching-to-sample task. When the patterns
indicated in the first column are detected, the production in the second column
fires. This results either in an action (e.g., pecking, head movement), a change in
the content of working memory (e.g., production of an image), or a change in the
external stimulus conditions (e.g., as a result of an action). The rules could be

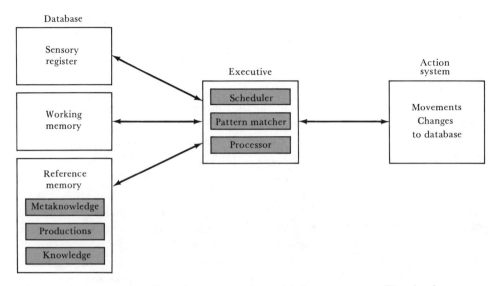

Figure 4.3. A general outline of a pattern-directed inference system. The database contains a sensory register, which transduces internal and external stimulus events, a working memory, which holds temporary or "scratch" information, and a reference memory, which contains knowledge, production rules, and information about the use of the system (metaknowledge). The executive controls the operation of the system, modifying the database and activating the action system. The action system operates on the environment.

TABLE 4.1 Delayed matching-to-sample pattern-directed inference system

Database pattern	Production
E: Warning signal	→ produce peck action
E: Sample	→ produce image of sample in working memory
WM: Sample image	→ produce image of correct choice in working memory
WM: Image of correct choice = E: Comparison stimulus	→ produce peck action
WM: Image of correct choice ≠ E: Comparison stimulus	→ produce head movement to different key
E: Food hopper available	→ produce peck action

Note: E: = external stimulus, WM: = working memory.

listed in any order because their activation depends on the pattern of information, not on the rules that precede or follow it.

Pattern-directed inference systems are very flexible in the kind of knowledge representations they may employ. Information may be represented procedurally—for example, as an if-then rule—as a semantic network of the sort used in neoassociationist theories, as analog quantities or measures, and at multiple levels of abstraction. In fact, there are few constraints, either on the kinds of information that can be represented or on the complexity or form of the particular modules included.

Learning in a pattern-directed inference system consists of the generation of new rules or modules from examples of behavior. Much work in artificial intelligence is directed toward developing explicit learning mechanisms within the pattern-directed inference system framework (e.g., Hayes-Roth & Waterman, 1978).

Conclusion

Each of the possible systems of representation described here has certain advantages and disadvantages. Each one captures easily some features of behavior and cognition but may be clumsy with others. In the rest of this chapter we will explore some of these systems as representations of learning.

REPRESENTATION OF INTEREVENT
RELATIONS: CONTENTS

Classical and instrumental conditioning are the two paradigm procedures most used to study learning. In fact, most of the analytic work has been limited to experiments using classical conditioning. In classical conditioning the experimenter controls the presentation of most, if not all, of the events about which the organism is supposed to learn—that is, the CS and the US in the context of an experimental chamber. This allows a high degree of experimental control. In contrast, in instrumental conditioning the experimenter has good control over only one of the nominal events about which the organism is supposed to be learning—the reinforcer. The other nominal event—the organism's behavior—is, by definition of the procedure, left free for the organism to control.

Classical conditioning is one of the most widely studied forms of learning. Its discovery in Pavlov's laboratory at the end of the last century marks a major change in the methods and characteristics of experimental psychology.

Three nominal events occur during classical conditioning. The CS and US are presented, in a certain contingent relationship, under the control of the experimenter, and the response (CR or UR) occurs as an index of the animal's learning. What does the animal learn about these three events that causes its behavior to change? What is the content of its representation, and how does it code this information?

We can identify at least three alternative forms of representation. For example, the representation could consist of an association between the CS and CR, or between the CR and the US, or the animal could learn about the relationship between the CS and US and behave according to its expectancies.

Pavlov's theory of conditioning

Pavlov was primarily a physiologist interested in the physiology of the cortex. He disliked psychology and psychological explanations.[5] As a result, he sought to describe learning in the same kind of objective terms he used to describe other physiological processes. He thought that the presentation of a relatively strong stimulus leads to activation of an area in the cerebral cortex. This activation then spreads across the cortex like ripples on a pond. Because of the structure of the brain, this activation also leads automatically to the occurrence of the UR. When the CS is presented, it initially activates a different area in the cerebral cortex. Because the CS is a weaker stimulus than the US, its activation is weaker, and does not spread as far as that of the US. With repeated presentation of the CS and US, however, the pathway between the two areas is reinforced and they become integrated into a united field. When the CS is then presented, it leads to activation of the US area via this pathway. The response then occurs just as it would if the US area were activated directly. Pavlov called this principle *stimulus substitution*.

Stimulus substitution

We now know that the particulars of Pavlov's physiology of conditioning are incorrect. For example, excitation does not spread in quite the way he proposed; the relationship between locations in the cortex and stimulation are not of the sort required by his theory, and so forth. Nevertheless, many of the themes he suggested continue to receive consideration, and many of the processes he proposed have counterparts in more recent notions of conditioning. Among the more prominent and still influential features of Pavlov's theory are the following: (1) Stimuli can be represented by the set of neural or memory elements they excite. (2) Conditioning results in the formation of connections between these elements, so that excitation of the elements corresponding to the CS leads to the excitation of the elements corresponding to the US. (3) Stimulus substitution, or the learned equivalence of CS and US, is the result of this connective process.

In its strongest form, the stimulus substitution hypothesis argues that the CS and the US are represented by a single code. In Pavlov's terms, they excite an overlapping area of cortex. If this hypothesis were correct, it would predict that animals would mistake the CS for the US and, therefore, fail to choose appropriately between them. They would sometimes choose the CS when both the CS and US are simultaneously present, because both stimuli would activate the same memory elements. Under certain conditions animals do show confusions of this sort. For example, "autoshaping" (Brown & Jenkins, 1968) is a classical conditioning procedure, in which the CS is an illuminated pecking key and the US is food delivered in a food hopper. After some number of light-food pairings, pigeons come to peck the key even if pecking it prevents food delivery (Williams & Williams, 1969). Further, if given a choice between a key light at one end of a long chamber and a food hopper at the other, birds prefer to peck a key that signals the food delivery, even if the key and food are so far apart that the bird cannot move from the key to the food in time to eat (Hearst & Jenkins, 1974). Some animals, such as turkeys and dolphins, have even been known to swallow stimuli, such as coins and rubber balls, that have been associated with food reinforcement (Breland & Breland, 1966). Certainly, these phenomena may be subject to other interpretations, but they show that confusion between the CS and US, as predicted by the strong stimulus substitution hypothesis, is at least not an absurd notion. Animals could represent the CS and US by a common code. This strong hypothesis also argues that the conditional response should be indistinguishable from the unconditional response because they are both the product of one area of activation.

Stimulus-stimulus learning

A somewhat weaker form of the stimulus substitution hypothesis argues that classical conditioning results in the formation of an association between the CS and the US. The CS and US are not represented by a common code; the separate elements representing these two stimuli are asssociatively linked. For example, after training, the animal's perception of the CS could activate memory elements representing that stimulus. Activation of these elements would then activate associatively connected elements, such as an image of the US. Activation of the US elements leads unconditionally to the performance of the UR. By this account the conditional response is expected to be very similar, although not necessarily identical, to the unconditional response. The similarity in the two responses comes from their common source in the activation of the elements representing the US. Differences between the CR and the UR may be caused by two factors: (1) The CS itself activates certain unconditional responses, which may modify the form of the CR. (2) Alternatively, directly activating an element by presenting the stimulus it represents may result in a different kind or different amount of activation than that produced when the element is activated via an associative link. The UR results from direct activation of the US elements by presentation of the US. In contrast, the CR results from associative activation of the US elements from those activated by the CS presentation (see Wagner, 1981).

In its most general form, the stimulus substitution hypothesis argues that, after training, the CS and US both activate a common set of memory elements in the animal. Activation of this set of elements then leads automatically to the production of a single response, either the unconditional or the conditional response. In this view learning is the formation of associative connections between the memory elements representing the CS and the memory elements representing the US.

Instrumental reinforcement

The instrumental reinforcement hypotheses claim that the conditional response is actually the result of instrumental conditioning. Animals produce the conditional response because this response is positively reinforced. According to one version of these hypotheses—the superstition hypothesis—the CR is learned because it is followed by a reinforcer—for example, the food US—and any response that is followed by the presentation of a reinforcer increases in strength. According to the second of these hypotheses—the US modification hypothesis— the animal learns to perform the conditional response because that behavior has a beneficial effect on its experience of the US.

Superstition.   Skinner has long argued for a process called adventitious reinforcement or "superstition." According to this account, the CR happens because its occurrence is "accidentally" reinforced by the presentation of the US. Temporal contiguity between the response and the reinforcer is all that is required to strengthen a behavior; no explicit contingency is necessary. For example, Skinner (1948) presented food to hungry pigeons every 15 s, independent of the birds' behavior. After a few of these presentations, nearly every bird developed a peculiar, recognizable form of stereotyped behavior during the interfood interval. One bird walked in circles, a second moved its head back and forth, and a third scratched the floor.[6] In describing this experiment Skinner said:

> The conditioning process is usually obvious. The bird happens to be executing some response as the hopper appears; as a result it tends to repeat this response. If the interval before the next presentation is not so great that extinction takes place, a second "contingency" is probable. This strengthens the response still further and subsequent reinforcement becomes more probable. (Skinner, 1948, p. 169)

The unconditional response normally occurs at about the time that the US is presented and in the context of the CS. According to the superstition account, the temporal contiguity between the animal's response and the reinforcing US is sufficient to strengthen this conditional response as a discriminated operant, occasioned by the CS. Lack of an explicit contingency between the response and the reinforcer did not prevent the formation of stereotyped behavior patterns in Skinner's superstition experiment, so its lack in classical conditioning should also not be critical.

According to the superstition account, the conditional response should normally resemble the unconditional response, because the unconditional response is the behavior that occurs in the context of the CS presentation and is reinforced by the presentation of the US. In principle, any behavior that occurs in temporal proximity to the US will be reinforced, so differences between the CR and UR may be due to the intrusion of any other behaviors that might happen to occur at the correct time.

US modification.   The second instrumental reinforcement hypothesis is based on the observation that there is usually a functional relationship between the UR and the US. Typically, the UR is a behavior that improves the US by making it more palatable, less painful, and so forth. For example, leg flexion reduces the aversiveness of a shock US by reducing the magnitude of the resulting muscle spasm. Similarly, eyelid closure protects the eye from airpuff US presentations.

The key feature of this hypothesis is that some behavior occurs prior to the US and is reinforced by the salubrious effect it has on the animal's experience of the US. Unlike the superstition hypothesis, mere contiguity between the behavior and the reinforcer is not thought to be sufficient. Rather, the animal makes the conditional response because of the particular effect the behavior has on its experience of the US.

Analysis of the instrumental reinforcement hypotheses.   The relationship between the CR and the US is crucial to evaluating the two instrumental reinforcement hypotheses. The superstition hypothesis predicts that any behavior occurring in close temporal proximity to the reinforcing US will be strengthened. For example, if shock is used as the CS signaling the presentation of food, then the flexion elicited by the shock should be strengthened by the presentation of food (Konorski & Miller, 1937). Brogden (1939a) tested this prediction. He trained dogs to make a flexion response to a bell in order to avoid shock. That is, if the dogs made the CR to the bell, then no shock was presented. This procedure is called an "omission procedure" because the US is omitted whenever the CR occurs. During the second phase of this experiment, Brogden disconnected the shock and presented food when the dogs made the flexion response following presentation of the bell. The avoidance training ensured that the leg flexion response occurred following the bell, presumably because it was reinforced by shock omission. The presentation of food also followed leg flexion. If temporal contiguity between the CR and the US is sufficient to reinforce the CR, then the contiguity between the leg flexion and the food should also be sufficient to continue to reinforce the dogs' leg flexion. Therefore, the dog should continue to make the leg-flexion response to the bell even when the reinforcer changes from shock omission to food presentation. In spite of these predictions, changing reinforcers interfered with the dogs' performance of the leg-flexion response. Contiguity of the response and the reinforcer was not sufficient to ensure that the response became a CR.

More recently, Skinner's interpretation of the superstition experiment has been questioned. Staddon and Simmelhag (1971) repeated Skinner's experiment. They presented food to hungry birds every 12 s and observed and recorded 16 different behaviors during the interfood interval. During the first few trials, they observed what Skinner had reported, namely that each bird exhibited a peculiar stereotypic response prior to the delivery of food. With further training, however, the particular behavior pattern exhibited by each bird began to appear earlier and earlier in the interfood interval, thus increasing the delay between the behavior and the reinforcer. Instead of continuing to be strengthened, the stereotyped behavior at the end of the interval, just prior to the food delivery, was replaced by a behavior related to the bird's ordinary food-getting behavior. Every bird pecked at the end of the interval. These two experiments provide powerful evidence against any adventitious reinforcement account of learning and, therefore, against adventitious reinforcement as a major determinant of what is learned in classical conditioning.

I described earlier an omission procedure used by Brogden to train a leg flexion avoidance response. This omission procedure is not limited to aversive stimuli; it also provides interesting information about the role of the relationship between the CR and the UR when the procedure is used with appetitive stimuli such as food. In an omission procedure there is no opportunity for the occurrence of the CR to modify the properties of an appetitive US because the US is presented only if the CR does not occur. Whenever the CR occurs, the US does not occur. Therefore, there is no opportunity for conditional response either to be paired adventitiously with the US or for the CR to modify the animal's experience of the US. If a CR still occurs, then it cannot be due either to adventitious reinforcement or to any reinforcement derived from its modification of the US.

Dogs continued to emit a reliable salivary response for more than 8000 trials, even though food was withheld whenever they salivated following the CS (Sheffield, 1965). Similarly, after 275 trials, rats continued to lick at a tube on more than 50 percent of the trials, even though licking prevented the delivery of water (Patten and Rudy, 1967).[7]

It is difficult to see how many of the examples of conditional responses could improve the quality of the US. For example, autoshaped pigeons peck at a key-light that signals the presentation of grain, even when the key is separated from the food, sometimes by large distances, or when pecking prevents the food's delivery. (Williams & Williams, 1969). Furthermore, Jenkins and Moore (1973) trained pigeons who were both hungry and thirsty in a chamber with two keys. Illumination of one key was followed by the presentation of water; illumination of the other was followed by the presentation of food. After some training on these two kinds of trials, the birds approached and contacted the keys when they were illuminated. The form of the CR, however, varied between the two keys. The birds pecked at the key signaling food in a manner similar to the way in which they peck at food, and pecked at the key signaling water in a manner similar to the way in which they drink.[8] In short, the pigeons tried to "eat" the key associated with food and "drink" the key associated with water. These differences in behavior cannot plausibly derive from either adventitious reinforcement or from modification of the US. Finally, conditioning can occur even when the animal is completely prevented from making the response, as for example, when paralyzed with the drug curare (Solomon & Turner, 1962; Zamble, 1974).

Conclusion. The most reasonable conclusion from these data is that an instrumental contingency between the CR and the US is not necessary for the occurrence of classical conditioning and so cannot be a necessary part of its representation. The content of an animal's representation during classical conditioning seems to be a stimulus-stimulus association between the representation of the CS and the representation of the US. The response, itself, may not be represented but is produced "automatically" from activation of the US representation. In other words, the most reasonable account of the representation formed by animals during classical conditioning is a modern version of Pavlov's stimulus substitution hypothesis.

Declarative representations

These S-S associations are declarative rather than procedural representations (Dickinson, 1980) because their content specifies the relations among stimuli, not the behavior that the animal must perform.

Strong evidence further supporting a declarative S-S rather than a procedural S-R representation for classical conditioning is the finding that changing the value of the US after training is complete also changes the behavior the animal performs in response to the CS (Adams & Dickinson, 1981; Dickinson, 1980; Mackintosh, 1983). If an animal uses procedural representations, then classical conditioning would cause it to learn a relation like "when the CS occurs, begin salivating." If instead, it uses a declarative representation, then classical conditioning would cause it to learn a relation like "when the CS occurs, it signals the delivery of tasty food."

We can test whether animals use declarative or procedural representations in classical conditioning by modifying the US after the animal has learned to make the CR. An experiment of this sort was performed by Holland and Straub (1979). They trained rats with a noise CS and food US and measured approach to the food dispenser as the CR. Then they changed the nature of the US from a tasty to a distasteful food by separately pairing it with an illness-inducing chemical.[9] They found that the animals integrated these two experiences. Rats who learned initially to approach a food hopper at the sound of the noise and who learned later that the food was aversive, then avoided the food hopper at the sound of the noise. During the first phase of the experiment, the rats had the opportunity to learn either a declarative representation—noise signals food X; food X is tasty—or a procedural representation—approach food hopper when noise occurs. During the second phase of the experiment, the rats learned that the food was distasteful. Tasty food was transformed into distasteful food. This separate experience during phase 2 could change the nature of a declarative representation from "noise signals food X; food X is tasty" to "noise signals food X; food X is distasteful." Because the noise was not presented during phase 2, however, the animals had no opportunity to change their procedural representation. Therefore, even after learning that the food was now unpalatable, the rats should have continued to approach the food hopper if they were using a procedural representation, like "approach food hopper when the noise is presented," but not if they were using a declarative representation, like "noise signals that food that is unpalatable." Consistent with the use of a declarative representation, Holland and Straub found that modifying the nature of the US immediately changed the nature of the animal's CR to the noise. Therefore, the animals were using a declarative, not a procedural representation of their classical conditioning experience.

REPRESENTATION OF INTEREVENT RELATIONS: CODES FOR REPRESENTING CLASSICAL CONDITIONING

Pavlov suggested that conditioning was the formation of connections between the neural elements corresponding to the CS and those corresponding to the US. Stripped of its inappropriate physiology, the modern version of this hypothesis argues that stimuli are represented by "stimulus elements" and conditioning is coded as connections between these elements. This section considers this hypothesis and alternative codes.

Associative codes

The Standard Associative model.   Earlier in this chapter I outlined several representational systems that rely on associative codes. The main features of these representational systems are summarized in the form of a model which I have called the Standard Associative Model (SAM).

SAM assumes that associations are directional connections between memory elements. Each memory element corresponds directly to a stimulus or a feature of a stimulus; SAM does not contain any memory elements that do not correspond to a stimulus feature. As experimenters, we present tones, lights, and so forth. These are the nominal stimuli of our experiments. Each of these nominal stimuli has many features, so each nominal stimulus is represented by a potentially large number of memory elements. SAM also assumes that there are two kinds of associative connections: excitatory associations and inhibitory associations. Once an element is activated by the presentation of its corresponding stimulus, excitatory connections lead to the activation within the animal of associated elements, whereas inhibitory connections reduce, cancel, or prevent their activation. Finally, SAM assumes that the behavior observed is determined by the set of activated and inhibited elements.

All learning consists of the formation or strengthening of connections between elements. For example, if the CS is reliably associated with the US, then excitatory connections are strengthened, so that when the CS is presented it leads to activation of the elements corresponding to the US. If the presentation of some stimulus reliably predicts that the US will not be presented, then inhibitory connections are strengthened so that presentation of the CS inhibits activation of the elements corresponding to the US. As connections become more excitatory, the presentation of the CS leads increasingly to an appropriate conditional response. As connections become more inhibitory, the presentation of the CS inhibits more strongly the occurrence of the conditional response. An equivalent way to describe the same system is to assume that only one kind of connection exists that can have either positive or negative "strength" corresponding to inhibitory and excitatory connections.

The Rescorla-Wagner model.   The Rescorla-Wagner model described in Chapter 3 (Rescorla & Wagner, 1972) is a specific example of the class of models represented by SAM. It assumes that representations of the CS and the US are connected by excitatory and inhibitory links. Before training, the strength of this connection is 0. Each pairing of the CS and US increases the excitatory "valence" or "value" of the connection, and each CS presentation that is not followed by the presentation of a US decreases its valence. All learning consists of changes along this single hypothetical dimension, ranging from inhibition (negative valences) to excitation (positive valences). Positive valences result when a CS reliably predicts the occurrence of a US. Negative valences result when a CS reliably signals that an otherwise expected US will not occur. Stimuli with negative strength are called "conditioned inhibitors," and the process of training them is called "inhibitory conditioning."

Measuring excitation and inhibition.   Associative models, such as SAM or the Rescorla-Wagner model, assume that learning can result in both excitatory and inhibitory connections. Measurement of excitatory connections is straight-forward. The animal does something when the CS is presented. Measurement of inhibitory connections is not so simple, however, because these connections in-hibit the animal's responses, rather than produce them.

Investigators have traditionally used two tests to measure below-0 inhibitory values. The *summation test* combines an allegedly negative CS− with a positive-valued CS+, which is known to support a CR. This test measures the ability of the CS− to reduce responding to the CS+. The CS− and the CS+ are pre-sented simultaneously, and the measured strength of the CR is compared to that obtained when the CS+ is presented alone. The reduction in responding gives a measure of the strength of the inhibitory connection between the CS− and the response. For example, if a light is trained as a CS+ predicting food, then the dog will salivate when the light is presented. The light clearly has an excitatory valence. If a tone is trained as a CS−, then the dog will not salivate in the presence of tone. All by itself, this failure to salivate could mean either that the dog has learned that the tone is a CS− or that it has failed to learn anything about the CS−. If the tone has become a CS−, then it should inhibit responding when presented in combination with the CS+. If the animal responds less to the combination of the tone and light than it responds to the light alone, we can con-clude that the tone is actually inhibitory.

The *reversal test* provides a second technique for detecting the presence of inhibitory associative connections within animals. A stimulus that was previously trained as a CS− typically takes more trials to train as a CS+ than one that was not trained at all. (See, however, Chapter 3, on the effects of overtraining on reversal.) Each reinforced presentation of the CS presumably increases the excit-atory strength of the CS, and it simply takes more trials to increase the strength from a negative to a positive value than to increase it from 0 to a positive value.

Thus, inhibitory conditioning has two effects: (1) A conditioned inhibitor "sums" with a simultaneously presented conditioned excitor, reducing the po-tency of the conditioned exictor to elicit the conditional response (Marchant, Mis, & Moore, 1972; Wessells, 1973). (2) A conditioned inhibitor takes longer, relative to a novel stimulus, to become a conditioned exictor (Konorski & Szwej-kowska, 1956; Rescorla, 1969). The evidence also suggests, however, that ani-mals learn about more than the excitatory and inhibitory values of stimuli (see Chapter 3).

Augmented associative codes

Path independence.   SAM and the Rescorla-Wagner model both assume that learning consists solely of changes in a single dimension: associative strength.

Pairing a stimulus with reinforcement increases its associative strength, and pairing it with the omission of reinforcement decreases its strength. There are four ways or paths by which a stimulus can have an associative strength of 0, that is, become a CS_0. If learning is no more than a change in the strength of the associative connection between a stimulus and a reinforcer, then it should not matter how the value of 0 was produced. The effects on subsequent learning should depend on the value of the stimulus, but be independent of the path—for example, the training procedure—by which that value was reached.

1. Path 1: No prior training. Before training, a stimulus has an associative strength of 0 because it has never been paired with either reinforcement or nonreinforcement.

2. Path 2: CS-only training. The CS can be presented by itself. In order for a CS− to gain inhibitory value, it must be paired with the omission of an otherwise expected US. If the US is never presented, then it cannot be expected, and the CS should gain neither excitatory nor inhibitory strength.

3. Path 3: 0-correlation training. It is possible to present the CS and US independently of one another. Sometimes the US occurs following the CS, and sometimes it does not. Sometimes the CS occurs prior to the US, and sometimes it does not. The US is neither more nor less likely to occur when the CS occurs than when the CS does not occur. The occasional pairings of the CS and US are balanced by the unpaired occurrences of the two, and the result is 0 associative strength (Rescorla, 1967).

4. Path 4: Conditioning followed by extinction. A balanced combination of excitatory training followed by inhibitory extinction should be able to return the associative strength of a stimulus to 0. Excitatory training increases associative strength and extinction decreases it. The result should be 0 associative strength.

SAM and the Rescorla-Wagner model predict that stimuli subjected to any of these four treatment paths should be associatively indistinguishable from one another. They should all have associative strengths of 0. In fact, they are not indistinguishable. Each of the paths has effects that are different from the others. Therefore, learning must consist of more than the formation of excitatory and inhibitory connections between the CS and the US. The kind of model represented by SAM and the Rescorla-Wagner model must be wrong.

As would be expected for a stimulus with 0 associative strength, all four paths lead to stimuli that are neither inhibitory nor excitatory when measured according to the *summation test*. A CS_0 paired with a CS+ does not diminish the CR (Marchant, Mis, & Moore, 1972; Wessells, 1973). The four paths lead, however, to different results when tested by the *reversal test*. Depending on the path by which the CS_0 was produced, retraining can be either slower or faster than original training with a novel CS (path 1). Compared to training with a novel

CS, many more trials are necessary to change a CS_0 into a $CS+$ when the CS_0 was produced by presenting it alone (path 2), or by training it with a 0 correlation between the CS and the US (path 3; Baker & Mackintosh, 1979; Lubow, 1973). These two training procedures apparently result in some kind of inhibition that interferes with the animal's later acquisition. This kind of inhibition is called "latent inhibition" to distinguish it from the conditioned inhibition resulting in a $CS-$ (Lubow & Moore, 1959). Finally, retraining is much faster than original training when the CS has been previously trained with the US and then extinguished (path 4; Bullock & Smith, 1953).

Because each of the four paths leads to different results, learning cannot consist only of the formation of associations between the CS and the US. In conjunction with the data presented in Chapter 3 on learning about dimensions and overtraining reversal effects, these data present a violation of the "path-independence" assumptions of SAM and the Rescorla/Wagner model. The path by which a value of 0 is reached does make a difference. Therefore, the animal knows more than simply the current associative value of a stimulus.

Two-dimensional codes.   The failure of path independence is consistent with the two-stage learning process described in Chapter 3 (e.g., Lovejoy, 1966; Mackintosh, 1975; Sutherland & Mackintosh, 1971). For example, the Sutherland-Mackintosh model describes learning in terms of a two-dimensional code. One code represents the excitatory or inhibitory values of the stimuli in association with other stimuli or with responses. The other code represents the degree to which an analyzer for that dimension is to be activated and, hence, the degree to which the animal attends to that dimension. Like SAM, these two dimensional theories assume that elements are connected to one another by a single kind of association—having either an excitatory or inhibitory value. These models also assume, however, that animals know more about stimuli than simply the strength of their connection to other stimuli. Their representations also contain information about the degree to which the stimulus they represent is informative. Learning is a change in the strength of associative connections and a change in the represented significance of the stimulus. For example, latent inhibition decreases the animal's representation of the significance of the stimulus without affecting its associative connections to other stimuli. In contrast, inhibitory conditioning strengthens inhibitory associative connections as well as the represented significance of the stimulus.

Temporal structure: inhibition of delay

Another body of data, also originating in Pavlov's lab (1927/1960, pp. 88–103), suggests that an animal's representation of a classical conditioning situation contains more structure than the simple connection between the CS and the US. When relatively long CS durations are used, the maximal CR is typically delayed until nearly the end of the CS (Bitterman, 1964; Smith, 1968; Williams, 1965). Pavlov called the delay in occurrence of the CR "inhibition of delay." This phenomenon was originally thought to be problematical for simple associative theories because one stimulus first inhibited and then elicited responding, and simple models could not accommodate a single stimulus having two associative values. Pavlov accommodated to this difficulty by noting that significant amounts of sensory adaptation may occur during a long CS presentation. Therefore, the effective stimulus that the animal perceives may change as a result of this adaptation. The initial portions of the CS would activate a somewhat different set of elements from the terminal portions of the CS. The animal could then form excitatory connections between the elements corresponding to the US and the terminal portions of the CS and inhibitory connections between the US and the elements corresponding to the initial portions of the CS. Only the activation of the elements corresponding to the terminal portion of the CS would result in the production of a CR.

Alternatively, inhibition of delay might result from temporal discrimination. There is a great deal of evidence that animals are capable of discriminating the passage of time (e.g., Church, 1978; Gibbon & Allan, 1984; see Chapter 6). In fact, "temporal conditioning" is possible in which the only obvious CS is the passage of time. The US is presented repeatedly, always with the same interval between successive presentations. After a while, animals come to make the CR just before the presentation of the US. The passage of time since the last US presentation is apparently the CS.

Inhibition of delay and temporal conditioning suggest that the representations animals form during classical conditioning have more structure than the simple connection of an element corresponding to the CS with an element corresponding to the US. At the very least, the animal must be able to represent a single nominal CS by several elements, each corresponding to discriminally different features of the stimulus. The data reviewed in Chapter 6 argue strongly against this interpretation, however. Instead, they support one that explicitly includes time as a represented feature of the conditioning episode.

Expectancy.   Another way to characterize classical conditioning is to suppose that the animal's representation is in the form of an expectancy. According to this view, organisms make one kind of response when they expect a particular US. During training they learn that the CS predicts the US; that is, they form an expectancy involving the CS and US. They make a similar response after the CS because it predicts the US. The main difference between a simple element-association account of classical conditioning and an expectancy account is the latter's potential for greater structural complexity. For example, an expectancy could include temporal information as well as information about characteristics of the US. Although this notion of expectancy holds promise as the code for the representation of classical conditioning, it has not yet been sufficiently well specified to be readily tested.

Wagner's SOP model

Whether they adopt the expectancy or the association version of representation, some theorists have found it necessary to augment not only the structure of the links and elements but also the structure of the other features of the memory system as well. The most elegant of these is Wagner's (1981) SOP model.

Wagner chose the acronym SOP, which stands for *standard operating procedure*, because he believed that this model represented the standard kind of mechanism employed by an animal in classical conditioning and habituation. He recognized that other, more complex, learning mechanisms may also be available to animals, but avoided any attempt to model the interaction of these other processes with the standard model.

The foundation of the model is a hierarchical memory structure, analogous to the type of memory structure used in neoassociationist theories. Memory consists of nodes that are interconnected via directional associative links. If node A "points" to node B, it does not imply that node B points to node A. For example, the CS node points to the US node, but the US node does not necessarily point to the CS. A node is a collection of informational elements identical to those proposed for SAM. Subsets of elements correspond to separable features of the events the node represents.

The model distinguishes three states of nodal activation. A node can be in the inactive state (state I), corresponding to long-term or reference memory, or it can be in either of two active states indicating different kinds or degrees of activation. The highest level (state A1) corresponds to focal memory or rehearsal. The second state of activation (state A2) corresponds to working, or short-term, memory that is not currently the "object of attention." The exact meaning of these activation states will become more clear after the functional implications of a node's state of activation are described.

An important feature of this memory model is the assumption that working, or short-term memory, consists solely of the activation of elements from the otherwise silent long-term memory—the collection of currently inactive elements. The working-memory state differs from other states of memory only in its level of activation, not in its structure. The number of nodes that can be simultaneously in each active state is also assumed to be limited.

The system is interfaced to the environment through a sensory register and a response generator. Presentation of a stimulus leads to its registration in the organism's sensory register and, thereby, to activation of its corresponding elements from the inactive state to the most active focal memory state, A1. Presentation of a stimulus has no effect on those memory elements already in the active state. Its only effect is to activate some proportion of the currently inactive elements into the A1 state. It neither prolongs the duration of an element in active memory, nor increases an element's level of activation from one active state to another.

Active elements eventually "decay" into the inactive state. Elements in state A1 decay into state A2, and elements in state A2 decay into the inactive state. Therefore, over time an element that is initially in the A1 state will eventually decay into the A2 state, and once in the A2 state it will eventually decay into the inactive state.

Decay is a stochastic process. This means that any given element is in only one state (inactive, A1, or A2) at a time and can change state with some probability. An element is never partially in one state and partially in another. For example, we could imagine that decay is controlled by the roll of a pair of dice. If "7" comes up, the element decays; if any other number comes up, it remains active. We can specify when the *average* item can be expected to decay from one memory state to another, but it is largely a matter of chance when any *particular* element will decay. As time passes, a given element, initially in the A1 state is more and more likely to have changed to the A2 state and from there to the I state. The rate at which these state changes occur depends on the relative capacities of the states. Wagner assumes that the elements of only 2 or 3 nodes can be in the A1 state and 10 to 15 nodes in the A2 state at any one time.

Behavior is produced by a response generator which is controlled by the combination of elements that happen to be in each state at the time. The actual response produced by the system may depend on the relative number of elements in each state. Under some circumstances, a given element in the A1 state will lead to one response, and the same element in the A2 state will lead to a different response.

Figure 4.4 illustrates the various parts of the SOP model and their connections. Imagine what happens when a tone is presented. Immediately after it is registered in the sensory register, all or most of the memory elements contained in the tone node become activated into the focally active A1 state. For example, there might be 100 elements which represent the tone and are activated by it. As time passes, some of these elements will have decayed to the A2 state. As more time passes, more and more elements will have decayed into the A2 state. As soon as they reach the A2 state, however, they begin decaying into the inactive state. Eventually, all of the elements activated by the tone will decay from the A1 to the A2 state and from the A2 to the inactive state. Another tone presentation will repeat the cycle.

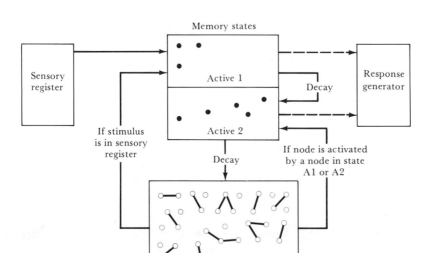

Figure 4.4. Wagner's SOP model. Each of the circles represents one memory node. Lines connecting nodes in the inactive state are intended to suggest associative links.

The SOP model includes two kinds of associative links. Excitatory links activate connected nodes and inhibitory links decrease the sensitivity to activation of the elements in the target node. The degree to which one node activates or inhibits another depends on three things: the valence of the connection between the two nodes, the strength of the connection, and the activation level of the first node. Activation of one node leads to activation of other nodes that are connected via excitatory links and to inhibition of other nodes that are connected via inhibitory links. The more elements the initial node has activated, the more it activates or inhibits the connected nodes. The stronger the association between the two nodes, the greater the degree of activation or inhibition of the connected node. The strength of an associative connection depends on the training history of the two stimuli rather than the number of nodal elements currently active. Finally, elements in the A1 state are more effective than are elements in the A2 state in either activating or inhibiting connected nodes.

When a node is activated directly by the registration of its corresponding stimulus in the sensory register, some of its elements change from the inactive memory state to active state A1. When a node is activated indirectly, through the activation of an associated node, its elements do not become fully activated into state A1, but are only partially activated into state A2. For example, if the tone just described becomes associated with food as the US, then its presentation will activate tone elements into state A1. The presence of tone elements in state A1 will then activate food elements into state A2 via the associative connection between the two.

The distinction between direct activation of an element by a stimulus and its indirect activation via an excitatory link is a central feature of the SOP model. Differential activation means that when an element is associatively activated it comes to be in the same state as an element that had been directly activated by a stimulus, but has since had time to decay into the partially active A2 state. This assumption is very different from that common in other associative models and is one of the features that makes the SOP model so powerful and interesting. For example, it contrasts with Pavlov's hypothesis that activation of the cortical area corresponding to the CS leads to activation of the area corresponding to the US in exactly the same way as does presentation of the US itself.

To summarize the workings of the model: Each stimulus is represented by a memory node consisting of a collection of elements corresponding to the features of the stimulus. The registration of a stimulus in the sensory register activates elements into the A1 state. At this point, all or some large proportion, of that stimulus's nodal elements are in the A1 state and none are in the A2 state. As time passes more and more of these nodal elements decay out of the A1 and into the A2 state. As elements decay from the focally active A1 to the less active A2 state, the number of focally active elements in the A1 state declines, and the number of partially active elements in the A2 state rises. The elements that have been transferred into the A2 state also begin to decay to the inactive state. When elements decay from the A2 state faster than they decay from the A1 into the A2 state, the number of elements in the A2 state then declines. The response generated at any point depends on the number of elements in each of the two active states. The form of the response reflects the proportions of elements in each active state and their change over time.

Learning in the SOP model.   Learning results from the formation of associative links between nodes. Two nodes (N1 and N2) that are both in the A1 state increase, or make more positive, the associative connection between them. On subsequent occasions activation of either node will facilitate the activation of the other. Conversely, the connection between a node in the A1 state (N1) and another node in the A2 state (N2) is decreased or made more inhibitory. As a result, on subsequent occasions during which the N1 node is activated, it will inhibit the activation of the N2 node. The reverse connection between node N2 and node N1 is unaffected.

Excitatory associative connections between the elements corresponding to the CS and those corresponding to the US occur when their nodal elements are both in the A1 state simultaneously. If the interval between the CS and the US is not too great, then many CS elements will still be active in the A1 state when the US elements are activated into the A1 state by the presentation of the US. An interesting feature of Wagner's SOP theory that differentiates it from other associative theories of classical conditioning is that the effect of a CS presentation is not to induce the animal into a state that is identical to that induced by a US presentation. Instead, pairing the A1 activation of the CS with the A1 activation of the US results in the formation or strengthening of an excitatory link between the CS node and the US node so that when the CS node is subsequently focally activated into the A1 state, the elements of the US node are activated into the partially active A2 state, not into the state occurring during the original pairing. Similarly, the conjunction of the CS in the A1 state and the US in the A2 state does not imbue the CS with the property of activating the US node into the A2 state on subsequent CS presentations. Instead, it strengthens an inhibitory connection between CS and US nodes and afterwards inhibits activation of the US node into any active state. Depending on the particular state of activation of the US nodal elements, a CS presentation forms either excitatory or inhibitory connections with the US node. The current state of the US nodal elements is constantly changing during the course of a conditioning session as a function of the time since the last US presentation, the time since the last CS presentation, and as a product of the resulting associative effects of these other changes. Hence, any conditioning trial results in the formation of both inhibitory and excitatory connections.

With this material for background it is possible to describe the sequence of events during conditioning as displayed in Figure 4.5. On the first conditioning trial, the CS presentation (time T_0) excites CS nodal elements into the A1 state, where they immediately begin decaying into the A2 state. When the US occurs (time T_2), it causes some of the US nodal elements to also be activated into the fully active A1 state. Because CS and US elements are both in the A1 state at the same time, an excitatory link is formed between the CS node and the US node. Its strength depends on the number of elements of each node currently in the A1 state. As Figure 4.5 shows, other links are also formed. Immediately following this first trial (times T_3 and T_4), some of the elements of the US will decay into the A2 state and so will form inhibitory connections with whichever CS elements remain in the A1 state. Since the CS was presented before the US, however, few CS nodal elements will remain in the A1 state. Therefore, the magnitude of the inhibitory connections will be small.

As training proceeds, the excitatory connection from the CS node to the US node will cause US elements to be excited into the A2 state when the CS is presented. Consequently, there will be many CS elements in the A1 state and some US elements in the A2 state during the interstimulus interval. This results in the formation of inhibitory connections between the CS node and the US node. After a number of trials, the formation of new inhibitory connections will balance the formation of new excitatory connections, and learning will reach an asymptote.

Other properties of conditioning can also be derived from the model. For example, if a light CS is pretrained with the US, then a tone CS—presented

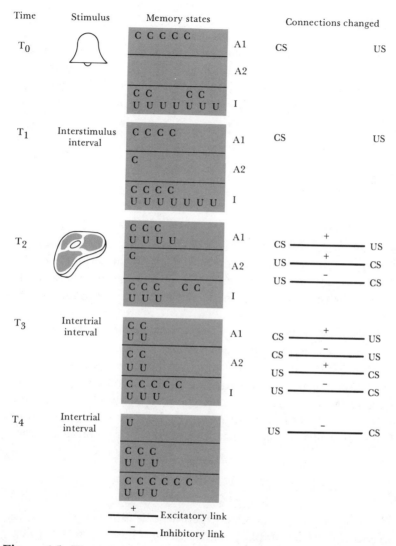

Figure 4.5. The sequence of events on the first training trial involving a bell as the conditional stimulus and meat as the unconditional stimulus. The letters C and U refer to nodal elements representing the conditional and unconditional stimuli respectively. Nodes for other stimuli are not shown.

simultaneously with the light—will not gain much excitatory strength. The light will have "blocked" acquisition to the tone (e.g., Kamin, 1969; see Chapter 3). The light activates US nodal elements into the A2 state. Therefore, the combination of tone elements in the A1 state and US elements in the A2 state results in the formation of inhibitory connections between the tone and the US that balance any excitatory connections formed as a result of the presence of tone-node elements in state A1 when the US occurs.

The SOP model is not without its difficulties. Some of these include its insistence, in common with many other associative models of conditioning, that there are only two kinds of connection—excitatory and inhibitory. Nevertheless, it represents a strong attempt to analyse classical conditioning and will undoubtedly lead to much further research.

REPRESENTATION OF INSTRUMENTAL BEHAVIORS: CONTENTS

In instrumental conditioning, just as in classical conditioning, there are three nominal events to each trial. The organism is exposed to some set of stimuli in its environment, it performs some response, and a biologically important event or outcome occurs. In this section we consider which of these events are actually maintained as part of the content of an animal's representation of an instrumental learning task.

Recall that S-R systems, of the sort suggested by Thorndike, hold that learning is the formation of connections between stimuli and responses. The sole function of a reinforcer is to stamp in the connection between a stimulus and a response, nothing more. The organism learns to make a response in a situation, but learns nothing about its outcome; the outcome serves only to modulate the connection between the situation and the behavior. In contrast to this simple notion, a great deal of evidence shows that features of the reinforcer *are* represented.

Representation of outcomes

The effects of changing outcomes.   One experiment by Brogden (1939a) has already been described: Brogden initially reinforced dogs for making a leg-flexion response by allowing them to avoid a shock. He then shifted to reinforcing the same response with food instead of shock-avoidance. He found that the animals stopped making the flexion response when the reinforcer changed. Simple S-R theory asserts that both reinforcers act identically to strengthen the connection between the stimuli and the response, but are not themselves represented. The deterioration in performance when the reinforcer changed indicates that the dogs knew that the reinforcers had been switched. Therefore, they had to have represented information about the nature of the outcome, not just about the connection between the stimulus and the response.

In another type of experiment on behavioral contrast, Elliott (1928) trained two groups of rats to run through a maze. One group was rewarded for running with bran mash, which rats love; the other was reinforced with sunflower seeds, which rats like. The group trained with bran mash ran faster and made fewer errors than did the group trained with sunflower seeds. On the tenth trial, Elliott changed the reward for the group that had been receiving bran mash so that both groups were now getting sunflower seeds. The group that had been shifted from bran mash to sunflower seeds now ran more slowly and made more errors than they had on earlier trials. In fact, they ran more slowly than did the group trained from the start with sunflower seeds! The change in performance following a change in the size or quality of the reinforcer is called "behavioral contrast."

An S-R theorist might attempt to attribute the lower-running speed and increased errors of animals trained with sunflower seeds to the lower effectiveness of sunflower seeds as a reinforcer. Rats in the sunflower group simply learned more slowly than did rats in the bran mash group. By the time of the reinforcer switch, however, the rats in the bran mash group had already learned to solve the maze. Even with a less effective reinforcer, they should have continued to perform at the same level, not drop their performance to a level below the group trained throughout with sunflower seeds.

A related experiment by Tinklepaugh (1928) depicts this phenomenon more picturesquely. Tinklepaugh trained a monkey on a delayed response task. In this task the monkey is shown a piece of food hidden under one cup or another. A screen is then lowered, blocking the monkey's view of the cup. After some delay the screen is raised and the monkey is allowed to lift one cup and consume the piece of food if the correct cup has been chosen. On the particular trial in question, Tinklepaugh showed the monkey a piece of banana being hidden. But while the screen was raised, he secretly substituted a piece of lettuce for the banana. Following the delay period, the monkey was allowed to lift one cup:

> She extends her hand to seize the food. But her hand drops to the floor without touching it. She looks at the lettuce but (unless very hungry) does not touch it. She looks under and around her. She picks the cup up and examines it thoroughly inside and out. She has on occasion turned toward observers present in the room and shrieked at them in apparent anger. After several seconds spent searching, she gives a glance toward the other cup, which she has been taught not to look into, and then walks off to a nearby window. The lettuce is left untouched on the floor. (Tinklepaugh, 1928, p. 224)

This monkey clearly represented the contents of that cup and behaved differently when her expectation was violated than if it had not been.

Other examples of behavioral contrast in which the shift is from a smaller or less preferred reward to one that is larger or more preferred have also been reported. For example, Crespi (1942) found that shifting rats from a small to a large reward led them to run faster than rats that had been trained from the start with the large reward. Similarly, Flaherty and Largen (1975) reported that rats licked faster for a 32 percent sucrose reward than for a 4 percent reward, but if the same rats were trained initially with the 4 percent solution and then shifted to the 32 percent solution, they licked faster still.

The effects of differential outcomes.   In a series of experiments with similar implications, Trapold (1970) began by training rats with a classical conditioning procedure. One group of rats was trained with a tone as the CS for food and with a clicker as the CS for sugar water. Another group was trained with the clicker as the CS for food and the tone as the CS for sugar water. He then trained both groups on a discrimination. The rats were reinforced with a food pellet for pressing one lever in the presence of a tone and with sugar water for pressing another lever in the presence of a clicker. Discrimination learning was faster when the relationship between the CS and the US was also the relationship between the discriminative stimulus and the outcome, than when different relations were used.

For example, consider the group trained with tone as the CS for food and clicker as the CS for sugar water. Presumably, this group learned to expect food when they heard the tone and to expect water when they heard the clicker. These animals were then trained in a discrimination task in which food was the reward for correct responses in the presence of the tone, and sugar was the reward for correct responses in the presence of the clicker. This group learned the discrimination very quickly, presumably because they used the expectancy of the reinforcer as part of the information that helped them to perform the discrimination. Now consider the group trained initially with food as the US following the clicker and sugar water as the US following the tone. The reinforcers used during discrimination training were the same as those received by the first group, but they were paired with the opposite stimuli. During classical conditioning these animals presumably learned to expect sugar water when they heard the tone and to expect food when they heard the clicker. During discrimination training, however, correct responses in the presence of the tone were reinforced with food, and correct responses in the presence of the clicker were reinforced with sugar water. This group learned the discrimination relatively slowly, presumably because each reinforcer violated their expectancy. In the presence of the tone, they expected sugar water but received food. In the presence of the clicker, they expected food but received sugar water. This experiment shows that expectancies regarding the outcome is part of the representation animals form in instrumental discrimination learning.

In another experiment, Trapold also found that naive rats acquired the discrimination faster if correct responses on each lever were rewarded with a distinctive outcome, than rats that were trained with both correct responses reinforced with the same outcome. Using discriminably different outcomes in a discrimination task made learning the discrimination easier than using a single outcome (see also Honig, 1984; Peterson, 1984).

Finally, a number of experiments show that changing the value of the reinforcer after instrumental training changes the animal's performance. The animals in these experiments are trained to make an instrumental response to obtain a certain reward. The reward is then separately made aversive by pairing it with an illness-inducing drug. The instrumental response is unavailable during this illness induction, so the animals have no opportunity to learn about the relation between the response and any of the stimuli involved. Once the food becomes aversive, as shown by the rats' refusal to eat it, they are again allowed to make the instrumental response. No reinforcers are delivered during this response test, so the aversive stimulus does not have the opportunity to punish the instrumental response. As a result of this training, most animals produce very few instrumental responses. By transforming the attractive food into an aversive stimulus, the experimenters decreased the rats' willingness to perform the instrumental response that produces that food (Chen & Amsel, 1980; Adams & Dickinson, 1981; Adams, 1982; Dickinson, Nicholas, & Adams, 1982). These experiments show that animals perform their instrumental responses at least in part because they have formed an expectancy that a particular outcome will follow. Therefore, an animal's representation of instrumental learning must include information about outcomes.

Representation of the response

Molecular versus molar descriptions.   There are many levels at which to describe the response that an organism learns. Weiss (1941) has identified six different levels of organization in behavior: (1) level of neuron, (2) level of muscle, (3) level of muscle group, (4) level of organ, (5) level of organ system, and (6) level of the whole organism, to which Tolman added (7) level of purposive behavior. Because of their emphasis on reflexlike mechanisms, S-R theories have concentrated on descriptions at the second or third level—that of muscle patterns. Theories of this type have often been called "molecular" or "muscletwitch" theories because they attempt to account for behavior in terms of the low-level muscle movements that comprise behavior in the same way that molecules make up matter. Other theorists, notably Tolman, have argued for descriptions at more molar levels, such as the global aspects of behavior that are necessary to reach some goal, such as go to the white star and turn left. Thus, Tolman (1932) suggested that purposiveness was an emergent property of behavior that could not be meaningfully reduced to sequences of muscle twitches.

The basic question is: At what level does the organism represent its own behavior? Although we can describe an animal's action at any level we choose, we are here concerned with determining how the animal represents its own behavior. If it represents its behavior at too molecular a level—for example, the precise pattern of muscular movements necessary to produce the instrumental response—then it loses flexibility in changing its behavior in response to changes in the environment. If the animal represents its behavior at too molar a level, then it may be, as Guthrie once accused Tolman, "lost in thought," knowing what its goals are, but not how to reach them (see Chapter 2).

Two kinds of evidence suggest that animals represent information about their behavior at a level above that of specific muscle movements. Many different patterns of movement can be used interchangeably by an animal to perform the same behavior, and evidence exists that they learn about "places" as separate from the behaviors necessary to reach them.

The experiments reviewed in Chapter 2 showed that animals continue to perform efficiently in a maze even when the test situation required a radically different pattern of movement from that they learned during training. For example, the pattern of muscular movements required to swim through a maze during training were very different from those necessary to run through the same maze after it had been drained. Yet the animals ran without error through the drained maze. They may have represented information about the specific pattern of movements necessary to swim through the maze, but they obviously also represented higher-level information about other properties of the task.

Similar results have been reported by Wickens (1938), who trained human subjects to avoid a mild electric shock by withdrawing their finger from a board when a light came on. The subjects were initially trained with their hands in a palm-down position. The appropriate response, then, was a flexion of the muscles on the back of the finger and an extension of the muscles on its front. So compelling was the learned response to the light, that at least one subject lost a bet that he could withold his response voluntarily. The subjects responded "automatically"; they did not have to "consider" the correct response.

After training, the subjects were tested with their hands in the palm-up position. Hand withdrawal now required the active response of the antagonistic muscle group; that is, subjects had to flex the muscles on the front of the hand—those required to relax during training—while extending the muscles on the back—those required to contract during training. In terms of the muscular response, exactly the opposite behavior was necessary during palm-up testing relative to that used during palm-down training. From a more molar viewpoint, however, exactly the same response was necessary, namely, withdrawal of the finger. All subjects adapted immediately to the new hand position, withdrawing their finger in an appropriate manner.

Finally, we have already discussed the data regarding place versus response learning (see Chapter 2). The evidence is clear that animals can learn about the locations of important stimuli. If place and response learning conflict, place learning is often faster.

The correct conclusion from these data is that the content of the animals' representations in instrumental conditioning includes information about stimulus context, molar descriptions of action, and information about the consequences of that action.

REPRESENTATION OF INSTRUMENTAL BEHAVIORS: CODES

Hierarchical behavioral control systems

Animals represent their behavior in a kind of hierarchical control network (Gallistel, 1980). This network may include information about low-level features of a behavior, such as the pattern of muscular contractions necessary to perform it. They also include intermediate levels of organization, such as coordinated action in a chain of responses. Finally, they also include high levels of organization, such as places and goals. In the following paragraphs, I develop Gallistel's hierarchical control system into a coherent system for representing instrumental action.

The six levels of organization suggested by Weiss (1941) are organized hierarchically. A single motor neuron controls the contraction of a number of muscles. In order to produce a coordinated movement, the action of several neurons and their attached muscles must be coordinated under the common control of some higher-level unit.

Every joint or moveable part, in turn, is controlled by several muscle groups. The relative timing and strength of their action determines the strength, speed, and orientation of the limb's movement. Furthermore, most limbs have sets of muscles that oppose one another. When one set of muscles contracts, the opposing set must relax or else rigid paralysis or fibrillation occurs.

Segmented structures, such as limbs or the spine, involve several joints whose movements must also be coordinated. Limbs must also be coordinated to produce coherent action instead of chaotic twitching.

Various motor "programs" guide relatively stereotyped behaviors that occur in the service of the animal as a whole. These acts consist of coordinated combinations of coherent actions, such as the so-called fixed-action patterns of ethology (e.g., the courtship behavior of the three-spined stickleback fish). Higher levels, more abstract than these, also exist.

The important point of this hierarchical notion of behavioral control is that at nearly every level, the same unit of coordination forms a component of many behaviors. The same muscles we use for typing a paper are used in a different coordinative pattern for swinging a baseball bat.

Elementary units.   At the bottom of the control hierarchy are the elementary units. Each elementary unit consists of a *contractor*, a *conductor*, and an *originator*. The contractor consists of one or more muscles, whose contraction is the mechanical cause of the movement. The conductor is the neural element that delivers a contraction-initiating signal to the muscle; and the originator is another neural element, that is the source of the contraction-initiating signal. These signals arise in the originator either spontaneously or in response to a stimulus (Gallistel, 1980). This combination of an originator, a conductor, and a contractor forms an elementary unit in the same sense in which the elements in chemistry are basic units. It is the minimum necessary to explain a naturally occurring movement. As in chemistry, an elementary unit can be broken down into lower-level units, but these lose their identity as elements.[10]

All chemical substances are compounded out of a limited number of chemical elements. Similarly, behavior is compounded out of the limited number of elementary behavioral units and the hierarchical structure that controls them. For example, we use our hands for many purposes, such as waving, writing, or dribbling a basketball. Each of these purposes involves more or less the same set of muscles, nerves, and so forth. They differ primarily in the coordination and organization of the basic units.

The elementary motor units form the "final common path" in all behavior. Their action is, in turn, organized by higher level units in the rest of the nervous system. In other words, the elementary units each "serve many masters."

Three kinds of elementary units have been described (Gallistel, 1980): reflexes, oscillators, and servomechanisms. A reflex is an elementary unit whose originating signal arises in the environment. Some stimulus impinges on a receptor, which sends a signal, perhaps via a number of neurons in succession, to one or more contractors, which by their contraction cause some movement. Although the performance of the reflex action may change the state of the receptor (for example, by turning the head) this resultant change is incidental to the reflex, not an intrinsic part of its operation. Reflexes still operate even if feedback is prevented. In S-R approaches to animal behavior, the reflex was assumed to be the only kind of elemental unit.

An oscillator is another type of elemental unit in which the signal originating the movement comes not from the sensory systems, but from some internal "pacemaker." An oscillator produces rhythmic muscular contractions whose rates are determined by properties of the pacemaker. For example, Brown (1914) found a definitive rhythm in the stepping and scratching movements of dogs. These movements could have been due to a combination of reflexes in which the per-

formance of one movement (e.g., the downward scratch) was the stimulus eliciting the performance of the next movement (e.g., the upward scratch). Instead,
Brown discovered that the rhythmic stepping and scratching movements of a dog
persisted, even when the higher brain centers were surgically disconnected, or
when sensory input was surgically prevented. These rhythmic movements are
generated by central oscillators in the dog's spinal cord, going "tick-tock." Each
tick sends a signal to one set of muscles (the downward stroke), and each tock
sends a signal to the opposing set of muscles (the upward stroke).

Central oscillators have been found in nearly every organism in which someone has sought them. They play an important role in such behaviors as eating,
drinking, swimming, and grooming. They are also important in controlling the
daily, or "circadian," rhythms of life. Feeding time, body temperature, and many
other bodily functions are controlled by circadian oscillators. Each of these functions shows the same daily variation, even in the absence of external cues regarding time of day. Under ordinary circumstances the oscillators that control the
daily bodily functions are themselves hierarchically controlled by a more central
pacemaker that serves to keep them all synchronized relative to the events of the
day (Aschoff, 1984).

The third kind of elemental unit is a servomechanism. It is unlike a reflex or
an oscillator in that feedback is important to its operation. The signal originating
a movement depends on the discrepancy between two input signals. The resulting behavior functions to reduce this discrepancy. A thermostat is a nonbiological
example of a servomechanism. One input signal is the temperature set on the
thermostat, the other signal is the room's temperature. A disparity between the
current room temperature and the setpoint of the thermostat causes the furnace
to turn on. Heat from the furnace then reduces the disparity. When the room
temperature matches the setpoint, the thermostat turns off the furnace.

Biological servomechanisms operate according to a similar principle. The
movements resulting from a servomechanism reduce the discrepancy between
some environmental variable and the "setpoint" of the organism, or the discrepancy between two environmental variables. This process is known as "negative
feedback" because the output of the servomechanism operates to reduce the discrepancy between its inputs.

When a servomechanism maintains an animal's orientation relative to a stimulus while the organism moves about, it is called a "taxis." For example, as
discussed in Chapter 2, certain caterpillars climb upward after hatching, toward
the top of a tree, because their crawling is controlled by a servomechanism that
operates to equalize the brightness of the light falling on the two eyes. If the light
falling on the left eye is brighter, they turn leftward; if the light falling on the
right eye is brighter, they turn rightward; otherwise, they constantly move forward. On average the brightest part of the visual environment of a caterpillar in

a tree will be the sky overhead. Hence, the bug crawls upward. If one eye of the caterpillar is covered, it crawls around in circles. If bright lights are placed beneath the tree, it crawls downward.

Figure 4.6 shows a schematic representation of the kind of hierarchical control structure necessary to coordinated action. Units at higher levels in the hierarchy control units lower in the hierarchy through selective potentiation and inhibition. A unit that is potentiated has a high potential for becoming active; a unit that is inhibited has a low potential for becoming active. Whether or not a given unit is active depends on the combination of potentiating and inhibiting signals it receives from higher-level units and on the sufficiency of its activating conditions. The activating conditions for a reflex are the sufficient eliciting stimuli. For an oscillator, they are the phase of the oscillation. For a servomechanism, they are discrepancies in its inputs. Other units at higher levels in the hierarchy may have other types of activating conditions.

Without the coordinating control of higher-level units, lower units could not serve any function for the animal. For example, an animal typically uses its legs for many purposes, such as walking, feeding, and grooming. If one of its legs groomed while a second made feeding movements and a third made walking movements, the animal would get nothing done. Purposive action requires that

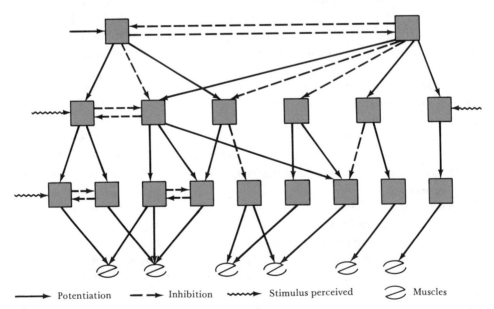

—————▶ Potentiation   — —▶ Inhibition   ⌇⌇▶ Stimulus perceived   ⌇ Muscles

Figure 4.6. A generalized representation of a hierarchical control system for coordinated action. Potentiation spreads from higher-level to lower-level nodes. A lower-level node may connect to more than one higher-level node. Outputs from the lowest-level nodes go directly to operate muscles.

higher-level units coordinate lower-level units, permitting only those movements that fit together while prohibiting others. It is important to remember that an animal's higher-level units do not directly control the muscles that produce the movement. Instead, they exert control by selectively potentiating or inhibiting lower-level units, for example, potentiating a reflex so that it can produce its movement when its adequate stimulus is present. The higher-level units do not themselves provide that adequate stimulus; they simply *permit* the reflex to respond to it.

Two examples can serve to illustrate this hierarchical layering of control (Gallistel, 1980). Roaches have six legs, which must be moved in an orderly fashion for the roach to run. Ordinarily, a rapidly running roach moves its front and back legs on one side at the same time that it moves its middle leg on the other. The front and back legs on the right side and the middle leg on the left side (labeled X in Figure 4.7a) move, while the other three legs remain stationary. Then the front and back legs on the left side and the middle leg on the right (labeled Y in Figure 4.7a) move together, while the other three remain stationary. In this way the roach's body is always supported by a stable tripod of legs.

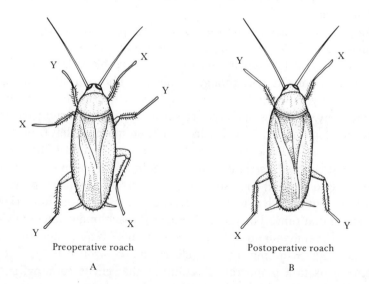

Preoperative roach   Postoperative roach

A   B

Figure 4.7. The coordinated action of a cockroach's running. Legs indicated by the letter X all move together in the same direction at the same time. Legs indicated by Y are all stationary when the X legs are moving, and all move together in the same direction and at the same time when the X legs are stationary. (A) shows the pattern of movement apparent in a normal intact roach. (B) shows the pattern of movement seen when the two middle legs are amputated. Legs that moved together in the intact roach move in opposition in the postoperative roach.

Simplifying a little, each leg is controlled by 6 muscles, so running involves the coordinated action of 36 muscles, each contracted and relaxed in an orderly manner. Roaches are also capable of other orderly gaits, which involve other stable configurations of legs.

This information tells us little about the organization of the control system that organizes roach running. It could function in a purely reflex manner like a player piano. The pattern of muscle twitches could be controlled by a fixed pattern of signals in the way that the holes in the piano roll control the melody produced by a player piano. A simple experiment is capable of demonstrating that this fixed program characterization is incorrect, however.

If one "amputates" one of the strings in a player piano, then the note produced when that string is struck will no longer function. Playing the piano roll will produce exactly the same melody it produced before the amputation, but whenever the missing note is scheduled, no sound is heard. The next note occurs at its usual time. Analogously, one can amputate the middle leg on each side of a roach. If a fixed program controls its behavior, then the other legs should continue to operate in the same manner as before. That leg will be missing whenever the motor program signals for it to support the roach, however, and the insect will fall over.

The postoperative roach, in contrast to the postoperative piano, does not fall flat on its mandibles. Before its middle legs were amputated, the roach ran with its front and back right legs moving together, followed by its front and back left legs. After amputation, its gait changes radically. The two legs that formerly moved in synchrony, now alternate, and the legs that formerly alternated, now move in synchrony. The postoperative roach moves its front right leg together with its back left leg (labeled X in Figure 4.7b) and moves its left front leg at the same time it moves its back right leg (labeled Y in Figure 4.7b). When the preoperative roach moved its right front leg, its brain sent a motor command to its right back leg to move at the same time. Conversely, when the postoperative roach moves its right front leg, its brain sends a motor command to its right back leg to stay still at that time. Thus the "intelligent" roach immediately modifies its pattern of motor commands to accommodate the new requirements of running without middle legs. Running, then, is clearly not controlled by a fixed motor program analogous to a piano roll. A stimulus that elicits running, such as a bright light, does not directly control the firing of motor neurons as it would in a simple reflex system. Rather, it signals a higher-level unit, which adaptively copes with changing conditions such as amputation. The roach represents its own action at a level higher than the direct connection of stimuli to muscular movements.

The mediterranean coastal snail provides another example of a hierarchical control structure in behavior. The snail feeds on algae growing on rock walls.

Under water it crawls toward shore because it has a negative phototaxis. That is, it turns so that the light hitting its two eyes is equal, but proceeds in a direction away from, rather than toward, the brighter light. If it comes upon a horizontal crevice under water, it will crawl into it. At the back of the crevice, it will crawl onto the roof. Now, upside down, its phototaxis reverses, the snail becomes attracted by light. It crawls out of the crevice and continues upward because of a negative geotaxis (crawls away from the attraction of gravity, responding to equalize the pull on its statocysts). If the sun is shining brightly, the snail stops at the waterline. If the light is dim or if it is dark, however, the snail continues upward out of the water. Once above water, if the snail comes to a crevice it will again crawl in, but it won't crawl out, because the phototaxis reverses only when the animal is both upside down and under water. The result is that the snail stays in the crevice, perhaps for a considerable amount of time, until the water reaches it—for example, during high tide—and it is again submerged.

This example illustrates that a given elementary unit, such as a reflex, servo-mechanism, or oscillator, is only allowed to act at certain times under the control of higher-level units. The snail displays a three-level hierarchy. At the lowest level are the motor units, which directly activate and deactivate the muscles. At the second level are the positive and negative phototaxes and the geotaxis. These units do not control muscle fibers directly; instead, they potentiate or inhibit the firing of the motor units. At the third level are decision circuits that determine whether the positive or the negative phototaxic units are to be activated. Decision circuits control behavior through the control they exert over the lower-level units, much as a general controls privates by influencing their officers.

At any given moment, only certain behaviors within the snail's repertory are activated. Other units, whose action would be incompatible with the activated actions, are inhibited, and their access to the final common path—the motor units—is blocked. By selectively potentiating and depotentiating particular sets of units, higher levels impose a general tendency or direction on behavior. This tendency plus the relevant auxiliary conditions, such as being upside down and under water, lead to the particular behavior observed (the reversal of the photo-taxis, and the snail crawls out of the crevice).

Hierarchical representations of instrumental learning

Similar kinds of hierarchical control structures might also be the basis for representing instrumental learning. The main characteristic of instrumental behavior is that it is purposive or goal-directed. It is controlled by its consequences. Therefore, the hierarchical control structure that represents instrumental learning must also include additional layers of units or nodes that represent the animal's goals or needs. Activation of one of these goal units leads to the potentiation of those behaviors that serve that goal and to the inhibition of those lower-level nodes and behaviors that are incompatible with it. By this hypothesis, instrumental learning is the formation of potentiating and inhibiting connections among nodes, along with stimulus-stimulus associations of the sort formed during classical conditioning.

Recall Tolman's concept of a cognitive map. Through learning the organism acquires relationships, called expectancies, between pairs of stimuli, which it then organizes into cognitive maps. Activation of the goal of food might activate an "image" or other representation of the goal box—for example, its location in the cognitive map. In turn, this might activate or potentiate images or representations of the choice point preceding the goal box, and so forth. Activation spreads through the cognitive map from the goal box to other points in the maze. As the organism progresses through the maze, those behaviors that are incompatible with the goal, for example, going in the wrong direction or entering blind alleys, are depotentiated, and those that lead toward the goal are potentiated.

Discrimination learning.   Figure 4.8 illustrates a hierarchical control system that an organism might use to represent a discrimination task. In this task the animal is rewarded for pressing the left-hand lever when a light is on and for pressing a right-hand lever when a buzzer is on. The animal's representation of this task consists of a hierarchy of goals, subgoals, and learned expectancies. When it is hungry, the highest-level node shown in Figure 4.8 is activated. Activation of this node potentiates the lower-level subgoals that lead to the delivery of food and inhibits other goals and subgoals that lead to incompatible behavior. Inhibition of a goal does not inevitably prevent that goal from controlling the animal's behavior; the inhibited node is simply made less likely to control it. For example, activating the food-motivation node may inhibit the simultaneous activation of the water-motivation node. If, however, the animal were to become more thirsty, then the water-motivation node might become sufficiently activated to inhibit the food-motivation node and come to control the immediate behavior. The important point is that activated nodes are mutually inhibitory to other nodes at the same level in the hierarchy. Activation of one node inhibits other nodes at the same level.

Activation of the animal's food motivation potentiates all actions that produce food. Some of these actions have been specifically learned, such as bar pressing, whereas others apparently are unlearned.

When the node labeled "Actions that produce food" is activated, it potentiates two sets of expectancies at the next lower level in the hierarchy. These expectancy nodes become activated when the conditions for their expectancy occur. The tone–left–bar–food expectancy is activated when the tone is present, and the buzzer–right–bar–food expectancy is activated when the buzzer is present. The tone–left–bar–food expectancy is analogous to an expectancy that when the left-

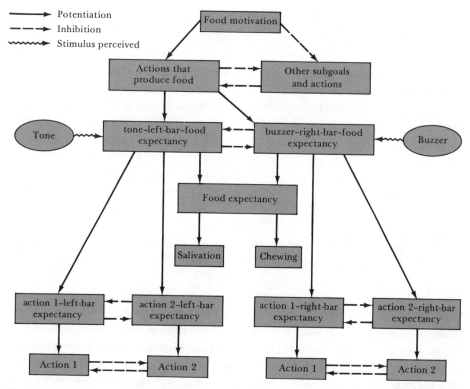

Figure 4.8. The hierarchical representation underlying an instrumental discrimination of the sort: respond on the left lever in the presence of light and on the right lever in the presence of a buzzer.

hand lever is depressed in the presence of the tone, then food will be delivered. Correspondingly, the buzzer–right-bar–food expectancy is analogous to the expectancy that when the right-hand lever is depressed in the presence of the buzzer, then food will be delivered. By design of the discrimination task, these expectancies are appropriate only when the proper stimuli are present. The animal should expect food following a right-bar press only if the buzzer is on. Therefore, detection of the buzzer is necessary to activate the buzzer–right-bar–food expectancy, even after it has been potentiated. Although both expectancies are potentiated, only one will be activated depending on whether the buzzer or the tone is presented. When one is activated, it inhibits the other.

Activation of one of these conditional food expectancies also potentiates other food-related behaviors, such as salivation and chewing. This widespread activation of all food-related behaviors accounts in part for the so-called constraints on learning and "misbehavior" of the sort observed by Breland and Breland (1961) and described in Chapter 2. For example, Shettleworth (1973, 1975) found that presentation of food to hungry hamsters led to an increase in such behaviors as scrabbling and digging and to a decrease in such behaviors as grooming and face washing. When reinforcement was made contingent on one of these behaviors, the behavior increased in frequency as long as it was one of the actions that also increased when noncontingent reinforcers were presented. When food reinforcement was made contingent on face washing or grooming, however, these behaviors decreased in frequency. According to the hierarchical control structure hypothesis, these results were obtained because activation of the food expectancy potentiated scrabbling and digging but inhibited face washing and grooming.

Activation of the tone–left-bar–food expectancy activates all of the behaviors the animal could use to press the left bar. For example, the rat could press the bar with its right paw (action 1), with its left paw (action 2), with its rear end, and so forth. Any one of these will result in the achievement of the subgoal specified at the next higher level in the hierarchy, and all are potentiated. Once one of these actions becomes activated, however, it inhibits all incompatible actions, and the result is the successful performance of the discrimination.

Maze learning.   A similar analysis can apply to the data obtained by MacFarlane (1930). Training rats to swim through a maze resulted in the formation of a hierarchical control structure that includes the muscle movements necessary to traverse the flooded maze as well as higher-level nodes corresponding to a cognitive map of the maze. Being in the maze activated higher-level nodes corresponding to locations and locomotion commands. These nodes then potentiated all of the possible kinds of movement patterns that would get the rat from the start to the goal box. For example, both swimming and running would be potentiated, but the activation of one or the other depends on the particular stimulus conditions that are present. If the maze is flooded, then swimming is activated and running is inhibited; if the maze is dry, then running is activated and swimming is inhibited. The stimulus conditions control which of the potentiated actions will actually be activated.

The most important feature of this representation system for instrumental learning is the notion that learning occurs at multiple levels in the hierarchy. It includes S-S associations, such as the tone + left-bar-down–food expectancies, as well as action representations. The higher-level nodes in the hierarchy correspond to declarative representations. They specify the relations among events, but they do not, themselves, specify the actions necessary to bring about those events. Lower-level units correspond to procedural representations. In contrast to higher-level nodes, these units do specify the exact form of the action. The translation from declarative representations to action is controlled by the pattern of lower-level units that are activated or inhibited. Although a system such as this one clearly requires further development, it appears to be physically realizable and capable of dealing with known problems in learning.

SUMMARY

Learning relies on memory. When an organism learns something, it must remember what it has learned if that past experience is to affect its later behavior. There are many ways in which an organism can represent its experience. These include reflexlike stimulus-response associations, stimulus-stimulus associations or expectancies, hierarchical associationist networks, imagelike systems, and pattern-directed inference systems. Each of these alternative systems has specific strengths and weaknesses. All may be used in different kinds of situations.

Classical conditioning is represented by animals in terms of stimulus-stimulus associations. The response is not directly contained in the animal's representation, but is derived from the nature of the unconditional stimulus. In contrast, the representations formed during instrumental conditioning include information about the response as well as about the outcome of the behavior. In general, animals appear to use hierarchically organized representations of their learning experience.

RECOMMENDED READINGS

Dickinson, A. (1980) *Contemporary animal learning theory*. Cambridge: Cambridge University Press.

Gallistel, C. R. (1980) *The organization of action*. Hillsdale, N.J.: Erlbaum.

Honig, W. K. (1978) Studies of working memory in the pigeon. In S. H. Hulse, H. Fowler, & W. K. Honig (Eds.), *Cognitive processes in animal behavior*. Hillsdale, N.J.: Erlbaum.

Wagner, A. R. (1981) SOP: A model of automatic memory processing in animal behavior. In N. E. Spear & R. R. Miller (Eds.), *Information processing in animals: Memory mechanisms*. Hillsdale, N.J.: Erlbaum.

CHAPTER 5

Working Memory

CHARACTERISTICS OF WORKING MEMORY

The previous chapter described reference memory. The primary characteristic of this kind of memory is that its contents are stable over time. Informally, we can say that reference memory contains knowledge—what we have learned. Responses to "questions" asked of reference memory do not depend on when the question is asked. For example, the name of the first president of the United States or the rules of a card game do not change with the time of day or day of the week. You may not know the president's name or how to play the game, but if you do, this information does not depend on your current status or on your recent experience. It also does not matter when or where you learned the information. Similarly, when an animal learns that a bell CS signals the delivery of food, the relationship does not change from trial to trial. Once the relation is learned, it does not matter whether it is tested on the next trial, the tenth trial, or a hundred trials later. All other things being equal, the same response is always appropriate.

Another sort of memory seems to be involved when you try to remember what you ate at your last meal. Typically, this information changes, depending on the time of day and when and where you last ate. Similarly, although the rules of a card game, such as bridge, are stable and unchanging, your behavior when playing changes over time, depending on the cards that happen to be in your hand and on your memory for cards, bids, and behaviors shown by your opponents. Appropriate behavior, that is, winning, depends on the successful integration of stable rules and ever-changing situations. Working memory is the memory that we use to keep track of the changing features of experience that, in conjunction with the stable features, determine appropriate behavior. Working memory holds information that is useful for only a limited time.

Working memory is the primary concern of the present chapter. It has been studied most commonly with some kind of delayed-response task. In such a task, some information is provided at one time and the subject's retention of that information is tested at another. For example, the sample that appears at the start of a delayed matching-to-sample (DMTS) trial provides the organism with the information necessary for it to choose the correct comparison stimulus at the end of the trial (see Chapter 3). A correct choice depends on maintenance during the retention interval of the information provided by the sample. Because the identity of the sample varies randomly from trial to trial, knowledge of the task, analogous to our knowledge of the rules of bridge, is not sufficient to ensure appropriate performance. The correct response depends on the present stimulus conditions (the array of comparison stimuli) and on an adequate memory for information from the recent past.

A typical delayed-response task uses only a small set of alternative stimuli as samples and comparisons. The to-be-remembered event is usually one member of this small set, not some arbitrarily chosen stimulus. As a result the subject does not need to hold all of the features of the event in working memory; it needs only enough information to discriminate the correct choice from its alternatives. Therefore, performance of a well-learned delayed-response task requires two distinct kinds of memory. While the animal is learning the task, it must encode the rules and enough of the distinctive features of the stimuli to identify them. Presumably, this information is maintained in reference memory throughout the experiment. Performance of the task also requires the animal to remember which of the possible stimuli is the to-be-remembered event for that particular trial. Presumably, this information is maintained in working memory for the duration of the trial.

On the distinction between working and reference memory

Operational distinctions between working and reference memory are often possible based on the stability versus the variability of the information. Physiological procedures also differentiate between the two kinds of memory. For example, lesions to certain parts of the brains of experimental animals result in a loss of working, but not reference, memory (Olton, 1983). That is, animals can still make choices based on stable sources of information, such as where food is always located, but cannot make choices based on changeable information (for example, where food has recently been eaten). Furthermore, electroconvulsive shock (ECS) produces amnesia (abnormal forgetting) in both working and reference memory, but the temporal patterns of the effect are very different in the two kinds of memory (Shavalia, Dodge, & Beatty, 1981). During learning, an immediate treatment is more disruptive than a delayed treatment; but when animals perform a working memory task in a radial maze, delayed treatment is more disruptive than immediate treatment.

The distinction between working memory and reference memory is related to a number of other proposals for the division of memory functioning. For example, the parallels between working and short-term memory and between reference and long-term memory should be obvious. To a large extent, these terms are equivalent. The most important difference between the two distinctions is that the short-term/long-term distinction operationally defines memory by the time at which it is tested, whereas the working/reference distinction classifies memory on the basis of its contents, codes, and use. The working/reference distinction does not compel us to invoke such concepts as "short long-term memory" or "long short-term memory" to explain a number of phenomena. The distinction between working and reference memory is related to Tulving's (1972) distinction between semantic and episodic memory, Bruner's (1969) distinction between memory with record versus without record, O'Keefe & Nadel's (1978) distinction between locale and taxon memory, Marshall's (1979) distinction between autobiographical and procedural memory, Dickinson's (1980) distinction between procedural and declarative memory, and Squire's distinction between "knowing how" and "knowing that" (Cohen & Squire, 1981; Squire, 1983). Olton (1983) has pointed out that these various distinctions share a number of common properties. For example, the type of brain lesions that affect working memory and not reference memory also affect episodic and declarative memory functioning without impairing semantic or procedural memory. Whereas strong conclusions may be premature, the distinctions are probably not mutually exclusive. With further investigation it may be possible to combine them into a unified theory of memory functioning. For present purposes, however, the distinction between working and reference memory is sufficient and useful.

Some investigators have attempted to develop theories that involve only one type of memory. According to these single-memory models (e.g., Gaffan, 1983; Staddon, 1984), animals do not retain information in working memory; they simply discriminate the time at which the alternative, to-be-remembered events occurred. For example, the subject does not encode the sample from the current delayed matching-to-sample (DMTS) trial; it discriminates which sample was most recently presented. By this view working and reference memory differ only in the "strength" of the various memory representations. In general, these models which assume temporal discrimination have not proved satisfactory (Roitblat, 1982a; see below), and some distinction between memory systems appears to be necessary.

Differences remain in determining the criteria that distinguish between the working and reference memory systems, but some division is necessary, because without it we are led to obvious contradictions. For example, it is well known that pigeons performing DMTS show higher choice accuracy with longer sample durations than with shorter sample durations (see Roitblat, 1982a). One possible explanation is that animals are originally trained with fairly long sample presentations. Therefore, they perform more poorly when short sample presentations are used because they fail to recognize these brief samples as similar to the long samples to which they are accustomed. If this "generalization decrement" hypothesis (see Chapter 3) were correct, it would also predict that subjects' choice accuracy should decline when samples longer than those used during training are presented. In contrast to this prediction, choice accuracy continues to improve with increasing sample durations, even when the birds are tested with samples that are several times as long as the durations used in the original training (Roberts & Grant, 1974).

Other difficulties with the distinction between working memory and reference memory also remain. For example, we do not know how frequently information must change in order to be stored in working memory instead of reference memory. This may turn out to be a difficult problem to solve operationally because the memory system the animal employs may depend more on its expectation as to how the information will be used than on the particular operations we employ to test for memory. Fortunately, enough clear cases exist that the distinction between working memory and reference memory can prove useful.

REPRESENTATION OF A SPATIAL TASK

The first working-memory task we will consider involves a radial-arm maze, an example of which is shown in Figure 5.1. The arms of the radial maze project outward from a central platform like spokes on a wheel. In most experiments a single piece of food is placed at the end of each arm before the start of a trial, and a rat is allowed to run around the apparatus until it finds the food. As each arm is chosen, it becomes a to-be-remembered stimulus for later choices. Once the rat visits an arm, no more food is available there, so the optimal strategy, and a sufficient demonstration that the rat remembers the previously visited arms, is for it to visit each arm once before returning to any arm.

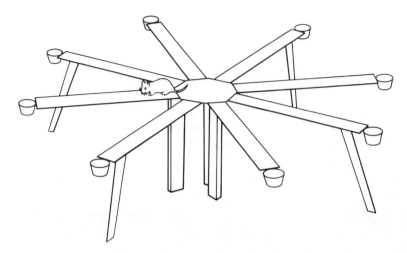

Figure 5.1. A top view of an eight-arm maze. A food cup is at the end of each arm.

Rats are very good at this task. They perform perfectly in a four-arm version of this maze after about 10 trials (Walker & Olton, 1979). They also do well in a 17-arm maze. After about 50 test trials, they choose 15 different arms in the first 17 choices, a level far above chance (Olton, Collison, & Werz, 1977). Most of the experiments, however, have been conducted with 8-arm mazes, in which rats typically enter about 7.5 different arms in their first 8 choices (Olton, 1978).

In order to perform accurately on this task, the rat must maintain information about where it has been, where food has been available, and/or where food remains available. Rats can perform this task on the basis of working and reference memory. Presumably, reference memory contains the stable information about the layout of the maze, for example, that each arm has food at the start of a trial. Working memory holds information about those arms that have or have not been visited so far on the trial. First, we will examine some alternative strategies that rats might use in performing this task; then we will consider some data regarding the nature of the representation they use.

Some alternative strategies

Algorithms.   There are a large number of strategies that would allow a rat to perform very accurately in a radial-arm maze by using a simple algorithm or rule to determine its choices. For example, when asked, most people say that they would use the algorithm of starting at one arm and then going around the maze in order, entering each adjacent arm. This is a very simple strategy because each successive response depends on the arm just chosen and not on any of the previously visited arms. As each arm is visited, it serves as a cue guiding the choice of the next arm. The algorithm could be paraphrased as "choose the arm to the right of the arm you are now leaving." This strategy is an algorithm because it specifies the solution to the problem of finding all of the food in the maze as a series of behaviors, which when executed flawlessly will guarantee correct performance in the maze. A rat employing an algorithm of this type would not need to use working memory at all. It would need only to maintain the rules of the procedure in reference memory and execute them flawlessly during the trial. The same sequence of arm choices would occur on each trial in the order specified by the algorithm.

The available data argue strongly against an algorithmic strategy. Figure 5.2 shows the distribution of choices made by a rat and a fish in a radial-arm maze. The graph shows the relative frequency with which the animal chose the next arm to the right ($+1$), the second arm to the right ($+2$), the first arm to the left (-1), and so forth. If the animals were using a simple algorithm, such as "always move one arm to the right," then all their choices would be in one particular column. Conversely, if they made random choices, they would enter each arm equally often. Both rats (Olton, 1978) and fish (Roitblat, Tham, & Golub, 1982) showed regularity in their response patterns. The fish were more regular than the rats. In neither species, however, was the degree of regularity sufficient to account for the observed choice accuracy. Hence, their performance cannot be explained solely in terms of a "memoryless" response algorithm. Furthermore, when rats were confined to the central platform of a 17-arm maze for 20 s following each choice, their accuracy remained high, whereas the regularity of the response pattern virtually disappeared (Olton, Collison, & Werz, 1977).

These data cannot rule out more complicated response patterns that depend on more than one prior choice. In order for the response to depend on more than one previous choice, however, the animal would have to remember those choices. Therefore, the discovery of these complex choice patterns would be a demonstration of the importance of working memory.

Odor cues.   A second obvious strategy would be for the rats to smell the food and go only into those arms that have a food smell. Alternatively, the same thing could be accomplished by leaving a scent marker (e.g., a spot of urine) on each arm as it is entered or left. The rats could then avoid the marked arms. They would not have to remember where they had been in the maze, because the scent marker would substitute for memory. As long as the scent remained, they could successively avoid entering already visited arms. Rats, however, do not seem to use these strategies.

Olton and Samuelson (1976) trained rats in an 8-arm radial maze until they performed quickly and accurately. The rats were then tested to discover whether their performance was controlled by such intramaze cues as scent markers or food cues, or by spatial location.

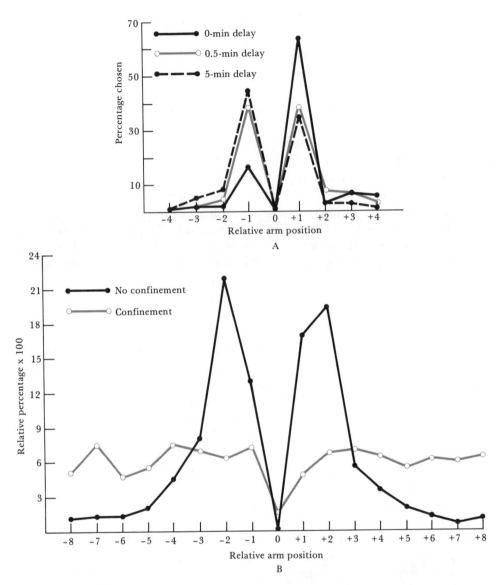

Figure 5.2. Proportion of arms chosen at each distance and direction from the just chosen arm. Arms in the positive direction were clockwise from the just chosen arm; arms in the negative direction were in the counterclockwise direction. The Siamese fighting fish (A) were tested with either no delay between choices or with a 0.5 or 5.0 min delay between choices. Rats in (B) were confined for either 0 or 20 s between successive choices.

Each test trial began with three free choices among the eight arms: The rats were released in the maze with the entrances to all eight arms open. They were allowed to choose three of these arms and then were confined to the central platform of the maze while the arms were rotated 45°. The rotation moved the three arms that the rat had already visited to new spatial positions. As Figure 5.3 shows, the arms that had the odor cues were now located in spatial positions that had not been visited. During the fourth choice, the central platform of the maze was also rotated in case scent markers had been left on the platform at the entrance to the visited arms. The subjects were then allowed four more choices. If the rats were following scent cues, then they should have avoided the arms with the scent cues, wherever their location. During the trial shown in Figure 5.3, they should have avoided visiting arms B, D, E, and G. If the animals chose arms by remembering the spatial locations they had visited, then they should have avoided the arms in the already visited positions, however they smell. During the trial shown in Figure 5.3, they should have avoided visiting arms C, D, F, and H. Olton and Samuelson found that the rats responded to spatial location and not to intramaze cues. They behaved as if they had not noticed the rotation and avoided previously visited spatial locations, whether or not they now had food in them. They entered previously visited arms, provided these were now in unvisited spatial locations.

Other data further indicate that rats represent the food locations relative to extramaze locations and have difficulty if the task requires them to respond to intramaze features. Olton and Collison (1979) trained rats in the standard manner in an eight-arm maze, and then tested them with one of two rotation conditions. For the intramaze group, the maze was rotated after each choice and the remaining food rotated along with it. As a result, the food stayed in a constant position relative to intramaze features, but moved relative to extramaze features. For rats in the extramaze group, the food remained behind while the maze rotated so that the food stayed in a constant position relative to extramaze cues, but moved relative to intramaze features. Choice accuracy on rotation test trials dropped to chance for the animals in the intramaze group and never recovered. In contrast, the accuracy of the extramaze group remained high. These results indicate that rats locate the food relative to extramaze locations not relative to intramaze cues.

The important distinction in these data is not whether the rats use intramaze or extramaze cues, but how they represent the information regarding the locations of food. There is nothing special about orienting with cues that are off the maze versus those that are on it. The importance of these findings is that the animals cannot change the extramaze cues when they visit an arm. Therefore, the environment cannot provide the information necessary to decide whether an arm has or has not been visited. The rats must maintain this information internally. An animal orienting to intramaze cues could still use memory to keep track of the visited arms, but we would then have difficulty discriminating the use of memory from the use of intramaze cues. The conclusion from these experiments is that rats use memory representations that contain information about

A

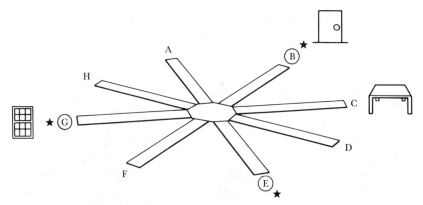

Stage 1: Three free choices to arms marked with stars. Stars indicate visited spatial locations. Circles indicate arms that could be sent marked.

B

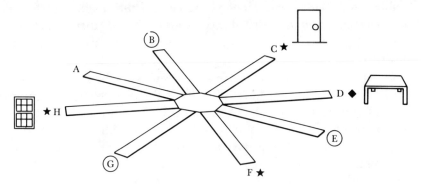

Stage 2: The rats are confined in the center while the maze is rotated 45°. The arm that was near the table is now near the door and so on. The rat is allowed a fourth choice. While the rat is making its fourth choice, the central platform is rotated to match the arms. The diamond indicates the arm chosen by the rat on its fourth choice.

C

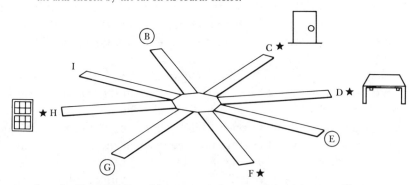

Stage 3: The rat is allowed four more choices among the eight arms. The arms with stars are in already visited spatial locations; the arms with circles are arms that could hold scent markers. Rats avoid arms that are in already visited spatial locations, not arms that could have been scent marked.

the locations in the maze and their status—whether they currently do or do not have food in them. Because the status of an arm changes when the rats visit it, this status information is presumably maintained during the trial in working memory. Next we examine how animals represent this information about maze locations and their status.

Representations

Cognitive maps.   Rats could internally represent the locations of a radial-arm maze in a large number of different ways. The most prominent of these is as an analog of the arms in their spatial location, that is, as a *cognitive map*. The notion of a cognitive map has a long history (e.g. Tolman, 1948; see Chapters 2 and 4) and much intuitive appeal. The essence of the hypothesis is that the animal carries in its head a representation of the spatial properties of the maze that correspond, point for point, with the physical properties. A cognitive map represents the maze in the same way that a paper map of a town, for example, has features that correspond to the streets and roads of the town. The simple presence of a map, however, is not sufficient for the rat to perform the radial-maze task or any other kind of navigation. Navigation requires some way to orient the map. In addition, rats in the radial maze must also keep track of the changing status of the arms as they visit them.

A map provides correct information about an environment only when it is oriented appropriately relative to that environment. People frequently use a magnetic compass to orient a paper map in correspondence with the environment. The north orientation is marked on the map and the compass indicates which way is north in the environment. Features of the environment or landmarks can also be used to orient. The evidence described above suggests that the rat uses one or more extramaze "landmarks" to define the spatial locations of the arms and, thus, the orientation of its cognitive map.

The rats could be orienting relative to one particularly noticeable extramaze stimulus or relative to more complex combinations of stimuli. They clearly are not orienting relative to intramaze stimuli because rotation of these stimuli did not result in an analogous rotation of the rats' choice pattern.

Figure 5.3. (*opposite page*) A test for control by intramaze versus extramaze cues. (A) shows the locations of arms and food prior to rotation. (B) shows the maze after rotation. The locations indicated by stars were visited before the maze was rotated. The arms indicated by circles in (B) are arms that were entered prior to rotation (in their former starred positions) and from which the food has been removed. (C) shows the maze after the center platform is rotated. [After Olton & Samuelson, 1976.]

Lists of arm-stimulus pairs.   The use of a cognitive map assumes that each significant point in the environment is represented in relation to every other significant point. This is a fairly sophisticated representation of the geometric properties of a space (see Cheng & Gallistel, 1984). Instead of a complete map of the maze environment, rats might use a simpler representation. They could associate each arm with a unique stimulus. Each spatial location in this kind of representation would be identified by a unique stimulus. The representation would not necessarily contain any information about the relations among these stimuli. A rat using this kind of representation could keep track of the status of each arm it has entered by activating a representation in working memory of the arm's identifying stimulus. Rats would then avoid any arms associated with stimuli whose representations are currently active. In many ways this scheme is simpler than using a cognitive map. A cognitive map represents stimuli and their relations; a list need represent only the stimuli.

Three alternative representational schemes have been proposed. The rats could maintain a map of the maze environment in reference memory and orient it according to a single salient stimulus. Alternatively, they could maintain a map of the maze environment in reference memory, and orient it relative to complex combinations of stimuli. Finally, they could maintain a paired-associate list of arms and identifying stimuli in reference memory and a list of currently active stimuli in working memory. All three hypotheses propose that rats use working memory to keep track of the status of the arms in the maze and reference memory to maintain the information necessary to identify the arms.

Orientation to the stimulus complex.   Rats appear to use cognitive maps and to orient them relative to complex combinations of stimuli. Suzuki, Augerinos, and Black (1980) carefully enclosed an eight-arm maze inside a large cylindrical chamber made of black curtains. In one experiment, they hung distinctive stimuli, such as Christmas tree lights and posters, on the curtain. There was one distinctive stimulus for each of seven arms, and none for the eighth. Presumably lack of a stimulus for this arm was itself distinctive. The relationships of each stimulus relative to the others, relative to the arms, and relative to the central platform of the maze were changed between trials.

Each trial consisted of three stages. First, the rats were forced to make three choices to arms randomly selected by the experimenter. All other arms were blocked by doors. Following the third choice, the rats were confined on the central platform for 2.5 min inside a holding chamber that prevented them from seeing the external stimuli. During the third stage of the trial, they were allowed free access to all arms.

One of three stimulus manipulations occurred during the confinement stage of each test trial. These are all shown in Figure 5.4. On *control* trials the stimuli

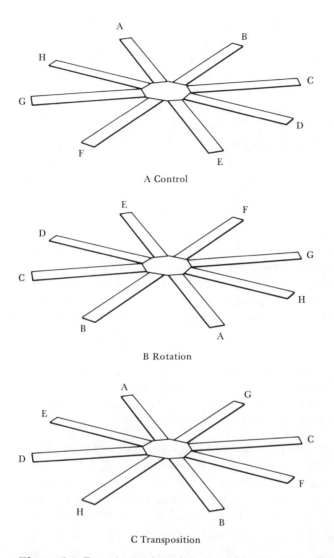

Figure 5.4. Experimental conditions used by Suzuki, et al., 1980. (A) shows control, (B) shows rotation, and (C) shows transposition. The letters at the end of each arm identify the stimulus associated with it. Food that was uneaten after the first stage of the trial moved along with the stimuli.

were rotated around the maze and then returned to their original locations. On *rotation* trials the stimuli, the walls, and the ceiling of the cylinder were rotated 180° and left there. In this condition the stimuli maintained the same relationship relative to one another, but moved relative to possible stimuli coming from outside the cylinder (sounds, smells, etc.). On *transposition* trials the stimuli were exchanged with one another, changing their relationship to each other and to outside stimuli. In all cases the food moved with the stimuli. For example, if the rat had not yet visited the arm near the Christmas tree light before the stimuli were moved, then food was still available in whatever arm was near the light after they were moved.

Choice accuracy on rotation trials did not differ from accuracy on control trials. The rats "tracked" the rotation, continuing to choose arms associated with previously unchosen stimuli. They rotated their choice pattern in correspondence with the rotated stimuli. This clearly indicates that they were using the particular stimuli provided by the experimenters to orient themselves and not the stimuli from beyond the black curtain. On transposition trials, in contrast, when the relations among the stimuli were changed, choice accuracy dropped to a level near chance. "Analyses of errors suggest that in the transposition trial the animals did not avoid the stimuli chosen in the forced choices and performed as if a new trial had been started after stimulus transposition" (Suzuki, et al., 1980, p. 11).

The rotation of choice patterns in correspondence with the rotation of the stimuli shows that the rats were using specifiable, extramaze, visual stimuli to orient themselves in the maze. The disruption in the rats' performance following transposition shows that the configuration and not just individual stimuli was important. These data are consistent with the hypothesis that rats use a cognitive map of the maze. In contrast, they are inconsistent with the hypothesis that a single stimulus determined the orientation of the map or that each arm was associated with a unique stimulus set. We turn next to the question of how animals maintain information about the status of the location.

Memory for arms visited.   In addition to a maplike representation of the maze, correct performance requires that rats also discriminate arms they have already visited from arms that they have not. Although this discrimination is between memories and not between stimuli, the methods developed for studying stimulus control can also be applied to the analysis of memory. These methods suggest that rats maintain information about the arms they have visited in a listlike format.

Systematic behavior relative to some stimulus dimension, such as brightness, requires that the organism be able to distinguish stimuli that vary along that dimension. Systematic behavior relative to some remembered dimension, such as whether or not an arm has been visited, similarly requires that the organism be able to distinguish memories that vary along that dimension. The experiments described above clearly show that animals use memory to perform in the radial-arm maze, and not any simple memoryless strategy.

In experiments on stimulus control, the pattern of generalization and the ease with which the animal learns a discrimination can tell us about how it codes the stimuli. For example, following training to respond to one stimulus, the animal will respond to similar stimuli. Typically, its rate of responding declines as the similarity between the test and the training stimulus declines. Hence, the degree to which a trained animal responds to a stimulus indicates its "judgment" regarding the similarity of the presented stimulus to its memory of the training stimulus. Further, the subject responds with more errors and learns more slowly when the stimuli to be discriminated are more similar to one another than when they are more different. Both generalization and the difficulty of the discrimination tell us about how the animal judges the similarity among the stimuli.

By analogy more-similarly coded items should be more often confused (more difficult to discriminate) than less-similarly coded items. For example, Conrad (1964) tested people's ability to remember lists of consonants, which he had displayed on a screen. Subjects were more likely to confuse letters that sounded similar, such as B and V, than letters that looked similar, such as B and R. On this basis he concluded that information about letter identities are stored in working, or short-term, memory in an acoustic code.

We can use the same logic to analyze the error patterns exhibited by a rat in a radial-arm maze as an indication of the way it codes information about the arms it has visited. Arms that are similar to the rat's representation of an unvisited arm should be more likely to be erroneously visited than arms that are dissimilar.

Visits to arms of a radial maze are distributed in space and in time: Some arms are visited before other arms, and some arms are located nearer to some arms and farther from others. Error responses may show systematic patterns based on the temporal position of the animal's previous visit or on the spatial location of the previous visit. Those errors that are systematic relative to the *time* at which the arm was previously visited show a "serial position effect." In contrast, those errors that are systematically related to the *locations* of previous visits show a "spatial position effect." Again, systematical behavior relative to some feature of the task, implies that the animal can differentiate alternatives according to that feature. In memory-based performance, the features that control behavior are not the overt observable stimuli, but features of the animal's representation.

Just as Conrad's subjects produced error responses that were similar in sound to the correct stimulus, animals in a radial maze might also produce errors that are systematically related to some aspect of the correct response. If they were to code the information regarding the status of an arm, that is, whether or not it currently held food, in a spatially organized code, then we might expect that when errors occur, they would substitute spatially similar arms for the correct choice. This suggests that errors would be more likely to arms near remaining correct arms than to arms distant from them. If, however, the animals remember the status of an arm by adding it to a list, then their error patterns should reflect the structure of that list, for example, its serial organization, and not the structure of the space. Either representational scheme for maintaining the current status of an arm would be consistent with the use of a maplike representation to represent the spatial aspects of the radial maze.

The method for investigating the code rats use to maintain information about the status of visited versus unvisited arms can be summarized as follows: First, differential responding of an animal relative to features of stimuli that are not immediately present implies that the organism has represented those features; they are part of the content of its representation. Second, errors are more likely to similarly coded than to dissimilarly coded items because similar memories, like similar stimuli, are harder to discriminate than dissimilar items from one another. The particular pattern of errors, then, provides information about the code of the representation.

Analyses of the error patterns rats make in a radial-arm maze indicate they have a listlike memory for arm status. Error entries to arms near correct arms occur no more frequently than would be expected by chance (Olton & Samuelson, 1976). Similarly, Roberts (1981) tested rats on two mazes simultaneously. The mazes were located in the same room 30 cm from each other. He gave the rats four forced choices in the first maze. That is, he provided access to arms, one at a time, rather than providing access to all arms simultaneously. Next he gave the rats four forced choices in the second maze. Then he tested their memory for the arms they had visited by returning them to the first maze for four free choices—all arms available—and eventually to the second maze, where they also had four free choices. He failed to find any evidence of interference, even when the first four choices in the second maze were forced to the arms that pointed in the same direction as those not yet visited in the first maze. The rats were able to keep distinct the arms they visited in each maze, even when the arms in the two of them were near each other or pointed in the same direction. This experiment showed that the rats behaved systematically relative to spatial position; therefore, spatial position was included as part of the *content* of their representation. The experiment did not, however, show any evidence that their errors were systematically related to spatial position. Thus, this experiment provided no evidence that spatial location was part of the working-memory *code* the animals use to keep track of already-visited arms.

Instead of discovering systematic patterns of spatial confusions, Olton and Samuelson found that erroneous choices were more likely to favor arms that were visited early in the trial over arms visited later, even when controlling for differences in the opportunities to make these different kinds of errors (Olton, 1978; Olton, Collison, & Werz, 1977; Olton & Samuelson, 1976; Roberts & Smythe, 1979). Thus, errors were not systematically related to the spatial properties but were systematically related to the serial properties of the arm entries. This serial-position effect implies that the serial or ordinal properties of the visits were encoded in the animal's working memory. If the spatial properties were also encoded in working memory their codes were sufficiently distinct from one another to avoid being confused: the limit on correct performance was temporal, similarity between items, not spatial similarity.

These data also argue that the animals remembered the arms they had already visited, rather than, or in addition to, the arms remaining to be visited. They behaved systematically relative to a feature of the already-*entered* arms, namely, the order in which they had been entered. Differential behavior with respect to order implies that order information was included in their representation.

In another example of the use of this technique, Cook, Brown, and Riley (1985) tested rats in a 12-arm radial maze. They inserted a 15-min delay after either the second, fourth, sixth, eighth, or tenth choice of a daily trial. Following the delay, the rats were allowed to complete the remaining choices on the maze. Relative to performance on control trials without a delay, the animals' choice accuracy was poorest when the delay occurred between the sixth and seventh choices and best when it occurred between either the second and third or the tenth and eleventh choices. When it occurred following the sixth choice, a pronounced serial position effect was observed. Error revisits were much more likely to be made to arms entered early in the trial than to arms visited more recently. In contrast, when the delay occurred following the eighth or tenth choices, error reentries were about equally likely to arms visited early in the trial as to those visited later.

These data imply that the rats were changing the code they used in order to minimize the number of arms they had to remember. Before the sixth choice, they remembered which arms they had visited. After the sixth choice they remembered the arms remaining to be visited. In other words they shifted from using a retrospective memory—remembering past events—to using a prospective memory—remembering the set of arms they would visit.

With a 60-min delay, however, serial position effects were observed no matter where the delay occurred. Whether the delay was before or after the sixth choice, the rats were more likely to enter arms visited early in the trial than to enter those they had visited more recently.

Dynamic properties.   The discovery of a serial-position effect with a 60-min delay suggests the possibility that rats' retrospective memory is more durable than their prospective memory. When a longer delay was imposed between successive choices, the rats adapted to this task demand by using the more durable memory. Alternatively, this finding might suggest that the speed with which the rat can develop a retrospective memory becomes increasingly slow as the number of arms to be remembered increases. When a brief delay occurs between the eighth and ninth choices, the animal does not have time to develop a retrospective memory and must rely exclusively on a faster-developing prospective code. When a long 60-min delay is used, however, the rat does have enough time to develop the retrospective code and shows this in its behavior.

For whatever reason, the rats appear to use different codes when a long versus a short delay intervenes between successive choices. That they can tolerate a 60-min delay between choices is itself remarkable. In fact, they are able to tolerate even longer delays. Beatty and Shavalia (1980) tested rats in an eight-arm radial maze, with a long delay between the fourth and fifth choices. After a 4-hour delay, rats were still able to complete the maze with better than 90 percent accuracy. Choice accuracy remained above chance even with a 12-hour delay between the fourth and fifth choices. The representation used by these rats is remarkably durable.

A large number of treatments known to affect performance on other tasks failed to interfere with postdelay accuracy. Neither variations in illumination or auditory level, removal from the experimental room, feeding, or exposure to a four-arm maze were effective in reducing choice accuracy on the last four choices (Maki, Brokofsky, & Berg, 1979).

Beatty & Shavalia (1980) tested the ability of rats to remember information from two mazes simultaneously. The procedure they used was similar to that used by Roberts (1981) described above. The main difference was the imposition of a 4-hour delay between the fourth and fifth choices on each maze. The experimental trials consisted of five parts: (1) four free choices on maze 1, (2) four free choices on maze 2, (3) a 4-hour delay, (4) four more choices on maze 1, (5) four more choices on maze 2. Choice accuracy on both mazes was uniformly high and not significantly different from that observed on those control days involving only one maze and a 4-hour delay. This means that the rats were able to remember information about the first four choices in both mazes while making their post-delay choices on maze 1.

Some treatments, however, do interfere with radial-maze performance. Roberts (1981) found interference when choices on three mazes intervened between the first and second four choices on the initial maze. The rats were given four forced choices on maze A, followed by four forced choices on each of mazes B, C, and D. They were then returned to maze A and allowed four free choices, followed by free choices on mazes B, C, and D. The rats made more errors during the free choices on maze A when they were simultaneously required to remember choices on the other three mazes than on control days when they were required to remember only their choices on maze A, and the other mazes were not presented. These findings suggest that under appropriate conditions it is possible to demonstrate a limited working-memory capacity, although this capacity is apparently quite large (e.g., 16 to 20 arms, cf. Olton's, 1978, estimate of a 12-to-13-arm capacity).

Electroconvulsive shock and working memory.   A different kind of interference effect has been obtained through the use of electroconvulsive shock (ECS). ECS results when an electrical current of sufficient strength is passed through the brain. In a number of experiments involving learning of a passive-avoidance task, ECS treatments have been found to induce amnesia, that is, forgetting of the preceding experience. A passive-avoidance task is one in which aversive consequences are avoided as long as the subject refrains from making some response. Two kinds of such tasks have been widely studied. In one type, the subject is placed on a platform in a chamber containing an electrified grid floor. As long as the animal remains on the platform, it receives no shock. As soon as it steps from the platform, however, it receives the shock. Retention, in this task, is measured by the time the animal takes to step from the platform. Longer latencies indicate better retention of the training experience. The other type of passive-avoidance task involves the learning of a flavor aversion. For example, in the previous chapter I described a study by Holland and Straub (1979), in which rats were injected with lithium chloride (LiCl) after eating some food pellets. The LiCl made the animals ill, and they stopped eating the pellets. Retention in this task can be measured by the degree to which animals subsequently avoid the flavor associated with illness.

In most experiments involving passive-avoidance and ECS presentations, ECS presented immediately after the learning episode produces greater amnesia than delayed ECS treatments. For example, animals who receive ECS immediately after a flavor-illness pairing will consume more of that flavor on a later test trial than animals that have not received the ECS or animals that receive the ECS after a delay. The animals receiving the immediate ECS apparently forget that the flavor was paired with illness. Therefore, they fail to avoid it on subsequent presentations. If the ECS treatment is delayed for some time after the experience, however, then retention is preserved, and the animals avoid the flavor that had been paired with illness.

In general, the effects of ECS on retention of a learning experience show a temporal gradient. Immediate treatments are more disruptive of retention than delayed treatments. This temporal gradient of the effect of ECS is often called a "consolidation gradient" because learning or the formation of long-term, or reference memories, is thought to depend on some kind of physiological transfer of the information in short-term memory into a more permanent form (Duncan, 1949; McGaugh, 1966). Presumably, the ECS interferes with this "consolidation" process before the information can be consolidated into long-term memory. Delayed shocks are less disruptive than immediate shocks because the delay allows the animal to consolidate some of the information before the ECS.

Although the consolidation theory is not as widely held as it once was (McGaugh & Herz, 1972; Spear, 1973), the form of the consolidation gradient, whatever its cause, remains unchanged. ECS generally produces more amnesia when presented immediately after a learning experience than when its presentation is delayed. The opposite pattern, however, is observed when ECS interferes with the animal's retention of previous choice information in a radial maze. ECS presented immediately after the fourth choice is *less* disruptive of performance than one delayed for a time. Figure 5.5 shows both patterns.

Shavalia, Dodge, and Beatty (1981) tested rats in an eight-arm radial maze, with a 4- or 6-hour delay between the fourth and fifth choices. The rats were allowed four free choices; then they were returned to their home cages for the delay period, after which they were returned to the maze and allowed four more choices. Shavalia and his associates administered ECS to the rats at various times during the delay. In contrast to the usual consolidation gradient obtained following a learning episode, they found that ECS presented within 15 min after the start of the delay had no effect on the choices made afterwards, ECS presented 30 min after the start of the delay had some disruptive effect, and ECS delivered either 2 or 4 hours after the start of the delay had a devastating affect on choice accuracy after the delay. In contrast to the pattern of effect observed following a learning experience, the effectiveness of a standard ECS treatment on material held in working memory increased with increasing age of the memory.

Errors after the delayed treatment consisted of revisits into arms entered during the first four choices (before the ECS), but not of revisits into arms entered during the second choice period. Furthermore, on control trials the rats were administered ECS prior to the first four choices. These pretrial ECS treatments had no effect on their performance. Finally, Maki (1985) required rats to remember their first four choices on two mazes. ECS was administered immediately after the fourth choice on the second maze and two hours after the fourth choice on the first maze. The rats' memory for the first maze was eliminated by the ECS treatment, but their memory for the second maze was undisturbed. Therefore, we can conclude that ECS interferes specifically with the rats' "old" memories about the arms they have already visited.

The "negative consolidation gradient"—the greater interference with a delayed than with an immediate treatment—observed by Shavalia, et al. has interesting implications for theories of working memory in general and for the radial-arm maze in particular. First, it suggests that the mechanism rats use to remember information about the first four choices on a radial maze is different from that used in maintaining the results of a learning episode. Not only are the contents of the two types of memory different, but their physiological bases also appear fundamentally different. Second, some change occurs in the way a memory is stored during a long delay. Consolidation does not appear to be the correct way to characterize this change, but some kind of recoding evidently does occur to take the memory from a state in which it is resistant to disruption by ECS to a

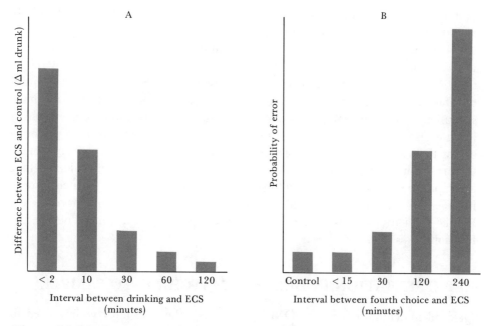

Figure 5.5. Idealized data from a taste-aversion learning experiment and a radial-arm maze experiment. (A) shows how electroconvulsive shock interferes with learning. (B) shows how it interferes with retention in working memory.

state in which it is susceptible. This change appears to occur at some time between 15 min and an hour after the fourth choice. Although it may be coincidental, Cook and Brown found that the rats changed from using a prospective to using a retrospective memory when the delay was an hour but employed a prospective memory when the delay occurred after the middle choice and was only 15 min long. Shavalia, et al. also presented the delay following the fourth choice. Under these circumstances exactly the same number of choices preceded and followed the delay. Therefore, neither prospective nor retrospective codes would be more beneficial. They too found that the first 15 min of the retention interval was important. This raises the possibility that by the end of 15 min animals have begun to recode the information about visited arms from a prospective, ECS-resistant form, to a retrospective, ECS-susceptible form. At present this is mostly a hunch, but an interesting one nevertheless.

A summary of a theory of working memory in the radial-arm maze

The content of reference memory used by rats in a radial-arm maze is a set of spatial locations they maintain in a maplike structure. Information about arms visited during a trial is maintained in working memory in a listlike structure and updated after each choice. Usually, this working memory contains an ordered list of already-visited arms, although under appropriate conditions, rats apparently also employ a prospective list of arms remaining to be entered. The particular working memory code they use apparently changes during the course of retention. At some points in time it can be disrupted by ECS; otherwise, it is quite durable. The role of external extramaze stimuli is to orient the map. Intramaze stimuli that are independent of extramaze cues are more difficult for a rat to learn to use than are extramaze stimuli. In other words, rats appear to prefer to orient themselves relative to more global, typically more stable, environmental features rather than to smaller, more localized stimuli. There is no evidence that the capacity of reference memory to remember spatial locations is limited. Working memory, on the other hand, does appear to have a large, but nevertheless limited capacity, capable of maintaining the status of only a limited number of locations.

REPRESENTATION IN DELAYED MATCHING-TO-SAMPLE

Delayed matching-to-sample (DMTS) has been the task most widely used to study working memory in animals. A number of examples of its use have already been described (e.g., see Chapter 3). Many different species have been tested, including monkeys (e.g., D'Amato & Cox, 1976; Mishkin & Delacour, 1975), dolphins (e.g., Herman & Gordon, 1974), and pigeons (e.g., Blough, 1959; Maki & Leith, 1973; Roberts, 1972).

The delayed matching task

Most DMTS tasks follow the same general procedure (see also Figure 3.6; Roitblat, 1982a). Each trial begins with the presentation of a sample stimulus. The sample is followed by a delay or retention interval (hence, the name "delayed matching-to-sample") and then by the presentation of two or more comparison stimuli. The identity of the sample stimulus determines which one of the comparison stimuli is the correct, rewarded choice. The sample is the to-be-remembered stimulus, and retention is indicated by the stimulus the animal chooses. Typical stimuli used in DMTS include hues, line orientations, and forms.

In most experiments two or three sample stimuli alternate randomly from trial to trial. For example, on one trial the sample might be a red disk, on the next a green disk, then a green disk, then a red disk, and so forth. At the start of a trial, the subject cannot know which of the colors will be used as the sample until it is presented.

Choice accuracy improves with increasing sample duration and declines with increasing retention-interval duration.

Finally, when the comparison stimuli appear, they alternate randomly from trial to trial between response positions so that during the retention interval the subject cannot know which response position—left versus right—will be the correct choice. As a result, the animal cannot reliably orient toward the correct alternative during the retention interval. Hunter (1913) found that when such orientation was possible, some animals tended to "remember" the correct location by posing in specific postures, usually oriented toward the correct choice.

In "identity delayed matching-to-sample" (called usually just "delayed matching-to-sample"; DMTS), one of the comparison stimuli is identical to the sample and is designated the correct choice. In a variant of the task called "symbolic delayed matching-to-sample," neither comparison stimulus physically matches the sample, and the experimenter arbitrarily designates the correct choice. Subjects learn both variants of the task with equal ease.

Because of the delay between presentation of the sample and presentation of the comparison stimuli, the sample stimulus is no longer present when the subject makes a choice. Therefore, accurate performance at the end of the retention interval requires the animal to encode and retain information about the identity of the sample. Because the sample alternates randomly from trial to trial, this information presumably is maintained in working memory.

The copy/trace theory and its alternatives

A number of theories have been developed to describe the representational system pigeons use in DMTS. I concentrate on pigeons mainly because most of the analytic work has been done with this species; however, the extent to which these models also apply to other species remains an open question.

Probably the most straightforward candidate for the representational system pigeons use in DMTS is suggested by the name of the task and is based on the assumption of a "matching" process: "Choose the comparison stimulus that *matches* the sample." This model has been highly influential and serves well to organize the DMTS findings. In this view the subject's observation of the sample stimulus results in the formation in working memory of a "trace" or copy of that stimulus. Following the retention interval, the bird compares the remembered trace with each of the comparison stimuli, then chooses the one that most closely matches the trace.

Features of the copy/trace model.   According to the copy/trace model (e.g., Roberts & Grant, 1976), the trace that results from a sample presentation is a basically unanalyzed record of its sensory features. The longer the sample is physically present, the stronger or clearer is the trace. Sample duration is analogous to exposure duration of a film image. Unlike a film, however, the trace or copy begins to "fade," or lose strength, as soon as the sample is removed. As a trace fades, it is less accurately compared to the relevant comparison stimuli and errors become more likely. If its decay is slow enough, however, the trace can last longer than the duration of the trial on which it is relevant. For example, a trial with a red sample stimulus, for which red is the correct choice, can be followed by a trial with a green sample stimulus, for which green is the correct choice. If the trace of red remains after the green sample has produced its trace, then both traces would be in working memory simultaneously and could compete for control of the subject's choice. The animal could, then, erroneously choose the comparison stimulus appropriate to the trace remaining from the previous trial. Therefore, according to the model, error responses occur either because the strength of the trace from the current trial is too weak or because the competitive trace from the previous trial is too strong. Table 5.1 summarizes this model.

Abstract versus stimulus-specific response rules.   A central assumption of the copy/trace model is the combination of an iconic working-memory representation with an abstract reference-memory representation. According to this model, working memory contains an analog (e.g., an image) of the sample that maintains many of its stimulus properties. In contrast, reference memory contains a general matching rule of the form, "pick the comparison stimulus that matches the trace in working memory." This rule is abstract since it does not refer either to a particular stimulus or to a particular trace. Instead, it refers to any comparison stimulus that matches the strongest current memory trace. These two assumptions of the copy/trace model can be investigated separately.

Pigeons' performance on symbolic delayed matching-to-sample, as well as suggestions from simultaneous matching-to-sample (see Chapter 8), indicate that similarity between the comparison stimuli and the sample, or its trace, is not necessary for accurate performance (Carter & Eckerman, 1975; Cohen, Looney, Brady, & Acuella, 1976; Roitblat, 1980). Recall that the relationship between the sample and the correct choice is arbitrary in symbolic matching-to-sample, so correct performance cannot require an identical match between the trace of the

TABLE 5.1 Features of the copy/trace model

---

1. Working memory contains a trace or analog of the physical features of the sample.
2. Trace develops gradually as a result of exposure to the sample.
3. Trace decays after sample ends but may last longer than the duration of a trial.
4. Reference memory contains a generalized matching rule.
5. Choice is determined by matching comparison stimuli with the trace of the sample.
6. When more than one trace is present in working memory, they compete for control of responding and errors can result.
7. Weaker traces are less likely to result in a correct match than stronger traces.

---

sample and the appearance of the comparison stimuli. Similarly, pigeons performing simultaneous matching-to-sample, in which the sample and comparison stimuli are present at the same time, have been found to use a generalized matching rule. After the birds are trained to match one set of stimuli, they show some (though not complete) transfer to new sets of stimuli (see Chapter 8 and Zentall, Hogan, & Edwards, 1984). Processes other than sample registration and trace formation also appear to be involved in pigeon DMTS performance.

Passive trace strength versus active processing.   The copy/trace model also implies that encoding of the sample information is a relatively passive result of exposure to the sample stimulus. Data from a number of experiments suggest that the memory process is more active than this. For example, Maki, Gillund, Hauge, and Siders (1977) trained pigeons in a two-alternative 0-delay matching-to-sample task. The sample stimulus was removed immediately before the comparison stimuli appeared. This experiment presented a combination of identity matching-to-sample and symbolic matching-to-sample. Two kinds of samples were used—colors and line orientations—but the comparison stimuli were all colors. Red was the correct choice following either the red or the vertical sample. Green was the correct choice following either the green or the horizontal sample.

During the first phase of training, the birds were required to make 10 observing-response pecks to the sample stimulus to initiate the presentation of the comparison stimuli. After they reached a high level of choice accuracy on both the identity- and the symbolic-matching trials, observing responses to one of the sample stimuli were extinguished. That sample stayed on for a fixed amount of time, independent of the bird's behavior, and was no longer followed by presentation of comparison stimuli. For example, if green were the extinguished sample, then it was presented for 5 s, whether or not the bird pecked at it, and was followed directly by the intertrial interval. All other samples were still presented for ten pecks and were still followed by the presentation of comparison stimuli. The birds quickly stopped pecking at the extinguished sample whenever it appeared. They did continue pecking, however, at the other samples when they appeared. By not pecking at the extinguished sample, the birds clearly indicated that they were able to identify it.

In the final stage of this experiment, a few probe trials were presented, in which the extinguished sample *was* followed by the red and green comparison stimuli. Choice accuracy on these probe trials was at the chance level. Although the birds had identified the sample well enough to avoid pecking at it, they behaved as if they had no information about its identity when the comparison stimuli were presented.

We can now see why the combination of symbolic and identity matching was important. One possible explanation of these data is that the bird learned to avoid pecking at one stimulus wherever it appeared. Recall, however, that both colors and line orientations served as sample stimuli, but only colors served as comparison stimuli. For example, if green were the extinguished sample, then the birds avoided pecking at green samples but continued to peck at the green comparison stimulus following horizontal samples. Hence, they were not avoiding green. Further, avoidance of one comparison stimulus predicts that matching accuracy on the probe trials would be below chance as the birds avoid pecking the correct comparison. In contrast, the birds neither avoided nor approached the correct comparison; they chose randomly between them.

Further evidence against a passive trace-strength hypothesis has been reviewed by Grant (1981), Maki (1984), and Roitblat (1982a). For example, changing the level of illumination—from light to dark or from dark to light—during either part or all of the retention interval interferes with DMTS performance (Cook, 1980; D'Amato, 1973; Herman, 1975; Kraemer & Roberts, 1984; Roberts & Grant, 1978; Tranberg & Rilling, 1980; Zentall, 1973).

The magnitude of the effect depends on the magnitude of the change in illumination level. Changes at the end of the retention interval are more detrimental than changes at the beginning. The effect also depends on the "surprisingness" of the change. After extended training with a particular light regimen, illumination changes lose their effectiveness (Tranberg & Rilling, 1980). Pigeons initially trained with a light on during the retention interval at first show interference when the light is turned off. Following continued training with the light off, however, the disruptive effect disappears, only to reappear when the light is turned on during the retention interval. Repeated cycles of light-on training alternating with light-off training show the same pattern. Disruption appears when the lighting regimen changes but then disappears with extended training. The same interference effect also appears when the sample is not a visual stimulus, but is the presentation or absence of food (Maki, 1984). Further, recovery from the retroactive interference of the light change was slower when the light change occurred only at the end of the retention interval than when it occurred at the beginning.

These experiments illustrate two points. First, neither the level of illumination, nor even the change in it was sufficient to produce interference. The presentation of light following training with a dark retention interval and the presentation of darkness following training with a light retention interval were both equally effective in producing interference. Extended experience with a change in illumination level was sufficient to remove the effectiveness of the change as a disrupter of performance. The illumination change presumably had to be "unexpected" or "surprising" to be effective in disrupting the birds' performance. Extended experience with an illumination change of one sort or the other, reduced the surprisingness of the change and, consequently, reduced its ability to disrupt performance.

One way in which surprising stimuli may interfere with retention of sample information involves supposing that ordinarily animals actively process the information about the sample during the retention interval. When a surprising stimulus is presented, they allocate a share of their attentional capacity (see Chapter 3) to the surprising stimulus and so have less capacity for processing the information about the sample.

The same notion can be used to explain why illumination changes later in the retention interval are more disruptive and are disruptive for more trials than changes occurring early in the interval. When illumination changes occur early in the interval, birds can predict both that they will occur and when they will occur. As a result the birds quickly learn not to be surprised by the change. In contrast, illumination changes that occur late in the interval are not as easily predicted. Delayed illumination changes are more difficult to predict than immediate changes, because animals are less accurate at estimating the duration of long than of short intervals (see Chapter 6). As a result, pigeons are more surprised by late changes and are slower in learning to predict them.

Second, note the similarity between the relative effectiveness of late versus early illumination changes on DMTS performance and the effect of early versus late ECS treatment on radial-arm maze performance. Both show a so-called negative consolidation gradient: Delayed treatments (either surprising illumination changes or ECS) are more effective at disrupting working memory than are immediate treatments. Whether working memory is generally more affected by delayed rather than immediate interference or whether the DMTS effect can be explained on some other basis is not yet clear; nevertheless, the parallel is striking.

These data are incompatible with a passive-trace strength notion. Apparently, the bird has to do something to maintain the information in working memory. Presentation of competing information, such as a surprising change in chamber illumination, interferes with the bird's ability to maintain the sample information. The effect of a stimulus presentation is not a uniform function of the stimulus properties themselves. Instead, it depends on the surprisingness of the presentation. The animal reacts or processes a stimulus differently when it is surprising than when it is expected. Therefore, the effect cannot be either passive or automatic.

In support of the proposition that animals process surprising stimuli differently from expected stimuli, surprising samples have been found to be more memorable than expected samples, presumably as a result of the animals allocating additional processing resources to them. Maki (1979b) trained pigeons in a symbolic DMTS task with samples of food versus no-food and red and green comparison stimuli. After DMTS training he separately trained the birds to discriminate horizontal from vertical lines by reinforcing pecks to verticals with the presentation of food. The two tasks were then chained. Figure 5.6

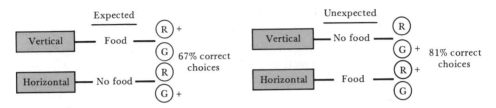

Figure 5.6. Surprising, or unexpected, versus expected samples in delayed matching-to-sample. The correct choice is indicated by +.

shows the procedure he used during this part of the experiment. On "expected" trials the vertical lines were presented and reinforced (that is, followed by food) or the horizontal lines were presented and not reinforced. This reinforcement/nonreinforcement then served as the sample in the subsequent DMTS trial. On surprising trials the horizontal lines were surprisingly reinforced or the vertical lines were surprisingly not reinforced. Again, the presence or absence of food served as the sample for a DMTS trial. The birds were 81 percent correct following unexpected samples, but only 67 percent correct following expected samples. The surprising unexpected food was better encoded and remembered than was the expected food.

Pigeons apparently allocate more processing capacity to surprising than to expected stimuli. When the sample itself is surprising, the birds increase the attentional capacity they allocate to processing it. As a result, they better encode and retain information about the sample, and their choice accuracy improves. The birds also allocate more attentional capacity to processing unexpected stimuli that follow the sample. As a result, they have less capacity available for processing the sample and so they encode and retain it more poorly. Their choice accuracy is lower.

Directed forgetting.   Directed forgetting also points to an active memory process in DMTS. In these experiments one of two "instructional stimuli" is presented during the retention interval. The R-cue signals that the trial will end in the usual manner with the presentation of the comparison stimuli. The F-cue signals that no comparison stimuli are forthcoming. The F-cue is analogous to an instruction to forget the sample information because it will not be tested.

This procedure can be seen as an extension of that used by Maki, Gillund, Hauge, and Siders (1977), involving the extinction of observing responses. Extinction of the observing responses is equivalent to permanently signaling that the extinguished sample will not be tested. The sample-extinction method is limited, however, in that (1) only a single sample is cued, and (2) the identity of the sample provides the information that it will not be tested. This raises the bility that the extinguished sample is not only remembered differently, but is also processed and encoded differently.

In contrast, the R- and the F-cues are presented equally often *after* each sample. Therefore, the subject cannot know whether or not that particular sample will be tested until after it disappears. This assures that all samples will be processed equally and that any effects of the cue can be attributed to processes occurring during the retention interval and after the sample presentation.

The interesting data from this kind of experiment come from occasional *probe* trials on which an F-cue *is* followed by the presentation of the comparison stimuli. A number of studies have found that DMTS choice accuracy on those few trials on which comparison stimuli do follow an F-cue is lower than on trials which present an R-cue. (Kendrick, 1980; Maki & Hegvik, 1980; Maki, Olson, & Rego, 1981). This result is exactly what we would expect if the F-cue were causing the subject to forget the sample information. It is also consistent, however, with at least three other explanations (Maki & Hegvik, 1980). (1) The F-cue could cause the animals to turn away from the keys so that they fail to orient correctly to the comparison stimuli when they are presented. (2) The F-cue typically signals not only that the comparison stimuli will not be presented, but also that the trial is ending and no reinforcer will be available. Reinforcer omission somehow extinguishes responses or processes that would otherwise be necessary to accurate performance. (3) The effect could be due to the bird directing its attention toward the F-cue, which then limits the capacity it has available for processing and maintaining the sample information.[1]

One alternative to directed forgetting as the explanation of the disruptive effects of F-cues is the possibility that it causes the subject to turn away from the keys on which the comparison stimuli will appear. According to this explanation, the birds remember equally well following R- and F-cues, but, because they are improperly oriented, they fail to respond appropriately to the comparison stimuli (Kendrick, 1980). This hypothesis receives some support from experiments showing that, when the F-cue signals comparison omission (i.e., that no more events are forthcoming on the current trial), the birds sometimes do turn away from the comparison keys. Furthermore, a simple change in the procedure can prevent the F-cue from interfering with performance. No interference is observed if the F-cue signals a nonconditional discrimination in place of the comparison stimuli (Kendrick, 1980; Maki & Hegvik, 1980). As in the standard procedure, presentation of the R-cue signals that the comparison stimuli will be presented, and the bird chooses appropriately between them. Presentation of the F-cue, however, signals that instead of the comparison stimuli, another nonconditional discrimination, that is, one that does not depend on the identity of the sample, is presented. Under these conditions, choice accuracy remains high when the comparison stimuli are presented on probe trials following the F-cue.

The F-cue still signals that the sample information will not be tested, but the substitute discrimination task does ensure that the birds will orient to the keys. This kind of result raises the possibility that the pigeons' bodily orientation is the crucial factor in directed forgetting.

Bodily orientation cannot be the entire explanation, however, because (1) F-cue effects are still observed under other conditions when the subject can be shown to be properly oriented, (2) F-cues that do cause a drop in DMTS choice accuracy do not interfere with "probe simple discrimination" performance, and (3) failure to orient to the keys during the retention interval does not automatically result in a drop in choice accuracy.

Replacing the comparison stimuli with a single stimulus on F-cued trials also ensures that the bird will orient to the comparison stimuli when they appear on the occasional probe trials. This type of substitution, however, reduces, but does not eliminate, the effects of the F-cue (Maki, Olson, and Rego, 1981). The birds in this experiment were trained with samples of food versus no-food and color comparison stimuli. For example, a choice of red was correct following a sample of food, and a choice of green was correct following a sample of no-food. For one group of pigeons, F-cued trials ended in the standard manner, with the omission of comparison stimuli. For the other group, F-cued trials ended with the presentation of a white cross as a replacement for the comparison stimuli. The cross was equally likely to appear on either of the two comparison stimulus keys. A single peck to this cross stimulus was reinforced. Presentation of the cross stimulus ensured that the birds oriented following an F-cue and that they were in an appropriate position to respond to one of the comparison stimuli.

As in previous experiments, a directed-forgetting effect was observed. Choice accuracy was lower on probe F-cued trials, during which the comparison stimuli were presented, than on R-cued trials. The group trained with comparison stimulus omission following F-cues showed a larger difference than the group trained with the cross as a substitute for the comparison stimuli, but both groups showed the directed-forgetting effect. Replacing the comparison stimuli with a single stimulus reduced, but did not eliminate, the effect of the F-cue.

In a second experiment, Maki and his associates trained pigeons to perform two tasks. One task was a simple simultaneous discrimination between horizontal and vertical lines. Pecks to the vertical stimulus were reinforced; pecks to the horizontal stimulus were extinguished. The other task was DMTS with color samples and comparison stimuli and F- and R-cues. When the F-cues appeared, they signaled the end of the trial—no further stimuli appeared until the next trial.

After training, two kinds of probe trials were presented. On some probe trials, the F-cue was followed by the comparison stimuli. On the other probe trials, the

F-cue was followed by the line-orientation stimuli. Consistent with the previous experiment, choice accuracy was lower on probe DMTS trials than on R-cued trials. In contrast, the F-cue did not lower choice accuracy when it preceded the simple discrimination. These results show that the F-cue works retroactively to interfere with retention of the sample information. It does not work pro-actively—for example, by disorienting the bird—to interfere with the performance of any discrimination that follows it. Although F-cues may cause animals to turn away from the comparison stimulus keys, this turning does not then cause the interference with DMTS performance.

Roitblat and Scopatz (1983a) found further evidence that orientation to the keys during the retention interval is not necessary to accurate DMTS performance. For two birds, the F-cue was an irregular white "blob" stimulus on the center key, where the sample appears, and the R-cue was food delivered in the usual food hopper. For another two birds, the F-cue was food and the R-cue was the blob. When food is the R-cue, it ensures that the bird does not orient to the key during at least that part of the retention interval occupied by the cue. If orientation is necessary to performance, then choice accuracy should be low on both R-cued and probe F-cued trials. In contrast to this prediction, the same level of disruption by the F-cue was observed whether food or the blob served as the F-cue. Although it interfered with the pigeon's orientation to the comparison keys, the food R-cue did not interfere with choice accuracy.

Another alternative explanation for the disruptive effects of F-cues suggests that they interfere with the bird's performance because R-cued trials end in reinforcement following a correct choice, but F-cued trials typically do not. Without reinforcement certain necessary processes that occur on R-cued trials do not on F-cued trials. By this argument the effect of the F-cue is an artifact of some kind of "adventitious extinction." This hypothesis is unlikely because the F-cue continues to disrupt when the trial ends in reinforcement, either as a result of a nondiscriminative response (Maki, Olson, & Rego, 1981) or as the result of using food as F-cue (Roitblat & Scopatz, 1983a).

Furthermore, the use of food as an R- or an F-cue (Roitblat & Scopatz, 1983) provides evidence against the remaining alternative explanation. There are few stimuli that are more memorable than food (Maki, Moe, & Bierley, 1977) or that are more likely to occupy the attention of a hungry pigeon. Yet, when food was the R-cue, the birds' choice accuracy remained high relative to that observed when the blob F-cue was presented.

These results mean that a pigeon's orientation to the key during the retention interval is not crucial to high choice accuracy. They also indicate that it is the F-cue, rather than some artifact of F-cued trials ending without reinforcement, that produces the decrease in choice accuracy. The occurrence of an F-cue ap-

pears to produce a change in the animal's cognitive state, reducing its maintenance of sample information. Maki (1981, 1984) suggests that the effect of the
F-cues is due to attenuation or elimination of rehearsal.

To summarize: At this point it seems clear that pigeons do more than passively
register stimulation falling on their receptors in the process of performing
DMTS. Instead, the birds appear to be more active in encoding and maintaining
the information in the sample. Simply registering and identifying the sample
is not sufficient to ensure accurate choice performance. Similarly, the fact that
maintenance of sample information can be brought under instructional stimulus
control by R- and F-cues further indicates that it is an active process under the
subject's control. According to trace theory, the code a pigeon uses in DMTS is a
copy of the physical properties of the sample stimulus. Although the physical
relations between sample and comparison stimuli may play a role, such a simple
code is inadequate to account for pigeon DMTS performance. The birds seem
also to use particular sample-comparison stimulus pairings.

Memory codes in DMTS

One assumption of the copy/trace theory, as shown in Table 5.1, is that matching performance is controlled by an abstract generalized matching rule, which
operates on iconic representations in working memory. A single rule, such as
choose the stimulus most similar to the current trace, is maintained in reference
memory and specifies the relation between all samples and choices. An alternative hypothesis is based on the assumption that more active coding uses multiple
rules relating samples and choices. According to this multiple rule hypothesis,
the subject maintains in reference memory one "rule" for each sample-test pair
(Carter, 1971; Carter & Werner, 1978; Cumming & Berryman, 1965). The rule
specifies the mapping of comparison stimuli onto sample stimuli, that is, the
correct choice, given each sample. At some point after the sample has been identified, the subject applies the rule to the identified sample and selects the choice it
will make at the end of the trial. By this view the subject translates from an identified sample to a representation of the correct choice.

The requirement to translate from identification of the sample to specification
of the correct choice is most apparent in symbolic DMTS, but the multiple-rule
hypothesis argues that it occurs in all forms of DMTS. This translation must
occur sometime between the onset of the sample stimulus and the time a choice is
made. Figure 5.7 shows four models, which differ in when they assume the
translation to occur.

The first model shown in Figure 5.7 is the copy/trace theory. It says that no
translation occurs. Instead, the animal matches the physical characteristics of the
comparison stimuli against those of the sample stimulus. Models 2 to 4 specify a

Alternative codes in pigeon DMTS

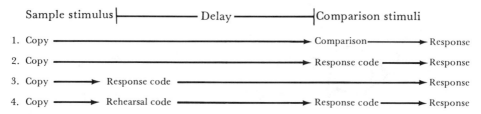

Figure 5.7. Alternative memory codes pigeons can use in symbolic delayed matching-to-sample. [From Roitblat, 1982a.]

translation process. According to model 2, the animal maintains information about the sample during the retention interval as a copy/trace and performs the translation at the end of the interval. Model 3 specifies that the translation occurs at the beginning of the retention interval. Therefore, during most of this interval, the animal maintains the sample information as a specification of the choice to be made. According to the last model, two translations occur. The first encodes the sample information into a "rehearsal code," and the second translates from the rehearsal code into a response code identical to that assumed by models 2 and 3. Models 2 and 3 are identical to one another, except for their assumption about when translation from sample to response code occurs. Model 4 differs from the other two in its assumption of two translation processes.

A considerable amount of evidence has accumulated showing that pigeons code the contents of working memory in terms of the correct comparison stimulus and its outcome. In other words, the data suggest that memory is prospective, relative to upcoming events, rather than retrospective, relative to features of the sample (Honig, 1978, 1981; Honig & Wasserman, 1981; Roitblat, 1980).

In symbolic DMTS, increases in the duration of the retention interval result in increased confusions between similar comparison stimuli, but not between similar sample stimuli. In one experiment (Roitblat, 1980), pigeons were trained in a symbolic DMTS task, in which the similarities of the sample and the comparison stimuli were carefully arranged. One sample and three comparison stimuli occurred on each trial. The sample set for two of the birds consisted of three colors: blue, orange, and red. For these birds the comparison stimulus set consisted of three line orientations of 0° (vertical), 12.5° and 90°. Vertical was the correct choice following the blue sample, the 12.5°-slant was the correct choice following the orange sample, and horizontal was the correct choice following the red sample. Figure 5.8 shows these stimuli and their relations. Notice that the orange and red pair of sample stimuli are similar to each other relative to the third stimulus (blue), and that these similar samples correspond to a

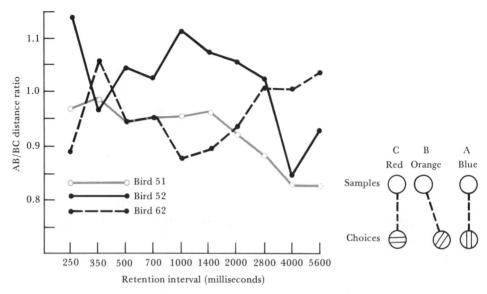

Figure 5.8. The ratio of discriminal distances between stimuli A and B relative to the discriminal distance between B and C. Discriminal distances are assigned in a manner analogous to that used in multidimensional scaling. Distance declines as confusion between the two stimuli increases. For birds 51 and 52, samples were blue, orange, and red (A, B, C, respectively), corresponding respectively to comparison stimuli of 0° (vertical), 12.5°, and 90° line orientations. For bird 62, the sample and comparison sets were exchanged relative to the other two birds (lines were samples and colors were comparisons). Therefore, from a theoretical point of view, an equivalent change is in the opposite direction for this bird. [From Roitblat, 1982a.]

dissimiliar pair of comparison stimuli (12.5 and 90°). Notice also that the similar comparison stimuli (12.5 and 0°) correspond to sample stimuli that are relatively dissimilar (orange and blue). As Figure 5.8 shows, an analysis of the confusion patterns indicates that, as the retention interval lengthens, the birds are increasingly likely to confuse similar comparison stimuli relative to similar sample stimuli.

The changing distribution of error responses obtained from this experiment and a subsequent replication indicate that the pigeons maintain the information about the presented sample in a form resembling the comparison stimuli. That is, they translate early in the retention interval from sample identification to response specification and maintain the information about the sample identity in a code reflecting the similarity relations among the comparison stimuli. One possibility for such a code would be an image of the correct comparison stimulus.

Another experiment by Grant (1982) also provides evidence that the birds have a prospective test code. Choice accuracy improved when three samples rather than one were presented at the start of a trial. It did not matter whether the three samples were identical to or different from one another, so long as they all signaled the same correct choice. Presenting three different samples had the same effect as presenting a single sample for three times the duration. The common comparison stimulus was sufficient to support summation of these different samples. This suggests that the birds code the sample "prospectively" in terms of the response they must make.

Memory for outcomes.   In addition to information about their upcoming choice, pigeons also include information in their representation regarding its outcome. When each correct choice is associated with a unique outcome, the information about the expected outcome is part of the information the animal maintains during the retention interval and contributes to the control of its choice. Acquisition is faster when correct choices after each sample are followed by unique reinforcers (Peterson, 1984). Differential reinforcement also makes the sample more memorable (Peterson, Wheeler, & Trapold, 1980). Finally, changing their expectancies regarding the outcome for a correct choice facilitates learning to change choice patterns, and interferes with maintaining the same choice patterns (Peterson & Trapold, 1980).

These data argue strongly for an active memory process, in which sample information is coded in a prospective form, resembling the comparison stimuli and the outcome of a correct choice. Both the coding and the maintenance of sample information is an active process under the subject's control.

The coding process

Pigeon's choice accuracy typically improves with increasing sample duration and declines with increasing retention-interval duration (Maki & Leith, 1973; Roberts, 1972; Roberts & Grant, 1974; Roitblat & Scopatz, 1983b). The copy/trace model attributes these changes to the gradual development and decay of a trace. Although the data just reviewed suggest that the encoding process is more active than the simple accumulation of a trace, the idea of a representation that grows gradually with increasing sample duration and decays gradually with increasing retention interval duration is appealing. The longer the sample is available, the greater the strength of its representation; the longer the retention interval, the weaker the representation. There are several alternatives to the gradual model that do not rely on gradual encoding but that would still produce an increase in choice accuracy with increasing sample duration. Instead of changing gradually, these models assume that the representation changes in a discrete, single-step, all-or-none manner.

The gradual model assumes that at the start of any trial, the "strength" of the representation is 0 and the subject knows nothing about the identity of the sample. The strength of the representation grows continuously during the sample presentation, and the subject gains more and more information about the identity of the sample. As the previous section showed, this information is coded in a form related to the correct choice. According to this model, memory consists of representations that can have any strength between 0 and some maximum.

The discrete-state models also assume that the strength of the trace is 0 at the start of every trial. According to these models, however, the representation can take only one of a limited set of values. The simplest discrete-state model assumes that there are two memory states: a know-nothing state and a know-all state. At the start of the trial, the subject is in the know-nothing state. It knows nothing about the identity of the sample. As the sample is presented, however, there is a certain probability that the memory will change from the know-nothing to the know-all memory state. Longer sample durations simply provide more opportunities for the jump from knowing nothing to knowing all. According to the "all-or-none" model, choice accuracy improves with longer sample durations because the bird is more and more likely to have changed from the know-nothing to the know-all state. Choice accuracy declines with increasing retention-interval durations because the bird is more and more likely to have forgotten the sample—that is, to have changed from the state of knowing the sample to the know-nothing state. This all-or-none model differs from the gradual model in assuming that there are no situations in which the subject has partial information about the sample. Either it knows perfectly well which sample had been presented or it is perfectly ignorant of it.

According to the all-or-none model, the gradual improvement in choice accuracy observed with increasing sample duration is the result of averaging large numbers of trials on which the subject is scored only as correct or incorrect. Hence, this change in performance could mean either that it knows more after longer sample presentations or that its memory system has had more opportunities to have encoded the sample in an all-or-none manner. The all-or-none model assumes that working memory is always in one of two possible states at any point in time. No information about the sample is available in the "know-nothing" state, so correct responses can occur only by chance. Complete sample information is available in the "know-all" state, so correct choices always result. Therefore, if the subject makes an error, this means that it knows nothing about the sample. Longer sample durations result in higher-choice accuracy because they provide more opportunities for the transition from the know-nothing to the know-all state.

According to the gradual model, coding is a gradual process. Longer sample durations improve the subject's choice accuracy because they provide more opportunities for it to accumulate sample information. Errors result from less than complete encoding. Therefore, they do not imply complete lack of information on the animal's part.

Both of these models predict exactly the same pattern of change in the frequency of a correct response with increasing sample duration (Roitblat, 1984a, b). With two alternatives we cannot distinguish between an all-or-none and a gradual model. We know only whether a response is correct. Discriminating between these two models requires that we know whether the subject knows nothing or knows a little after it makes an error. We must have a means to assess the subject's memory a second time following an initial error. By presenting three comparison stimuli on every trial, we can allow second choices following first-choice errors. According to the all-or-none model, errors can result only from the know-nothing state. Consequently, second choices must also be pure guesses. Choice accuracy on second choices following first-choice errors is thus predicted to be at chance. In contrast, the gradual model assumes that errors can occur when the subject has partial information about the sample. Therefore, second choices, following first-choice errors, should also reflect this partial information.

I tested pigeons in a three-alternative DMTS task, in which second choices were allowed if the first choice was an error (Roitblat, 1980). As Figure 5.9 shows, second-choice accuracy, as well as first-choice accuracy, increased with increasing sample duration. These data thus allow the rejection of the simple all-

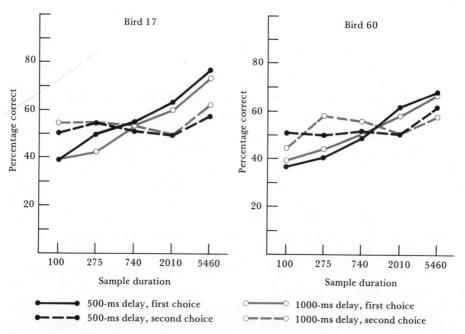

Figure 5.9. Choice accuracy on first and second choices as a function of sample duration. Chance accuracy is 33 percent correct for first choices and 50 percent correct for second choices. [From Roitblat, 1980.]

or-none model because second choices were more accurate than the chance level predicted by the all-or-none model. Other available data also force us to reject a number of other discrete-state models. These data are reviewed elsewhere (Roitblat, 1980, 1984a, 1984b; Roitblat & Scopatz, 1983b). They demonstrate that subjects have information about the sample even when making errors, and that second choices are based on memory for the sample, not just for the previous choice. Whatever processes function to produce errors, they do so at the same time as the processes that operate to produce correct responses. The choice actually observed is a combination of these two kinds of processes.

These data argue against any moderately complex discrete-state model. Any adequate model of this type would have to have far more memory states than the number of stimuli used in the experiment. It seems much more likely that the pigeon's memory process involves a gradual accumulation of sample information with increasing sample duration.

Intertrial proactive interference

If, as the above data suggest, the birds' representation of the sample information forms and decays gradually, then some information about one sample may still be present during a subsequent trial involving another (Roberts & Grant, 1976). Proactive interference (PI) occurs when the events of one trial affect the choice made on the next.

Two types of PI effects have been observed. Choice accuracy of pigeons (Grant, 1975; Maki, Moe, & Bierley, 1977; Roberts, 1980), monkeys (Jarrard & Moise, 1971), and dolphins (Herman, 1975) is lower when short intertrial intervals (ITI) separate trials than when long ITI durations are used. In addition, both monkeys (Moise, 1976; Worsham, 1975) and pigeons (Grant, 1975) show a decline in matching accuracy when the stimulus corresponding to the incorrect choice on one trial was the correct choice on the previous trial.

Roberts and Grant's (1976) copy/trace model attributes both kinds of PI to intrusions of the trace from the previous trial. Choice accuracy is higher with longer ITI durations because the traces from the prior trials have longer to decay before the later trial's test. Choice accuracy is lower when the correct choice from the earlier trial conflicts with that from the later because of competition between these traces, each indicating an incompatible response.

An alternative to the copy/trace model holds that the drop in the pigeon's choice accuracy observed with short ITI durations and the drop observed with conflicting choices result from different mechanisms. The ITI effect derives from general decrements in the overall efficiency of the information-processing system, perhaps due to fatigue, temporary satiation, or something else. The intertrial-conflict effect results from competition or intrusion of the memory from one trial into the next.

Robert Scopatz and I (Roitblat & Scopatz, 1983b) used 3-alternative DMTS to investigate PI, assessing separately the role played by specific intrusions and general interference. If PI exists solely in the form of a general deficit in the bird's ability to process information, then its responses should be less accurately related to the sample from the current trial and unrelated to the events of the previous trial. If, however, as the copy/trace model suggests, information from one trial intrudes into, that is, competes with the information from, the subsequent trial—then the distribution of choices should be affected by the previous interfering events. The copy/trace model asserts that these are not separable effects; choice accuracy increases with longer ITI durations specifically because competition between previous and current traces is reduced.

We found evidence for proactive interference in 3-alternative DMTS. Choice accuracy was higher with longer than with shorter intertrial intervals. We also found evidence for intrusions. The choice made on one trial (the prechoice) and not the sample from it (the presample), affected the choice made on the next trial (also see Roberts, 1980). These results are consistent with the data just reviewed (Roitblat, 1980; Grant, 1982), which also argue that subjects code sample information in a form related to the choice they are to make.

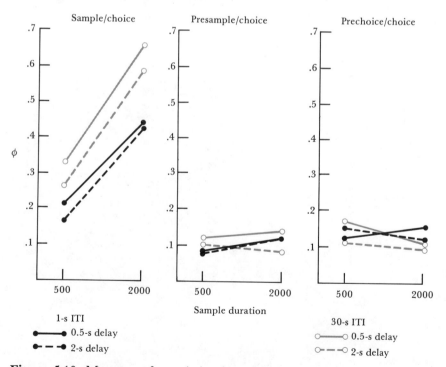

Figure 5.10. Measures of association between samples and choices, presamples and choices, and prechoices and choices. Presamples and prechoices are the sample and the choice, respectively, presented on the previous trial. [From Roitblat & Scopatz, 1983b.]

In contrast to the predictions of the copy/trace model, however, the magnitude of the intrusions—that is, the strength of the relationship between prechoice and choice—does not depend on the duration of the intertrial interval or of the sample or retention interval duration. Increasing ITI duration improved the relationship between the sample and the choice, but did not reduce the relationship between either the presample, or the prechoice, and the choice. See Figure 5.10 (Roitblat & Scopatz, 1983b).

A "drift" model of working memory

One way of conceptualizing a gradual memory process that encodes sample information in terms of the comparison stimuli involves a spatial metaphor (Roitblat, 1984a, b). This model, shown in Figure 5.11, consists of two separate mechanisms: an analyzer, which identifies the sample stimulus, and a "memory space." Each of the comparison stimuli is represented as a point in this memory space; the distances between points represent the dissimilarities between the corresponding stimuli. Similar stimuli are located near each other, and dissimilar stimuli are located far from each other. The 3-alternative DMTS task described above is modeled in a two-dimensional space, though other, higher-dimensional spaces may be necessary to model other tasks or more complex sets of stimuli.

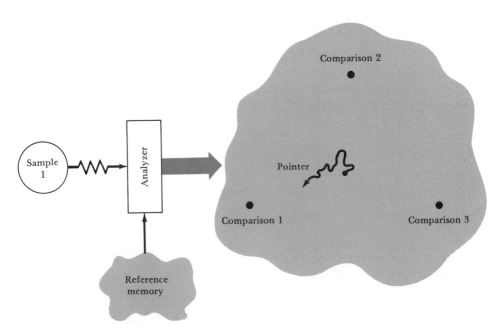

Figure 5.11. The drift model of pigeon DMTS working memory. Sample 1 was presented. The pointer walked randomly from the center of the memory space more or less in the direction of Comparison 1.

The metaphorical memory space has nothing to do with real space, the location of the keys, the bird's position in the operant chamber, or any topological aspect of the bird's brain. We can just as appropriately describe it as a system of mutually inhibitory neurons, but the spatial metaphor helps to conceptualize it.

During the sample presentation, the analyzer identifies the sample stimulus through standard signal-detection processes. For example, it might compare the presented sample to a representation in reference memory of each of the samples. This comparison takes some time. Furthermore, the more frequently the bird uses the analyzer, the longer it takes to produce an identification. Hence, the model accounts for the general interference effects of brief ITI durations by postulating that brief ITI durations slow the functioning of the analyzer, perhaps as a result of fatigue.

Once an identification is made, reference memory specifies the correct comparison stimulus for that sample, and the output of the analyzer drives a "pointer" through memory space on a random walk in the general direction of the correct comparison stimulus. A random walk means that the pointer only tends toward the correct alternative. At any time, it might take a step toward the correct alternative or toward one of the others. With some probability, it takes a step in the correct direction; with some other probability it takes a step in a random direction. Although we cannot predict the direction the pointer will move at any particular time, on average it will move toward the correct choice.

Once identification is complete, the random walk continues as long as the analyzer maintains its identification (about 0.5 s longer than the duration of the sample; see Riley & Roitblat, 1978). Higher choice accuracy is obtained with longer sample durations because the pointer has more time to take more steps. The speed with which the pointer moves is unaffected by the duration of the ITI. Its distance from some central point is analogous to strength in the trace theory. In this model, however, choice accuracy does not depend solely on the distance of the pointer from the neutral point. The use of three alternatives requires at least two dimensions to properly characterize the pattern of choices the subjects make.

At the end of the analyzer-driven random walk—when the sample is no longer present and new information is no longer coming in—the pointer begins to drift randomly. The evidence from the directed-forgetting experiments previously described suggests that two rates of drift may be possible: one when the comparison stimuli are expected and another when they are not. In any event the subject's loss of information during the retention interval is also a gradual process described by the location of the pointer in memory space. Forgetting, however, is not simply a reversal of the encoding process, that is, a random walk in the general direction of the central origin. In this model forgetting is simply a matter of gradually substituting one alternative for another with or without a modification of trace strength. That is, the pointer may or may not move toward the center of the space, as it moves from the vicinity of one alternative to another.

When the comparison stimuli are presented, the subject chooses the one that corresponds to the point in memory space closest to the pointer's current location. If the resulting choice is an error, the subject chooses the alternative corresponding to the next-closest memory point. Therefore, first-choice errors, as well as correct responses, will contain information about the sample presented because on average the pointer will be closer to the more-similar than the less-similar comparison stimulus. Further, because the second choice is made to the next-closest stimulus, second choices will have some relationship to first-choice errors, but may also have additional information about the sample's identity.

Between trials the pointer resets to a point a fixed distance from the central origin, but in a direction determined by its final position. This ensures that there will be some choice-specific proactive interference but that interference will not depend on the duration of the intertrial interval.

Conclusion

In this section we have seen the development of a theory of working memory from an early trace hypothesis to a more sophisticated multidimensional view of the processes involved in DMTS. Table 5.2 presents a comparison of the assumptions of these models. Although the trace theory appears to be incorrect or at least inadequate, it does not mean that it was not a good theory. On the contrary, the large number of specific predictions it makes, and the ensuing critical analysis of them, means that it was an excellent theory. I have little doubt

TABLE 5.2 Comparison of the copy/trace and the drift models

Copy/trace model	Drift model
1. Sample reception passively produces trace.	1. Sample is analyzed actively and encoded.
2. Working memory contains a retrospective copy of the sample.	2. Working memory contains prospective features of choice and outcome.
3. Trace increases strength with sample duration and loses strength with retention interval duration.	3. Pointer moves gradually away from neutral origin on random walk during sample and drifts during retention interval.
4. Trace strength—absolute and relative—determines matching accuracy.	4a. Relative distance of pointer from alternatives determines choice made.
	4b. Pointer does not reset to center of space.
	4c. Analyzer can be fatigued.
5. Reference memory contains general-matching concept.	5. Reference memory contains sample-choice relations and rules relating memory space and behavior.

that the spatial model of DMTS performance I have described here will also be found eventually to be inadequate. At the present time, however, it seems to describe the available data well.

WORKING AND REFERENCE MEMORY

Wagner's SOP model, described in Chapter 4, argues that working memory is a state of activation within a general memory system. The only distinction between working and reference memory is the level of activation or inactivation. The SOP model seems to explain many phenomena within classical conditioning, but the data reviewed in this chapter suggest that its conceptualization of the relation between working and reference memory is inappropriate.

When rats perform in the radial-arm maze, they seem to use two separate, but related, memory systems. The reference-memory system seems to contain an analog of the spatial properties of the maze. In contrast, the working memory system seems to contain a temporally organized list of arms the subject has already visited. The apparent list representation in working memory refers to the locations specified in reference memory, but the two appear to be separate systems.

One way to conceptualize the lists of working memory in the radial-arm maze is to assume that working memory consists of pointers or "flags" that the animal sets when it enters an arm. These flags each refer to one location in the rat's cognitive map. As the animal enters an arm, it sets the flag and then avoids revisiting any arm indicated by a flag in the representation. Errors occur when a flag spontaneously resets, and the arm becomes indistinguishable from an unvisited arm. Flags could either reset in an all-or-none fashion, or they could slowly "fade." Therefore, the longer the time since the rat visits the arm, the more likely they are to have reset. This, in turn, increases the likelihood that the animal will revisit the arm. By this hypothesis, working memory consists of pointers located in a memory space.

Similarly, the drift model of pigeon DMTS also supposes that working memory consists of a pointer located in a memory space. According to this model, too, reference and working memory are distinct, though interacting, systems. The difference between the proposed working memory for DMTS and the proposed working memory for radial-maze performance is the way the pointers change—set and reset in the maze, drift in DMTS—and their number. At present the similarities between the two working memory systems are largely speculative, but they raise interesting possibilities.

Among the problems remaining to be addressed with regard to these working memory models is the source of a cognitive map in memory space. Tolman argued that cognitive maps are synthesized from families of means-end expectancies. Exploration of the radial maze would clearly provide sufficient information for construction of a cognitive map. In DMTS, however, the means by which an analogous map could be produced are not immediately obvious. One possibility is that in learning to perform the task, the pigeon first learns means-end expectancies regarding each sample and the outcomes of various choices following them. With continued training it combines those separate expectancies into a more general, metaphorically spatial organization. Only further research will determine whether these two views of working memory are anything more than suggestive speculation.

SUMMARY

Working memory holds information that is typically useful only for a limited amount of time or in a limited context. We usually study working memory with some kind of already well-learned delayed-response task, in which the animal receives information at one time that controls the correct response it will make at a subsequent time.

Working memory processes for two kinds of task were described. The working memory of rats performing in a radial-arm maze contains a list of arms that they have already visited. The rats' reference memory contains a map of the maze. In contrast, the working memory of pigeons in DMTS is generally prospective. It contains a gradually strengthening representation of the choice the animal will make at the end of the retention interval. Reference memory contains the rules necessary to the bird's performance of the task. The drift model describes the working memory processes of pigeons performing DMTS.

RECOMMENDED READINGS

Honig, W. K. (1981) Working memory and the temporal map. In N. E. Spear & R. R. Miller (Eds.), *Information processing in animals: Memory mechanisms.* Hillsdale, N.J.: Erlbaum, pp. 167–197.

O'Keefe, J., & Nadel, L. (1978) *The hippocampus as a cognitive map.* Oxford: Clarendon Press.

Olton, D. S. (1978) Characteristics of spatial memory. In S. H. Hulse, H. Fowler, & W. K. Honig (Eds.), *Cognitive processes in animal behavior.* Hillsdale, N.J.: Erlbaum.

Olton, D. S. (1979) Mazes, maps, and memory. *American Psychologist, 34,* 588–596.

Roitblat, H. L. (1984) Representations in pigeon working memory. In H. L. Roitblat, T. G. Bever, & H. S. Terrace (Eds.), *Animal cognition*. Hillsdale, N.J.: Erlbaum, pp. 79–97.

CHAPTER 6

Time and Serial Order

Animals live in environments that change over time in three ways. First, there are cyclical changes, such as the succession of day and night, the progression of the seasons, and the ebb and flow of the tides. Organisms have evolved general and specific mechanisms for adapting to and anticipating these changes by representing them internally. Second, all events have duration. Time is spent foraging, searching for a mate, and so forth. Animals have evolved specific mechanisms for determining rates and durations and use these to guide their behavior (see Chapter 7). Third, events occur in succession. Phenomena such as classical conditioning indicate that organisms are highly sensitive to the order in which events occur.

For centuries philosophers have been concerned with the relationship between time and change. Is time nothing more than the succession of changes perceived by an organism or does time have its own existence as a dimension of the world? When an organism anticipates cyclical events or measures a duration, is it simply responding to the succession of events imposed on it, or is it measuring their duration relative to some internal clock? If an animal does have an internal clock with which to time events, is this clock the basis for its response to succession? These are the main questions of this chapter.

TIME AS A DIMENSION OF EXPERIENCE

All of the effects of time on an organism might be passive like the erosion of a river bank or decay of a radioactive element. When animals appear to be responding to the passage of time, they could actually be responding to changes in the environment. Early behaviorists tried to explain all apparent examples of animal timing as responses to changes in the environment because no single observable stimulus corresponds to the passage of time. Showing that an animal was responding to the passage of time, and not directly to stimuli that change with time, would be equivalent to showing that it was responding to something that could not be observed, but had to be inferred from changing experience. Hence, true animal timing would be incompatible with a straightforward stimulus-response account of behavior. Such attempts to attribute animals' responsiveness to time exclusively to changes in the environment have generally failed. Instead, the evidence is clear that animals are capable of forming internal representations of the temporal properties of events and measuring them against an internal clock. This evidence is presented next.

Circadian rhythms

Animals exhibit many behaviors that occur at regular intervals. Some are repeated at very brief intervals: heartbeats, the wingbeats of birds, or the breathing of a panting dog, for example. Others, such as feeding patterns, or sleeping and waking, occur on a daily, or circadian, rhythm. Still other behaviors, such as the migratory flights of robins, occur according to an annual cycle. These rhythms have been widely studied over the last 20 or 30 years by chronobiologists.

Among the most studied of these rhythms are the daily or circadian rhythms, such as body temperature, sleep/wakefulness, activity level, and feeding. For example, many rodents exhibit a daily activity cycle in which they are most active at night and least active during the day. This pattern of activity continues, even if the animals are maintained in completely constant conditions. Under ordinary conditions the biological clocks that underly these rhythms become entrained or synchronized to the environmental cycles called "zeitgebers," but they also continue indefinitely in the absence of zeitgebers. The most usual zeitgeber is the daily oscillation between light and darkness, or day and night.

A circadian rhythm results from the functioning of one or more pacemakers (e.g., see Rusak & Zucker, 1975; Silver & Bittman, 1984). Pacemakers are located within certain areas of an animal's brain—for example, the suprachiasmatic nucleus—and produce outputs with a regular rhythm. These neural pacemakers are disrupted by certain chemicals, such as lithium chloride and deuterium, but they are unaffected by many of the other factors that have been found to modify the functioning of neurons. For example, most neurons change their rate of firing when their temperature changes. In contrast, neural pacemakers compensate for temperature changes, maintaining their rhythms over wide variations in temperature (see Saunders, 1977). The behavioral rhythms are controlled by the pacemakers, not by the external zeitgebers to which the pacemakers are synchronized. For example, bees were trained in New York to forage for food between 1 P.M. and 2:30 P.M. Eastern Standard Time (EST). They were then flown during the night to California. Pacific Standard Time (PST) is 3 hours earlier than Eastern Standard Time. If the time at which the bees forage is controlled by the location of the sun, then they should forage at about 1 P.M. PST, corresponding to 4 P.M. EST. If, however, the time at which the bees forage is controlled by an internal biological clock, then they should forage at 10 A.M. PST, corresponding to 1 P.M. EST. On their first day in California, the bees began to forage at about 10 A.M. PST. Then, as their internal rhythms became synchronized with the zeitgeber, they gradually shifted over several days, until they were again beginning to forage at 1 P.M. PST (Renner, 1960). The bees experienced "jetlag" until their internal clock became synchronized with the local time in California.

That we can identify the parts of the brain responsible for producing the rhythmic activity underlying the circadian clock does not detract from the fact that these rhythms are representations or models of the earth's rotation or day/night cycle.[1] The model allows the animal to take advantage of the regularities in the day/night cycle and thereby anticipate when events such as dawn are to occur. An animal can wake up before dawn, while it is still dark, and begin making its preparations for efficient daytime activity. Some birds use the time before the sky begins to lighten to adjust their body temperatures and begin singing.

Circadian rhythms also allow animals to fill in parts of the immediate or recent past that they have not experienced directly. For example, it would be disastrous for a burrowing animal to behave as if it were night every time it entered the darkness of its burrow. It would be equally unfortunate if the animal could not begin its daytime activities until after it had experienced the light of dawn (by already having emerged from its dark burrow). Circadian rhythms also insulate the animal from unimportant variations in the environment, such as the darkness brought by a passing thunderstorm.

The evidence is clear that circadian rhythms represent the regularities of the day/night cycle. Animals who respond in anticipation of daily events (e.g., feeding time; see Terman, Gibbon, Fairhurst, & Waring, 1984) are not reacting to direct external stimuli, rather they are using internal clocks to determine the time of day.

Event duration

Timing and conditioning.   In addition to timing events on the order of a day, animals can also be observed to time very brief events on the order of seconds to minutes. At least three phenomena in classical conditioning indicate that animals can use elapsed time as a variable controlling their performance. These include the existence of an optimal CS-US interval, inhibition of delay, and temporal conditioning. Early explanations of these phenomena suggested that animals were responding to changes in the environment rather than to the passage of time. More recent evidence, however, forces us to discount such explanations in favor of direct temporal discrimination. As in circadian rhythms of activity, animals respond on the basis of internal clocks and measured durations, not simply to changes in the external stimulus. They have duration clocks that are generally accessible to a wide range of stimuli or tasks, not specific to any one of them.

Conditioning is typically best when the interval between the start of the conditional stimulus and the start of the unconditional stimulus is neither too short nor too long. For many kinds of conditioning, a CS-US interval of about 0.25 to 0.5 s is the best; for other kinds, longer durations are optimal (Gormezano, 1972; Kimble, 1961; Mackintosh, 1974). The limits of this range could indicate that animals time the interval between the CS and the US, perhaps because some amount of time is optimal to most usefully anticipate the US, or it could result from other factors. For example, Pavlov (1927/1960) and later Hull (1943) argued that some minimal time is necessary for the neural activity produced by presentation of the CS to reach its maximum level and become associated with the US. Similarly, conditioning might be poor with longer CS-US intervals because contiguity between the CS and US is poorer when the interval is longer or because the CS is less predictive of the US. Neither of these explanations is actually adequate however.

Pavlov and Hull argued that inhibition of delay results from changes in the effective CS, as perceived by the animal. Because of sensory adaptation, the CS excites different "elements" at the start of a CS presentation than at the end of it. An excitatory connection forms between the US and the elements activated at the end of the CS, and an inhibitory connection forms between the US and the elements activated at the start of the CS (see Chapter 4). The animal then withholds its responses until late in the CS presentation, thereby showing inhibition of delay.

Temporal conditioning is the third phenomenon that would seem to indicate that animals can time the duration of events. In temporal conditioning the US is presented at regular intervals without any explicit stimulus, other than the passage of time, to predict its occurrence. In contrast to the other conditioning phenomena, which Pavlov sought to explain on the basis of factors other than temporal discrimination, he explained temporal conditioning by arguing that the passage of time served directly as the CS (Pavlov, 1927/1960). Like inhibition of delay, however, temporal conditioning can also be explained as the result of changes in the effective CS. Although the experimenter presents no explicit stimuli to serve as the CS, many events are still available to potentially serve as the CS. For example, if the experimental dog closes its eyes whenever food is delivered, its sensitivity to the lights in the room could potentially, if not plausibly, serve as an external stimulus whose effect would change with the passage of time.

The basic question is: Do animals time the duration of events, or are all the examples that appear to indicate timing actually the result of a succession of changes in the effective properties of external stimuli? According to the first alternative, animals possess the ability to discriminate the duration of intervals on the basis of internal clocks. According to the second, all examples of animal timing are the result of discrimination of differences in the properties of external stimuli or their effectiveness.

The use of an internal clock does not preclude temporal discriminations based on changing stimuli. The use of a clock does not mean that no stimulus is involved in timing. For example, when we employ a kitchen clock to time a cake's baking time or to anticipate the beginning of an interesting television show, we are responding to a stimulus that varies systematically with the passage of time. The important point of this example, however, is that we can use this clock to time practically any event. Variations in the clock control our response to the event we are timing, not variations in the event itself—such as the temperature of the oven. Animals, who do not have access to kitchen clocks, do, nevertheless, appear to have access to an internal clock with many of the same functional properties. This internal clock varies systematically with the passage of time in the same way that an external clock does. Animals use this variation as a measure of the passage of time. The primary question is whether they use such internal event-independent timers or whether they respond merely to intrinsic variations in the events themselves.

If the optimal CS-US interval were the result of the time necessary for optimal stimulus effectiveness, then we would expect that the optimal CS-US interval should depend only on the type of CS. Tones might take longer to become effective than lights. In contrast, the optimal CS-US interval depends on the conditional response being measured, even when identical conditional and unconditional stimuli are used. Vandercar and Schneiderman (1967) recorded simultaneously the nictitating-membrane (a kind of eyeblink response) and the heart-rate conditional responses of rabbits.[2] They found that the optimal CS-US interval was about 0.5 s for the nictitating-membrane response but was 6.75 s for the heart-rate response. The optimal duration for the heart-rate response was too long for any nictitating-membrane response to be observed. The presence of a nictitating-membrane response with a 0.5-s CS-US interval indicates that the CS was fully effective within 0.5 s, and that the animal could fully process the US in time to associate it with the CS. The same CS that reached full effectiveness in 0.5 s could not also have needed 6.75 s to reach full effectiveness for heart-rate conditioning. Slow behaviors, such as changes in heart rate, have a relatively long optimal CS-US interval. Behaviors that can occur quickly, such as the rabbit's nictitating-membrane response, have a relatively short optimal CS-US interval. These differences suggest that the optimal CS-US interval is not a simple product of the stimuli presented, but is timed by the animal to maximize the usefulness of the information to the behavioral system involved.

Although inhibition of delay could be explained by the animal responding to changes in the effective stimulus, the results of other kinds of experiments are incompatible with this hypothesis. For example, Dews (1962) trained pigeons to respond to a fixed interval 500-s schedule (FI-500). Figure 6.1 shows that on this schedule the birds produced the typical fixed interval scallop: they responded slowly at the beginning of an interval and then accelerated their rate of response as the time of reinforcement approached. The interesting data come from a subsequent portion of the experiment, in which Dews turned the houselight on and off in successive 50-s intervals, but still presented the reinforcer for the first response after a total duration of 500 s. The reinforcer was always presented during a light interval, never during a dark. As a result, the birds soon decreased responding when the light was off, but continued to respond when the light was on at rates that were comparable to those observed in the corresponding period of

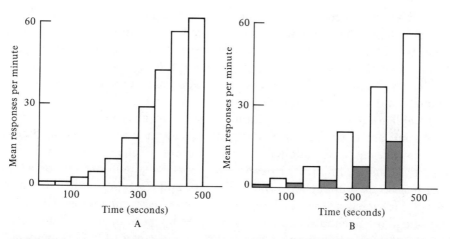

Figure 6.1. The rate of pecking in successive 50-s periods. Reinforcers were delivered on a fixed-interval 500-s schedule. (A) The pattern of responding observed when a constant signal filled the entire interval. (B) The pattern of responding observed when a light (open bars) and a dark (black bars) period alternated during the interval. [After Dews, 1962, Figure 2.]

the standard fixed-interval schedule in which the light remained on for the entire 500 s. Turning the light on and off ensured that the sensory effects at the end of the 500-s interval would significantly differ from those in the uninterrupted schedule. In the standard interval, the animals had 500 s of sensory adaptation to the light. In the alternating interval, they had only 50 s at a time to adapt to the light. Animals regulating their response rate on the basis of sensory effects, then, should always respond as if they were within the first 50 s of the fixed-interval schedule. Instead, they continued to accelerate their response rate in a way appropriate to the time until reinforcement, not to the time in the presence of the stimulus. Furthermore, because the birds responded more slowly when the light was off, many properties of their response pattern also changed; consequently, these properties were also unavailable as cues to correct responding. This experiment shows, then, that the animals were responding to the passage of time, not to changes in the sensory properties of the discriminative stimulus.

Some techniques for studying timing. The experiments that show temporal discrimination to be important in conditioning are consistent with other experiments that study animal timing more directly. (For reviews see Church, 1978, 1984; Gibbon & Church, 1984; Roberts, 1981, 1983.) Just as an animal can discriminate the length of a line, so can it discriminate the duration of an event. Similar techniques can be used to study both kinds of discriminations, and similar properties are observed for both.

Table 6.1 shows some of the situations in which investigators have studied timing in animals. Others are described in greater detail below.

As in all discriminations, animals indicate their ability to discriminate along the temporal dimension by responding differentially to the different stimuli along that dimension. One technique that has been used to study timing in animals is to train an animal in a conditional discrimination similar to delayed matching-to-sample. The "sample" in this task is the duration of a "timing stimulus," and the animal's task is to discriminate "short" from "long" timing stimuli. Short timing stimuli are those that have a duration less than a given criterion, and long timing stimuli are those that have a duration greater than the criterion. Each trial begins with the presentation of the timing stimulus, followed by the presentation of two choice stimuli. Responses to one of these stimuli are reinforced if the trial had begun with a short timing stimulus, and responses to the other are reinforced if it had started with a long one. Temporal discrimination is shown by the increase in the likelihood of a LONG response by the animal as the duration of the interval increases. Figure 6.2 shows the likelihood of a LONG response as a function of the duration of the timing signal (Stubbs, 1968). When the durations are plotted on a log scale, the resulting curve is in a form, called an "ogive," similar to that observed in many psychophysical procedures relating choice prob-

TABLE 6.1 Some situations in which temporal discrimination has been observed

Duration	Method/finding	Example
Duration of stimulus	One response after brief stimulus, another response after a long stimulus.	Stubbs, 1968; Church & Deluty, 1977; Stubbs, et al., 1984
	Temporal generalization. Maximal response probability after stimulus of target duration, decreases to shorter and longer stimuli.	Gibbon & Church, 1981
Duration of response	Rats reinforced for emitting response longer than criterion. Median response duration increases as a function of criterion.	Platt, Kuch, & Bitgood, 1973
Duration of reinforcer	Relative rate of responding to two keys approximately equal to the relative duration of the reinforcers provided for the two keys (pigeons).	Catania, 1963
Response-response interval	Reinforcement provided only if the interval between responses greater than criterion or DRL schedule. Distribution of interresponse times a function of criterion.	Kramer & Rilling, 1970
Inter-reinforcer interval	Temporal conditioning. Unconditioned stimulus presented at regular intervals.	Pavlov, 1927; LaBarbera & Church, 1974
Stimulus-stimulus interval	Inhibition of delay. Food delivered at fixed delay after signal onset. Response rate increases over the delay, peaking at about the time food scheduled to appear.	Pavlov, 1927
Reinforcer-response interval	FI scallop. Response rate increases as time to next reinforcer approaches.	Dews, 1970

Source: After Church, 1978.

ability to a stimulus dimension like brightness. Furthermore, when pigeons are trained with only two timing stimulus durations—the shortest and the longest— then the duration at which they are equally likely to respond SHORT or LONG (called the indifference, midpoint, or bisection point) is the geometric mean of the shortest and the longest interval (Church & Deluty, 1977; Meck, 1984; Stubbs, 1976). The log of the geometric mean is the mean of the log of the shortest and longest durations used during training. The bisection point is the point judged by the animal to be halfway between the shortest and the longest duration because it is the point at which SHORT and LONG responses are equally likely. That this point is the geometric mean has important implications for the kind of clock the animals use to time the duration of the timing stimulus. These implications will be considered below.

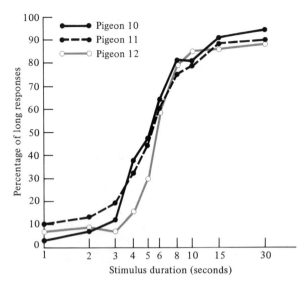

Figure 6.2. The percentage of LONG responses as a function of stimulus duration. Durations are plotted on a logarithmic scale. [From Stubbs, 1968.]

Temporal generalization is another technique that produces essentially identical results. For example, Church and Gibbon (1982) used temporal generalization to study timing in rats. Each trial presents a timing stimulus to the animal. After the end of this stimulus, a response lever is inserted into the box, and the rat is allowed to respond. If the timing stimulus had been exactly some specified duration, called the reinforced duration, then responses are reinforced. If the duration of the timing stimulus had been either shorter or longer than the reinforced duration, then responding is not reinforced. Animals are most likely to respond to the reinforced duration and are progressively less likely to respond as the duration of the timing signal becomes either progressively shorter or longer than the reinforced duration. Figure 6.3 shows typical results of such an experiment.

The peak procedure is still another technique that investigators have used to study temporal discrimination in rats (Meck, 1984; Roberts, 1981, 1983). In this procedure two types of trials are randomly intermixed. On "FI" trials, the rat is reinforced on a fixed-interval (FI) schedule. The timing interval begins with the start of the trial and lasts for a specified duration. As in standard FI reinforcement schedules, the first response following the timing interval is reinforced and ends the trial. On "empty" trials, no reinforcers are presented, and the trial lasts for at least twice as long as an FI trial. A typical FI scallop is observed during the FI trials. The animals respond very slowly at the start of the interval and

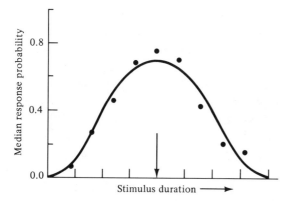

Figure 6.3. Temporal generalization. The median response probability as a function of signal duration. The reinforced duration was 4 s. [From Church & Gibbon, 1982.]

increase their response rate regularly until the end of the interval (cf. Dews, 1962, described above). The interesting data come from the occasional empty trials. Because the rat cannot discriminate FI from empty trials, its response rate also increases at the start of the empty trial and reaches a peak at about the time that the reinforcer would be presented on an FI trial. Response rate then declines for the rest of the trial. Figure 6.4 shows an example of the data obtained from this peak procedure.

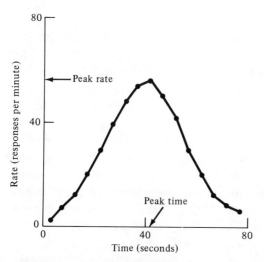

Figure 6.4. The peak procedure and some typical results. On FI trials food was presented after 40 s. On empty trials no food was presented. The time at which the maximum response rate occurred is called the peak time. The maximum rate is called the peak rate. [From Roberts, 1981.]

The time at which the maximum response rate occurs is called the peak time, and the maximum rate is called the peak rate. The time of the peak response rate indicates the time at which the rat expects the reinforcer. This time is independent of the rate of responding. Certain operations affect the peak rate without affecting the peak time. Certain other operations affect the peak time without affecting the rate at which the rat responds. For example, increasing the proportion of empty trials lowers the animal's response rate, but does not change the time of its peak response rate. On the other hand, prefeeding the rats with food high in carbohydrate, but not high in protein, postpones the peak time (Roberts, 1981).

Changing the proportion of empty trials and prefeeding affect different mechanisms. Reducing the probability of reinforcement by increasing the proportion of empty trials reduces the animal's motivation to respond and thereby reduces its peak response rate. It does not, however, change how the animal times the interval. In contrast, prefeeding does change the way in which the rat times the interval, presumably by slowing its internal clock. Other kinds of treatments also have been found to change the temporal location of the peak response. For example, injection of methamphetamine shortens the time to the peak response rate, presumably because it speeds the operation of the clock (Maricq, Roberts, & Church, 1981).

The properties of an internal clock

The data obtained from these timing tasks all lead to the conclusion that animals have access to an internal clock, which they can use to time events. Furthermore, the available data suggest the kind of timing system shown in Figure 6.5. The system is composed of four major parts (Gibbon & Church, 1984; see also Church, 1984; Gibbon, Church, & Meck, 1984); a *clock*, a *working memory*, a *reference memory* and a *comparator*. The *clock* consists of a pacemaker, a switch, and an accumulator. The pacemaker is similar to the electronic "tuning fork" that provides the time base for electronic watches in that it produces pulses at a more or less fixed rate. When the switch is "on," and the animal is timing some event, the pulses are directed into the accumulator, where they add up or accumulate counts. The value of the counts in the accumulator can be either transferred to the working memory, or the value of the accumulator can be combined with the value in the working memory. The system can then compare the value in the accumulator and/or the working memory with a value stored in reference memory. The value in reference memory might represent the total standard duration of the event being timed, for example, the time at which a reinforcer will be delivered on an FI trial. When the value in the accumulator is close enough to the value in reference memory, then some response is enabled; other-

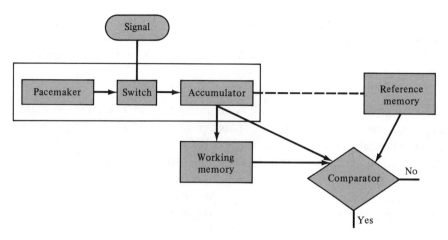

Figure 6.5. The timing system proposed by Gibbon and Church. [From Church, 1984.]

wise, the response is not enabled. When a response is made and reinforced, the information in the accumulator and working memory is transferred to reference memory for future use.

Animals could use this system for timing in the peak procedure as follows: At the start of the timing signal, the switch engages and allows pulses to travel from the pacemaker to the accumulator. Reference memory contains the number of counts that have in the past been followed by reinforcement. As the duration of the signal wears on, the count in the accumulator increases. The comparator compares these counts with those remembered in reference memory. As the value in the accumulator approaches that stored in reference memory, the animal becomes increasingly likely to respond. On an empty trial the reinforcer does not occur at the expected time—that is, the time at which the accumulator matches the value stored in reference memory. Instead, the accumulator continues to accumulate counts, and the difference between accumulator and reference memory grows. As a result, the likelihood of a response declines as the difference between the accumulator and the value in reference memory grows.

The clock contained in the timing system described in Figure 6.5 is similar to a man-made stopwatch. For example, both contain a pacemaker. In electronic stopwatches the pacemaker is an electrically oscillating crystal. When the watch is timing, impulses from the crystal are transferred to an electronic counter. The accumulator is then displayed on the face of the watch. At any point in time, you can consult the display and compare it with some criterion duration, for example, the record time for running the 50-meter dash. When the event being timed has ended, you can stop the watch. It can also record lap time in a "working memory" or notebook while continuing to accumulate time in the accumulator.

Both the electronic and the animal's internal clock begin timing from 0 up to some value. Both scale time linearly. The difference between 5 and 10 s is the same as the difference between 25 and 30 s. Both can be stopped temporarily, and both can be used to time different events.

Clock times up from 0.   The timing system described in Figure 6.5 contains both an accumulator and a memory. In order for the clock to be useful in performing temporal discriminations, such as those involved in the peak procedure, the animal must compare the elapsed time with the criterial remembered time. There are two ways in which it can perform such a comparison. A *countdown timer* starts with the criterion value in the accumulator and counts down to 0 with each pulse. When the clock reaches 0, the interval is complete. A kitchen timer is an example of a countdown clock. If you want to bake a cake for 40 minutes, you set the kitchen timer to 40 minutes, and take the cake from the oven when the bell rings at 0. A *countup timer* starts with 0 in the accumulator and counts up to the criterion with each pulse. When the value in the accumulator matches the criterion in reference memory, the interval is complete. A stopwatch is an example of a countup timer.

Shift experiments indicate that rats constantly compare a countup clock with the criterion value in reference memory. The rat in this kind of experiment begins to time an interval in the presence of one stimulus and finishes timing it in the presence of another. The stimuli each predict different times of reinforcement. For example, in the presence of a light, food might be presented 20 s into the interval, whereas in the presence of a tone, it is presented 40 s into the interval. Shift trials start with the light for 5, 10, or 15 s and then shift to the tone for a combined total duration of 80 s. No food is presented on shift trials.

If the rats are using a countdown timer to time the light, then they would expect the food to be delivered 20 s after the start of the trial. They should ordinarily show an accelerating-response pattern with a peak response rate at about 20 s. The rat's countdown timer would read "5 s left" if the shift occurs after 15 s, "10 s left" if the shift occurs after 10 s, and "15 s left" if the shift occurs after 5 s. By hypothesis, a countdown timer can only be reset to the value specified in reference memory; it includes no mechanism for combining the current value in the accumulator with the standard value in reference memory. Therefore, following the shift, the animals could do one of two things in the presence of the tone. They could either continue to count down from their original preset interval and show a peak response rate when the countdown clock reaches 0, 20 s after the start of the trial, or they could reset the clock to the duration associated with the tone and show a peak-response rate when the clock reaches 0, 40 s after the shift.

If, however, the rats were using countup timers, then their clocks would read "15 s elapsed" if the shift occurs after 15 s, "10 s elapsed" if the shift occurs after

TABLE 6.2 Predicted time of peak response rate with two types of timer

Type of timer	Clock resets	Clock does not reset
Countup	40 s after shift	40 s after start of trial*
Countdown	40 s after shift	20 s after start of trial

Note: * indicates the outcome observed by Roberts (1981). Rats use countup timer and continue timing rather than resetting clock to 0 after shift (see text).

10 s, and "5 s elapsed" if the shift occurs after 5 s. By hypothesis, a countup timer can only be reset to 0, but its current value can always be compared to the standard value appropriate to the current stimulus. Therefore, following the shift, the animals could do one of two things in the presence of the tone. They could reset their clocks to 0 when the shift occurs and show a peak response rate 40 s after the shift, or they could continue to count up, showing a peak response rate 40 s after the start of the trial. Table 6.2 presents the predictions associated with a countup and a countdown timer.

Consistent with a countup timer, Roberts (1981) found that the rats showed their peak response rate 40 s after the start of the trial. Figure 6.6 shows these results. The rat continued timing from the start of the trial and constantly compared the current value in the accumulator with the standard in reference memory appropriate to the current signal. Of particular importance is the sudden drop in response rate when the shift from light to tone occurred 15 s after the start of the trial. Immediately before the shift at 15 s, the animals were responding at a rate of about 40 responses per minute. Immediately after it, their response rate dropped to about 20 responses per minute. A high response rate is appropriate 15 s after the start of a light trial, because it is only 5 s before the impending reinforcement, but a low response rate is appropriate 15 s after the start of a tone trial, because the reinforcer is still 25 s away. As soon as the tone was presented, the rats shifted from the response rate appropriate to the light to that appropriate to the tone.

Clock times along a linear scale.   The proposition that the pacemaker produces pulses at more or less regular intervals implies that subjective time is a linear function of real time, as is measured by an electronic watch. On the surface this proposal seems inconsistent with some of the known facts of animal timing. Specifically, Weber's law holds for animals' temporal discriminations. The discriminability of two temporal intervals decreases as the duration of the intervals increases. Two temporal intervals are equally discriminable if the ratio of one to the other is constant, no matter what their absolute duration. For example, people and animals can discriminate fairly easily between 5 and 10 s, but have difficulty discriminating between 1 hour and 1 hour plus 5 s without a

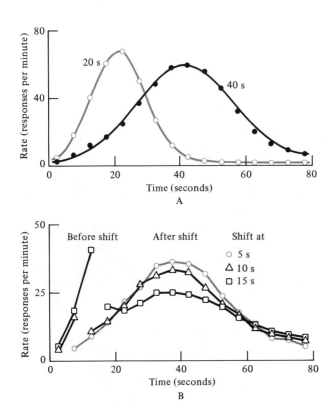

Figure 6.6. The shift experiment. (A) The response rate as a function of time on baseline trials during which the reinforcer was presented on an FI-20 s schedule for tone and on an FI-40 s schedule for light. (B) The response rate both before and after the shift from tone to light. Note the sudden drop in response rate following the shift. [From Roberts, 1981.]

mechanical clock. Further, the bisection point, the point judged by an animal to be the temporal middle between two durations, lies at their geometric mean (Church & Deluty, 1977; Meck, 1984; Stubbs, 1968). Both of these findings would be explained if the animal's subjective time scale were the logarithm of real time. Differences measured on a log scale correspond to ratios on a linear scale, and the mean of the log of two durations is their geometric mean.

Gibbon and Church (Gibbon, 1977; Gibbon & Church, 1981, 1984) have argued cogently that animals cannot be using a logarithmic subjective time scale. The difference on a log scale between 5 s and 10 s (1.0 − 0.699 = 0.301) is equivalent to the difference between 10 s and 20 s (1.301 − 1.0 = 0.301) because the ratios of the two durations are constant. The difference between durations depends on the starting point at which the intervals begin when time is measured on a log scale, but does not depend on the point at which they begin when time is measured on a linear scale. If time is measured on a logarithmic scale, intervals in the future are discounted relative to intervals in the present. Differences between two intervals in the future are judged to be smaller than the same differences in the present. Similar discounting does not occur if time is measured on a linear scale. Gibbon and Church took advantage of the difference between currently elapsing and future intervals by requiring subjects to compare an ongoing duration with a fresh duration.

In one experiment rats were trained with two FI schedules available on separate levers that could be inserted into and removed from the operant chamber. One lever produced reinforcers on a fixed-interval 60-s schedule (FI-60); the other lever produced reinforcers on a fixed-interval 30-s schedule (FI-30). The trial began with the presentation of the FI-60 lever. Either 15, 30, or 45 s later the FI-30 lever was inserted. When the FI-30 lever is inserted into the operant chamber, the rat has the choice of continuing to respond on the FI-60 lever or on the FI-30 lever. We would expect the animal to switch from the FI-60 to the FI-30 lever if it judged the subjective time left to reinforcement on the FI-60 lever to be greater than the time left to reinforcement on the FI-30 lever. It would continue responding on the FI-60 lever if it judged the subjective time to reinforcement to be shorter on the FI-60 than on the FI-30 lever. If the subject judges time along a linear scale, then it should prefer the FI-30 lever if it is presented after 15 s on the FI-60 lever. The FI-60 schedule will deliver food in 45 s, whereas the FI-30 s schedule will deliver food in 30 s. The animal should be indifferent if the FI-30 lever is presented after 30 s. Both levers will deliver food after 30 s. Finally, it should continue responding on the FI-60 lever if the alternative is presented after 45 s. FI-60 will deliver food in 15 s, but FI-30 will not deliver food for 30 s. On the other hand, if the animal judges time along a logarithmic scale, then it would compare a partially elapsed interval with a fresh one. In every case we would expect the animal to judge the elapsing time to reinforcement on the FI-60 lever to be less than the fresh time to reinforcement on the FI-30 lever, no matter when the FI-30 lever is made available. For example, Figure 6.7 shows the relationship between subjective and real time when the FI-30 lever is presented 15 s after the FI-60 lever. The interval between a and b is the subjective time to reinforcement on the FI-60 schedule, and the interval between a and c is the subjective time to reinforcement on the FI-30 schedule. Figure 6.7A shows the relationship between subjective and real time when subjective time is logarithmic. Figure 6.7B shows the relationship between subjective and real time when subjective time is linear. If subjective time is logarithmic, the subjective duration to reinforcement on the FI-30 s schedule is greater than the subjective time to reinforcement on the FI-60 schedule. If, however, subjective time is linear, then the subjective time to reinforcement on the FI-30 schedule is shorter than the subjective time to reinforcement on the FI-

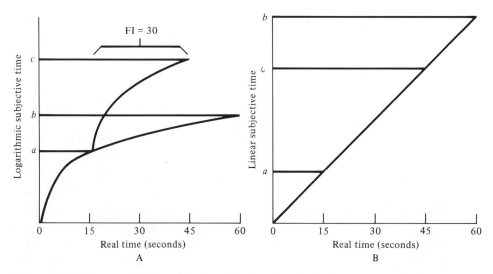

Figure 6.7. Linear versus logarithmic subjective time in the duration comparison experiment of Gibbon and Church (1981). After 15 s of responding on an FI-60 s schedule, the animal is given a choice between continuing on the FI-60 s schedule and responding on an FI-30 s schedule. (A) Logarithmic subjective time as a function of duration. (B) Linear subjective time. The interval between *a* and *b* indicates the subjective duration to reinforcement on the elapsing FI-60 s schedule. The interval between *a* and *c* indicates the subjective duration to reinforcement on the new FI-30 s schedule. Animals prefer the FI-30 s to the FI-60 s schedule when the choice is provided after 15 s on the FI-60 s schedule. This result is incompatible with logarithmic subjective time because the subjective duration to reinforcement on the FI-30 schedule is predicted to be greater than the subjective duration to reinforcement on the FI-60 schedule.

60 schedule. Therefore, we would expect the animal to prefer the FI-60 schedule if subjective time is logarithmic and to prefer the FI-30 over the FI-60 if subjective time is linear. Consistent with the prediction of linear subjective time, subjects preferred the FI-30 over the FI-60 schedule when the FI-30 was made available after 15 s, but not when it was made available after 45 s. They were indifferent when the FI-30 schedule was provided after 30 s of access to the FI-60 schedule. A fresh interval was judged to be the same duration as an ongoing interval of equal physical duration.

The data from this and other experiments are quite convincing evidence for the use by animals of a linear subjective time schedule. Gibbon (1977) employs a scalar-timing theory to explain these data, to accommodate the apparent contradictions presented by Weber's law, and to explain why the geometric mean is judged to be the midpoint between two durations. Scalar-timing theory proposes that the variability of judgments, not the scale along which those judgments are made, increases with the duration being judged. For example, the pacemaker may itself contain some variability in the regularity with which it produces pulses (Gibbon & Church, 1984). This variability would add up over the duration of the interval being timed so that longer durations would show more variability in the relationship between subjective and real time than would short durations. The scalar-timing hypothesis further proposes that durations are compared by taking their ratio, rather than their arithmetic difference; that is, the comparator compares the ratios of the duration in reference memory with the duration indicated in the accumulator. This theory has been applied in a wide variety of situations and to a wide variety of tasks and is entirely consistent with the obtained data.

Clock can be stopped.   The timing system proposed by Gibbon and Church contains a switch that gates impulses from the pacemaker to the accumulator and a working memory that maintains the contents of the accumulator for relatively brief times. Rats have been found capable of using the switch and accumulator to time the total duration of an interrupted signal. Roberts (1981) trained rats on a peak procedure of the sort shown in Figures 6.4 and 6.6. Trials were signaled by a light. On standard FI trials, the rats received food for their first response after 40 s. As in earlier experiments, these standard FI trials were intermixed with occasional empty trials on which the food was omitted. They were also accompanied by probe trials, in which a 5- or 10-s blackout interrupted the signal. When a blackout interrupted the signal, the rats delayed their peak responding. With a 10-s interruption, the time of their peak response rate was delayed by an average of 13.3 s. With a 5 s interruption, the time of their peak response rate was delayed by an average of 7.2 s. In both cases, only the peak time was changed. The pattern of responding following a blackout was identical to that on trials without a blackout, except that it was delayed for about the duration of the gap. This experiment indicates that rats can stop their clocks when the signal is absent and resume timing when it returns. It is also interesting to note that rats' peak times are consistently longer when a gap is used than when the signal is continuous. This apparently reflects a difference in the speed with which the switch is opened and closed. Once the signal starts, some minimum latency must elapse before the switch closes and allows pulses to travel from the pacemaker to the accumulator. Similarly, there will be a short latency between the time that the signal ends and the switch opens, terminating the transfer of pulses. If the switch opens and closes only once, the relative durations to open and to close are irrelevant because the same latencies to open and close were present when the animals were learning the food duration. Therefore, reference memory contains the total number of pulses that correspond to the signal, including those gained by a slow switch opening and those lost by a slow switch closure. The introduction of a gap, however, necessarily causes two switch openings and two switch closures. Reference memory has compensated for one opening and closure, but, without further specific experience, it cannot compensate for two. Thus, the judged duration reflects the difference between those pulses gained from a slow switch opening and those lost from a slow switch closure. The difference is apparently on the order of 0.2 to 0.5 s. In other words, it takes about 0.2 to 0.5 s longer for the switch to close than to open, and the peak time is delayed for a corresponding amount of time (see also Meck, Church, & Olton, 1984).

Clock times different events.   Like a man-made wristwatch, the rat's clock can time many different kinds of events. This flexibility is important because it demonstrates that the rats are timing the duration of signals; they are not responding to temporally changing properties in the signals themselves. For example, the shift experiment (Roberts, 1981), described above, showed that rats can continue timing an interval when the signal shifts from one modality to another. Similarly, rats that are trained to time a light show transfer to timing a sound. Roberts (1982) trained rats to press one lever after a 1-s signal and to press another lever after a 4-s signal. Half of the rats were initially trained with light and the other half with tone signals. After training with one signal, they were tested with the untrained signal. The animals continued to respond differentially to the long versus the short signal, indicating that they timed the transfer signal as well as the originally trained signal, and according to the same memory and clock.

Summary.   Animals' timing systems consist of four distinct parts: a clock, a working memory, a reference memory, and a comparator. The clock consists of a pacemaker, which produces pulses at more or less regular intervals; a switch; and an accumulator. The switch controls whether or not pulses from the pacemaker reach the accumulator, and the accumulator counts the number of pulses reaching it. Subjective time for the animals studied is measured along a linear scale that is proportional to real time, as measured by an electronic or mechanical clock. The variability of a time judgment increases as the duration increases. The timing system is flexible: it can be started and stopped, and it times a variety of different signals.

SEQUENTIAL BEHAVIOR AND SEQUENTIAL REPRESENTATIONS

The data presented in the previous section clearly demonstrate that animals can time stimulus events; the ability to time is not simply the product of a sensitivity to successions of stimulus events. In addition, the succession of sensations is not sufficient to yield a sense of succession. Each sensation occurs by itself in its own moment of time. Therefore, in order to appreciate the succession of events, the organism must not only represent the events in succession, but information about their order. James stated this distinction clearly:

> A succession of feelings, in and of itself, is not a feeling of succession. And since, to our successive feelings, a feeling of their succession is added, that must be treated as an additional fact requiring its own special elucidation . . . . (James, 1892/1962, p. 292)

The study of the representation of sequences requires tasks that are sensitive to this difference between memory for the items in the sequence versus memory for the items *and* their sequence. The goal of this study is to determine whether animals are capable of forming a coherent, ordered representation of the events in a sequence.

Sequential behavior without sequential representations

A coherent, ordered representation of a sequence is one in which the elements of the sequence and information about their succession is represented simultaneously and as a unit. This kind of representation is distinct from the kind of simple association thought to underlie classical conditioning (see Chapter 4). For example, in Wagner's (1981) model of classical conditioning, the animal does not represent the sequence CS-then-US. Instead, presentation of the CS is assumed to activate a representation of the US. The requirement that the CS precede the US for effective conditioning is a product of the patterns of activation, not evidence for an explicit representation of order.

Maze learning.   A number of tasks that appear to provide information about animals' abilities to represent sequences are actually inadequate. For example, in learning to run through a multiple-unit maze, an animal must somehow represent the sequence of responses necessary to move from the start to the goal box. To the extent that each choice point is unique, however, it can be associated with a single response. Therefore, an adequate representation would contain the information necessary for the animal to identify each choice point and the appropriate response at that choice point. No information about the order in which the choice points are encountered is necessary. In fact, if the maze is constructed so that a certain choice point can be reached by different paths, or if the animal is sometimes started from different locations in the maze, a serial representation— for example, a series of left and right turns—might actually interfere with performance. The subject need not know about the particular responses that brought it to a choice point, only the correct response at that point (Bever, Straub, Terrace, & Townsend, 1980). As each response takes the animal to the next choice point, the stimuli produced by that point become associated with the correct response. The next response leads to the next choice point and its stimuli, and the chain continues. The serial organization of the behavior need not derive from a serially organized representation of the maze within the animal, but from the physical layout of the maze and the serial connections of the runways between choice points. Hull (1931) and Skinner (1934) viewed this type of stimulus-response chain learning as the prototype for all kinds of sequence learning. They argued that the performance of one response produces the stimuli associated with the next response, that response produces another set of stimuli, and so forth. The essence of this proposal is that the sequence of performance observed in a maze is thought to be due to unordered representations of choice-points/response pairs.

Alternative heuristics.   In addition to unordered list representations of the kind thought to underlie maze performance, an organism could use other heuristics to respond appropriately to some sorts of sequences. For example, in one experiment, pigeons were trained to discriminate a sequence of two colors (call them A and B) from their reverse order (BA). Accurate discriminative performance on this kind of task does not imply that the organism has a representation of the sequence AB (Weisman, Wasserman, Dodd, & Larew, 1980). A pigeon could respond differently to AB and BA because it remembers only the item that came first (primacy) or only the item that came last (recency). In order to rule out the primacy and recency explanations, we must show that the animal can discriminate other sequences that are equivalent in either their first or last stimuli. For example, the recency heuristic is ruled out if the organism can discriminate the sequence BB from AB. The most recent stimulus in these two sequences is B. If the animal were responding only to this stimulus, then it should treat these two sequences as identical. Similarly, the primacy heuristic can be ruled out if the organism can discriminate AA from AB.

Although many tasks involving sequential behaviors can be explained on the basis of simple unordered pairings of stimuli and responses, a number of other tasks cannot be similarly explained. They seem to require the use of a serially integrated representation in which the events in the sequence as well as information about their order is simultaneously represented.

Speed of response and serial organization

In contrast to performance in multiple-unit mazes, certain sorts of tasks seem to require serial representations because the response occurs before the nervous system has time to process the stimulus that precedes it. For example, Lashley (1951) explored the nature of the representation that underlies sequences of skilled movements, such as those used in typewriting or piano playing. In many examples of piano music, the finger movements follow one another so rapidly in succession that there is not enough time for the nerve signals to travel from the ear hearing one note to the finger playing the next. Hence, unlike performance at a choice point in a maze, the sensory result of one response cannot be the stimulus controlling the next response. If a stimulus-response-type representation were to work at all as an explanation for such skilled movements, then each response—say pressing the key for the fifth note—would have to be controlled, not by the immediately preceding note, but by one played much earlier. Because at least some animals are capable of such intricate and rapid responding, it suggests that organisms are capable of representations of serial patterns that are more complex than stimulus-response chains.

The nature of sequences

A number of different tasks have been used successfully to study sequence learning in animals. These tasks all use elements that have a stable ordering. These ordered elements make up an "alphabet." Like the alphabet of Roman characters that are used to form English words, an "alphabet" is a stable set of events or stimuli that can be ordered independently of the sequence in which they happen to be presented on any particular occasion. As children we learn that the alphabet is ordered A, B, C, D, . . . Each particular word that we learn, however, also presents its own unique sequence of letters. We learn that the ordered elements of the alphabet can be arranged in different ways to make particular words. Some of the alphabets that have been used in animal sequence-learning tasks are food rewards of different sizes, lights of different colors, and spatial locations. Some of the responses that have been used include running down a runway, pecking at a test stimulus, and pecking at a sequence of colored lights.

SERIAL ANTICIPATION LEARNING

In many experiments on human serial pattern learning, the subject is shown an example of a sequential pattern and then asked to continue or to reproduce the same pattern. For example, a subject might be shown the sequence 4 5 1 2 3 4 4 5 1 3 4 5 4 5 . . . , and asked to write down the next five numbers in the sequence. The general finding is that complex patterns are more difficult to learn and to remember than simpler patterns. Analogous experiments with rats have arrived at similar conclusions. These experiments use an alphabet consisting of food rewards of different sizes, and the rat is required to anticipate each subsequent item in the series. With sufficiently long sequences, acquisition is faster when the order in which the elements are presented corresponds to their alphabetic ordering.

The serial anticipation task

In *serial anticipation learning* experiments, rats are trained to run down a long alleyway for some food pellets at the other end. The rat's running speed is taken as a measure of its expectation of the size of the food reward—that is, the number of pellets—at the other end of the alleyway. Provided that the sequence is sufficiently simple, the animals typically run quickly in anticipation of large food rewards and slowly in anticipation of small food rewards. In order for the rat to anticipate the next item in the series, it must know the order in which the items are presented as well as which item in that sequence is coming next—that is, the current location in the series.

In an initial experiment of this sort with rats (Hulse & Campbell, 1975), the patterns consisted of various orderings of the elements: 0, 1, 3, 7, and 14 food pellets. One group of rats received an ascending series, with 0 pellets on the first run of a trial, 1 pellet on the next, 3 on the next, 7 on the next, and 14 pellets on the fifth (0-1-3-7-14). Another group received the same five elements in descending order (14-7-3-1-0). Three other groups received the elements in random orderings that varied from trial to trial. For one group the series always ended with the 0-pellet element—for example, 14-3-1-7-0 or 3-1-14-7-0—and each trial had a different sequence. For a second group the series always ended with the 14-pellet element—for example, 1-0-7-3-14 or 7-3-0-1-14—and for the third group it ended with a randomly chosen element—for example, 3-14-7-0-1 or 1-3-14-0-7. After some training rats in the increasing- and decreasing-order groups ran with speeds proportional to the reward magnitude. The more pellets in the element, the faster they ran. Figure 6.8 displays these data. The difference in running speed was most pronounced between the nonzero elements and the terminal 0-pellet element in the monotonically descending series. Rats in the other groups ran with the same speed to every element in the series.

Hulse and Dorsky (1977) found that rats trained with the monotonic sequence 14-7-3-1-0 learned in fewer trials to anticipate—that is, run slowly to—the 0-pellet element than did rats trained with the weakly monotonic sequence 14-5-5-1-0 or with the nonmonotonic sequence 14-1-3-7-0. Similar results were obtained with similar sequences by Hulse and Dorsky (1979). In each of these studies, the remarkable feature is that both the monotonic and the nonmonotonic sequences were built of exactly the same elements. Every animal received the elements in a consistent order. Nevertheless, they found one arrangement of

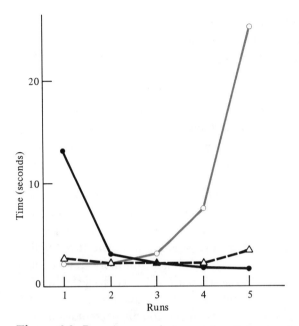

Figure 6.8. Running speeds in serial-anticipation learning. The solid dots indicate the running speed to the increasing sequence 0-1-3-7-14. The open dots indicate the running speed to the decreasing sequence 14-7-3-1-0. The triangles indicate the running time to the random sequence. [From Hulse & Campbell, 1975.]

these elements easy to learn, whereas the other arrangement was very difficult to learn. Those sequences that were easy to anticipate can be described by a simple monotonic rule, either of the form $E(i) > E(i + 1)$ or of the form $E(i) < E(i + 1)$. The first rule says that each successive item is smaller than the last; the second rule says that each successive item is larger than the last. Those sequences that were difficult to anticipate could not be described by a similarly simple rule. For example, the nonmonotonic sequence 14-1-3-7-0 is described by a decrease from element 1 to element 2, an increase from element 2 to element 3 and from element 3 to element 4, and a decrease from element 4 to element 5.

Alternative representations for serial anticipation

There are a number of alternative representational systems animals could use in performing serial anticipation tasks. The rats could respond to changes in hunger, they could respond via temporal anticipation, or they could count the number of successive elements (Hulse, 1978). In recognition of the effects of pattern complexity on ease of learning, Hulse (1978) suggested a rule-based concept. Rats learn the rule that each successive item is smaller or larger than the preceding item. In contrast, Capaldi and his associates (e.g., Capaldi, Verry, & Davidson, 1980), have argued for an associative stimulus-stimulus representation. Finally, work from my laboratory suggests that rats form more complex representations of the sequence.

Increasing satiety. According to the satiety hypothesis, rats decrease their running speeds as their hunger declines progressively during a trial as they satiate. As they consume each element in the sequence they are less hungry and, therefore, less motivated to run quickly to the next element in the sequence. This hypothesis cannot account for the changes in running speed, however, because it does not explain why rats more easily anticipate a monotonic than a nonmonotonic sequence. First, the rats have consumed exactly the same number of food pellets in each type of sequence by the fourth run of the trial. Therefore, the satiety hypothesis would predict that both groups should anticipate the 0-pellet element with equal success. They do not. Second, animals run more quickly, not more slowly, when each successive item in the sequence is larger than the last, as Figure 6.8 shows. Third, no decrease in running speed is evident over successive trials of a day. Running speeds to the elements in the fourth presentation of a sequence are no slower than the running speeds to the elements on the first presentation, despite the fact that the animals have already eaten all of the pellets from the first three trials.

Temporal anticipation and counting. According to the temporal anticipation and the item-counting hypothesis, rats anticipate the 0-pellet element not on the basis of the previous elements, but on the basis of the time passed or the number of previous elements since the start of the trial. This hypothesis also fails, however, to explain the difference in the ease with which animals anticipate the monotonic and nonmonotonic sequences. Both the time and the number of elements in the series were identical in each of the two sequences. Further, the animals were unable to anticipate a final fixed element in the series when the earlier elements were randomly selected (Hulse & Campbell, 1975). Even in these random sequences, the final 0-pellet element occurred in a stable serial position and at a stable time.

Rule encoding. The rule-encoding hypothesis is based on the idea that learning of a pattern is easier when the pattern can be described in a simple manner. According to the strong version of this hypothesis, the rat anticipates each successive element in the sequence by applying the rule to the element just received. In a sequence described by a monotonic decreasing rule, each successive element is smaller than the previous element. The same smaller-than rule applies on every successive run. Thus, on the basis of the rat's memory for the previous element, it can anticipate that the next element will be smaller. In contrast, nonmonotonic sequences are described by more complex rules, and the animal must know its current position in the sequence in order to apply the correct rule; the next item is greater than the previous one at some points in the sequence and less than the previous one at others. From the rule-learning point of view, nonmonotonic sequences are more difficult to learn than monotonic sequences because non-monotonic sequences require more complex rules.

In support of a generalized rule representation, Hulse and Dorsky (1979) found that training rats with irregular patterns that conformed to a monotonic rule resulted in quicker learning of a new regular pattern that conformed to the same rule. Two groups of rats were trained with sequences that were either two, three, or four elements in length. The elements were 0, 1, 3, 5, and 10 food pellets. One group was exposed to patterns that were always monotonically decreasing. Table 6.3 displays the set of sequences presented to the monotonic group. A random control group received exactly the same elements in sequences of the same length, but the elements were scrambled into a random order. For example, if the monotonic group received the sequence 10-5-3, the random group received some other ordering of these elements, such as 10-3-5.

After training with these sequences for 70 trials, subjects were transferred to one of two five-item sequences. One group was transferred to a new monotonic pattern (16-9-3-1-0), and the other group was transferred to a nonmonotonic pattern (16-1-3-9-0). Transfer from the variable-length monotonic sequence to the fixed-length monotonic sequence produced the fastest learning of the fixed-length sequence. Transfer from the variable-length monotonic to the fixed-length nonmonotonic sequence produced the slowest learning. The two groups trained initially with the random sequences were intermediate in their acquisition of the fixed-length sequence.

Because the sequences used during the first stage of training were of variable length and were made of variable elements, their most salient consistent feature

TABLE 6.3 Sequences used by Hulse and Dorsky in the monotonic training condition

Four-element	Three-element	Two-element		
10-5-3-1	10-5-3	10-5	5-3	3-1
10-5-3-0	10-5-1	10-3	5-1	3-0
	10-3-1	10-1	5-0	
	10-3-0	10-0		

Source: After Hulse & Dorsky, 1979.

was the monotonically descending relation between successive elements. Hence, this experiment provided an optimal opportunity for rats to extract this monotonic rule from the sequence, and those in the monotonic group apparently did so. Learning the monotonic rule during the first phase of the experiment promoted their ability to learn another monotonic sequence. The random group differed from the monotonic group only in the relevance of the monotonic rule. Both groups received exactly the same elements. The random group had the same opportunity to become familiar with the elements that the monotonic group had, but it did not have the opportunity to learn the monotonic rule. It was slower than the monotonic group in transferring to the new monotonic sequence. These results suggest that the animals stored the formal properties of the monotonic sequence as part of the representation. This representation aided transfer to another monotonic sequence and interfered with transfer to a nonmonotonic sequence.

Association/generalization. Capaldi proposes to account for the same data through an association/generalization model. Running speed is controlled by the excitatory potential associated with the cues for that item. For example, in the sequence 14-7-3-1-0, the 14-pellet element serves as a cue for the anticipation of the 7-pellet element, the 7-pellet element serves as a cue for the 3-pellet element, and so forth. Each element in the sequence is both anticipated and serves as a cue for the anticipation of the next item in the sequence. The actual excitatory potential connected to a cue depends on a complex combination of factors. First, it depends on the element that the cue signals. Cues that signal large elements (e.g., 7 pellets) have high excitatory potential, cues that signal small elements (e.g., 0 pellets) have low excitatory potential. Second, cues gain excitatory potential through generalization. Animals respond in a similar way to similar cues. For example, the 7-pellet element gains some excitatory potential from its signaling of the 3-pellet element. It also gains excitatory potential from its similarity to the 14-pellet element (which signals 7 pellets) and from its similarity to the 3-pellet element (which signals one pellet). It also gains some smaller amount of excitatory potential from the 1-pellet element (which signals 0 pellets). The amount of excitatory potential one item gets from another depends on that item's independent excitatory potential and the similarity of the two items. A similar process applies to each of the other elements in the series. For example, the 1-pellet element directly predicts 0 pellets. In addition, it is most similar to the 3-pellet element, which predicts the relatively small 1-pellet element, less similar to the 7-pellet element, and still less similar to the 14-pellet element. Thus, the total sum of excitatory potential declines from the 14- to the 1-pellet element across a monotonic sequence. In contrast, in a nonmonotonic sequence (14-1-7-3-0), the 3-pellet element directly predicts the terminal 0-pellet element. This element is most similar to the 7-pellet element, which predicts 3, and to the 1-pellet element, which predicts 7. Hence, this element will have a higher net excitatory potential in a nonmonotonic sequence than would the 1-pellet element in a monotonic sequence. The result of the generalized sharing of excitatory potential is that the nonmonotonic sequence does not show a simple decline in excitatory potential over the course of the sequence, whereas the monotonic sequence does. As a result, the hypothesis predicts correctly that running speed should decline over successive items in a monotonic sequence, but not over successive items in a nonmonotonic sequence.

The usefulness of this representational scheme is not its ability to explain the data obtained by Hulse and his associates. In general, it cannot do so because it makes predictions that are inconsistent with the data (see Roitblat, 1982a). Instead, the hypothesis is important for the attention it calls to the similarity among elements in the sequence. Capaldi and his associates (e.g., Capaldi, Verry, & Davidson, 1980) have presented extensive evidence indicating that the magnitude of the stimuli used in a sequence plays an important role in the ease with which animals anticipate the sequence.

The rule-based and the association/generalization models differ in their emphasis and in the type of representations they attribute to animals. The rule-based model emphasizes the relationship among elements in terms of an overall generalized rule structure, such as monotonic versus nonmonotonic sequences. The subject is not assumed to represent explicitly in reference memory the elements in the sequence. Rather, its reference memory contains primarily the pattern with which they change. In contrast, the association/generalization model emphasizes the relationship among the specific elements in terms of paired associates and a generalized spread of excitation. Although the complexity of a pattern clearly affects the ease with which the animal learns it, the association/generalization model asserts that learnability is controlled by associative patterns rather than by the rules themselves. Sequences that can be described by simple rules also contain consistent patterns of generalization and association. Sequences that cannot be described by simple rules contain inconsistent patterns of generalization and association. Although both models differ in a number of ways, each asserts that anticipation of the next item in the sequence depends on the remembered size of the previous item. According to the association/generalization view, running speed is controlled by the cueing provided by the previous element. According to the rule-learning hypothesis, anticipation of the next item in the series is controlled by applying the rule to the previously received item. Whatever value is remembered in working memory for that item, the next one will be smaller in the monotonic-descending series.

Coherent sequence representation.   Work from my laboratory (Roitblat, Pologe, & Scopatz, 1983) indicates that both models need modification to describe what the rats learn when they learn to anticipate sequences. In one experiment rats were trained to anticipate a monotonic sequence (14-7-3-1-0) of food pellets. Once acquisition was complete, we tested them on occasional probe trials in which one of the elements in the sequence was replaced by a a 0-pellet element. Thus, a probe sequence would present either 14-7-3-**0**-0, 14-7-**0**-1-0, 14-**0**-3-1-0, or **0**-7-3-1-0. The crucial data are the rats' running speeds on the element following the probe 0-pellet element. Both models described so far predict that presentation of a 0-pellet element should disrupt performance because no element is possible that has a lower value—as predicted by the rule hypothesis—and, because the 0-pellet element has been learned as the final element in the sequence, it has no cueing function associated with it. We found, however, that occasional probes of this type had no effect. The rats' running speeds on the runs after the probe 0-pellet element were indistinguishable from their speeds on comparable runs of a standard unprobed trial. These results show clearly that rats use more than the single previous element in anticipating the next element.

Although the generalization is correct that rats more easily learn simpler than complex sequences, this learning does not appear to be in the form of paired associates between successive pattern elements nor in the form of a rule applied in an abstract manner to the previous element. Instead, the animals appear to learn about more global properties of the sequence that are not disrupted when a novel element occasionally replaces one element in the series. These experiments provide strong evidence that rats ultimately represent the sequence as an integrated series. It remains to be seen, however, how they go about forming this representation. The possibility remains that interitem associations and rules may both play a role in the formation of this integrated representation.

SEQUENCE DISCRIMINATION

Animals have also been trained in sequence-recognition tasks. The previously described experiments on serial-anticipation learning tested the ability of animals to anticipate a sequence that was always consistent from trial to trial and that provided feedback at each point in the sequence in the form of the value of the element at the end of the runway. In contrast, experiments on sequence discrimination test the ability of animals to discriminate one sequence of elements from other sequences of the same events, when feedback is delayed until the end of the trial.

One sequence discrimination experiment has already been mentioned (Weisman, Wasserman, Dodd, & Larew, 1980). Pigeons were required to discriminate a two-event sequence, designated AB, from several alternatives. The complete experiment used three different stimuli as events in the sequence. Stimulus A was a green light, stimulus B was a red light, and stimulus X was a dark, unfilled interval. Each stimulus was presented for a brief time and was separated from the other stimulus in the sequence by a short interstimulus interval (ISI). The sequence AB (green-red) was designated as the positive sequence, to be discriminated from all other combinations of the three events, that is, from AA, AX, BA, BB, BX, XB, and XX. A test stimulus was presented following each sequence. Pecks to the test stimulus following the positive sequence were reinforced; pecks following a negative sequence were extinguished. Discrimination was indicated by the difference in the rate at which the bird pecked the test stimulus following the positive sequence versus the rate at which it pecked following the negative sequence.

Pigeons in this experiment were able to discriminate positive from negative sequences after training. The negative sequences AA, XA, and all the sequences that ended with X were the earliest to be discriminated from the positive sequence, AB. In contrast, the birds had the greatest difficulty with sequences ending in B (XB and BB). Finally, the sequence BA was intermediate in its difficulty.

This experiment demonstrates that pigeons are capable of learning a discrimination that depends on the order in which two stimuli are presented. Discrimination of the XB sequence from the positive AB indicates that the birds' performance is not based on the second stimulus alone (recency). Discrimination of the AX sequence indicates it also is not based on the first stimulus in the sequence.

Schemes for performing sequence discrimination

Discrimination of the positive from the negative sequences requires the pigeon to compare the sequence being presented with a representation of the positive sequence. As in serial-anticipation learning, however, the birds could use many alternative schemes to perform this discrimination.

Retrospective scanning.   According to one scheme, the subject holds in working memory each stimulus as it is presented and compares the remembered list of stimuli with an analogous list of the positive sequence in reference memory. This is a retrospective scheme in that it assumes that the bird postpones its decision regarding the sequence until the test stimulus appears, at which point it "scans backwards" and compares the stimuli that had appeared with those in the positive sequence. This model is consistent with many views of working memory, with the hypothesis that temporal discrimination is the basis for sequence recognition, and with numerous experiments on human list learning.

Prospective conditional discriminations.   There is one major difference, however, between the sequence discrimination task and most human list-learning experiments. In experiments with humans, the lists are typically formed of novel items that had not previously appeared in the experiment. The subject must then remember each of these items in order to be able to reproduce them later. In contrast, in sequence discrimination experiments, the same small number of stimuli appear on virtually every trial. Therefore, as in delayed matching-to-sample, a pigeon performing a sequence discrimination experiment need not remember the characteristics of each stimulus, only its identity. In the sequence discrimination experiment described above, identification of the B stimulus at the start of a trial is sufficient to classify the sequence as negative. This provides a potential to greatly simplify the task for the pigeon and to greatly reduce its memory load. Table 6.4 describes a production system that would be adequate to discriminate the two-item sequences described above.

According to this scheme, the subject must be able to discriminate the stimulus events signaling the start and the end of the trial and those that make up the sequence. The first column in Table 6.4 shows the state or content of the pigeon's working memory before the stimulus listed in the second column is presented. The combination of a working-memory state and a stimulus produces either a change in the state of working memory or an action. The rules specified in Table 6.4 are contained in the pigeon's reference memory in no particular order. They do not specify explicit information about the sequence, other than the information embodied in the conditional structure of the individual rules. The memory system simply activates whatever action is appropriate to the combination of memory state and stimulus. Therefore, this scheme allows the bird to discriminate among sequences without having a coherent representation of that sequence. It is analogous to the scheme outlined above for the solution of a maze on the basis of associations between choice points and responses. The combination of the current memory state and the current stimulus correspond to the

TABLE 6.4 A production system for sequence discrimination

Memory		Stimulus	Memory production	Action production
Start	+	Green	Peck	
Start	+	Red	No peck	
Start	+	X	No peck	
Peck	+	Red	Peck	
Peck	+	Green	No peck	
Peck	+	X	No peck	
Peck	+	Test		Pecking
No peck	+	Any stimulus	No peck	No peck

stimuli of the choice point. The memory state produced by the production rule corresponds to the response.

Working memory contains information either that the trial is starting and no stimuli have been presented yet or that the trial is in progress and the current decision is to peck or not peck. Presentation of a green stimulus at the start of the trial causes a decision of PECK to be made and remembered in working memory. This is a conditional discrimination. Presentation of the green stimulus causes the bird to make one decision or another, depending on the current state of its working memory. Presentation of the same green stimulus in the context of the memory that another stimulus has appeared—represented by either a peck or a no-peck decision—results in a no-peck decision.

This prospective scheme differs from the retrospective scheme described above in important ways. First, according to the prospective scheme, the bird does not wait for the test stimulus to be presented before making a temporal discrimination; rather, it makes decisions as the sequence is presented. In fact, it is the decision, rather than information about the characteristics of the stimuli that is maintained in working memory. Reference memory contains only the rules or productions relating stimuli, decisions, and actions, and the information necessary to identify the stimuli.

With only two stimuli in a sequence, a memory for decisions (peck versus no-peck) is sufficient to produce appropriate sequence discrimination. With three-event sequences, however, such a scheme would be inadequate. A number of studies have used three-event sequences. Among the first was an experiment by Weisman, et al. (1980), in which a sequence of two colors (designated "A" and "B") was followed by the presentation of one of two line-orientation test stimuli (horizontal, designated "C" and vertical, designated "D"). These line stimuli replaced the white test stimulus used in the previously described sequence-discrimination studies. Hence, the line orientation stimuli served both as conditional test stimuli and as the third item in the sequence. The sequences ABC (e.g., green, red, horizontal) and BAD (e.g., red, green, vertical) were both positive. That is, the birds were rewarded for pecking at the horizontal stimulus if it followed the sequence green-red, and for pecking at the vertical stimulus if it followed the sequence red-green. The sequences involving repeats of A and B (AAC, AAD, BBC, and BBD) and the sequences ABD and BAC were negative.

Use of line-orientation test stimuli meant that the fixed relation between color and position inherent in the earlier procedure was now eliminated. In the first experiment (discriminating AB versus BA), the presentation of B in the first position meant that the sequence must end as a negative sequence. Therefore, the bird could make a negative decision on half of the trials based only on the first stimulus in the sequence. In contrast, inclusion of the line-orientation stimulus meant that trials starting with B could still be positive if the next stimulus were

A and the final stimulus were D. Only after the third stimulus is presented and identified can the bird make a decision whether or not to peck.

Acquisition of this three-event sequence discrimination problem was about as rapid as acquisition of the simpler two-item sequence. As in the other experiments, pigeons readily discriminated positive sequences from others involving the same stimuli. This discrimination would seem to require the birds to maintain in working memory the identity of the first stimulus until the second was identified and, if the second was not a repeat of the first, to maintain information about the identity and order of both until the line-orientation stimulus was presented. Hence, this task would appear to demand a retrospective decision process. Performance on this task can also be explained, however, on the basis of a prospective production system similar to that used to explain two-item discriminations. Table 6.5 shows the analogous production system for the discrimination of these three-event sequences.

The model described in Table 6.5 is similar to that described in Table 6.4. The first column shows the state of working memory before the stimulus displayed in column 2 appears. The major differences between the systems described in Tables 6.4 and 6.5 are the number of rules they contain and the number of memory states they assume. The two-event system contains two memory states: "peck" and "start." The three-event system, described in Table 6.5,

TABLE 6.5 A production system for sequence discrimination

Memory	Stimulus	Memory production	Action production
null	+ Green	green	
null	+ Red	red	
green	+ Red	red	
red	+ Green	green	
green	+ Green	null	
red	+ Red	null	
red	+ Vertical		Peck
green	+ Vertical		No peck
red	+ Horizontal		No peck
green	+ Vertical		Peck
null	+ Vertical		No peck
null	+ Horizontal		No peck

Note: Stimuli and responses are indicated by upper case, memory states by lower case.

contains three memory states. For convenience I have labeled these states with the names of stimuli (and "null"), but in principle they need not reflect information about the properties of the stimulus. As in the two-event system, working memory is in exactly one state at any point in time, and the only information the bird has about the sequence currently being presented is the current state of working memory. The combination of a memory state and a stimulus controls the transitions from one memory state to the next. For example, presentation of the red stimulus while the memory is in the null state causes it to change to the red state. Similarly, presentation of the green stimulus while the memory is in the null state causes a transition to the green state. The identification of the red stimulus while in the green state causes the memory to change to the red state. In contrast, identification of the red stimulus while in the red state occurs only in negative strings so it produces a return to the null state.

This scheme, like the two-event decision scheme in Table 6.4, allows sequence discrimination without a coherent, ordered representation of the sequence. An unordered set of transition rules that treat the sequence as a set of conditional discriminations provides it with sufficient information to support discrimination. In principle, a discrete-state memory scheme would be sufficient to discriminate any sequence of events from any other. As long as the positive sequence does not involve repeats of one or more stimuli, a sequence of any length can be represented using one memory state more than the number of stimuli in the positive sequence. More complex strings simply require more states.

Although these straightforward conditional discrimination models describe any set of positive strings sufficiently well to allow their discrimination, this does not imply that animals necessarily use this kind of system to perform these discriminations. Even strings as complex as sentences uttered by humans can often be described using similar "finite-state grammars," but these grammars fail to capture psychologically important features of the way people understand sentences. The key feature of the production models described so far is the assumption that each memory state corresponds more or less directly to a single stimulus. Each stimulus is treated as an independent unit. The positive string is judged to have been presented when the set of productions terminating in a peck decision has operated. A negative decision is made if any other set of productions has fired. If we are to argue that animals can actually represent the sequence as a unit, we must show that they represent the sequence in units that are more complex than individual stimuli.

Hierarchical sequence representations.   Some experiments from my laboratory on the discrimination of three-event sequences show that animals can use higher-level combinations of stimuli as basic units (Roitblat, Scopatz, & Bever, 1986). In one experiment we trained pigeons to discriminate three-item se-

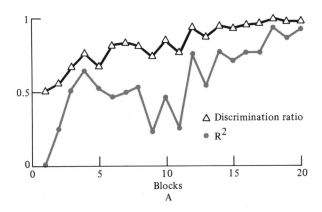

Blocks
A

quences made from colored stimuli projected onto a pecking key. The sequence ABC was positive (the actual colors assigned to A, B, and C varied from bird to bird); the other 26 combinations of A, B, and C, such as AAB, AAA, CBA, and CCB were negative. The same white test stimulus followed every sequence. Pecks to the test stimulus following the positive string were reinforced; pecks following the negative strings were extinguished. Discrimination among sequences was measured by the rate at which the bird pecked at the test stimulus following positive sequences relative to its peck rate following negative sequences.

Each individual stimulus can contribute to the control of responding by itself or in combination with the other stimuli in the sequence. For example, a pigeon using a primacy heuristic would respond to the sequence on the basis of only the first stimulus in the presented string. It would respond if the first stimulus was positive, but not if it was negative. In either case, the identity of the remaining stimuli would not affect the bird's peck rate. When there are three events in the sequence, then combinations of stimuli can also contribute to the control of responding in a way that is separate from the control by individual stimuli. For example, the combination of the first two stimuli in the sequence could control responding. The bird would respond whenever both of these match the positive sequence, but not if either is different from the corresponding stimuli in the positive sequence. The identity of the third stimulus would not affect the bird's peck rate. Instead of being all-or-none, the units can contribute to varying degrees. For example, the bird could increase its peck rate a small amount for every stimulus in the string that matches the positive sequence. If A in the first position, B in the second position, or C in the third position appears, then the bird pecks at the test stimulus. If two stimuli appear in the correct positions, then it pecks faster, and if three stimuli each appear in the correct position, it pecks still faster.

We used mathematical techniques to assess the control exerted by the seven possible units in a three-event sequence that could contribute to the control of responding: (1) the first stimulus (symbolized in Figure 6.9 by C1); (2) the second stimulus (C2); (3) the third stimulus (C3); (4) the combination of the first

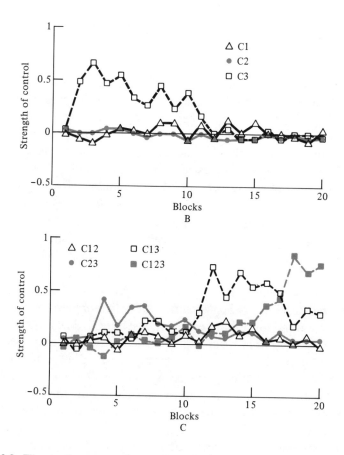

Figure 6.9. The performance of one bird on a three-item sequence discrimination task. (A) (*opposite page*) Two measures of stimulus control. Discrimination ratio is the ratio of responding on positive relative to negative sequences (rate to positive / rate to positive + rate to negative). A ratio of 0.5 indicates no discrimination; a ratio of 1.0 indicates a perfect discrimination. The R^2 curve indicates the degree to which the animal responded systematically to the various sequences in the experiment. A value of 0 indicates no systematic responding; a value of 1 indicates that responding was controlled perfectly by the sequences. (B) The degree to which the first (C1), second (C2), and third (C3) stimulus in the sequence controlled responding. (C) The degree to which the combination of stimuli 1 and 2 (C12), stimuli 1 and 3 (C13), stimuli 2 and 3 (C23), and the entire string (C123) controlled responding.

and second stimuli, considered as a single unit (C12); (5) the combination of the first and third stimuli, considered as a unit (C13); (6) the combination of the second and third stimuli, considered as a unit (C23); and (7) the entire string, considered as a single unit. Each of these units can contribute to the control of responding to various degrees. Figure 6.9 displays their magnitude of control. The more a unit controls responding, the more the bird's rate of pecking to the test stimulus depends on the identity of the stimuli appearing in the corresponding positions of the presented sequence.

225

During the early stages of training, the birds tended to use a recency heuristic. They responded more and faster if the third stimulus in the presented sequence was C than if it was either of the other two stimuli. After some amount of training, however, control by the combination of stimulus 1 and stimulus 3 replaced control by the third stimulus alone. In other words, the bird initially responded to the sequences on the basis of individual stimuli, then switched to responding on the basis of serially organized combinations of stimuli.

This experiment shows quite clearly that pigeons learning a sequence discrimination task do not perform it in the way suggested by the production models described above. Thus, they do not treat the stimuli in the sequence as independent units; instead they integrate combinations of stimuli into coherent sequentially ordered units. These higher-order units control discriminative performance in a way that is independent of the control exerted by the individual stimuli that make up the higher-level units. For example, an individual stimulus, such as B in the second position, might not increase response rate by itself, but the combination of B in the second position and C in the third, would increase responding. Interestingly, the higher-level units frequently consisted of combinations of nonadjacent stimuli. For example, Figure 6.9 shows that the combination of stimuli in the first and third position served as a unit. This further strengthens the conclusion that pigeons used true serially integrated representations in sequence discrimination.

The evidence obtained from pigeons performing sequence discrimination is consistent with that from rats performing serial anticipation. Both species in both tasks organize the events of their sequences into coherent, serially organized representational structures. Like people, animals are capable of forming and using a representation of a sequence that is different from a sequence of representations.

SEQUENCE PRODUCTION

Of the two sequence tasks described so far, one required rats to anticipate the next item in the series on the basis of the item or items just received, and the other required pigeons to discriminate sequences on the basis of stimuli as they were presented. The serial anticipation experiment gave the subject explicit feedback after each element in the sequence. In addition, both of these tasks required the animal to respond to the sequence on the basis of external stimuli that changed at each stage of the sequence. Another approach to studying the representation of serial patterns requires pigeons to produce a sequence of responses when the external stimuli are constant throughout the production trial and no explicit feedback is involved, either in the form of rewards after each response or in the form of explicitly changing stimuli. In these experiments (Richardson & Warzak, 1981; Straub, 1979; Straub, Seidenberg, Bever, & Terrace, 1979;

Straub & Terrace, 1981, a set of four differently colored keys is presented simultaneously to a pigeon—for example, red, white, blue, green. The arrangement of the colors on the keys varies randomly from trial to trial, but the pigeon is always rewarded for pecking at them in the same sequence, say red, white, blue, green, no matter what their physical order. The trial terminates if the bird pecks any color in the wrong order. With extensive training (Straub, et al., 1979), birds can learn to peck the four colors in order at a level of reliability, (62%) far above the accuracy predicted on the basis of chance (9%).

The types of sequential tasks we have been considering in this chapter have progressively decreased the amount of feedback available to the animal within the sequence. Both the sequence anticipation and the sequence discrimination tasks could be solved using the same stimulus-response chain scheme that is available to rats in a multiple choice point maze. (The fact that they appear not to use such a scheme is irrelevant at present.) Each subsequent stage in the sequence of these two tasks is accompanied by a unique set of experimenter-supplied stimuli. In contrast, performance on the sequence-production task is interesting, because it provides the opportunity to investigate the representation of serial strings in a situation without explicit sensory changes at successive points in the sequence. The set of stimuli are presented at the beginning of the trial and do not change as long as the pigeon continues to perform correctly. Therefore, the bird must either produce its own changing stimulus situation or represent the task in another way if it is to perform the sequence production task correctly.

Alternative schemes for sequence production

At least two alternative schemes that do not involve a coherent sequence representation are available by which a pigeon could perform the sequence production task. One scheme suggests that pigeons represent each arrangement of stimuli on the keys and the response pattern that goes with it. The other scheme suggests that they do solve the problem by using stimulus-response chains, but the stimuli are those produced by pecking at the experimenter-provided stimuli.

Configural hypothesis.   According to the configural hypothesis, pigeons learn a set of stimulus-response pairs. In each pair, the stimulus is the spatial arrangement of the four colors and the response is a patterned sequence of pecks at particular locations. Note that this hypothesis is not totally incompatible with a sequential representation; it merely argues that the important sequence is spatial, rather than temporal. Nonetheless, this may be an important distinction because a spatially configured set of primitive stimuli is what defines objects in the world (cf. Chapter 8), and the mechanisms responsible for processing of spatial configurations may be different from those involved in processing temporal configurations (see Honig, 1981).

Straub et al. (1979) tested the configural hypothesis. There are 24 possible configurations of four colors displayed in four locations. During training the pigeons saw only 15 of these configurations. When the animals were subsequently tested on the full set of 24 configurations, their performance was nearly perfect. Thus, there is no evidence that the particular spatial arrangements of the stimuli were a significant part of the animal's representation of the sequence. This finding has since been replicated by Straub and Terrace (1981), with a different set of birds and a more complex set of configurations—four colors displayed on six possible keys.

Response-produced stimulus-response chains.   According to a second hypothesis, the animal codes the sequence as a chain of stimulus-response-stimulus-response units such that its response to one stimulus produces characteristic feedback, which then serves as the cue for its next response, and so on. For example, each time the bird pecks at a color in the sequence it moves its head and beak closer to the key. The color on the pecked key then fills a larger portion of the bird's visual field than before the bird began pecking at that key or when it was pecking another color. This characteristic effective stimulus could then serve as the distinctive cue for its next response. If this hypothesis were correct, the bird would code the sequence as a series of unordered conditional rules analogous to "when red fills the visual field, then find and peck white."

Data forcing rejection of this hypothesis were obtained by testing sub-sequences (Straub & Terrace, 1981). The chaining hypothesis implies that a correct response to one stimulus is necessary in order for the bird to respond correctly to the next stimulus. Therefore, if any of those stimuli are missing, the chain would be broken, and the bird would not have a cue to direct its next peck. Its next choice should then be random. Straub and Terrace (1981) found that the birds could perform accurately, even when some of the stimuli in the sequence were missing and therefore unavailable as cues for the next response.

Following initial training with the entire array of four stimuli (designated "A," "B," "C," "D"), each bird was tested with sub-sequences of the pattern (e.g., BCD, ABD, BD, AD). The chaining hypothesis predicts that choice accuracy should be low with those sub-sequences, such as AD or ACD, that are missing one of the middle stimuli. It also predicts that choice accuracy should be poor on those sub-sequences, such as BCD, BD, and BC, that are missing the initial A stimulus. In these sub-sequences the chain either fails to be started, because A is missing, or it is broken before the end, because one or more of the middle stimuli is missing. Straub and Terrace, however, found that the pigeons' choice accuracy was above chance on all sub-sequences. This finding implies that the birds used a representation that did not require the correct performance of one choice in order to cue the next.

These results clearly indicate that the pigeons are capable of forming a representation of a sequence of four colors. Their ability to cope with remote transitions from one stimulus to a sequentially nonadjacent stimulus in the subsequence test indicates that they do not rely solely on paired associates between response-generated characteristics and subsequent responses, or between adjacent stimuli. Instead, they seem to represent each of the stimuli in their sequential position in a manner analogous to that found with other sequential tasks (e.g., Roitblat, Pologe, & Scopatz, 1983).

The Avian models.   Bever, Straub, Terrace, and Townsend (1980) developed a series of computational models that account quite well for the error patterns and response latencies reported by Straub and Terrace (1981). Figure 6.10 presents one version of their model, AVIAN-F. The model's main feature is the

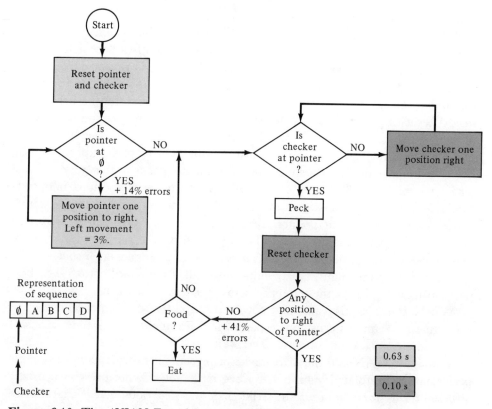

Figure 6.10. The AVIAN-F model proposed by Bever, Terrace, and Townsend to account for response patterns and latencies in the sequence production task.

assumption that the birds have a representation in reference memory analogous to a list of the entire sequence. The representation consists of one element for each stimulus in the sequence and an additional element serving as a "reset" position.

Production of the sequence requires three operations. One operation moves a "pointer" from one position on the list to another position on the list. Each movement takes 0.63 s. Another operation moves a "checker" from one position on the list to another. This operation is assumed to take 0.10 s. A third operation generates a peck. No specific time is allocated to this process; it operates in parallel with the others. When the pointer and the checker both point to the same element in the list, then a peck is produced to the indicated stimulus.

At the start of a trial, the pointer and the checker are both reset to the Ø position. The first decision point asks whether the pointer is at Ø. If it is, then the pointer is moved, and its position is again tested. On 14 percent of the tests, the system will decide that the pointer is at its reset position, even when it is not. When this happens, the pointer is moved one position to the right, and a "forward skip" error occurs. The bird erroneously skips the correct stimulus and pecks at the next one. If the pointer is not at Ø, then the system tests to see if the checker points to the same list element as the pointer. If it does not, then the checker is moved one position to the right and the test is repeated. When the checker and pointer match, then a peck is generated to the stimulus corresponding to the element indicated by the pointer and checker, and the checker is reset to Ø. After each peck the system checks to see if any elements remain to the right of the pointer. If the pointer is not pointing to the end of the list, then it is moved one position to the right and the tests are repeated. On 41 percent of these tests, however, the system erroneously decides that the pointer is at the end of the list when it is not. The bird then erroneously checks to see if the food hopper is available. If no food is present in the hopper, the system checks again for coincidence of the checker and pointer. Because nothing has occurred to move the pointer, a repeat peck is generated. The final source of error also derives from moving the pointer. On 3 percent of its moves, the pointer goes erroneously to the left instead of to the right. This results in so-called backward errors: The bird pecks at the stimulus in the sequence before the correct stimulus.

AVIAN-F is a sophisticated and powerful model that does an excellent job of predicting the error patterns and response latencies (the time between responses) of the birds trained by Straub and Terrace (1981).

Although AVIAN and the drift model of pigeon delayed matching-to-sample performance (Roitblat, 1984a, b, described in Chapter 5) are presented in very different forms, they contain some striking similarities. Both models characterize reference memory following acquisition as a static structure representing the pertinent events and the operations involved in processing them. For the drift model, this structure includes the memory map and the spacing of its points, the rules relating sample identity to comparison-stimulus choice, and the other rules of operation of the analysis and random-walk processes. For the AVIAN models, this structure includes the listlike representation and the processes indicated in Figure 6.10.

Working memory in both models is characterized by the location of a pointer, which moves through memory space in the drift model and through a list representation in the AVIAN model. In both models the content of working memory is the location of the pointer. Both models are nonassociative in the sense that they assume that stimuli are not represented in the form of interitem associations, but rather in the form of one- or two-dimensional quasi-spatial arrays. The AVIAN model could be made more similar to the drift model by asserting that the pointer does not move in discrete steps of fixed size, but merely moves with an average step size of just less than one cell in the representation. Such a mechanism could replace the decisions responsible for producing skips and backward errors. It might also partially explain the occurrence of repeat pecks, but this and any other benefits of such a translation attempt remain to be seen. In any event the possibility of nonassociative models of this type is intriguing.

REPRESENTATION OF SEQUENCES IN WORKING MEMORY

The above sequence tasks have been concerned mainly with the question of whether or how easily animals can form coherent representations of various sequences in reference memory. Each task has required the animal to learn about a stable sequence of events and respond according to that sequence. The tasks have varied in the degree to which they provide explicit feedback at each point in the sequence. The main function—if any—of working memory in these tasks is to allow the subject to keep track of its current position in the sequence, for example, by remembering the previous item. Other tasks, more analogous than those considered so far to human list-learning experiments, have investigated the ability of animals to represent sequences of events that change from trial to trial. Presumably, in performing these tasks, the information about the sequence that had been presented must be held in working memory.

Serial probe reproduction

Shimp (1976) trained pigeons to reproduce elements from a presented sequence. He trained them to peck at a three-item sequence of X-shaped forms presented in random order on the side keys of a three-key operant chamber. For example, the first X might be presented on the left key, the second on the right, and the third on the right; alternatively, the sequence could be left, right, left, or right, right, left, and so forth. Each X was presented for a fixed amount of time with a fixed interstimulus interval (ISI). A retention interval followed the presentation of the third X. Finally, a probe stimulus was presented consisting of a color on the center key. The color indicated which of the three serial positions containing an X would be reinforced. Red signaled that pecks to the side key on which the first X had appeared would be reinforced. Blue indicated that pecks to the side key on which the second X had appeared would be reinforced. White indicated that pecks to the side key on which the third X had appeared would be reinforced.

The animals could report with good accuracy which location they had pecked first, second, or third. Furthermore, a strong serial-position effect was apparent. When all three stimuli were presented for 0.5 s each, separated by a 0.1-s interstimulus interval, choice accuracy was markedly higher when the third item was probed than when the earlier items were probed. No primacy effect was observed unless the duration of the first X was increased to 4 or 10 s while the other stimuli continued to be presented for 0.5 s. Only then did the birds' choice accuracy when the first element was tested improve relative to its accuracy when the second element was tested. This experiment indicates that pigeons can represent in working memory, as well as in reference memory, a sequence of items.

In a similar experiment (Devine, Burke, & Rohack, 1979), two monkeys were trained to reproduce a list of two presented stimuli in a variation of the delayed matching-to-sample task. In this task, called delayed matching-to-successive-samples (DMTSS), two samples were presented in succession. The monkey's task was to respond to comparison stimuli in the same order, first choosing the comparison stimulus corresponding to the first sample and then choosing the comparison stimulus corresponding to the second sample. Three comparison stimuli were presented on each trial: one that matched the first sample, one that matched the second, and one that matched neither. If on the first choice the monkey correctly selected the stimulus matching the first presented sample, then it was permitted a second choice between the remaining two stimuli. Incorrect choices terminated the trial. This technique differs from the three-alternative matching task described in Chapter 5 (Roitblat, 1980) in that the monkeys saw two samples on every trial, and second choices were permitted only if the first was correct. In contrast, the pigeons saw only one sample on a trial and second choices were permitted only if the first was an error. Where three-alternative DMTS provides two opportunities to test the pigeon's memory of a single sample, the DMTSS task used by Devine, et al. requires the subject to make two choices in order to indicate what it remembers about the identity and order of two samples.

Two kinds of samples (and comparison stimuli) were used: four solid white shapes consisting of a triangle, an "X," a square, and a vertical line, all on a black background; and four colors, red, green, yellow, and white. A sequence of samples could then be either a color followed by a shape, a shape followed by a color, two colors, or two shapes. Similarly, the comparison stimuli could be two colors and a form, two forms and a color, three colors, or three forms. These various combinations of samples and comparison stimuli were important to the results. The monkeys made more errors when the two samples were both forms or were both colors than when one was a form and the other a color. Hence, similarity among items played a role in controlling the extent of the monkeys' memory for the sample sequence.

After extensive training the animals were able to perform the task with better than 80 percent accuracy at short retention interval durations. Choice accuracy depended on the particular combinations of samples and comparison stimuli presented. Some combinations were more difficult than others. Table 6.6 displays the various testing combinations and the proportion of errors obtained with each. During training, the monkeys had great difficulty if the two samples and the third, distractor, comparison stimulus were all from the same dimension, either all colors or all forms. In fact, so difficult were these same-dimension sequences that they were dropped from analysis for one monkey (Houdini) and only considered during a second test phase for the other (Don).

TABLE 6.6 Percent errors by stimulus combination tested by Devine, Burke, and Rohack

Stimulus combination	Subject	First choice		Second choice
		Sample 2	Distractor	
CCS-SSC	Don	16.15	0.00	9.52
	Houdini	25.63	1.25	11.11
CSC-SCS	Don	2.50	2.82	17.16
	Houdini	21.25	3.75	16.67
CSS-SCC	Don	2.60	0.42	14.72
	Houdini	14.38	1.25	8.15
CCC-SSS	Don	26.67	4.17	20.48

Note: C = color, S = shape; for stimulus combinations the first two letters indicate the first and second sample presented, and the third letter indicates the distractor. Don's data are averages of the first (all sequences tested except CCC and SSS) and second test phases (all sequences tested including CCC and SSS). The CCC-SSS data were only collected during phase 2. Second-choice error proportions were corrected for opportunity.
Source: After Devine, Burke, & Rohack, 1979.

The results of this experiment indicate that the animals maintain item and order information independently. First, the more experienced monkey, Don, showed a decline in first-choice accuracy only when the two samples were drawn from the same dimension. This suggests that as the delay increased, he confused similar samples, from the same dimension, with one another, but not dissimilar samples from different dimensions (cf. Roitblat, 1980). In contrast, the less experienced monkey, Houdini, showed a decline with all combinations. Second, choice accuracy was lower for both monkeys on trials with similar samples than with dissimilar samples. Third, 90.2 percent of both monkeys' first-choice errors were to the comparison stimulus corresponding to the second sample—order errors. Finally, even when all of the comparison stimuli and the two samples were from the same dimension, that is, all three were colors or all three were forms, Don still made almost six times as many first-choice errors to the second sample as to the distractor stimulus. Thus, these errors clearly reflect loss of order information, rather than loss of identity information. When errors occurred, they were systematically related to either the item or the order. Errors were not haphazard.

These results, and those described above for pigeons (Shimp, 1976), clearly indicate that these animals can represent both item and order information in working memory as well as in reference memory.

CONCLUSION: DURATION AND SUCCESSION IN ANIMAL COGNITION

The experiments reviewed in this chapter indicate quite clearly that animals are capable of using an internal clock to time the duration of events and that they are also capable of forming internal representations of sequences. Animals treat time as a stimulus. They can judge its length just like any other psychophysical dimension. The passage of time corresponds to no single specific stimulus, but rather to a change in stimulation. Thus, the timing ability of animals is interesting both by itself and because it implies that they can form abstract representations that cannot be reduced to changes in specific stimulus properties.

At least in principle, all of the experiments on discrimination of duration involved tasks that could have been solved by responding to changes in the effective stimuli. In every case, however, evidence was found that the animals were timing the experimental stimuli, not responding to changes in their effectiveness. Duration timing for animals is distinct from a simple response to succession.

Experiments also showed that animals are clearly capable of dealing with succession. In all of the experiments on sequences considered in this chapter, the animals performed tasks that could have been solved on the basis of representations of associations between two stimuli. In every case, however, the evidence is compelling that such paired associate schemes are not the basis for sequential behavior. Instead, animals are clearly capable of forming and using sequential representations reflecting at least large portions of the string to which they must respond.

Timing and serial organization appear to be an important feature of an animal's cognitive ability. Many events in the world contain serial structure, and animals seem to have evolved to represent this kind of information.

SUMMARY

Circadian timers control many of the daily rhythms of animal behavior. These timers depend on the functioning of one or more internal pacemakers. These pacemakers ordinarily become entrained or synchronized with external daily events, such as changes in the light level between day and night. Rhythmic behaviors, however, are controlled by the internal rhythm, not by the external stimulus changes.

Animals can also time brief events. Animals do not respond directly to changes in stimulus conditions—for example, as a result of sensory adaptation—but compare stimulus conditions with the time indicated on an internal clock, which can be used for many tasks and stimuli. The clock times up from 0 along a linear scale. It can be stopped and started as the task demands.

Animals also learn to locate events in time. They can learn to anticipate sequences of events and to discriminate some sequences from others. They represent the events in this task as items in specific temporal locations.

RECOMMENDED READINGS

Church, R.M. (1978) The internal clock. In S. Hulse, H. Fowler, & W. K. Honig (Eds.) *Cognitive processes in animal behavior.* Hillsdale, N.J.: Erlbaum, 277–310.

Fraisse, P. (1975) *The psychology of time.* Westport, Conn.: Greenwood Press.

Gibbon, J., & Allan, L. (Eds.) (1984) *Timing and time perception.* Annals of the New York Academy of Science, vol. 423. New York: New York Academy of Sciences.

Hulse, S. H. (1978) Cognitive structure and serial pattern learning by animals. In S. Hulse, H. Fowler, & W. K. Honig (Eds.), *Cognitive processes in animal behavior.* Hillsdale, N.J.: Erlbaum, 311–340.

Richelle, M., & Lejeune, H. (1980) *Time in animal behavior.* London: Pergamon.

Roberts, S. (1983) Properties and function of an internal clock. In R. L. Mellgren (Ed.), *Animal cognition and behavior.* New York: North Holland, 345–397.

Saunders, D. S. (1977) *An introduction to biological rhythms.* Glasgow: Blackie.

CHAPTER 7

Cognition and Natural Behavior

While comparative psychologists were developing a cognitive approach to animal behavior, based on the assumptions of information processing and the like, behavioral ecologists were developing a similar view, based on the assumptions of evolutionary theory. According to this view, animals are seeking to solve a maximization problem. Ultimately, this problem is the evolutionary problem of maximizing the reproduction of their genes.[1] More directly, this ultimate problem translates into many more immediate problems, such as maximizing the rate of food intake, the chances of finding a suitable mate, and so forth. From the perspective of behavioral ecology, animals are optimal decision makers who choose their behaviors to maximize the benefit they provide.

ANIMALS AS OPTIMAL DECISION MAKERS

Optimal decisions as trade-offs

Life is a compromise. It is a compromise among competing demands, among potential and realizable goals, and between benefits and costs. No matter how great its potential benefit, every behavior also has costs. The animal must always compromise between minimizing costs and maximizing benefits. For example, in order for an organism to reproduce, it must find a mate and obtain sufficient food to produce sperms or eggs. It could spend its time seeking food, or it could spend its time seeking a mate, but many animals cannot do both simultaneously. One of the costs of seeking food is a decrease in the time available for seeking a mate. One of the costs of seeking a mate is a decrease in the time available for seeking food. The animal must decide how much effort to spend seeking food and how much to spend seeking a mate. An optimal decision maker will choose the combination of time spent in each activity that maximizes its benefit. A little more food may help a female produce one more egg, but without a mate, all her eggs will be useless. Her success depends on the compromise she makes between mate seeking and food seeking.

If the organism had no competing demands—if it had only one life problem to solve—then its life (and ours) would be simpler. For example, if an animal's single problem were to get as much food as it could, then the most successful animal would be the one that found the most food. Even if life were that simple, however, no organism could ever take in food at an infinite rate and thereby achieve infinite success. Its life would still be a compromise between its "goal" of an infinite food-intake rate and its practical limits. Further, every behavior also entails costs as well as benefits. Finding food provides an obvious benefit, but it also costs the time, energy, and effort necessary to search for it. Some foods may provide more benefit than others, but they may cost more effort to obtain. The organism's success depends on the appropriate compromise between minimizing costs and maximizing benefits.

Behavioral ecologists recognize that all behavior involves conflicts of this sort. The premise of the optimal decision view is that organisms "choose" their behaviors so as to maximize their net benefit—that is, the benefit minus the cost. The behavior or set of behaviors that maximizes benefit is called, respectively, the optimal behavior or optimal strategy.

Optimality currencies

If an animal is to trade competing demands against each other—for example, the demand to find food and the demand to avoid wasting energy—it must have some common currency in which to value the competing activities. The animal's "goal," then, is to maximize this currency. The ultimate currency for any animal is Darwinian fitness, that is, the number of copies of its genes that it leaves through reproduction for subsequent generations.[2] The logic of this assumption derives from modern conceptualizations of evolution; according to which evolution itself is viewed as a maximization process: selection favors those organisms that are maximally successful at leaving copies of their genes for future generations (see Dawkins, 1976).

Although the ultimate currency is fitness, it is usually difficult to measure fitness directly. Animals may live a long time and may produce few offspring. As a result, measuring fitness, and the effects of various individual actions on it, is problematical. Thus, for practical reasons, many optimal-behavior models make simplifying assumptions. For example, they try to simplify the ultimate optimization problem by assuming that the animal's success in maximizing its fitness is related to its success in maximizing some other, more proximate, "currency," such as energy obtained per unit of time. The success of this simplifying assumption depends on the extent to which maximizing energy intake is consistent with maximizing fitness. In real life many more variables than energy intake may contribute to an animal's ultimate fitness. Fortunately, the simplified models, using an energy currency such as calories, have often been found to be close approximations to the actual behavior observed. Therefore, the simplifying assumption often seems to be reasonable. Future models, however, will have to take into account more of the variables that affect an animal's fitness.

Implications for comparative cognition

The optimal decision views introduced by behavioral ecologists are important to comparative cognition for a number of reasons (Kamil & Yoerg, 1982; Roitblat, 1982b; Staddon, 1983). Foremost among these is the shared assumption that evolution has equipped animals with appropriate mechanisms to allow them to maximize their fitness. For an organism to perform behaviors appropriate to its ecological niche, it must have adequate cognitive—and other—capacities to make the appropriate decisions. Therefore, we would expect that natural selection has resulted in certain cognitive specializations related to the animal's ecology. For example, an organism that makes its living by remembering the locations where it has previously fed is likely to have a better memory for spatial locations than one that always feeds in the same location.

Behavioral ecologists developed their analyses from the principles of evolution and their inferences regarding what an efficient animal ought to be able to do in its particular environment. These considerations led them to suppose that animals had the capacities and skills that they inferred were necessary. In many instances the behavioral ecologists were correct. Animals often do seem to have the capacities predicted for them. More recently, behavioral ecologists and comparative psychologists have combined their efforts in an attempt to understand both the nature of the animals' decision rules and the mechanisms by which they make those decisions (e.g., see Kamil & Roitblat, 1985). This collaboration has so far proved fruitful. Such collaborations are necessary because a complete understanding requires that we know both the mechanisms of cognition and how those mechanisms and processes perform in conferring a selective evolutionary advantage on the organisms that possess them.

One of the goals of comparative cognition is to understand the evolution of intelligence and cognitive mechanisms. In the remaining parts of this chapter, I will present some examples of how the analysis of natural behaviors can lead to insights on the nature of animal cognition and its evolution. The range of examples was chosen to illustrate both the ways that the natural behavior of animals can inform us about the mechanisms of behavior and some of the areas in which students of comparative cognition and students of behavioral ecology can work together. All of the examples concern either how an animal finds food or how it avoids becoming food for some other animal. First is an example of how animals choose their diet in the context of optimal decision making. This is followed by a description of the role of memory in foraging, then by a consideration of the benefits and costs of learning. Finally, I will describe two examples of animal communication that serve both as demonstrations of relatively complex cognitive capacities and as an introduction to the consideration of language learning in the next chapter.

DIET SELECTION AS OPTIMAL DECISION MAKING

MacArthur and Pianka's diet selection model

One of the earliest applications of optimal-decision theory to animal behavior was an optimal-foraging model arguing that animals seeking food are attempting to solve a maximization problem, obtaining the maximum amount of food in a limited time (MacArthur & Pianka, 1966). For example, an animal must find an optimal trade-off between the costs of spending time and effort in searching for and handling a particular kind of prey against the benefit provided by eating that prey, when it is found. The time spent searching and handling prey are costs. Food energy, measured in calories, is the benefit. Some prey will be more profitable than others. More profitable prey provide more food value for the same amount of time spent handling the prey.

MacArthur and Pianka (1966) divided foraging time into two components: the time the predator spends searching for prey and the time it spends handling the prey that it has found. They argued that a predator should always include the most profitable prey in its diet. If these prey are common, then the predator should concentrate exclusively on them. If they are less common, however, the predator may spend too much time searching for them. It should then broaden its diet to include additional, less profitable, prey. These additional prey will decrease the amount of time the animal has to spend searching, but, because they are more difficult to handle—for example, perhaps because they have harder shells—they will increase the amount of time the predator spends handling them. The diet that maximizes the rate of food intake will add less profitable prey as long as the decrease in search time compensates for the increase in handling time. A number of studies have found data that are in general agreement with this optimal diet model (see Krebs, Stephens, & Sutherland, 1983, for a review).

Constraints

Optimal foraging models, such as that proposed by MacArthur and Pianka (1966), contain assumptions about the currency in which alternative actions are to be compared and the constraints that limit performance. The currency in their diet selection model is the rate of energy intake per time spent foraging. These models also make assumptions about the constraints that limit the animal's efficiency. Among these are (1) "accidents" of its ancestry—for example, the "raw material" on which natural selection can operate; (2) limits on the speed with which it can change the form of its decision rules in response to changes in the environment; (3) limits on its ability to obtain and process information from the environment, including psychophysical limitations (counting, timing, and size measurement) and memory limits; and (4) limits on the availability of resources. Studies of optimal foraging cannot be used to test whether organisms are "nicely adapted to their environmental niche." Instead they seek to discover the competing demands and constraints an organism faces, and the means it employs to meet these demands. Many studies have discovered relatively close agreement between the observed foraging behavior and the assumptions of the model. Three examples follow.

Crows and whelks

Northwestern crows (*Corvus caurinus*), on the west coast of Canada, feed on shellfish, insects, berries, and the young and eggs of seabirds. Zach (1978, 1979; Zach & Smith, 1981) observed crows on Mandarte Island, British Columbia. He found that they hunt during low tide for whelks (*Thais lamellosa*), a kind of marine snail. When a crow finds a whelk, it carries the snail in its beak while it flies to a rocky area at the back of the beach. There, it flies up into the air and drops the whelk onto the rocks. If the whelk breaks, the crow can eat the meat inside; if it does not break the crow retrieves it, flies up, and drops it again.

A crow foraging for whelks faces clear trade-offs. Smaller whelks are more common and are easier to find than larger whelks, but the larger whelks are both easier to break and provide more food value. Dropping a whelk from a greater height increases the chances that it will break but requires the crow to use more energy to reach that height, and increases the probability that the whelk will bounce away or become shattered into tiny, difficult-to-eat pieces. Dropping whelks on the sandy part of the beach means that the crow has to spend less time and energy carrying the whelk to the rocky back of the beach but greatly decreases the probability that the snail will break. Whelks also differ in the brittleness of their shells. A crow could conceivably get a particularly tough whelk and spend a lot of energy trying to break it, or the bird could abandon a tough whelk and try to find a more brittle one. In short, efficient foraging depends on making optimal choices in four decisions: (1) the height from which to drop a whelk, (2) the size of whelk to drop, (3) the surface onto which to drop it, and (4) the number of times to drop a whelk before giving up and finding another.

Through calculations of the energy needed to fly to various heights and his own attempts to break whelks, Zach discovered that 5 m was the optimal height from which to drop them onto a rocky surface. On the one hand, flying higher required more energy but did not substantially increase the probability that a whelk would break. On the other hand, dropping a whelk from a lower height substantially reduced the probability that it would break. Therefore, although a lower than optimal drop height would require less energy on any given flight, more flights would usually be necessary to break a given whelk. Actual observations of the crows indicated that the average drop height was 5.2 m, slightly higher than Zach's estimate.

Whelks on the beach ranged in size from about 1 to about 5 cm. As Figure 7.1 shows, the crows chose only the largest whelks, which averaged 4.1 cm in length. Whelks of this size were not significantly more difficult to carry or manipulate, but they were more easily broken and provided more food value. Zach (1979) estimated that the crows expended approximately 0.55 kilocalories per whelk in finding, breaking, and eating it. The larger whelks provided approximately 2.04 kilocalories each. Therefore, each provided about 1.49 more kilocalories than it cost the crow to obtain it. Because of the difficulty in breaking the smaller whelks, a crow would have to expend about 0.90 kilocalories to find, break, and eat a medium-sized whelk, but because these snails are also smaller, the crow would obtain only 0.60 kilocalories from eating one, a loss of 0.30 kilocalories per whelk. Thus, it actually takes more energy for the crow to obtain a medium-sized whelk than it could gain from eating one. A crow who ate only medium-sized whelks would eventually starve to death! Zach also found that even when

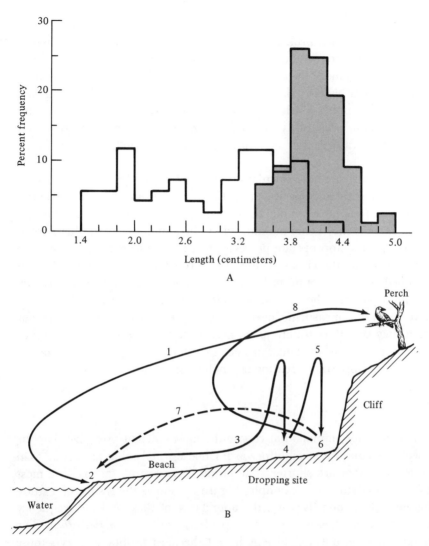

Figure 7.1. (A) The percentage of whelks of each size class that were present in the intertidal zone (open histogram) and the proportion in the diet (shaded histogram). (B) The activities of a crow capturing whelks; (1) flight from perch to water, (2) search for a whelk, (3) flight to dropping site and first drop, (4) handling of whelk between drops, (5) subsequent drop, (6) extraction of meat following last drop, (7) flight back to water, and (8) flight back to perch. [From Zach, 1978, 1979.]

the number of smaller whelks was experimentally increased, the crows continued to concentrate exclusively on only the largest sized preferring to switch to other foods rather than take smaller-sized whelks. Both these findings are consistent with the predictions of MacArthur and Pianka (1966).

Large whelks required an average of 4.36 drops to break. The crows continued to drop a whelk until it broke; they were never seen to abandon one whelk
and seek another. Zach found that whelks did not become brittle as they were
dropped. They were no more likely to break after five drops than after one drop.
Because finding a new whelk takes time and energy, the crows should always
prefer to continue dropping a whelk rather than to abandon it and search for
another with the same probability of breaking. Zach found that the crows followed this optimal strategy; they continued dropping a whelk, as many as 20
times, until it broke.

These findings illustrate how calculation of the costs and benefits of a behavior can lead to interesting and specific predictions. They imply that the ecological
analysis of the situation, for example, the optimizing criterion that Zach chose, is
close to the actual currency being maximized by the animal. In turn, this implies
that the animal has the appropriate processes and mechanisms to measure those
variables. For example, the crows "chose" to drop whelks from the height that
Zach determined to be the optimum height. Zach had the advantage of measuring height with a pole that he had marked off with a tape measure. The crows
did not have a similar measuring device, but the regularity of their behavior
indicates that they could accurately judge height without a pole. How animals,
such as crows, process the information necessary for these optimal decisions is
likely to become an important area for psychological research.

Wagtails

Crows are not the only animals that choose the most efficient prey size. For the
crows the selection rule was straightforward: Choose whelks that are about 4 cm
long and reject any that are shorter. The largest prey are not always the most
profitable for all predators. For example, Figure 7.2 shows the results of a study
on the relationships among fly sizes, the abundance of flies, and the frequency
with which they were chosen as prey by pied wagtails (*Motacilla alba*). The
most abundant flies were 8 mm in length, but the most profitable prey—those
that provided the greatest number of calories per second of handling time—were
the 7 mm flies. Those that were either longer or shorter than 7 mm were less
efficient sources of food. The size of the fly most frequently taken by the bird was
neither the most abundant nor the largest size, but the most efficient (Davies,
1977).

Sunfish

Werner and Hall (1974) studied the selection of prey of various sizes by bluegill
sunfish (*Lepomis macrochirus*) in a laboratory. They allowed the fish to search
for three size classes (small, medium, and large) of *Daphnia* in a large aquarium.

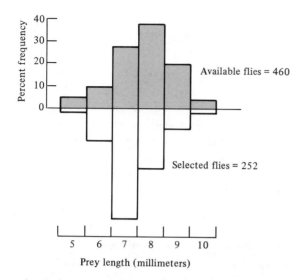

Figure 7.2. The relative abundance of flies in the environment (shaded histogram) and the frequency with which they were captured by pied wagtails (open histogram). [From Davies, 1977.]

Handling time for each prey size was about equal, and the *relative profitability* depended on the size of the prey. Larger prey were more profitable than smaller prey. The major variable was the density of prey in the tank.

MacArthur and Pianka's (1966) optimal foraging theory predicts that the range of prey taken should depend on the situation. When the most profitable prey are abundant, the predator should concentrate exclusively on the most profitable prey. (When they are less abundant, then it should include a broader range of successively less profitable prey until the inclusion of another prey type reduces the overall rate of food intake.) The sunfish conformed closely to the prediction of MacArthur and Pianka.

At low densities—20 *Daphnia* of each size—the sunfish were not at all selective. Instead, they took each size about equally, as predicted. Unlike the whelks, even small prey could contribute more calories than were necessary to obtain them. At high densities the encounter rate for each prey size was high, but the fish concentrated almost exclusively on the largest *Daphnia*, ignoring the smaller prey.

These experiments indicate that the decisions controlling the foraging behavior of crows, wagtails, and sunfish were quite sophisticated. All three predators allocated their search effort in a pattern that maximized their net gain in energy. All three were able to make profitability judgments and to base their behavior on these judgments. At this point we do not know too much about the mechanisms these animals use in making profitability judgments, and we should be cautious in attributing too sophisticated a cognitive system to them on the basis of these performances. Sometimes, seemingly complex judgments are based on a simple mechanism. An animal may use a "rule of thumb" to simplify its decision problem: All other things being equal, an animal with more information about its environment will do better than an animal without that information (Houston, Kacelnik, & McNamera, 1982; Krebs, Stephens, & Sutherland, 1983). Analogously, all other things being equal, an organism with a greater capacity to process relevant information would be better off than an organism with a lesser capacity. At some point, however, the benefit to be derived from an additional increment in information-processing capacity or in information would be outweighed by the costs (e.g., Janetos & Cole, 1981; Orians, 1981). Therefore, many animals can be found to use mechanisms that only approximate the ideal of an omniscient predator with infinite information-processing capacity. For example, Hubbard and Cook (1978) found that the parisitoid wasp *Neritis canescens* allocates its search time for hosts approximately as specified by an optimal decision model based on an ability to measure the rate at which it encounters hosts. Waage (1979) subsequently found that this creature's rule for deciding when to stop searching in a particular area is based on its habituation to the host's scent. Dishabituation occurs when the insect lays an egg on a host. It then continues searching in that area until it again reaches a certain level of habituation whereupon it leaves that area and searches another. A potentially complex variable—the rate of host encounters—is implemented by a relatively simple mechanism. Even these simple mechanisms, however, provide rich material for psychological analysis. It is no less interesting because it is simple. One important contribution of psychologists can be in identifying precisely the variables controlling the animal's behavior, the information it has, and how it represents and processes this information.

Diet selection is only one area in which optimal decision-making has been studied in animals (for a review see Kamil & Roitblat, 1985). The same kinds of decision rules have been studied in other problems animals face, such as life history strategies (e.g., whether to live long and produce few offspring per year or to live a brief time and produce many offspring at once; Horn, 1978), mating strategies (Parker, 1978), and territorial defense (Pyke, 1979), among others. Investigation of these problems and the mechanisms animals use in their solution is likely to be an exciting area of research during the next few years.

MEMORY AND FORAGING STRATEGIES

In order for foraging strategies to be successful, animals must have evolved the sensory and cognitive mechanisms necessary to implement those strategies. The crows studied by Zach must be able to judge height, whelk size, the caloric content of food, and so forth. Other foraging strategies also require specific cognitive mechanisms for their implementation, such as the sophisticated spatial memories evolved by species that feed on food sources that are distributed over an area and depleted as the animal feeds. For example, the spatial memory of rats has already been discussed in Chapter 5. In those experiments, the rats were allowed to obtain food from the arms of a radial maze. Finding the food at the end of an arm depleted that location, and the optimal strategy was to visit an arm only once. In solving this problem, the rats showed evidence of a well-developed spatial memory.

Honey creepers' spatial memory

Similar memory capacities have been observed in other animals that feed on a patchily distributed depleting food source. The Hawaiian honey creeper, or amakihi (*Loxops virens*), is a bird that feeds primarily on the nectar of the mamane bush, sucking the nectar from the flower clusters with its long tongue and beak. Each bird maintains a home territory, in which it nests and feeds, and from which it works to exclude other amakihi. Because a bird tends to remain in its own territory, researchers can keep track of the behavior of a single bird throughout the day.

Nectar is available only in certain limited locations or patches, namely the flowers. Once the bird visits a flower cluster and extracts the nectar from it, the plant takes some time to generate new nectar. Thus, the optimal strategy for the amakihi is to visit flowers only when they have nectar and to avoid revisiting them until the plant has had time to regenerate its supply of nectar. This is essentially the behavior pattern Kamil (1978) observed. The birds were more likely than chance to visit a marked flower cluster exactly once and less likely than chance to visit it either no times or more than once. The shaded bars in Figure 7.3 show the pattern of visits that would be observed if the birds were simply visiting flowers at random. The white bars show the actual pattern of visits Kamil observed. Like the diet-selection performances previously described, the amakihi were selective in the distribution of their foraging effort.

As with the performance of rats in radial-arm mazes, a number of different strategies could account for the amakihi's behavior. For example, the birds could adopt a uniform pattern of movement, perhaps always choosing flowers that are to the right of or below previously chosen flowers. Alternatively, they could somehow sense the presence of nectar in the flowers, for example, by seeing or smelling it, and only visit those flowers showing signs of having nectar. For example, many birds can see colors that for us are in the invisible ultraviolet range. Some nectars also absorb light in this range, so it is possible that the birds

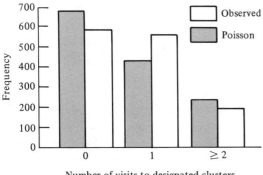

Number of visits to designated clusters

Figure 7.3. The observed and expected distributions of visits to marked flowers by Hawaiian honey creepers. The expected distribution of visits was derived from the Poisson distribution. [Data from Kamil, 1978; Figure from Roitblat, 1982b.]

could see nectar that would be invisible to us. Finally, the birds could leave some kind of indication on a flower after they have drained it. For example, some bees obtain nectar by cutting the petals at their base. The bees can then forage efficiently simply by avoiding flowers with freshly cut petals. Amakihi may use a similar strategy.

Despite careful examination, no evidence could be found for any of these alternative foraging strategies. The amakihi were clearly using memory for the flowers they had visited in order to avoid revisiting them. For example, other amakihi sometimes intruded into the territory under observation and "stole" nectar. These intruders were just as likely to visit a flower that had been visited by the resident bird as one that had not. In turn, the resident bird was also unaffected by the particular flowers on which the intruder bird had fed; that is, it was neither more nor less likely to avoid a flower cluster visited by the intruder than an unvisited flower. These data indicate that in determining which flowers they would visit, the amakihi were neither relying on signs produced by the presence of nectar nor relying on signs left by an amakihi. Instead, like the rats in the radial-arm maze, they were relying on their memory for where they had fed.

Caching and retrieving

Specialized memory capacities are also found in those species that cache or store food for later use. For many species, especially in temperate or desert habitats, food is superabundant for short periods of time and then scarce for the remainder of the year. Animals that can store food when it is superabundant and use it during the lean part of the year would have a clear advantage over those that cannot.

Animals could store food for later use in three ways. One way is to consume the food on the spot and store it as fat within their own body. Many hibernating animals employ this strategy. They increase their prehibernation foraging activity markedly and their body weight by as much as 50 percent. A second alternative is to cache, or store, food in one large fixed location such as the animal's nest. For example, acorn woodpeckers store many items in a single site such as a large tree. Retrieval of this type of concentrated hoard presents few difficulties, except, perhaps, for problems inherent in defending a centralized store and nest site against competitors, spoilage, and infestation. A third storage strategy uses distributed caches. The animal scatters its hoard in several storage sites, placing a small amount of food in each.

Scatter hoarding has certain benefits over concentrated hoarding. Among these are a relatively low probability that all the sites will be pilfered. Discovery of one site by some thief will not automatically result in substantial losses, as it would if the thief discovered a concentrated hoard and the owner could not defend it. Similarly, because the food is distributed in many sites, the chances for spoilage or infestation are also lessened. The major difficulty for an animal employing scattered hoards is to keep track of the cache sites. Birds of the family *corvidae* (crows, jays, nutcrackers, etc.) are widely known to use distributed caches and appear to keep track of their cache sites using memory. They store food, such as seeds, in many different sites during the fall and then retrieve it during the winter and early spring. Birds of the family *Paridae* (e.g., marsh tits and chickadees) also cache food in scattered hoards. Unlike the corvids, however, they typically hide and retrieve it within a single day. Both families of birds appear to rely on memory to retrieve the food they have stored.

Alternatives to memory.   One possible scheme that animals employing distributed caches could use as an alternative to memory is to store food only in certain types of locations. For example, they might store it only next to large rocks, on the south sides of trees, and so forth. An animal using this type of strategy would not have to remember any particular storage sites; it would only need to search sites of the chosen type. Alternatively, the caching animal could leave a mark of some kind, such as a twig damaged in a certain way or a feather on the cache site, and only search sites that have the necessary mark. Evolution would not favor either of these nonmnemonic strategies, however, because any animal using the same kind of recovery strategy could take advantage of the caches, retrieving the food without having stored it. A thief would have just as much success in recovering cached food as the animal that did the caching, but without expending the effort necessary to gather and hide the food. Thus, the "honest" animal would be at a disadvantage relative to a "cheater." Evolution does not favor the development of systems in which "cheaters" prosper (Maynard Smith, 1978). Instead, it favors storage strategies that allow recovery by the caching individual, while resisting theft by other individuals of the same or of competing species.

Nutcrackers.   Because of the disadvantages of employing nonmnemonic strategies to locate stored food, the use of distributed food caches would appear to require certain particular adaptations. For example, Clark's nutcracker (*Nucifraga columbiana*) feeds primarily on seeds of the white pine tree. These seeds are superabundant for only a short period during the late summer and fall. During this time of abundance, a single nutcracker may bury as many as 33,000 seeds in small groups of 5 to 6 seeds each (Vander Wall & Balda, 1977; Tomback, 1983). Field evidence indicates that the nutcracker retrieves and subsists primarily on these seeds throughout the winter and spring (Giuntoli & Mewaldt, 1978; Mewaldt, 1956). These birds also have beaks that are specially adapted for the extraction of seeds from pine cones and a specialized seed pouch under their tongues in which they can carry many seeds at one time. For example, the nutcracker depicted in the X-ray photograph in Figure 7.4 has 38 seeds weighing 30.6 grams in its pouch.

If it is to survive the harsh winter of its alpine environment, the nutcracker must recover between 850 and 1200 caches, somehow locating them, even after a 4- to 5-month delay. During the spring nesting season, nutcrackers rely almost exclusively for their food supply on seeds they retrieve from their caches. Therefore, these caches are clearly important to the animals' survival and reproduction.

The nutcrackers husk recovered pine seeds at the cache site. Tomback (1980) used characteristic markings left by the birds when they dug for the caches to estimate the number of probes they made and used the presence of hulled seeds as evidence that they had recovered seeds at that site. She estimated that 72 percent of the nutcrackers' probes for caches resulted in the recovery of seeds. This estimate may actually be an underestimate of the birds' success, however, because they sometimes carry seeds away from a cache site before husking them, and caches are sometimes stolen by rodents. A pilfered site would contain evidence for digging but none for seed recovery. Even this level of accuracy, however, is impressive.

Balda and Turek (1984) report a series of experiments that further argue that Clark's nutcrackers are capable of remembering their caching sites for considerable amounts of time. Each experiment consisted of two phases, a caching phase and a recovery phase, separated from one another by a long retention interval. The experiments were conducted in a large indoor aviary, whose floor was covered with several centimeters of sand. During the first phase, Balda and Turek provided the bird with a tray of seeds and allowed it to cache them in the sandy floor. They then removed the bird from the aviary for a period of up to 31

A

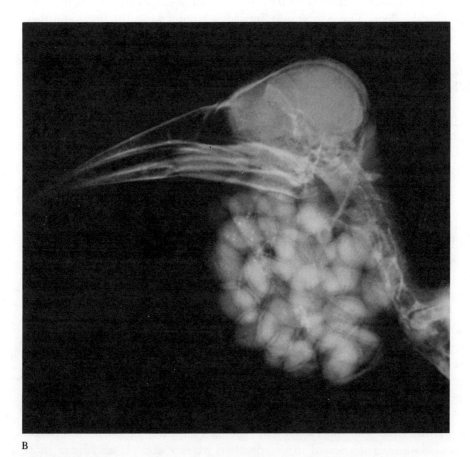

B

Figure 7.4. (A) Anatomical specializations of Clark's nutcracker include a long sharp bill with which it pries open pine cones to get at the seeds and a sublingual (under the tongue) pouch in which it carries them. (B) This X-ray photograph shows the nutcracker carrying 38 seeds weighing a total of 30.6 grams. [From Shettleworth, 1983. Photograph by S. Vander Wall.]

days. While the nutcracker was out of the room, they dug up all caches, recorded their location and the number of seeds in each, and reburied half the caches in their original locations. Digging up the caches enabled Balda and Turek to count the seeds stored at each site. It also disrupted any particular cues the bird might have left in the sand. Finally, by removing the seeds from half the caches, they were able to control for the possibility that the birds could smell or otherwise sense the presence of the seeds. They also took care to remove any signs, such as empty seed hulls, that might cue the locations of the caches and carefully raked the sand floor smooth. After the long retention interval, the nutcracker was returned to the room and allowed to dig up caches.

During the caching phase the bird carried some seeds in its seed pouch to a location on the floor. There, it would hop, look around, scan the floor, and then begin to insert the seeds into the sand with a jab of its beak. The nutcracker then used a swiping bill motion to cover the cache with sand and went to the food dish for more seeds.

When the bird was reintroduced to the room during the recovery phase, it first acted agitated, hopping from perch to perch and giving loud calls. Eventually it flew to the floor, hopping slowly about while scanning the floors and walls. Sometimes it would examine a spot on the floor and then either hop away or search for a cache. Searching was accomplished either by jabbing its beak straight down into the sand or by making a swiping motion in the sand with its beak. If it found a cache, the nutcracker typically loaded all the seeds into its seed pouch and flew to some other location where it opened and ate them. If it probed at a site from which the seeds had been removed by the experimenters during the retention interval, it often repeated the probe a number of times with increased vigor, sometimes extending this searching behavior to nearby areas.

In the first experiment reported by Balda and Turek, the bird made 26 caches in 22 minutes. After the 31-day retention interval, it recovered 18, or 69 percent, of these caches, using a total of 28 probes. Two probes were made to sites where no cache had been placed, and eight probes were made to cache sites from which the seeds had been removed. Probing accuracy was thus 90 percent in a room whose floor was covered with smooth sand. Later experiments added features to the surface, such as rocks and logs. The addition of these conspicuous features did not materially improve the bird's probing accuracy in experiment 2. In experiment 3, however, the features were removed during the retention interval. In the recovery phase of this experiment, the bird appeared agitated for a longer period of time than it showed in the previous experiments. It also spent more time hopping about on the floor without making any probes. When the nutcracker did eventually begin probing for caches, its accuracy dropped to 50 percent, but this was still substantially above chance. In experiment 5, the logs and rocks were replaced for the caching phase of the experiment. During the retention interval, however, all of the objects in the room were displaced 40 cm to the north. Under these conditions the bird made 27 caches during the caching phase; it recovered 8 of them with 44 probes during the recovery phase. Of the error probes, 15 were repeat probes to a cache site that the bird had already emptied, and 21 were to locations without caches. Of the 21 probes to locations without caches, however, 4 were approximately 40 cm north of an actual cache site, within 1 cm of a location that would have held a cache if the sites had moved along with the objects in the room.

The accuracy of probing in each of the five experiments Balda and Turek reported is far higher than would be expected by chance.[3] Because the bird probed at locations from which the seeds had been removed as well as at locations in which the seeds had been replaced, it is unlikely that its probing accuracy was due to any direct cues emanating from the cache itself, such as odor or marks left by the bird. Although the caching sites chosen in the various experiments overlapped somewhat, the overlap was also not sufficient to account for the nutcracker's high probing accuracy.

Kamil and Balda (1985) found further evidence that the birds were not retrieving their caches by hiding them only in specific conspicuous locations. They studied an additional four Clark's nutcrackers in a room containing 180 sand-filled holes. They controlled the caching sites the birds could use by covering most of the holes in the room with wooden plugs. All of the holes were open during the recovery phase of the experiment. Kamil and Balda found the birds accurately retrieved the seeds even when they, and not the birds, controlled the caching site.

Finally, Vander Wall (1982) allowed two Clark's nutcrackers to cache seeds in an aviary. When they were each later allowed to recover these caches, each bird was highly accurate in retrieving its own caches, but virtually never recovered those made by the other bird. This experiment also indicates that the nutcrackers were not responding to any signal produced by the seeds themselves in recovering the caches. If they had been using cache-produced cues, then each should have recovered the seeds stored by the other as well as its own seeds. These experiments with Clark's nutcrackers argue very strongly for a long-lasting spatial memory for the location of caches.

Marsh tits.   Similar hoarding and recovery behavior was observed in marsh tits (*Parus palustris*). In nature, these birds employ a hoarding pattern different from that used by nutcrackers. Instead of burying the seeds, tits tend to hide them in already existing holes, they also tend to recover the seeds after much shorter periods of time—typically measured in hours—than nutcrackers do. Cowie, Krebs, & Sherry (1981) provided 50 radioactively labeled seeds to marsh tits in Wytham woods. Many of the seeds were cached by the birds and then discovered by the experimenters using scintillation counters. The tits stored an average of 1.03 seeds per minute. When the experimenters discovered a caching site, they hid a control seed either 10 or 100 cm away, in as close to an identical site as they could manage. They then measured the time that the control and the cached seeds remained in their caching sites. Seeds that had been cached by a bird were recovered much earlier than seeds that had been hidden by the experimenters. This suggests that the birds remembered their storage sites and returned to them to recover their seeds.

Laboratory experiments provide even stronger evidence that the tits use memory to recover their cached seeds. Shettleworth and Krebs (1982) tested the birds in a large indoor aviary, depicted in Figure 7.5, in which various tree limbs and logs had been arranged. Holes were drilled in these artificial "trees" and covered with black cloth. The holes provided the birds with ready caching sites, and the black cloth ensured that an easily measurable behavior—lifting the black cloth—would be associated with every examination of a hole.

The tit was admitted to the aviary, which contained a dish full of hemp seeds. After eating a few, it began storing them in the holes provided. The bird was then removed from the aviary for a retention interval of 2 to 3 hours. During this time Shettleworth and Krebs removed the seeds from their storage sites and recorded their location. On control trials the seeds were moved to new holes during the retention interval. On experimental trials, they were replaced in the holes chosen by the bird.

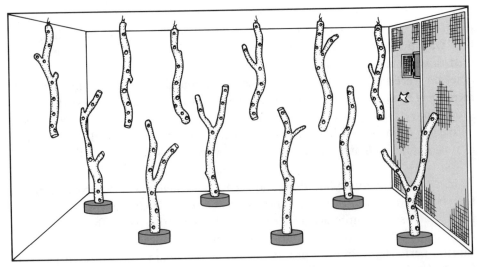

Figure 7.5. The experimental environment used by Shettleworth and Krebs. [From Shettleworth, 1983.]

Like the nutcrackers studied by Balda, the marsh tits were also found to rely heavily on memory in recovering their caches. In the first experiment, 97 potential storage sites were provided to store 12 seeds. The birds recovered a median of 65 percent of the stored seeds. They inspected 30.5 of the 97 different holes and made 4.8 errors while finding the first 5 seeds. Hence, their memories are not perfect, but this level of performance is far better than one would expect on the basis of chance.

Over trials, the birds were more likely to store seeds in some locations than in others, but this tendency was not sufficient to account for the accuracy of their performance. The birds also tended to avoid visiting holes they had previously investigated during the recovery phase but showed no signs of using a fixed search path.

On control trials, in which the seeds were moved during the retention interval, the birds searched significantly more holes and made many more "errors" than on experimental trials, in which the seeds were returned to the holes the birds had actually used to hide the seeds. Therefore, the birds were not finding seeds on the basis of smells or other cues emanating from the seeds.

In a second experiment, the tits were permitted two hoarding opportunities. In place of the usual recovery session, they were allowed into the aviary with a second bowl of seeds. After eating a few of these seeds they proceeded to cache the remainder. The birds showed evidence of remembering the storage sites from the first caching session by avoiding those sites during the second caching session. Two to three hours after the second caching session the birds were again allowed into the aviary to recover the seeds they had stored. During this recovery phase, they showed a preference for recovering seeds stored during the second caching session over seeds stored during the first. This is consistent with the possibility that some forgetting occurred during the retention interval. It is also consistent with the increasing likelihood that a cache in the field will have been pilfered, the longer it is stored.

Convincing evidence that the information about storage locations is maintained in the tit's brain was obtained by Sherry, Krebs, and Cowie (1981). One peculiarity of bird brains is that, unlike those of most mammals, they have no corpus collosum connecting one cerebral hemisphere with the other. Further, because of the placement of the eyes of most birds, the information from each eye feeds exclusively to one hemisphere and not to the other. Sherry and his associates had marsh tits store seeds with one eye covered and then tested their ability to recover those seeds with either the same eye or the opposite eye covered. When the same eye was covered, and hence the same side of the brain could "see" during both storage and retrieval, retrieval accuracy was high. When one eye was open during storage and the other eye was open during retrieval, the birds performed very poorly. Their left eye was unaware of what the right eye had seen. Other factors such as odor, markings left by the bird, or preference for certain sites were equivalent no matter which eye had been used during each phase of the experiment. The difference in performance when one eye is uncovered during caching and the other during recovery of the food makes the possibility of control by such external variables extremely unlikely.

The problems faced by a caching animal, such as the nutcracker or marsh tit, are very similar to those faced by animals, such as rats or amakihi, feeding on depleting food sources. In both situations the animal must keep track of the status of many spatial locations—that is, whether they contain food. There are some differences between these two feeding strategies. For instance, the caching species make their own storage locations. In order to avoid pilferage, they typically choose inconspicuous sites. In contrast, the foraging animals use food sites that are determined by the food (or the experimenter), not by the foraging animal. These sites are typically conspicuous. The main task of the foraging animal is to remember whether a given site has been visited or not. In contrast, the caching species must remember not only the status of potential cache sites, but also where they are located.

Nevertheless, in both types of animals, evolution has clearly favored the development of large-capacity stores for spatial information. The capacity of the nutcracker's spatial memory is apparently sufficient to allow it to maintain several thousand cache sites. From an evolutionary viewpoint, these large capacities may not be surprising. Given that an appropriate ecological niche is used, such a capacity seems necessary. From the viewpoint of comparative psychology, however, they are amazing and we have yet to explore their limits. For example, we do not know how general these memory capacities are. Can they be used to keep track of other sorts of information beside food sites? What kind of evidence of forgetting can we observe? How many sites can an animal remember? Are the physiological mechanisms responsible for such large-capacity memories similar to or different from those used in other kinds of memory? These and other questions will undoubtedly be important in the future development of comparative cognition.

PREY SELECTION AND IDENTIFICATION

Decision making, memory, and related cognitive processes are clearly critical to the ways animals make their living. For example, they must decide what prey to eat and be able to identify those prey. Learning and attention play a significant role in these decisions. In this section we consider the role played by learning about the characteristics of prey, the costs and benefits of generalization, and the role of selective attention in detecting prey. These topics have long been of interest in the laboratory. This chapter suggests some ways in which they affect animals in the field and raises some possible reasons for their evolution.

Certain animals, such as the great panda (*Ailuropoda melanoleuca*) or the koala (*Phascolarctos cinereus*), are so specialized in their diets that no learning is necessary for them to identify their food sources. Each of these animals eats basically one food. Other animals, such as rats and humans, are generalists in their diets. They will eat many different foods, depending on what happens to be available. Some of the items in their world make good food sources; others are either poor or actually dangerous. Learning plays an important role in determining what potential foods are acceptable and what are unacceptable. For example, some people find the idea of eating caterpillars or grasshoppers to be disgusting. Others see them as acceptable foods. Preferences such as these are clearly the result of the "tastes" and mores of the diner's culture. Animals show similar kinds of "taste" in their feeding patterns.

Generalists have evolved certain strategies for determining which foods are acceptable and which are to be avoided (see Zahorik & Houpt, 1981). For example, many studies with rats show that these animals are neophobic; they avoid consumption of novel foods. A rat confronted with a novel food will typically consume only a small portion of it and often will eat no other food during the same meal. If the animal becomes ill within a few hours of this meal, it will avoid eating any more of that novel food (Garcia, Ervin, & Koelling, 1966). The rat has formed a learned taste aversion. Similarly, it will learn to select a new food that is associated with recovery from illness. Rats on a thiamine-deficient diet will prefer a novel food over the familiar thiamine-deficient one and if the deficiency is corrected soon after eating this novel food, for example, by a thiamine injection, they will prefer this food over others that have not been associated with illness nor with recovery (Rozin, 1969).

An extensive amount of work has been done on the learning of taste aversions and preferences in animals, and a number of excellent reviews are available (see Barker, Best, & Domjan, 1977; Logue, 1979). Learning clearly plays an important role in determining what animals will eat and what they will not. We will turn instead from the factors that determine whether or not a food will be palatable to the role of learning and attention in the detection and utilization of prey.

Predators and prey: Learning and generalization

For most organisms, it is advantageous to avoid being eaten,[4] and animals have evolved a number of "defenses" to prevent this (see Curio, 1976; Edmunds, 1974). These defenses include signaling, alarm calling, rapid running, fighting, mobbing, and many others. The particular defense "adopted" by an organism depends on the characteristics of its ecology and its predators. Prey species evolve to resist predation, and predators evolve so as to maximize their ability to obtain prey.

Aposematic coloration and model-mimic systems.   Some prey species avoid being eaten by signaling conspicuously to their potential predators that they are distasteful or even harmful if eaten. Other prey avoid being eaten by concealing themselves among inedible objects. Against both kinds of defense, the predator is faced with the problem of discriminating—harmful from harmless and edible from inedible. Learning plays a definite role in these discriminations as well as in the effectiveness of the prey's defense.

Some prey species have evolved poisons, stings, or venoms that are dangerous or distasteful to predators. These species take advantage of the predator's ability to learn about and detect salient prey characteristics by also employing highly salient "warning (aposematic) coloration." Thus, these prey gain their protection by being conspicuous. Black, bright orange, and red are the typical colors of species using this kind of defense. The salience of these bright colors apparently increases the ability of potential predators to learn about the aversive properties of the prey, and the use of a common set of colors allows the predator to generalize from one prey species to another. As a result, the similarly colored prey all receive protection from the predator's experience with one of them.

Some animal species have taken advantage of predators' generalization by evolving appearances that mimic an aversive prey species with or without evolving its toxic components. When two species resemble each other and are both aversive, their similarity is called *Mullerian mimicry*. Individuals of both species gain protection from experiences a predator has had with the aversive properties of individuals of either species.

When a nonaversive species resembles an aversive one without actually having its aversive properties, their similarity is called *Batesian mimicry*. The aversive species is called the model, and the nonaversive species is called the mimic. The mimic gains protection from a predator's experience with the aversive model species. The protection conferred on these nonpoisonous species by resembling poisonous species is analogous to the protection from burglars conferred by placing in the window warning decals such as "These Premises are Guarded by an Acme Burglar Alarm" without installing a burglar alarm. Presumably, burglars would rather not attempt to break into a house that is protected by an Acme Burglar Alarm. Thus, the house with the decal gains as much protection from burglary as the house with the decal and the alarm.

One of the most familiar and most interesting model-mimic systems involves the monarch butterfly (*Danaus plexippus*). These butterflies serve as the models for Batesian mimicry by the nonpoisonous viceroy butterfly (*Limenitis archip-*

pus), and also show a third kind of mimicry called *automimicry*. Monarch butterflies gain their distastefulness from the particular kind of milkweed on which they fed as caterpillars. Certain kinds of milkweed contain a poisonous cardiac glycocide, which makes vertebrate animals vomit. In large enough quantities, it can actually kill them. Monarch caterpillars are immune to this poison but can store it within their bodies. After they metamorphose into butterflies, the poison remains effective for any vertebrate animal unfortunate enough to eat the butterfly. Other monarchs, raised on different plants, do not have these poisons and are quite palatable to birds. Nevertheless, these nonpoisonous monarchs gain protection because of their similarity to their relatives who are poisonous. This is called automimicry because the model and the mimic are both of the same species. A bird, such as a bluejay that has once eaten a poisonous monarch, will avoid all similar-appearing butterflies including both the automimic monarch and the Batesian mimic viceroy.

Brower (e.g., 1971) has found that a very hungry bluejay can be induced to eat a monarch butterfly. If this one was not raised as a caterpillar on poisonous milkweed, the bluejay will readily eat several other monarchs as well. If the same bird is then offered a toxic monarch, it will also consume it, but eating the toxic butterfly induces severe retching and vomiting. After this experience, some birds develop such a strong aversion to monarch butterflies that they actually retch on seeing one. Bluejays that have experience with distasteful monarchs will also reject viceroys on sight.

Viceroy and nonpoisonous monarch butterflies gain their protection from the ability of bluejays to learn about the visual characteristics of aversive butterflies and generalize to other butterflies. Once a butterfly is eaten, of course, it cannot gain any further protection from its appearance. Its similar-appearing relatives, however, do gain protection because they are less likely to be eaten. The mimics gain when a predator learns to avoid the model. The bluejay also gains protection from aversive butterflies by learning to avoid prey with their conspicuous colors. This protection is not without some cost, however. By avoiding monarchs, the jay also avoids other tasty butterflies, such as the viceroy, that it could safely eat. In fact, field and laboratory research indicates that the ratio of distasteful to tasty butterflies—like the ratio of houses with alarms and decals versus those with only decals—influences the extent to which bluejays and other predators learn to avoid models and their mimics.

Predators protect themselves from aversive prey by avoiding prey with aposematic coloration. If they generalize too broadly, however, they also deprive themselves of a potentially valuable food source in the mimics. Hence, as in other examples of animals foraging for food, there is an optimal trade-off between behavioral alternatives—between avoiding all aposematic animals and discriminating mimics from models.

Cryptic prey and specific searching images.   Aversive prey gain protection by virtue of their conspicuousness. Their salience makes it easy for the predator to learn to avoid them and other species that appear similar. Other species that are not poisonous or otherwise aversive to their predators gain protection by being inconspicuous. They resemble their characteristic background so closely that the predator has difficulty detecting their presence. This means of defense is called *crypsis,* and the prey who employ it are called *cryptic prey.* In many cases predators have to learn how to find such cryptic prey. For example, De Ruiter (1952) presented stick caterpillars (*Geometridae*) to hungry bluejays. These caterpillars ordinarily are found in woody areas, and their resemblance to small sticks make them very difficult to find. When the insects were presented to bluejays on a neutral background, such as on cardboard, they were readily taken by the jays, indicating that they could be easily recognized as food. When the caterpillars were presented among twigs, however, the birds did not take any of the now cryptic insects until they were "accidentally" encountered, for example, when the jays stepped on them. Once the first caterpillars were encountered in this manner, others were subsequently taken. It is reasonable to conclude from this experiment that the jays could identify a stick caterpillar as food once one was seen, but that they had to learn to see it among the twigs.

Von Uexkull described a similar phenomenon:

> During an extended stay at the home of a friend, an earthen water jug was always set before my place at lunchtime. One day, however, the servant broke the jug and in its place put a glass carafe. At the next meal, when I looked for the jug, I did not see the carafe. Only after my host assured me that the water stood in its accustomed place did the various glittering reflections off knives and plates suddenly fly together through the air to form the glass carafe. . . The searching image obliterates the receptor image. (Von Uexkull, 1934, p. 83)

Von Uexkull proposed a kind of perceptual-attention hypothesis to explain his reactions to the water carafe, and, as an analogy, to explain the means by which predators find cryptic prey. Since von Uexkull proposed it, more and more evidence for such an attentional process has been accumulating not only in cases such as that reported by De Ruiter on the changes necessary to first identify a prey item, but also in cases when predators search for familiar prey.

Luuk Tinbergen (1960) used the searching-image hypothesis to explain the results of a monumental study he conducted in a Dutch pine woods. He examined the foraging pattern of tits (*Parus* spp.) bringing food back to their nestlings. He and his associates placed cameras in the nest box and photographed or observed the parent bird everytime it came into the nest. During the spring and summer of 6 years, 52,509 items and 92 different broods were observed. Tinbergen and his associates spread cheesecloth around the box and collected feces produced by these birds. They then analyzed the feces for the remnants of the insects that the birds had eaten. A substantial number of insect species could be identified on the basis of the undigested fragments remaining in the feces. They also trapped insects in the woods and collected twig samples, which were then taken to the laboratory and analyzed for the presence of insects. In this way Tinbergen and his associates could determine the availability of the various insect species in the wood and the rate and pattern in which they were taken by the tits.

Tinbergen found that the birds tended to make several foraging trips in a row in the same direction from the nest, although not typically to the same locations. They also tended to bring prey back to the nest in runs. If they brought a caterpillar of a certain species on one trip, they tended to bring another caterpillar of the same species on the next trip.

During the course of the nestling season (spring and early summer) the availability of various insect species in the woods is constantly changing as some insects hatch, others pupate, and others become adults. If prey were captured randomly, then the bird would be expected to bring them to the nest at a constant rate that was approximately the same as the prey's frequency in the forest. Instead, Tinbergen found that the probability that a tit would capture a prey item varied depending on the frequency with which the item occurred in the environment. Edible prey species that were rare in the area were captured less often than one would expect if captures were determined solely by random selection. As a given prey species became more common, however, the tits eventually began taking them more often than one would expect simply on the basis of random selection. Finally, when a prey type was very common, they took fewer of that type than would be expected by chance. In other words, rare and very common prey types were avoided relative to their frequency of occurrence and prey with moderate frequencies were sought.

The relatively low rate with which the tits captured very common prey types can be explained if the birds need to maintain some diversity in their diets, for example, to balance nutrients. There is a limit to how many prey of one type a bird can eat, and no single prey can provide it with all the necessary nutrients (e.g., see Belovsky, 1978). The initial low rate of predation on rare prey types, and the lag until they began to be taken, is more interesting. Tinbergen was able to rule out a number of possible explanations for the lag between appearance of prey in the forest and their appearance in the birds' diet. It was not due to (1) rejecting prey after first finding them, (2) preferences for different layers of the woods as foraging locations (e.g., the floor versus low branches versus high branches), (3) differences in foraging techniques, (4) avoidance of novel foods (for example, the tits readily accepted painted mealworms), nor (5) changes, such as growth, in the size of the prey items (there was also a delay between the appearance of large moths, which do not grow, and the time at which they were taken heavily). Instead, Tinbergen attributed the change in predation frequency to learning by the predator about features of the prey. In particular, he proposed that, as a result of several random encounters with a prey item, the birds adopted a "specific searching image," which allowed them to detect more easily the presence of similar prey items. The specific searching image, he argued, was a "highly selective sieving operation on the visual stimuli reaching the retina" (Tinbergen, 1960, p. 332). At low prey densities the bird would be unlikely to encounter the prey by chance. Therefore, it would be unlikely to form a searching image for it and, consequently, would underutilize it. Once the density increased, however, multiple encounters would be more likely. A searching image could then form, and heavier predation would result. According to the searching-image hypothesis, the bird learns to attend selectively to the prey for which it has a searching image. It becomes more efficient at detecting those prey and, presumably, less efficient at detecting other prey.

Searching images were also studied in other birds (e.g., Dawkins, 1971). For example, Croze (1970) studied the foraging behavior of carrion crows on artificial prey. In one experiment he attracted wild crows to a beach on which he had placed a number of cryptically colored shells. Under each shell he had put a piece of meat. He used three different colors of shell: muted red, black, and yellow, colors that were similar to those of pebbles on the beach. As a result, the shells were cryptic against the background of the beach and difficult to find. On some days he used all three colors of shells. On other days he used shells of only one color.

The crows' searching was much more successful on days when only one shell type was present on the beach than on days when three shell types were used. Croze attributed this difference to the ability of the crows to form searching images for a single shell type on those days when only one was present, but not on those days on which all three shell types were present. Like Tinbergen, Croze argued that the formation of a searching image improved the crows' ability to find the cryptic shells.

Although both Tinbergen's and Croze's experiments are consistent with the hypothesis that the formation of a searching image results in an attentional change that renders cryptic prey more noticeable, they are also consistent with a number of other explanations. For example, finding one prey item of a particular type could increase the subjective palatability of another prey of the same type. This is analogous to the "salt-peanut" effect. For many people, eating one peanut increases the attractiveness of subsequent peanuts. The best support for an attentional change would be to show that the ability to detect cryptic prey improves when other factors are controlled. Such a demonstration has been reported by Pietrewicz and Kamil (1979, 1981) using bluejays searching for extremely cryptic *Catocala* moths. Their experiments employed photographic images of the moths projected onto a pecking key. "Positive" images contained moths; "negative" images did not contain them. Each positive image had a corresponding negative image that was identical, except that it did not contain a moth. Pecks to the positive images were reinforced with a piece of mealworm. Pecks to negative images were extinguished.

Pietrewicz and Kamil used two different kinds of moths, each cryptic on a different kind of background. *Catocala retecta* has gray forewings with brown and black markings. It normally rests head-down on oak tree trunks. *Catocala relicta* has white forewings with black and gray lines. It typically rests head-up on birch tree trunks. Both moths are cryptic on their respective backgrounds.

A session consisted of 24 trials. On each trial a single stimulus slide was presented. Half of the slides were positive and contained moths, the other 12 slides were the matched negative slides. Of the 12 positive slides in a session, 6 contained *C. relicta* and 6 contained *C. retecta* on their respective cryptic backgrounds. The birds had extensive experience detecting these moths on these slides.

The first 8 trials of a session consisted of "warm-up" slides. The remaining slides were either presented in runs or were randomized (nonruns). In the nonruns condition, the four slides with the *C. relicta* moths and their matched negative slides were randomly intermixed with the four *C. retecta* slides and their matched negatives. In the runs condition, all the slides containing one species of moth were presented first, intermixed with their matched negatives, and followed by all of the slides containing the other species of moth, and their matched negatives. In other words, the experiment either imposed a series of encounters with one species or intermixed encounters with two. In all other respects, the two conditions were identical. The same reward was presented, the same slides were used, and so forth. Only their order differed. If the jays were forming searching images as a result of repeated encounters with one species, and if the searching image functioned to improve their ability to detect cryptic prey, then their choice accuracy should improve over runs relative to that obtained during nonruns sessions. As Figure 7.6 shows, this is exactly what occurred. Choice accuracy averaged about 88 percent correct on runs sessions and about 75 percent correct during nonruns sessions.

These data strongly support the hypothesis that searching images result from repeated encounters with a particular prey and that the searching image itself is a change in the predator's ability to detect similar prey. The increase in detectability cannot be attributed to learning where to hunt; the same slides were used in both conditions and moth location varied randomly between slides. Similarly, it could not have been due to a change in the preference for prey type because all correct detection responses were reinforced with the same reward.

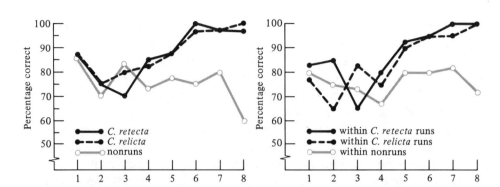

Figure 7.6. Mean percentage of (A) correct detection and of (B) correct rejection of a moth in a photographic slide during runs and nonruns. Position refers to the slide's position within the session. [From Pietrewicz & Kamil, 1981.]

Instead, the increase appears to be due to changes in the birds' attentional set. This conclusion is further supported by the finding that detectability of the second moth species in a runs session began at a lower level than the detectability of either the same species in the nonruns condition or the detectability of the first species of the day. Detectability then improved over the course of the run with the same species. Apparently, formation of a searching image for one moth species made detection of the second species even more difficult than if no searching image was being used. This trade-off also indicates that the formation of a searching image is a selective-attention process (see Chapter 3).

COMMUNICATION

The previous section described some of the defenses such as crypsis, mimicry, and aposematic coloration that animals have evolved to avoid predation and the strategies and processes that predators have evolved to cope with them—for example, searching image formation. The defenses discussed were primarily individual defenses. Other defenses depend for their success on the cooperation of groups of individuals.

Group defense

Many species of birds, primates, antelopes, and other animals defend against attacking predators by mobbing. For example, pairs of blackheaded gulls (*Larus ribidundus*) will attack a crow if it flies too near their nest. If the crow flies near the center of a gull colony, where several nests are close together, a substantial number of gulls may attack it simultaneously, driving it away from the nests (Kruuk, 1964).

Many mobbing species have developed special, easily localized mobbing calls, which they emit when a predator is nearby. Mobbing calls and other alarm calls that animals emit probably serve two communicative functions that aid survival. First, they alert other members of the prey species and call them to the location of the predator. Second, they signal the predator that it has been detected and that capture is likely to be significantly more difficult. In addition to alarm and mob calling, many species employ other signals of various sorts in their social interactions.

Communication as transfer of information

Communication can be roughly defined as action on the part of one individual that alters the probability or pattern of behavior in another individual. The resulting change in behavior is adaptive to either one or both of the participants. Communication is neither the signal itself, nor the response to the signal, but the relation between the two.

In fact, an adequate definition of communication, like an adequate definition of cognition, has proven to be elusive. Perhaps this is because communication is not a unitary concept. We cannot point to the essential features that are sufficient to define communication and exclude all actions that are not purely communicative. Instead, acts of communication bear a family resemblance to one another. Communication involves transmission of information from one organism to another. Furthermore, it is the information transferred, not the energy conveying the information (e.g., the sound waves) that is being communicated. For example, pushing a man off a bridge clearly affects the pattern of behavior he is likely to emit during the next few minutes (assuming he survives the fall), but this act is definitely not purely communicative. The information being transferred from the pusher to the victim is probably negligible in controlling the latter's behavior relative to the force of the push. In contrast, telling the same man to jump from the bridge is communicative. The force exerted by the sound waves is negligible.

The same problems about what constitutes communication occur when we study animals. For example, some of the pheremones excreted by animals fulfill a communication function, but other chemical excretions, such as the irritating spray of a whip scorpion, do not seem to be used communicatively, although they also affect the behavior of the recipient. Fortunately, there are enough clear cases that the study of animal communication is both interesting and fruitful. In any case, there may be nothing gained by attempting to divide behaviors into those that are communicative and those that are not. It may be more appropriate to consider a continuum in which noncommunicative behaviors, which provide some information as well as force, grade imperceptibly into communicative behaviors.

In this section we will consider two communication systems, both related to foraging and predation. To start we will discuss the so-called dance language of honey bees. Next we will examine the alarm calls of vervet monkeys. The first behavior system is used predominantly to support the bees' foraging for food, the second is used predominantly to avoid predators.

Dance communication of bees

Honeybees communicate to each other regarding the location and quality of food (see, e.g., von Frisch, 1967). When a worker bee discovers a food source near the hive, she returns, performs the "round dance" in the hive, and regurgitates some food to her nest mates, who follow the dancer closely, with their attennae touching her. The dancing bee runs in a small diameter circle, occasionally reversing direction. Between two reversals she may make two or three complete circuits, but sometimes she completes only part of a circle before a reversal. The dance lasts for a variable amount of time, ranging from only a few seconds to more than a minute. The round dance contains no directional or distance information about the food source except that it is fairly near the nest. Quality of the food source is correlated with the dance's vigor and duration. The scent and taste cues provided by regurgitation provide some information about the identity and quality of the food source, but not about its location. Because the food is located nearby, however, these cues are often sufficient to allow other workers to locate the food source.

As distance between the hive and the food source increases, the returning bee becomes increasingly likely to perform the "waggle dance" instead of the circle dance. The distance at which they shift from the circle dance to the waggle dance differs, depending on the species and race of bee. In the common honeybee (*Apis mellifera*), the waggle dance is used exclusively when the food source is more than 100 m from the hive. During this dance, as illustrated in Figure 7.7, the bee runs straight ahead for a time while wiggling its body to and fro and buzzing. At the end of the straight run, she turns in a semicircle, back to the starting point where she repeats the straight run. Semicircles to the left alternate regularly with semicircles to the right. The quality of the food source is indicated by the distribution of odor and taste samples of regurgitated food, by the vigor of the dance, and by the loudness of the buzzing sound that accompanies the straight run. Loud buzzing indicates a high-quality food source.

The straight run of the dance indicates the distance to the food source and its direction: the farther the food source from the hive, the longer the duration and

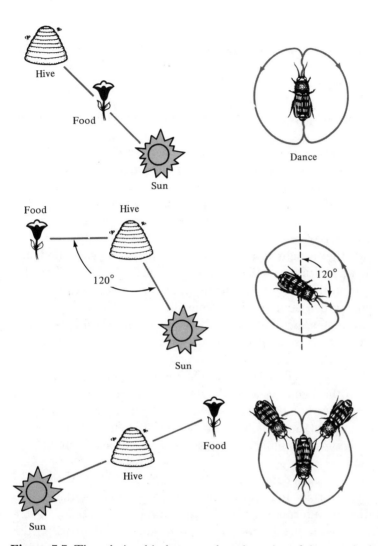

Figure 7.7. The relationship between the orientation of the waggle dance in the hive and the location of a food source. [After von Frisch, 1967.]

length of the straight run. Typically, the bee performs the waggle dance in the dark hive on the vertical surface of the combs. Navigation cues are communicated by the angle between the straight portion of the waggle dance and vertical line. A straight run that is oriented vertically indicates a direction directly from the hive toward the sun. If the food source is located 20 degrees to the left of the sun, then the bee's straight run is oriented 20 degrees to the left of vertical, and so forth. If the food source is located in the direction from the hive opposite the sun, then the straight run is directed downward.

Sometimes, on very warm days, the waggle dance is performed outside the hive in the light. Under these conditions the bee's straight run is always oriented relative to the sun, and hence, directly toward the food source. In other words, the frame of reference bees use to interpret the dance relative to the location of a food source has some flexibility. The relationship between the angle of the dance and the direction of the food depends on the conditions under which the dance is performed.

Gould (1975, 1976) has presented convincing evidence that the length and angle of the waggle dance within the hive is the actual source for direction and distance information. He took advantage of the bees' tendency to change the frame of reference for interpreting direction depending on the level of illumination. When bright light is present during the dance, the bees orient their dance relative to this light instead of relative to gravity. They respond to the light as if it were the sun. When the straight run of the dance is directly toward the light, the bees interpret it as indicating a flight directly toward the sun. When the dance is at an angle from the direction of the light, the bees interpret this angle as indicating a flight with a similar angle from direction of the sun. Gould painted over the eyes of some workers so that they were less sensitive to light than unpainted workers. Because it appears dim to them, these workers will now ignore a light in the hive and dance with respect to gravity. The unpainted bees, however, will detect the light and orient to it. They will interpret any dance as being made relative to the light. As a result, the painted bees will describe a direction relative to gravity but the other workers will interpret it as another direction, relative to the light, and go off in the "wrong" direction. This is what Gould observed. A significant number of bees arrive at a checkpoint in the misinterpreted location.

A bee performing a waggle dance may repeat it several times, with some variability each time. Recruits follow from 6 to 12 repetitions of the dance, apparently integrating the information from successive repetitions.

The foraging bees estimate the distance to the food source on the basis of the amount of energy it takes them to get there (not there and back). If the flight toward the food source is upwind from the hive, then they perform a longer straight run than if the food source is located downwind. Similarly, if the bee is artificially hampered in flight by the addition of small weights or by aluminum foil mounted on its thorax to increase wind resistance, it will also increase the duration of the straight run. Bees with these handicaps will systematically mislead their unencumbered hive mates.

The navigation and communication of honeybees requires them to have sophisticated cognitive processes. For example, they use a time-compensated sun compass. The location of the sun moves from east to west as the day progresses, and the bees are able to adjust their flight directions to take this movement into account. The dance language is clearly symbolic and reasonably flexible. The bees can transform angles described on a vertical surface relative to gravity or relative to a bright light into directions along the horizontal plane of the earth's surface. The dance is also flexible enough that its coordinate system can change under appropriate circumstances, such as when the dance occurs outside the hive or when a bright light is present in the hive versus when the dance is done on the vertical surface of a darkened hive. Furthermore, the dance can communicate a number of different food or water sources, and, under some conditions, it can even indicate the location of sites that are wholly unrelated to food. When bees are ready to start a new hive, workers go out and search for adequate nest sites. They use the same waggle dance to indicate the direction, distance, and quality of this potential nest site (Lindauer, 1955). Hence, it is probably appropriate to describe the bees' dance communication system as a semantic system that encodes symbolically various features of distant sites.

Alarm calls of vervet monkeys

Vervet monkeys (*Cercopithecus aethiops*), studied in the Amboseli National Park in Kenya, also show complex communicative skills (Cheney & Seyfarth, 1980; Seyfarth & Cheney, 1979; Seyfarth, Cheney, & Marler, 1980). This part of Kenya is a semiarid grassland dotted by occasional clumps of acacia trees and shrubs. Vervet monkeys give acoustically different alarm calls to each of their four main types of predators: leopards (*Panthera pardus*), martial eagles (*Polemaetus bellicosus*), baboons (*Papio cynocephalus*), and pythons (*Python sebae*). The acoustic properties of the calls are readily discriminable to humans and are unrelated to acoustic or behavioral features of the predators.

In general, the first monkey in a group to detect the presence of one of these predators gives the appropriate alarm call, and then all of the monkeys take the evasive action appropriate to that predator. Leopards generally attack by con-cealing themselves within bushes and springing on any monkey that happens to walk by. Hence, the monkeys are most vulnerable to leopard attacks when they are on the ground. Their typical response to either sighting a leopard or hearing a leopard alarm call is to run up into a tree. In contrast, eagles swoop down on monkeys that are in trees or in the open on the ground. In response to eagle alarms, the monkeys typically look up and/or run into dense bush near the ground. Pythons can attack monkeys either on the ground or in trees. The monkeys' usual response to a python is either to mob it—several monkeys attack the snake communally—or run away. Their response to python alarm calls is typically to look down and/or to approach the snake. Baboons, primarily the adult males, attack by isolating juvenile vervets from the rest of their group and then chasing them. Few attacks by baboons were observed (Seyfarth, Cheney, & Marler, 1980), so the typical response by vervets to baboon alarms could not be specified.

Playback experiments confirmed that the monkeys responded to the alarm calls themselves, rather than to the sight of the predator. For example, the alarm call for each type of predator may be coincidental, or it may result from the preparations the monkey must make to take the appropriate evasive action. (These preparations may be analogous to the sound people make when they take a deep breath.) According to this hypothesis, the only function of the alarm calls is to indicate generalized alarm, which increases the likelihood that the monkeys will detect the predator and act appropriately. If this were the case, then playing tape-recorded alarm calls should result in increased searching for predators, but it should not elicit any systematic evasive behavior.

Seyfarth, Cheney, and Marler (1980) recorded the alarm calls of identified individuals and played them back to the other members of the group. The researchers took care to avoid playing an alarm call when the recorded individual could be seen by the other members of the group. Direct visual cuing by the signaling individual was thereby ruled out. They also took care not to play alarm calls within 15 minutes of a naturally occurring alarm call or when a predator was detectable. Any response under these conditions could be a direct response to the predator, and not to the recorded alarm call.

The researchers found that playback of an alarm call increased the probability that the monkeys hearing the call would turn toward the speaker and the probability that they would visually scan the area. As expected, playback of leopard alarms also caused the monkeys to run into trees, eagle alarms were more likely to result in running toward cover or looking up, and snake alarms were more likely to result in looking down than were the other calls. This experiment clearly shows that the alarm calls themselves conveyed information about either the type of predator that was nearby or the appropriate type of evasive action. In other words, the calls had semantic content about predators even in the absence of those predators. The calls provided new information to the animals hearing them.

Seyfarth and Cheney (1980) studied the development of the various types of alarm calls. Infant and juvenile vervets, as well as male and female adults, were found to produce them, but the range of animals that elicited these calls grew progressively more narrow as the monkeys matured. Adult vervets produced the leopard alarm call primarily in response to leopards (74 percent of all leopard alarms) but also occasionally in response to lions, cheetahs, and jackals. Figure 7.8 displays the relative frequencies with which leopard or eagle calls followed the sighting of the various predator species. Infants were relatively unlikely to be the first to give a leopard alarm, but they were rather indiscriminate in giving eagle calls. Only 4 percent of infants' eagle alarms were made in response to martial eagles. Other species that elicited the call with equal frequency included storks, herons, geese, and pigeons (see Figure 7.8 on pages 272 and 273). In contrast, juveniles were intermediate in their selectivity.

Adult vervet monkeys classify the animals in their world according to predators and nonpredators. They further classify the predators more specifically, indicated by the different types of alarm calls associated with the different species of predator. Even infants were somewhat discriminating in their tendency to give certain alarm calls primarily in response to certain classes of potential predators. For example, although the infants did not discriminate as well as adults among avian species—they responded to 15 different species or objects—eagle alarms were given only in response to birds and never to any other type of animal. Their leopard alarms were restricted to nonprimate terrestrial mammals, and their snake alarms were restricted to reptiles. This indicates that even infants could make at least primitive taxonomic classifications. As they matured, they progressively learned to refine their representations of these taxonomic classes and to make more precise discriminations.

CONCLUSION

The natural behavior of various species requires sometimes sophisticated cognitive capacities. One major area of development in comparative cognition will be an analysis of these cognitive capacities that will include the features to which the organisms attend, the nature of the coding and memory processes employed, and their neural foundation. The success of this work, and perhaps of the discipline itself, rests on active communication between behavioral ecologists, whose main interest is in the function of behavior, and those psychologists whose main interest is in the mechanisms and processes of behavior. The work described in this chapter provides rich opportunities for further investigation by comparative psychologists.

Finally, communication between animals would seem to provide an area of investigation that is ripe for cognitive investigation. As we will see in the next chapter, communication is fundamentally important to our understanding of human minds and to the relation between human and animal minds.

SUMMARY

Behavioral ecologists have developed a cognitive view of animal behavior in which animals are seen as optimal decision makers. This view developed in partial independence of the similar view within psychology and from the basic assumptions of evolutionary theory. Many studies have shown that animals have the appropriate cognitive and sensory apparatus necessary for guiding their behavior in ways that maximize their rate of food intake. The optimal-decision view has proven very useful in understanding animal behavior.

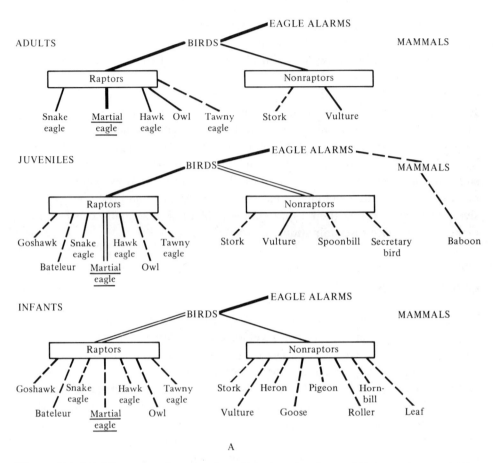

Figure 7.8. (A) The types of targets that elicited eagle alarms. (B) (*opposite page*) The types of targets that elicited leopard alarms. Both A and B show the increasing specificity of alarm calls with increasing age. The broken line represents 6 to 10 alarms, the double line represents 11 to 15 alarms, and the solid line represents more than 15 alarms. [From Seyfarth & Cheney, 1980.]

Animals also have specialized cognitive capacities that promote their survival in their particular ecological situation. For example, amakihi remember where they have fed, and some corvids, such as Clark's nutcracker, and some tits, such as the marsh tit, store their food and remember where they have stored it. These behaviors require remarkably large memory capacities. We do not yet know how general these capacities are—that is, whether they can be applied to tasks other than foraging.

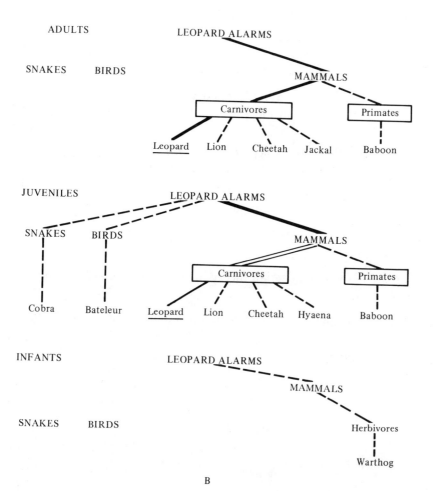

ADULTS

LEOPARD ALARMS

SNAKES   BIRDS

MAMMALS

Carnivores   Primates

Leopard   Lion   Cheetah   Jackal   Baboon

JUVENILES   LEOPARD ALARMS

SNAKES   BIRDS

MAMMALS

Carnivores   Primates

Cobra   Bateleur   Leopard   Lion   Cheetah   Hyaena   Baboon

INFANTS   LEOPARD ALARMS

MAMMALS

SNAKES   BIRDS

Herbivores

Warthog

B

Learning and attention play an important role in the relationship between predators and prey. Prey that are obnoxious have evolved salient color patterns that have made it easier for predators to learn to avoid them. Other prey have evolved cryptic coloration that predators have difficulty detecting. In turn, predators have evolved discriminative abilities that allow them to distinguish aversive prey from mimics and attentional mechanisms that enhance their ability to find cryptic prey.

Communication also plays an important role in the relationship between predator and prey. Honeybees communicate to one another regarding the location and quality of food or other resources. Vervet monkeys communicate with each other about the location of potential predators. Both of these communication systems appear to involve some level of symbolic communication.

RECOMMENDED READINGS

Dawkins, R. (1976) *The selfish gene*. Oxford: Oxford University Press.

Kamil, A. C., & Roitblat, H. L. (1985) The ecology of foraging behavior: Implications for animal learning and memory. *Annual Review of Psychology, 36*, 141–169.

Kamil, A. C., & Sargent, T. D. (1981) *Foraging behavior: Ecological, ethological, and psychological approaches*. New York: Garland Press.

Krebs, J. R., & Davies, N. B. (1978) *Behavioural ecology: An evolutionary approach*. Oxford: Blackwell Scientific Publishers.

Krebs, J. R., & Davies, N. B. (1981) *An introduction to behavioral ecology*. Sunderland, Mass.: Sinauer.

Maynard Smith, J. (1978) Optimization theory in evolution. *Annual Review of Ecology and Systematics, 9*, 31–56.

Sherman, P. W. (1979) Nepotism and the evolution of alarm calls. *Science, 197*, 1246–1253.

Shettleworth, S. J. (1983) Memory in food hoarding birds, *Scientific American, 248* (3), 102–111.

CHAPTER 8

Language, Concepts, and Intelligence

THE EVOLUTION OF COMMUNICATION

Communication is a necessary part of social living. Its value to the two communicative species described in the previous chapter is obvious: Social-living bees that can cooperate in finding distant sources of food or nest sites will be more likely to survive and reproduce than bees that do not. By avoiding predators that other monkeys have discovered, the vervet monkeys also gain an obvious survival advantage. These are only two examples of the powerful evolutionary advantages associated with communication abilities (see Sebeok, 1977; Smith, 1977, for more examples). As impressive as they are, however, there are still obvious differences between the communicative behavior of animals and that of humans.

Although some people view language as a uniquely human phenomenon, unrelated to the communication of animals (e.g., Lenneberg, 1967; cf. Chomsky, 1972), and see it as the very essence of being human, it is now generally accepted that humans evolved in essentially the same way as other animal species. Human language capacity must also have evolved from precursors that may be present in other animals and were certainly present in our ancestors. It is an important theoretical issue to discover the means by which our capacity for language evolved.

We have essentially only two ways to enquire into the evolution of language capacities. The first is to examine the fossil record of early hominids and the artifacts associated with their remains (e.g., Lieberman, 1975; Marshack, 1984). Figure 8.1 shows one possible "cladogram," or evolutionary tree, of the early relatives of human beings derived from such fossil records. The evolution of hominid species is very difficult to reconstruct on the basis of hard remains such as bones and artifacts. Any particular evolutionary tree is a conjecture that remains controversial. Reconstruction of the linguistic capacities of humans' ancestors is even more difficult because spoken language leaves no fossil record. By the time writing began, linguistic evolution was substantially at the point it is today.

The second approach to understanding the evolution of language is the comparative analysis of the communicatory behaviors of current species. Although no current species is truly ancestral to our own (see Figure 8.1), many apparent precursors of human characteristics can be found in current species that may have been present in the species that are truly ancestral to our own. Investigation of these apparent precursors can aid us in understanding the evolution of linguistic competencies.

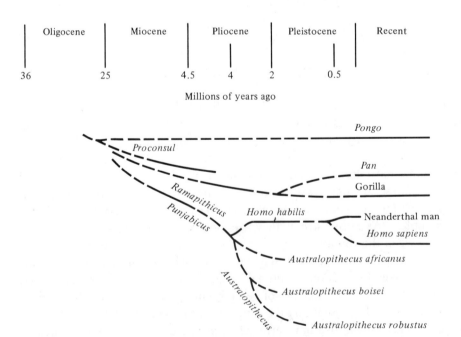

Figure 8.1. A hypothetical evolutionary tree showing the relationship among great apes and hominids. The genus *Pongo* includes orangutans, the genus *Pan* includes chimpanzees. Dashed lines indicate that the line of descent is speculative.

The comparative approach to the understanding of linguistic evolution has led to two lines of research. The first analyzes the "natural" communication systems of animals; the second studies the possibility that animals could be trained in a communication system that closely resembles human language. The first line investigates the precursors that are readily apparent as part of the animal's communication system. (Some of this kind of evidence was presented in the previous chapter.) The second attempts to discover those capacities that may be present in the animal's repertory but are not readily apparent in its communicative behaviors. Special training presumably allows the animal to demonstrate the presence of its capacity.

The relation between animal communication and human language

In order to detect the precursors of language in other species, we need some theory telling us how to identify precursors. This theory will develop in tandem with accumulating evidence, but it could start with an attempt to define the characteristics that distinguish language from other forms of communication. For example, Hockett (1958) identified 16 design features that he judged to be characteristic of human language, but apparently lacking in at least some animal communication systems. Hockett and Altmann (1968) later modified this set of criteria into five frames or dimensions. In part, they recognized that the discrete all-or-none criteria advanced originally by Hockett may be inadequate. Animals may differ in the extent to which they meet some criterion. Marshall (1971) proposed that there were at least three stages or grades of "language." At the lowest level, the "language" fulfills an indicative function. Expressions at this stage are simply responses in the sense of stimulus-occasioned acts: "The observations of significant correlations between 'states of the world' . . . and responses constitutes the evidence that something more than random babbling is going on. We can conceptualize this stage in fairly straightforward stimulus-response terms" (Marshall, 1971, p. 32). These responses simply indicate that some particular event has occurred. At Marshall's second level, the expressions serve a releasing function. The act of one organism releases behavior in another. Warning calls are in this class as are the clucks of a mother hen to call her chicks to her. The critical features of this level is that the performance of an expression is reinforced by the action of a second organism. At the highest level, the expressions serve a symbolic function. The organism is capable of using language symbolically. It "realizes" that it can "talk" about anything. There is a general rule that it is appropiate to say X, even if the organism does not know what X is. This stage is characterized by enquiry into names of things, increases in vocabulary, and the ability to perform an act of judgment and to express that judgment by means of a proposition. In more than a simple stimulus-response sense, the expressions represent the objects and events they are about.

Five paralinguistic features.   Although proposals such as Hockett's and Marshall's are attractive, they are not without problems. For example, how do we determine whether an animal *realizes* that it can talk about anything it perceives? It is difficult to develop any criteria that will accept human language and reject all other forms of communication, except the definition that human language is the communication system used by humans. Like communication, language resists strict definitions. We can, however, identify a number of characteristics of language that, while not definitional, are typical of human language and present to greater or lesser degrees in other communication systems. These features include reference, grammar, productivity, situational freedom, and communication of new information.

> **Reference:** The organism has a lexicon of arbitrary signals that symbolically stand for objects, events, concepts, and features. Organisms divide the world into categories and label those categories with symbols from the lexicon. At the highest level, the symbols not only refer to objects, and so forth, but they have meaning that goes beyond immediate stimulus-response connections.

> **Grammar:** Language structure can be described by a finite list of rules that can be used to produce an indefinitely large number of expressions. These rules control the meaning of a string of symbols. The same symbols in different orders—or with different inflection patterns—can express different meanings. For example, the sentence, "John hit Mary" is different from the sentence, "Mary hit John." Knowing a language is knowing the rules; it is not knowing every possible expression in the language.

> **Productivity:** Novel ideas can be expressed. The grammar can be used to produce novel, meaningful expressions.

> **Situational freedom:** Expressions are not fixed in the stimulus conditions that elicit them. They are not a reflexlike fixed response to a fixed class of stimuli. Prevarication (lying) provides evidence for this property, as does discussion of events displaced in space and time.

> **Communication of new information:** The sender provides information to the receiver that the receiver did not have. The sender does not simply repeat expressions used by the other member in the conversation.

I have chosen to emphasize these features because they seem to summarize a substantial amount of the thinking on the relationship between animal communication and human language and because many studies involving attempts to teach a humanlike language to animals have explicitly examined them. These features do not constitute a criterion for deciding whether or not an animal has language; they are simply some important ways in which humans and animals may or may not differ. It is probably fundamentally misleading to ask whether the communication behavior of some animal is truly language. Instead, it will probably be more rewarding in the long run to investigate the characteristics of animal communication, whether natural or human-trained, as features of a communication system. This will help us to understand both animal communication and our own.

The traditional ethological view of animal communication

According to the traditional view of animal communication, it involves only graded signals that communicate only about the emotional states and immediate needs of the organism. For example, some baboons and mandrills develop a characteristic, brightly colored "sexual skin" as a result of their physiological readiness to mate. This sexual skin communicates sexual readiness to potential mates, but it is the purely reflexive product of the animal's physiological state. Traditional ethology treats all forms of animal communication similarly as by-products of the communicator's physiological state. According to this view, the communication function of the behavior is either incidental or a later evolutionary adaptation, benefiting from being able to respond to the physiological state of another.

Those communicatory acts that are not so obviously connected to patterns in the animals' physiology were attributed to reflexlike mechanisms called "fixed-action patterns" (Tinbergen, 1951). A "sign stimulus," such as the sight of a competing male, releases a fixed sequence of behaviors. The sign stimulus does not cause the behavior; rather it unlocks it by affecting a certain area of the brain (the innate-releasing mechanism) in the same way that a key allows a locked door to open or the pull of the handle permits a toilet to flush. The unlocked behavior, such as the head-bobbing display of certain lizards (See Barlow, 1977), can itself function as a releasing stimulus. The performance of a fixed-action pattern by one individual can elicit a fixed-action pattern in another animal. This fixed-action pattern then releases another behavior in the first animal, and so forth. In this way long "conversations" can be produced in a simple manner analogous to a reflex chain.

Natural symbolic communication by animals

More recent thinking in ethology, especially as influenced by recent developments in behavioral ecology, has deemphasized a reflex-based approach to behavior in favor of one that emphasizes its informational properties (see Chapter 7). In this view animal communication conveys information from one organism to the other in a way that serves the adaptive needs of one, the other, or both organisms (See Smith, 1977). Whereas some communications, such as blushing in humans, are undoubtedly reflexively produced, not all communication can be similarly characterized. The behaviors that were formerly thought to be released by sign stimuli were found to be neither so fixed as the name "fixed action pattern" would imply nor were they as reflexively elicited. Animals can often be observed to make widely different responses to the same stimulus, depending on the context in which that signal arose. For example, a threat display of a monkey will have different effects on other monkeys depending on whether they are more or less dominant than the displaying monkey.

The data reviewed in the previous chapter provide what seems to be strong evidence for symbolic animal communication. For example, dancing bees typically signal the type of food source by regurgitating small amounts of food, but they signal its direction and distance by the pattern and direction of their dance. Type of food is communicated in an apparently nonsymbolic manner, but direction and distance information are clearly symbolically encoded. Bees use the same dance to communicate about the location and quality of a nest site that they use to communicate about food sites. Their communication about nest sites, however, must be wholly symbolic, because the bee has nothing to regurgitate. All information about the potential nest site must be contained in the pattern and vigor of the dance.

Whether the bee's dance is about food or nesting locations, its object is distant from the hive and from the dance. This displacement provides evidence for symbolic reference. The dance's flexibility in its reference provides evidence for situational freedom. Because the bees following the dance have not yet visited the site about which the scout is dancing, but are able to do so afterward, the dance clearly provides new information. In summary, the dance "language" appears to share three important features with human language: reference—although apparently limited—situational freedom, and the communication of new information. Productivity and the use of a grammar have not, however, been demonstrated.

Reference in vervet monkey communication is indicated by the specificity with which adult monkeys use calls and the apparent development of a classification system as the infant monkey matures. Similarly, playback experiments indicate that a monkey's alarm calls typically provide new information to other monkeys hearing them.

Other suggestive evidence for symbolic referential communication in non-human primates is seen in some of the sexual behavior of pygmy chimpanzees (*Pan paniscus*). Males in captivity have been observed to use certain hand signals to direct the female into various copulatory positions (Savage-Rumbaugh, Wilkerson, & Bakeman, 1977). Some of these signals involve touching the female, but others are made from a distance. No evidence has yet been offered suggesting the use of a grammar, productivity, hierarchical structure, or situational freedom in vervet monkey communication or in the sexual communication of pygmy chimpanzees.

Other animals do provide data indicating that they may use certain kinds of grammars and hierarchical organizations. For example, many bird songs consist of sequences of syllables organized into phrases and songs. For some species the repertory consists of a number of songs, each made from rule-governed rearrangements of basic elements. Most of the components in the song of the mistle thrush (*Turdus viscivorus*) are not repeated, whereas others are always repeated (Isaac & Marler, 1963). In contrast, the song of the olive-backed thrush (*Hylocichla ustulata*) tends to contain a sequence of elements, in which each element is a variation on the preceding one (Nelson, 1973). Unlike human languages, however, there is no evidence that the rule-governed variations in song pattern are associated with differences in song meaning or function (cf. Kroodsma, 1980).

Dennett (1983) quotes an anecdotal observation (by Seyfarth) of lying by vervet monkeys, which may indicate situational freedom. Two bands of monkeys were engaged in a territorial skirmish. One group was slowly losing ground to the other, until one of the monkeys on the losing side suddenly gave a leopard call, causing all of the monkeys to take up the cry and head for the trees—their typical leopard-evasion technique. No leopards could be observed at the time. The result of this maneuver was a sudden truce between the two bands. The losing side then regained the ground it had lost.

The status of the vervet monkey observation is mere anecdote. Except second (and now third) hand, it has not been reported in the scientific literature and may not pass scrutiny even if it were. It does illustrate, however, the kind of evidence one could use to establish that animal communications show situational freedom.

Under more controlled conditions, Woodruff & Premack (1979) report the development of lying by a language-trained chimpanzee. The chimps in this experiment were exposed to two kinds of experimental "trainers." The "good guy" wore regular lab clothes and shared any food he found with the chimp being tested. The "bad guy" wore dark glasses and a bandit's mask. He ate any food that he found. During an experimental trial, the chimp was shown food being hidden in one of two containers. The chimp was then restrained behind a wire mesh partition and could see the food container, but not get to it. Next, one of the two trainers came into the room, and the chimp was to indicate which container held the food. All of the chimps being tested initially made certain responses that indicated where the food was. For example, one would stand against the screen near the food box, another would rock back and forth, accelerating when the trainer approached the container with the food, and so forth. All four of the chimps tested learned to suppress these "involuntary" behaviors when the bad guy was observing but continued to perform them in the presence of the good guy. Two of the animals eventually learned to misdirect the bad guy to the empty box while continuing to direct the good guy correctly to the box with the food. Two of the chimps also learned to detect lies. They avoided the box indicated by the bad guy and chose, instead, the other box. In contrast, they did go to the box indicated by the good guy.

These examples of lying are suggestive of situational freedom, but they can also be interpreted in other ways. For example, a simple reinforcement account would suffice: the chimpanzees were punished for producing the "involuntary" indicative behaviors and differentially reinforced for responding in one way to the good guy and in the opposite way to the bad guy. Such an interpretation misses the point however. The importance of this experiment is that the chimps were able to modify their communicative behavior—both pointing and "involuntary" indicating—depending on the context (good versus bad guy) and its outcome.

LANGUAGE TRAINING IN APES AND DOLPHINS

An interest in the comparative approach to the understanding of paralinguistic competencies has also led investigators to attempt to train animals in a humanlike language. Although animals clearly do not spontaneously use a communication system that even approaches the complexity of human language, there has long been an interest in whether animals can be taught a humanlike language. (See Fouts & Rigby, 1977, for a review of the early history of this research.)

The interest in training animals in a humanlike language has many motivations. For example, researchers would like to know whether the absence of spontaneous humanlike language in animals is due to fundamental differences between the cognitive capacities of humans and other species or to such factors as motivation, opportunity, and so forth. Are chimps speechless because they have nothing to say, and, therefore, have no reason to learn language? Further, even though no nonhuman animal has yet been found to be capable of all aspects of human language, it would still be interesting to know which features they are capable of demonstrating. One approach to this question—studying the natural communication of animals—has already been described. Another is actually to try to train animals in a humanlike language and then to investigate the properties of the communication system that results. For example, to what extent are the universal properties that have been observed in all human languages due to biological characteristics of humans, and to what extent are they due to the requirements of efficient communication or of a cognitive system? To what extent are the skills demonstrated during language acquisition paralleled by the skills seen during other sorts of acquisition? To what extent does language training affect the organism's capabilities in other types of cognitive activity? These questions are interesting, whether or not the animals have truly learned a language, because they tell us about the animals being studied, about communication in general, about our training methods, and about the presence or absence of certain cognitive mechanisms, which could serve as the basis of language. Finally, studying language training in animals can help us to gain perspective on what it means to know a language. This perspective requires an impersonal attitude toward a phenomenon that is such a central part of our lives. One way to gain that perspective is to look at human language in comparison with other forms of communication (Miller, 1981, p. 11).

Training chimpanzees to speak

The attempts to train chimpanzees to speak are remarkable mainly for their consistent failure. Two of these studies tried to train language by raising infant chimpanzees as "surrogate children" in a human household (Hayes, 1951; Kellogg & Kellogg, 1933). The underlying assumption in these studies is that the chimpanzees do not spontaneously use humanlike language because their natural environments do not afford them the appropriate opportunities to acquire it. In contrast, the natural family environment obviously affords human children the opportunity to acquire language. Therefore, if the difference between humans and apes is one of environment, then raising a chimpanzee as a child would lead to its use of language.

Viki, the chimp trained by Hayes, did learn to "say" four words: "cup," "up," "mama," and "papa," and to understand a number of additional words. The Kelloggs raised an infant chimp named Gua along with their son. The boy learned to speak; the chimp did not.

One possible explanation of the failure of these early studies is the difference between the vocal tracts of chimpanzees and humans. Chimps appear to be physically unable to produce some of the sounds contained in human speech (Lieberman, 1975). If lack of an adequate vocal apparatus were all that prevents chimpanzees from learning language, they should be able to learn to speak, but with poor articulation. Instead, they do not speak at all. In contrast, the lack of an adequate vocal apparatus does not prevent humans from learning certain kinds of visual languages so, at least in principle, it also should not prevent apes from learning similar nonvocal languages. Yerkes (1925) speculated that apes might be able to learn languages that took advantage of their manual dexterity and their tendency to produce gestures. In this speculation he anticipated much of the work on language training in animals that was to begin in the 1960s.

Nonvocal languages

More recent investigations into language acquisition by apes have used some form of visual communication medium. The most common medium employed in these studies (e.g., Gardner & Gardner, 1969; Miles, 1983; Patterson, 1978; Terrace, Petitto, Sanders, & Bever, 1979) is a simplified or pidgin form of American Sign Language (Ameslan or ASL), the gestural language used by deaf people in North America. In this language each sign stands for a word. Examples of signs used in ASL are shown in Figure 8.2. Some of them bear an iconic resemblance to the things they denote. That is, the signs "look like" their referents in a way analogous to onomatopoeia in acoustic languages (e.g., buzz, pop). Most signs, however, are only arbitrarily associated with their meanings.

Figure 8.2. Some American Sign Language (ASL or Ameslan) signs learned by chimpanzees.

Other studies use plastic tokens (e.g., Premack, 1971) or computer keyboards (e.g., Rumbaugh, 1977). Figure 8.3 shows a keyboard used in recent experiments at the Yerkes Primate Center with two chimpanzees. Each key on the panel corresponds to one lexical item in the "Yerkish" language. The chimps communicate by pressing the keys in sequence until a whole "sentence" is produced. As keys are depressed, the corresponding symbols are simultaneously displayed and recorded by the computer. Among the benefits of using a computerized language of this sort is that the computer automatically generates a written transcript of any conversations. Some of the disadvantages will be discussed below.

The success of these modern language-training experiments is currently the subject of debate (see Ristau and Robbins, 1982, for a critical review). At this point it is unclear to what extent it is appropriate to say that any animal has been taught a humanlike language. Nevertheless, the animals have learned

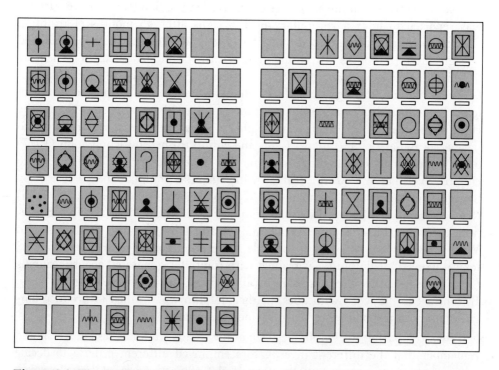

Figure 8.3. The Yerkish keyboard used by the chimpanzees, Sherman and Austin. Each key corresponds to one lexical item. Lexograms were made up from combinations of nine geometric elements superimposed on one another in random combinations. [From Savage-Rumbaugh, Pate, Lawson, Smith, & Rosenbaum, 1983.]

something. The following is a summary of some of the paralinguistic features in the communication systems learned by animals.

Paralinguistic characteristics of learned communication systems

Reference: word use.   One of the most important and striking characteristics of human language is that it contains symbols, such as words, which refer to objects, events, concepts, features, and the like. It seems clear that apes are capable of learning the words—more formally called lexical items—of a visual language and associating them with their respective objects, events, and so forth. What is less clear is the extent to which they can be said to use the lexical items as symbols referring to objects, events, and so forth (See Savage-Rumbaugh, Pate, Lawson, Smith, & Rosenbaum, 1983).

Gardner and Gardner (1969) report that their chimpanzee Washoe's vocabulary included at least 132 signs after 51 months of training. Nim, the chimp trained by Terrace and his associates (Terrace, Petitto, Sanders, & Bever, 1979), was reported to have a vocabulary of 125 signs after 45 months of training. Chantek, the orangutan trained by Miles (1983) was reported to have acquired 56 signs after 18 months of training. The record vocabulary seems to be held by the gorilla, Koko, who was reported by Patterson (1978) to have a vocabulary of between 185 and 264 signs. Similarly, chimpanzees trained with other kinds of token languages also seem readily to acquire comparable vocabularies. Sarah, the chimpanzee trained by Premack with plastic lexigram tokens, was reported to have a vocabulary of 130 items. Lana, the chimp trained by Rumbaugh (1977) on a computer-based language system, had a vocabulary of 75 items. Two chimps, Sherman and Austin, trained with a similar computer-based system by Savage-Rumbaugh and Rumbaugh (1978), had a vocabulary of over 90 items (Savage-Rumbaugh, Pate, Lawson, Smith, & Rosenbaum, 1983). Two bottle-nose dolphins (Phoenix and Akeakamai), trained by Herman, Richards, and Wolz (1984), were reported to be able to respond correctly to more than 28 lexical items. One dolphin was trained with computer-generated acoustic signals (see Figure 8.4), the other with a gestural language (see Figure 8.5 on page 288). In contrast to the work with apes, neither dolphin was trained to produce language, only to respond correctly to various commands.

When comparing the vocabulary size of the various animals tested, we should remember that the different investigators employed different criteria to decide when a given item was actually part of the subject's vocabulary. Moreover, vocabulary size was not stressed to the same degree in every study. Especially, in the dolphin studies, and to some extent in studies by Savage-Rumbaugh and her associates with the chimpanzees, Sherman and Austin, the goal was to train only

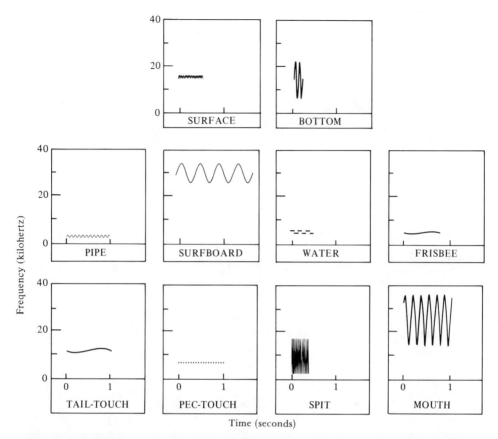

Figure 8.4. Modulation waveform characteristics of lexical items from the acoustic language learned by the dolphin Phoenix. [From Herman, Richards, & Wolz, 1984.]

the minimum vocabulary necessary to investigate other linguistic properties. Hence, vocabulary size is not necessarily indicative of the subjects' capacities.

The lexical items in these animals' vocabularies are intended to refer to items, features, or actions in their environments. Each of these studies consisted, at least in part, of specific training on labeling objects. The subjects were shown objects and then taught the name of the object. Although the animals were capable of associating labels with objects, this does not necessarily imply that they used those labels to refer to the objects. For example, Lana, who was trained in the mechanical Yerkish language, would readily "type" into her machine requests of the form PLEASE MACHINE GIVE M & M in order to get a candy. Despite her ready ability to do this, it took 1600 trials for her to learn to respond when shown an M & M or a banana and asked the question (typed on the experimenter's keyboard) ?WHAT NAME OF THIS with the correct reply M & M

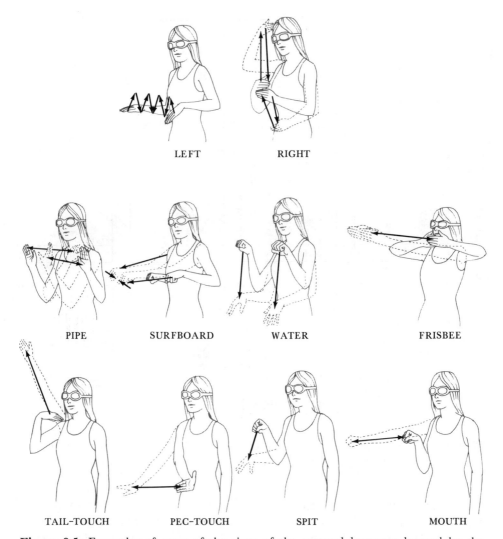

Figure 8.5. Examples of some of the signs of the gestural language learned by the dolphin Akeakamai. [From Herman, Richards, & Wolz, 1984.]

NAME OF THIS or BANANA NAME OF THIS. "M & M," "BANANA," "NAME," "THIS," etc. were each keys on Lana's Yerkish keyboard. Following this initial difficulty, Lana was able to correctly answer subsequent naming questions. After a considerable amount of training she was eventually able to answer a naming question the first time it was asked (Rumbaugh & Gill, 1977). Lana's difficulty in learning to answer naming questions suggests that she had used the lexigrams of her language, not as names for the objects, but as an instrumental means for producing these objects. The point of this finding is that, using a given lexical item in an appropriate, though limited manner is not the same as understanding its meaning.

If knowing the name of an object requires no skill more sophisticated than the formation of an association between the object and the label, then symbolic matching-to-sample performance by pigeons could also be construed to involve naming (see e.g., Chapter 5). The presentation of the comparison stimuli can be construed as a question regarding the identity of the sample that had appeared. When the comparison stimuli are presented, the bird reacts to them as alternative labels for the sample and chooses the one comparison stimulus that correctly labels it. By this interpretation, the pigeon also exhibits displacement; when making its choice, it is using a symbol that stands for an object—the sample—which appeared at another place and time.

Attributing naming to a pigeon performing delayed matching-to-sample seems inappropriate, because the symbols are used in such a restricted context and manner in the operant chamber and as instrumental in producing reward. Adult human language is characterized by a more abstract use of symbolic reference, in which words are not only associated with the appropriate objects, but can serve as symbols for those objects in many different contexts and for many different purposes.

One line of evidence that would indicate that an animal uses lexical items as symbols referring to objects would be to show that the animal can categorize the lexical items in a way that is appropriate to the items they represent. For example, Premack reports that Sarah chose the same features as descriptive of the token for an apple—which happened to be a blue triangle—that she chose as descriptive of a real apple (e.g., Premack & Premack, 1983). Gardner and Gardner (1975) report that their chimp, Washoe, could respond appropriately to "Wh—" questions, such as WHO THIS, WHAT COLOR OF THIS, WHERE X, and so forth. Who questions should be answered by a proper name, where questions by a location indicator, and so forth. When Washoe did make mistakes, her replies still tended to show good agreement between the type of question asked and the grammatical category of her reply. Thus, she answered who questions with the name of a person, where questions with the name of a location, and so forth. The agreement between the type of question and the type of reply suggests that Washoe understood the semantic class to which the symbols belonged.

Savage-Rumbaugh (1984) reports categorization of items according to functional categories. Sherman and Austin were taught the generic symbols for "food" and for "tool" using three familiar examples of foods and three familiar examples of tools. They were then tested with new objects and asked to categorize them as food or tool. Sherman classified 9 out of the 10 objects correctly. Austin classified 10 out of 10 correctly. After this first test, they were further trained to classify the lexigrams for the three items from each category used in the first phase of training. Finally, the chimps were tested for their ability to classify the lexigrams of items they had never previously been asked to classify—nor had they been taught the classification for these objects. In this test Sherman correctly classified 15 out of 16 lexigrams according to the category of the item represented, and Austin correctly classified 17 out of 17 items. These results suggest strongly that Sherman and Austin had learned that the lexigrams could function as symbols representing objects.

Productivity. Productivity refers to the organism's ability to form novel expressions according to the rules of a language's grammar. There is considerable controversy over whether or not language-trained apes have shown evidence of productivity. One type of evidence for productivity would be the appropriate use of familiar lexical items, either alone or in combinations, to describe new situations. For example, Washoe is reported to have signed WATER BIRD the first time that she saw a swan (Fouts, 1974). Although this appears to be a novel combination of lexical items indicating a new concept, in fact, both water and a bird were present when the signs were produced. Therefore, this example is ambiguous. It is impossible to know whether Washoe was naming the water-bird or was signing separately in response to the water and the bird. That she later repeated this combination in other contexts is also suggestive, but not conclusive, because of the reinforcement she received when she first produced the combination in the presence of a swan.

Another problem in assessing novel word combinations in the presence of previously unnamed objects is that the frequency with which the animals put together various lexical items in uninteresting combinations is not generally reported. As a result it is difficult to determine whether the striking examples that are reported reflect the animal's spontaneous production of new meaningful expressions or are simply selected from otherwise meaningless combinations. For example, Patterson has said, "Although Koko has produced uninterpretable strings (as do some children), most of her utterances are appropriate to the situation and some are strikingly apt" (1978, p. 88). It may be true that children produce uninterpretable utterances, but without a way to assess the apt expressions of either animals or children in comparison to their meaningless productions, any claims about them as examples of novel conceptualizations is problematical.

This criticism highlights a fundamental difficulty with research intended to critically appraise animal language. On the one hand, researchers recognize that productivity is an important characteristic of language use. A word combination must be spontaneous, novel, and appropriate to provide evidence for productivity. On the other hand, anecdotal reports of rare occurrences are not acceptable as scientific evidence, in large part because such anecdotes are particularly susceptible to what might be called "wishful interpretation." Similarly, repetition of a novel combination by the animal is not evidence that it has spontaneously named something because these striking productions—whatever their source—are almost certainly strongly, if inadvertently, reinforced by the human trainers. The dilemma is that, by definition, one cannot replicate spontaneous and rare events at will, but they are exactly what is needed to scientifically establish the existence of language productivity in animals. As a result usages of the sort described by Fouts (1974), Patterson (1978), and others will always be problematical.

Grammar: sentence use.   In addition to using words, human language is also characterized by the expression of propositions in the form of clauses. A clause is a combination of words, formed according to rules of the language's grammar, that expresses a proposition. The same set of lexical items arranged in a different order can produce clauses that express different propositions. (In some languages this same information is indicated by word inflection instead of, or in addition to, word order.) The rules of a language can be used to produce an indefinitely large number of different expressions. They also govern the interpretation of these expressions. Among the necessary conditions for demonstrating the use of grammar is the formation and/or understanding by the organism of novel clauses, which are composed according to the rules of the language, but contain words that had never before appeared together.

To know a language is to know the rules for producing and understanding clauses. When a language contains few lexical items, it is difficult to discriminate whether the "speaker" knows the rules of the language or knows each of its possible clauses. For example, Straub, Seidenberg, Bever, and Terrace (1979) trained pigeons to peck a set of simultaneously presented colored lights in an arbitrarily ordered sequence (e.g., in the order green, white, red, blue; see Chapter 6). Pecking at the colors in the appropriate order was reinforced with a food presentation. After some training, the birds came to produce this sequence reliably, even when they were confronted with novel arrangements of the familiar colors. Although the pigeons were capable of producing an organized string of behavior, it does not seem appropriate to claim that they were producing the sentence PLEASE MACHINE GIVE FOOD or that they were producing their sequences according to some set of rules. It seems much more reasonable to assume that they had learned the single string: green, white, red, blue, and produced it in a more or less mechanical as opposed to communicative manner.

An animal producing arbitrary strings of symbols in some "language" may also be producing them in the same mechanical manner in which the pigeons produce theirs. For example, Lana, the chimpanzee trained in the Yerkish keyboard language, was trained to produce strings such as PLEASE MACHINE GIVE BANANA, or PLEASE MACHINE GIVE M & M. These strings were produced by pressing arbitrary symbols in a fixed pattern. The question is: Do these expressions result from learning strings of the form ABCD and ABCE, or do they result from the rule-governed use of symbols that can be appropriately translated as PLEASE MACHINE GIVE BANANA?

Thompson and Church (1980) analyzed over 14,000 of Lana's expressions and found that they could account for most of them on the basis of a simple model involving paired associates and conditional discriminations. They argued that Lana learned paired associations between lexigrams and objects—that is, she learned names or labels for those objects—and conditional discriminations of six stock strings such as PLEASE MACHINE GIVE X. She then simply substituted the labels into the stock lexical strings. When no experimenter was present and Lana was interacting only with the computer, 91 percent of the strings she produced were one of the six stock sentences. When an experimenter was present, 66 percent of her strings were stock sentences, 19 percent were errors, and 14 percent were nonstock sentences. By this analysis, Lana's sentences consisted of, at best, two lexical units: the stock phrase and the substitutable label. At worst, this analysis suggests that Lana did not learn the "meaning" of any of her strings, only fixed patterns of behavior—analogous to that of the pigeon—accompanied by substitutable labels.

We must interpret Thompson and Church's conclusion with some caution, however. The limitations of the Yerkish language and the method used to train Lana in it may have overemphasized the use of sentences with a similar structure. It may be that Lana was producing a high proportion of stock sentences not because she was restricted to mechanical forms of production, but because she had been trained intensively in the production of these stock sentences. The high proportion of nonstock sentences she constructed when a human experimenter was present, relative to when no humans were available, suggests that social interactions and the attendant opportunities for true communication were important in controlling the range of her productions. Pate and Rumbaugh (1983) subsequently analyzed another, later block of Lana's productions. These productions could not be explained on the same simple basis as the block analyzed by Thompson and Church. Apparently, Lana became more proficient in her "language" with further training. If she were using stock phrases in her later productions, then she had about 45 of them, rather than the 6 detected by Thompson and Church. Paired associates and conditional discriminations could not plausibly account for these later productions.

Another criterion for demonstrating the use of rule-governed grammar is the relation between changeable word order and the meaning of the sentence. All of the investigators studying gestural language in apes agree that at least the two-sign strings produced by their subjects showed some regularity in sign order. Patterson has said that in 82 percent of Koko's productions involving a verb preceding a pronoun, the pronoun indicated the object of the indicated action. For example, TICKLE ME indicated that Koko was to be tickled, not that she would do the tickling. Similarly, in 76 percent of her pronoun-verb productions, the pronoun was the subject, or agent, of the action. For example, KOKO TICKLE indicated that Koko would do the tickling, not that she requested to be tickled. Similar regularities were noted in Nim's productions.

The use by animals of regular word orders with relatively small vocabularies does not provide very strong evidence for their use of grammar because these symbols can be combined in only a few ways. Furthermore, without some means of assessing the intentions of the animals, we cannot know whether their regular word order results from fixed patterns, from biases of various sorts, or from other causes. For example, Koko could have a bias to want to be tickled rather than to do the tickling and a bias to produce TICKLE KOKO rather than KOKO TICKLE. If these biases are strong enough, they would appear to indicate a co-variation between intentions and expressions when they are actually independent. (This hypothesis can be statistically tested.) More convincing evidence for the use of word order to determine an expression's meaning occurs when animals understand sentences that change their meaning with changes in word order. For example, "put the cup into the box" is different from "put the box into the cup." Comprehension of sentences of this type would indicate that word order is a salient property controlling the meaning of the string. Moreover, the problems of intention and bias are removed because the experimenter controls the sentences that are produced.

Premack (1971) trained his chimp Sarah with a lexical token for "on." He trained her to put a red card on top of a green one when presented with the sequence of lexical tokens RED ON GREEN and to put the green card on top of the red one when presented with the sequence GREEN ON RED. She was then tested for her ability to describe the position of colored cards. The tests presented her with colored cards and tokens for their colors neither of which had previously been used in this sort of task. She was required to order the lexical items—that is, the two colors and the lexigram for "on"—to correspond to the arrangement of cards. Sarah solved these description problems with high levels of accuracy.

Sarah may have solved the description problems not by understanding the meaning of the lexical token ON, but in a straightforward stimulus-response manner. For example, an appropriate description would result from placing the lexical token representing the top card first, the token representing the bottom card last, and the remaining token in the middle (Macphail, 1982). Similarly, she could match the arrangement of lexigrams to the arrangement of cards by placing the card corresponding to the first lexical token on top of the card corresponding to the bottom token, that is, by matching the card with its corresponding token and position. These performances would require little more than the existence of paired associates between colors and tokens.

More convincing evidence that an animal can understand sentences has been obtained by Herman and his associates (Herman, Richards, & Wolz, 1984) in their study of bottlenosed dolphins. The dolphin, Phoenix, was trained with three-word strings of the form:

direct object + FETCH + indirect object
FRISBEE   FETCH   BASKET

The dolphin was required to move the object signified by the first symbol in the sentence to the object indicated by the final symbol. For example, if instructed FRISBEE FETCH BASKET, the correct response would be to find the Frisbee, which could be floating anywhere in the pool, and to place it in the basket, whose location also changed from trial to trial. The most telling examples of this type of construction occur when either the direct or the indirect object can be moved. In those cases PIPE FETCH FRISBEE and FRISBEE FETCH PIPE clearly indicate different commands.

The other dolphin, Akeakamai, was trained with three-word strings of the form:

indirect object + direct object + FETCH
BASKET   FRISBEE   FETCH

This sentence order was used in order to divorce word order from the order in which the objects were contacted; that is, the dolphin's performance could not be interpreted as the result of a rule such as "first approach the first object, then take it to the second object."

Phoenix performed correctly 65.9 percent of novel reversible strings involving FETCH. Akeakamai performed correctly 53.3 percent of these novel strings. Of all the errors that occurred with these strings, however, only one error by Phoenix involved a reversal of the direct and indirect object. In most other instances, the dolphins' errors were failures to find the indirect object while transporting the direct object on their rostrum—the top of their "nose". Hence, these dolphins provide quite good evidence that they are capable of using word order as a source of information in a sentence.

OTHER ANIMALS THAT HAVE BEEN LANGUAGE TRAINED

In addition to apes and dolphins, language training has also been attempted with at least two other species of animals. Schusterman and Krieger (1984) have trained two California sea lions (*Zalophus californianus*) in a gestural language similar to that used by Herman and his associates. After 24 months of training, Rocky, a 6-year-old female, had a comprehension vocabulary of 20 signs— 5 modifiers, 10 objects, and 5 actions. After 20 months of training Bucky, a 3-year-old male, had a vocabulary of 16 signs—2 modifiers, 8 objects, and 6 actions. Both animals were capable of performing the instructions contained in three-sign combinations of the form:

modifier +   object   +   action
BLACK   FRISBEE   FLIPPERTOUCH

The animals were also able to comprehend sentences that referred to objects that were not immediately available. For example, if asked to mouth a pipe, and a pipe was not present in the tank, both animals searched for a longer time than if the pipe had been present. If the indicated object was not present, they also refused to mouth any object rather than to mouth an inappropriate object. One animal also showed generalization of actions the first time it was asked to respond to an object that was out of the water. For example, the behavioral patterns for tail touching are very different in water versus out of the water, but Bucky correctly responded in both media. At the time of the report, Rocky had not been similarly tested.

Pepperberg (1981, 1983) has trained an African grey parrot (*Psittacus erithacus*), named Alex, in a vocal language consisting of English words for objects, actions, numerical quantities, colors, shapes, and functional use of the word "no." The bird can accurately request, identify, quantify, refuse, and comment on about 50 different objects. Its vocalizations are apparently not simply mimicry of utterances just heard, although such mimicry may have played a role during early stages of acquisition.

For example, the bird was taught the concepts of color and shape. During tests it was presented with objects that differed in substance (wood, key, rawhide chew, or clothespin), color (rose/red, green, blue, and gray), and shape (number of corners ranging from a two-cornered football-like shape to a pentagon). The parrot was asked to classify these objects according to their various dimensions by answering questions such as, "What's this?", "What color?", or "What shape?" He then responded appropriately. For example, when shown a green wooden triangle and asked for its color, the parrot responded "GREEN WOOD." He answered shape questions by describing the number of corners. The bird made the correct response more than 80% of the time when asked about the properties of familiar objects.

These studies of language training suggest that the kinds of tasks subjects are asked to perform tap cognitive capacities that are fairly widespread in the animal kingdom.

THE RELATIONSHIP BETWEEN ANIMAL LANGUAGE AND HUMAN LANGUAGE

One of the main motivations of all of the animal language projects has been to see if animals are capable of learning a humanlike language. Answering this question, however, is very difficult. It is difficult to define language and difficult to determine those features that are essential to demonstrating its presence. The task is also hampered by differences in the standards the various researchers have applied to their data recording and interpretation. When an animal such as a chimpanzee is raised in the home of the experimenter and treated as a surrogate child, it becomes progressively easier to "overinterpret" the animal's utterances and progressively more difficult to obtain the necessary data to critically assess the project's success. We cannot know to what extent overinterpretation has colored the evidence. Similarly, it is difficult to know to what extent an overzealous application of Occam's razor and Morgan's canon has led to underinterpretation of the data. For example, the mere fact that Lana's utterances conformed to those that could have been produced by a mindless production model does not necessarily imply that they were produced in that way. We cannot adequately understand the meaning of the correlation between Lana's productions and those predicted on the basis of a simple model without similar data from humans interacting in a similarly structured situation. For example, consider the utterances of fans overheard at a sporting event. Most of them could probably be explained by a production model even simpler than that necessary to explain Lana's expressions. If we tried to apply the same sorts of criteria to humans that we apply to animals, and if we tested each under similarly constrained situations, we might be forced to conclude that humans do not have language.

Ristau and Robbins (1982) list approximately 18 features of human language (based on proposals by Hockett, 1958; Hockett & Altmann, 1968; Thorpe, 1974) and the evidence that similar features are present in the behaviors of language-trained animals. The general conclusion they reach is that the evidence, with regard to many of these features, is scanty at best but uniformly suggestive that with enough effort and carefully controlled observations, many of these features will also be found to be characteristic of animals' linguistic behavior.

Perhaps, however, it is a mistake to ask whether animals are capable of learning a humanlike language. No matter how many criteria an ape may meet in demonstrating its linguistic capacity, one can always construct other criteria that it will fail to meet. Because language is such a complex phenomenon, we may be unable to obtain universal agreement on its criteria. Instead, it may be more fruitful to investigate the properties of an animal's cognitive and linguistic capacities in their own right. In other words, rather than trying to prove that an ape can learn human language, we might more fruitfully study the "psycholinguistics" or, perhaps more appropriately, "psychosemiotics" (the psychology of sign usage) of whatever natural or artificial communication system animals do manage.

LANGUAGE TRAINING AND ANIMAL COGNITION

In recent years, many investigators have, in fact, begun to change the emphasis of their investigations from attempts to demonstrate humanlike language to attempts to discover the effects of language training on other cognitive processes in animals. One of the currently best-developed investigations of the effects of language training on animal cognition is that presented by Premack (1976, 1983; Premack & Premack, 1983). According to him, the result of language training of chimpanzees has been apes with upgraded minds. Specifically, language training "convert[s] an animal with a strong bias for responding to appearances into one that can respond on an abstract basis" (Premack & Premack, 1983, p. 125).

In Premack's view, language training changes the types of categories that animals form. Categorization is to treat discriminally different stimuli as equivalent and respond to them on the basis of their category rather than their unique properties. All animals categorize to some extent. For example, a predator must be able to recognize its prey from many different angles, in different positions, with sometimes different colors, and so forth. The predator's ability to classify various sensory images as views of the same object indicates it has some degree of categorization. The essence of Premack's proposal is that non-language-trained animals form these categories strictly on the basis of physical features of the stimulus objects. In contrast, language-trained animals form abstract categories, such as function, that cannot be reduced to or identified by specific physical features of the objects.[1]

In order to evaluate Premack's claims that language training modifies the kinds of categories that animals can use, we must first consider the kinds of categories used by animals that have not been language trained. Much of this work has been done with pigeons.

Conceptual categories

Artificial concepts.   The most basic categorization occurs when the members of the class can be discriminated from nonmembers on the basis of a single stimulus dimension. Levine (1970) studied this kind of concept learning in human subjects (see Chapter 3). He presented stimuli that vary along a small number of dimensions, such as large versus small, black versus white, X versus T, and left versus right. Category membership was usually defined by a single dimension—for example, all large stimuli are positive, all small stimuli are negative—and all other dimensions are irrelevant. The subject must identify the relevant dimension and the values of the stimuli along that dimension, for example, that size is relevant, "large" is indicative of the positive set, and small is indicative of the negative set. The subject is said to have identified the correct concept when responses are made systematically according to the feature or set of features that the experimenter has chosen to define the concept. If the subject consistently chooses the larger stimulus, this would indicate the use of the concept "size."

People are also capable of learning more complicated concepts, defined in terms of combinations of simple features. A *conjunctive concept* is defined by the simultaneous presence of two stimulus values. For example, the positive stimuli might be those that are both large and black. When the stimulus is both large and black it is a member of the positive set, but if it is small and black, or large and white, and so forth, it is a member of the negative set. A *disjunctive concept* is defined by a logical "or" relation. A stimulus is positive if it is either black or small.

Natural concepts.   Artificial concepts, such as those investigated by Levine, are all studied using relatively small sets of stimuli consisting of well-specified dimensions having only a few discrete values. Further, the concepts being studied can all be described according to simple rules. In contrast, natural concepts typically accommodate an unspecified large number of stimuli, which do not consist of well-specified dimensions. Often, we cannot describe the rules for their categorization using simple combinatoric rules. For example, consider the concept of a "strike" in baseball:

Among other things, a strike is:

  A missed swing at a pitched ball.

  A pitched ball that passes through the "strike zone" with or without
   the batter swinging at it.

  A ball hit into "foul territory," except if this would produce the
   third strike and is not the result of a "bunt."

Alternatively, consider the concept "furniture." What are the common features of club chairs, kitchen chairs, beanbag chairs, sofas, kitchen tables, coffee tables, floor lamps, desk lamps, beds, coatracks, credenzas, and so forth that allow us to classify them all as furniture? Attempts to determine the distinguishing features of concepts such as furniture have been popular occupations for philosophers and psychologists of language.

The consensus solution to the definition of fuzzy concepts, such as furniture, communication, or language, is to use the notion of *family resemblance*. You share some features of your appearance with your mother, some with your father, and some, perhaps, with your second cousin. Although there is usually no single feature that brands you as a member of your family and excludes others—(for example, you do not have to be a Hapsburg to have a Hapsburg lip)—people are still able to detect a family resemblance. Similarly, although no single feature can characterize the entire class of objects we call furniture, each member of the class shares some combination of features with many (but not all) of the other members.

Other categories we use are based on even more abstract concepts. The most abstract of these are concepts like truth, beauty, and goodness. In a more mundane vein, we use relational concepts, such as sameness, identity, and difference. Whether two things are the same or different is determined not by their individual characteristics, but by the relation between the features of one object and the features of the other. At present we have no way to know whether animals use concepts like truth, but there is good evidence that at least some animals can use relational concepts such as sameness.

Conceptual categorization by animals

Simple concepts.   Discrimination-learning experiments demonstrate that animals are clearly capable of solving discrimination problems in which the stimuli can be divided on the basis of critical features into a positive and a negative set (see Chapter 3). For example, Fields (1932) trained rats in a form-discrimination task. The stimuli varied in geometric form, size, orientation, and drawing styles—for example, outline versus solid—yet the rats were able to learn that form was the critical feature, triangles defined the positive set, and other dimensions were irrelevant.

Abstract concepts.   Other experiments have found that animals can respond on the basis of more abstract characteristics that are not specifically associated with any particular stimuli. For example, the overtraining-reversal experiments discussed in Chapter 3 indicate that animals can learn about the importance of stimulus dimensions as well as about specific stimuli along those dimensions (Reid, 1953). Learning-set experiments (e.g., Harlow, 1949) show that they can also learn about strategies for solving discrimination problems that are unrelated to any physical parameters of the stimuli. In these experiments animals are trained on many discrimination problems, one problem after another. Each problem involves a novel pair of objects. Each pair is typically presented for only a few training trials. One member is associated with reinforcement; the other is not. On the first trial, the animal cannot know which object is positive and which is negative, but afer training on many problems of this type, monkeys reach near-perfect discrimination on the second trial of a problem. Because different objects appear in each problem, the improvement in choice accuracy over successive problems cannot be due to the formation of associations between specific stimuli and reinforcement. Instead, Harlow argued that the monkeys were forming a "learning set" or conceptual strategy, which they could apply to any problem.

Animals have also been shown to use a concept of similarity. For example, Zentall and his associates (e.g., Zentall & Hogan, 1974, 1976, 1978; Zentall, Edwards, Moore, & Hogan, 1981; Zentall, Hogan, & Edwards, 1984) have found that when pigeons are trained on matching-to-sample or oddity-from-sample, they learn a generalized matching concept. In these experiments the sample and two comparison stimuli are present simultaneously. One comparison stimulus matches the sample; the other does not. In matching-to-sample, the subject must choose the comparison stimulus that is identical to the sample. In oddity-from-sample, it must choose the comparison stimulus that is different from the sample. Except for the rule relating the sample and the correct choice, these two tasks are identical. Hence, they allow an assessment of the role played by *matching* and *oddity relations* and by a generalized matching concept.

The general procedure in making this assessment is to train subjects to perform either matching-to-sample or oddity-from-sample and then to test them with new stimuli on either matching or oddity tasks. This experimental procedure requires four groups as Table 8.1 shows. Two groups are trained during the first phase of the experiment to perform matching-to-sample, and two are trained to perform oddity-from-sample. All animals during phase 1 are trained with the same set of stimuli—for example, red versus green. During the second phase of the experiment, they are all tested with new sample and comparison stimuli—for example, yellow versus blue or horizontal versus vertical. One of the groups trained to match during phase 1 is tested with a matching task during phase 2 (congruent transfer). The other matching group is tested with oddity during phase 2 (incongruent transfer). Similarly, one of the groups trained to perform oddity during phase 1 is tested with oddity during phase 2 (congruent transfer), and the other group is tested with matching (incongruent transfer). The only differences among the groups during phase 2 are the rules relating the sample and the correct choice and the congruency/incongruency of the rule used in phase 2 with the rule they learned during phase 1.

There are at least two hypotheses for what the birds learn during phase 1 of the experiment. Either they learn sample-specific associations: for example, peck at the red comparison when red is the sample or peck at the green comparison when red is the sample; or they learn a generalized matching concept: Choose the comparison that matches the sample or the comparison that is different from it. Actually, these two hypotheses are extreme positions and a combination of

TABLE 8.1 Assessment of a role for an abstract matching concept: Experimental groups and choice accuracy on the first transfer session

Initial training	Transfer test	
	Congruent	Incongruent
Color matching 85% correct	Line matching 60% correct	Line oddity 40% correct
Color oddity 85% correct	Line oddity 60% correct	Line matching 40% correct

Note: Data are a summary of many studies by Zentall and his associates. For example, see Zentall, 1984.

them is also possible. If the birds learned exclusively in the form of sample-specific associations, then there should be no evidence of transfer from the end of phase 1 to the beginning of phase 2. Choice accuracy during the first session of phase 2 should be approximately at the chance level because no associations have yet been learned for those samples. If the birds learned more general information about the task, however, then there should be significant transfer from phase 1 to phase 2. Their choice accuracy during the first session of phase 2 should be above chance following congruent transfer because the same rules as well as the same concepts apply in both phases. Their choice accuracy during the first session of phase 2 should be below chance following incongruent transfer because application of the same rules and concepts learned during phase 1 will lead to systematic errors in performance. Therefore, the difference in performance during the first session of phase 2 between the subjects receiving congruent transfer and those receiving incongruent transfer shows the degree to which performance was controlled by a matching concept.

As Table 8.1 shows, transfer to a congruent task typically results in about 60 percent correct performance during the first transfer session and transfer to an incongruent task typically results in about 40 percent correct performance. Chance is 50 percent correct. The difference between congruent and incongruent transfer indicates that stimulus similarity between the sample and one of the comparison stimuli, independent of the actual stimuli being compared, plays a role in controlling the pigeons' simultaneous matching and oddity performance (cf. D'Amato, Salmon, & Colombo, 1985). Table 8.1 also shows, however, that the matching concept is not the only factor controlling performance. At the end of phase 1 pigeons are typically performing either oddity or matching with about 85 percent accuracy. When transferred to a congruent task, their choice accuracy typically drops to about 60 percent correct. With further training on these stimuli, the birds do typically recover their former level of choice accuracy, presumably as they gain information that is specific to the stimuli involved. Therefore, we must conclude that pigeons' matching and oddity performance is controlled by a combination of a generalized matching concept and sample-specific information.

The congruence between the rules of phase 1 and the rules of phase 2 is important, but the rules themselves are not. The same degree of transfer is observed when transferring from matching to matching as when transferring from oddity to oddity. This suggests that the same abstract concept is responsible in both matching and oddity tasks. In matching-to-sample, the pigeon finds the matching stimulus and responds to it; in oddity-from-sample, the pigeon finds the matching stimulus and pecks at the alternative. As a further test of this hypothesis, Zentall and his associates trained pigeons to perform either matching or oddity tasks and then tested them by replacing one comparison stimulus with a novel one (Zentall, Edwards, Moore, & Hogan, 1981). Performance on both the matching and the oddity tasks was disrupted when the matching stimulus was replaced but was not disrupted when the odd stimulus was replaced. These data argue for the use of an abstract "same" concept by pigeons performing simultaneous matching-to-sample and oddity-from-sample (Zentall, Hogan, & Edwards, 1984).

Similarly, monkeys have shown evidence of the use of a "same" concept in matching-to-sample (D'Amato, Salmon, & Colombo, 1985) as well as in serial probe-recognition experiments. In the latter experiments, the monkeys are presented a list of stimuli, for example, pictures of objects projected with a slide projector, followed by a probe stimulus (see Sands, Urcuioli, Wright, & Santiago, 1984; Wright, Santiago, Sands, & Urcuioli, 1984). The monkey is reinforced for making one response if the probe slide is the same as one of the slides appearing in the list and for making another response if it does not match one from the list. Pigeons have also been found to be able to perform this task (Wright, et al., 1984). Like matching-to-sample and oddity-from-sample, this task appears to require the subject to use a concept of "same" versus "different" for successful performance because the slides are varied from trial to trial. Subjects presumably encode significant features of the visual stimuli as the list is presented and compare the encoded features with those appearing in the probe. The same/different judgment consists of a comparison of the remembered physical features of the list items with the features present in the probe.[2] Animals have also been found able to make same/different judgments based on class membership in addition to physical similarity.

Natural-concept discriminations

Herrnstein and his associates (see Herrnstein, 1984) have trained pigeons to perform discriminations between natural categories, such as trees versus nontrees, whose members cannot be unambiguously identified with unique physical features. These experiments are important because they imply that the pigeons are capable of a level of abstraction beyond that needed for tasks such as serial probe recognition. In addition to requiring an abstract concept for comparing the similarity of the physical features of stimuli, performance in these natural-concept experiments appears to require an abstract representation of the class being discriminated.

In natural-concept discriminations, subjects are trained to classify photographs that exemplify open-ended categories, such as people, individual persons, alpha-numeric characters, fish, and others. For example, in one experiment (Mallott & Siddall, 1972), pigeons were trained to discriminate photographs containing people or parts of people from photographs without people. The birds learned to perform this discrimination readily—typically with between 6 and 36 positive and negative examples—and with a high level of accuracy. Furthermore, they generalized this discrimination to pictures seen for the first time.

The slides used during training and generalization testing varied widely. Sometimes they contained only small parts of people. Other times they depicted crowds or whole persons, either clothed or naked. In short, no distinctive features such as specific hues, angular orientations, or brightnesses, could be used to discriminate consistently examples of the category from nonexamples, yet the birds learned to differentiate between the two sets.

A more dramatic demonstration required pigeons to discriminate photographs of a particular individual from similar photographs of other people. The positive slides contained the same woman in various settings, wearing different clothes, in company with various other people, and so forth. Negative slides, in which the woman was not present, included other individuals in similar settings—for example, her apartment—or wearing similar clothing. Nevertheless, the birds' discriminative performance in this experiment was also quite good (Herrnstein, Loveland, & Cable, 1976).

In another experiment, Cerella (1979) trained pigeons to discriminate between leaves of the white oak tree and leaves from other trees. All leaves were presented as black and white silhouettes. Only a single example of a white oak leaf was presented during training, yet the birds generalized immediately to subsequent examples of leaves from the same species. They responded positively to novel oak leaves and negatively to novel leaves from other species of tree. Although white oak leaves clearly resemble one another in certain ways, no obvious metric properties of the leaves used in training were responsible for the discrimination of novel leaves. For example, neither the number of lobes, their depth, nor the overall height of the silhouette, among other things, could account for the accuracy of the pigeons' discrimination. Figure 8.6 displays some examples of the leaves used by Cerella.[3]

Figure 8.6. Examples of some of the leaf silhouettes used by Cerella. The leaves in the top row are white oak and show the variations in oak leaves recognized by pigeons; those in the bottom row are nonoak leaves. [From Cerella, 1979.]

Although the physical appearance of the leaves was undoubtedly important to the birds' ability to perform the discrimination, Cerella also found it difficult or impossible to train pigeons to discriminate an individual white oak leaf from other white oak leaves (cf. Herrnstein, Loveland, & Cable's, 1976, success in training a pigeon to discriminate one person from other persons). In other words, the pigeon's ability to perform the discrimination is not indifferent to how the set of stimuli is divided—for example, *between* versus *within* species. Although individual oak leaves differ significantly from one another, these physical differences were difficult for the pigeons to learn. In contrast, physical differences between species of leaf were easy to learn, although they are of the same type, if not the same magnitude, as the differences within species.

In a related study, Poole and Lander (1971) trained pigeons to discriminate portraits of various breeds of pigeons from photos of other birds or objects. One of the striking features of pigeon breeds is that they are all derived from the common pigeon, but, through selective breeding, have come to develop appearances that are more different from one another than some species are from other species. Figure 8.7 shows several different breeds of pigeons. Despite differences of this sort, pigeons learned the discrimination and showed good generalization to new breeds.

Data such as these suggest that physical dissimilarity by itself is not sufficient to explain the classification schemes that the birds use. Instead, pigeons seem to be employing something related to taxonomic classes. One might suppose that these classes are related to classes experienced previously by individual pigeons or are even the result of genetically determined classification schemes. For exam-

Figure 8.7. Examples of some different breeds of pigeons: (A) wild rock pigeon, (B) fantail, (C) satinette oriental frill, (D) Pomeranian pouter, (E) carrier. [Based on drawings in W. M. Levi (1965) *Encyclopedia of pigeon breeds*. Jersey City: T. F. H. Publications.]

ple, the pigeons tested by Cerella (1979) may possibly have had experience with oak trees of various sorts and thereby learned to discriminate among them. The pigeons may have learned about them because of differences in the perches or acorns they provide, or simply as the result of having seen them through the walls of their natal coops. In the laboratory the pigeons merely behaved according to a discrimination they had learned elsewhere. One must be dubious of this type of explanation, however, because it still does not tell us how they manage to discriminate between leaf species, even if it does explain how they learned to do so. Furthermore, it is unlikely that these particular pigeons had ever had the opportunity to learn to discriminate oak leaves. Finally, pigeons have been found capable of learning to sort underwater photos according to whether or not they contain fish (Herrnstein & de Villiers, 1980). No pigeon ever tested in any laboratory has ever had any exposure to fish. Because pigeons originally derived from desert-dwelling species, it is also doubtful that they have had any adaptive pressure to be able to identify fish innately. Nevertheless, the birds did learn to perform the discrimination.

The rate at which the pigeons learned to discriminate between fish and non-fish was comparable to the rates observed in learning to discriminate other stimuli more typical of their environment. Similar to Cerella's (1979) findings that discriminating oak leaves from other leaves was easy, whereas discriminating among oak leaves was difficult, Herrnstein and de Villiers (1980) found that pigeons learned to discriminate fish from nonfish more easily than they learned an arbitrary discrimination in which some of the slides were assigned to the positive category, independent of their contents, and the remaining slides were assigned to the negative category. Further, in learning to discriminate fish from nonfish slides, the pigeons often responded correctly to a slide on its first appearance, before any reinforcers were given for pecking at it and continued to respond to the positive slides at rates that were unrelated to the number of reinforcers the birds received following those specific slides. These findings indicate that the pigeons were not basing their performance on their experience with the particular slides, but were performing relative to more global properties. These results lend further credence to the hypothesis that they form abstract representations of the discriminated concepts, rather than learn to identify individual examples of the two sets.

The pigeons indicated their discrimination by pecking at the slides showing examples of the positive set and pecking less or not at all at the slides showing the negative set. Ranking the stimuli on the basis of the peck rate to each gives an index of the ease with which the pigeon discriminated that slide. A high peck rate could mean that the slide was a very good member of the positive category, and a low peck rate could mean that the slide was a very bad representative of the positive category—that is, a member of the negative set. Using this measure, there was good agreement among the pigeons as to which slides were more difficult and which less difficult to categorize. Side views, corresponding to humans' canonical notion of a fish, were also best judged by pigeons as examples of fish. The pigeons were more likely than humans to misclassify ambiguous objects as fish and were more likely to judge other animals (e.g., sea cucumbers) as fish, but they usually classified divers and turtles correctly. People were slow to classify skates as fish, but pigeons, who have few if any preconceptions and extra-experimental knowledge of sea-animal classification, readily classified them as fish.

On the basis of these and similar data, Herrnstein and de Villiers (1980) suggest that animals may have evolved cognitive/perceptual systems specifically adapted to making discriminations at the taxonomic level that ignore differences at lower levels. ". . . We would expect the perceptual dynamics to equip the pigeon more for possible environments than for the much narrower class of actual environments, just as its appetite is equipped for possible diets rather than for specific foodstuffs" (Herrnstein & de Villiers, 1980, p. 87).

Pigeons apparently respond to the slides as representations of three-dimensional objects. For example, under certain schedules of reinforcement, pigeons will peck at other pigeons that happen to be available. Similarly, they will peck at the head region of a color photo of a pigeon (Looney & Cohen, 1974). This phenomenon is known as "schedule induced aggression." For present purposes the interesting point is not that pigeons show this aggression, but that they are willing to peck at the relevant portion of a picture of a pigeon in place of a live pigeon. Further evidence indicating that pigeons respond to photographs as representations of objects is that they immediately generalize to new slides of objects, photographed from different angles. They appear to be able to compensate for phenomena of perspective, such as foreshortening (see Hollard & Delius, 1982). Finally, they can transfer a discrimination from objects to pictures of those objects (Cabe, 1976) but apparently cannot transfer to line drawings of them.

Pigeons have an easier time discriminating between classes of objects than within classes of objects. Although we still do not know how pigeons and other animals define their object categories, the available evidence strongly suggests that they employ relatively abstract taxonomic classifications, which are difficult to describe in terms of simple physical characteristics or combinations of characteristics that unambiguously define the category.

LANGUAGE AS AN ENHANCER OF INTELLIGENCE

Premack's (1983) view is that language training affects animals' ability to use abstract concepts by allowing them to form abstract representations regarding the relations between relations and class membership. In contrast, non-language-trained animals are constrained to use only imaginal representations—information that can be represented by images. In Premack's view, each of the concept-discrimination tasks we have considered so far can be performed on the basis of physical features and judgments regarding their similarity or difference. Tasks such as simple discriminations and matching-to-sample and oddity-from-sample clearly can be solved on the basis of physical similarity or dissimilarity between features of the stimuli involved. Discriminations involving natural concepts such as trees, people, and fish can also be performed on the basis of physical similarity because "it is not clear what constitutes a 'simple feature.' Moreover, it does not seem that imaginal representation would itself set any limits on the complexity of what could serve as a feature" (Premack, 1983, p. 133). Only language-trained organisms are capable of solving problems that require the apprehension of relations between relations, because these tasks require the animal to use information that images cannot represent. In support of this claim, Premack has found a number of tasks that language-trained animals can perform, but non-language-trained animals cannot, and a group of tasks that both language-trained and non-language-trained chimpanzees perform equally well.

Tests that differentiate between language-trained and non-language-trained chimpanzees

Simultaneous same/different judgments.   In the simultaneous same/different task, the chimpanzee is confronted with two objects and required to respond either SAME, if they are identical, or DIFFERENT, if they are not. Figure 8.8 shows an example of this problem. In the first version of the task, the chimp must replace the bell-shaped symbol, which signals a question, with the correct symbol—either SAME, if the two objects are identical, or DIFFERENT, if they are not. In the second version of the task, the chimp must replace the question symbol with the correct item—either the matching object if the SAME symbol is used, or the nonmatching object, if the DIFFERENT symbol is used. Premack's language-trained chimpanzees perform this task, but his non-language-trained chimpanzees cannot. Apes, monkeys, and even to some extent pigeons (see Chapter 5) perform successive versions of this task, in which one item is presented and then followed by another item that is either identical or different (successive matching-to-sample and serial probe recognition). These same animals are also capable of performing simultaneous matching-to-sample. Premack's non-language-trained chimps, however, fail in performing the simultaneous version of the task. Premack claims that the non-language-trained animals succeed in the successive version of the task because they can solve the discrimination problem on the basis of familiarity. If the second stimulus is familiar, then they can respond SAME. If it is not familiar, then they respond DIFFERENT. Judgments of old/new, or familiar/unfamiliar are available to non-language-trained animals and are conceptually distinct from judgments of "same" versus "different." Non-language-trained animals fail on the simultaneous version of the task,

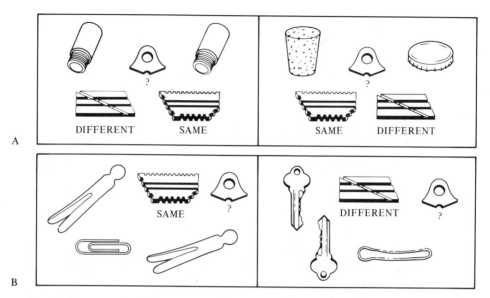

Figure 8.8. Four of Sarah's same/different problems. In the trial depicted in (A), she had to replace the interrogative marker (the bell shaped object above the question mark) with either the symbol for same or the symbol for different. In (B), Sarah had to replace the interrogative marker with an object to make the statement true. [From Premack & Premack, 1983.]

however, because it truly requires the animal to make a "same" versus "different" judgment. Familiarity is not sufficient.

On the surface, the simultaneous same/different task appears to be similar to simultaneous matching-to-sample, a task that pigeons can easily be trained to perform. The main difference between these tasks is the presentation of the nonmatching alternative. This alternative allows the animal to solve a matching-to-sample task on the basis of relative physical similarity. In the simultaneous same/different task, there is no nonmatching alternative and the animal must either make absolute judgments of similarity or it must decide on the basis of class membership. According to Premack, decisions regarding class membership require the abstract representations provided by language training.

Analogies.   The language-trained chimp, Sarah, can perform analogies of the form "A:A' ? B:B'" and of the form "A:A' SAME B:?" The first analogical test can be translated as "what is the relationship between the relation of A to A' and the relation of B to B'?" For example, the test might present two apples (A and A') and two bananas (B and B'). Because the relation between the apples is the same as the relation between the bananas—that is, the two apples are identical as are the two bananas—SAME is the correct response. The first task requires the chimp to fill in the symbol corresponding to the relation by choosing either SAME or DIFFERENT. The second task requires her to fill in the object corresponding to the relation. This might be translated as "what object would be appropriate as B' in order to make the relationship between A and A' the same as the relationship between B and B'?" For example, Sarah might be presented with two apples on one side and a banana on the other, separated by the token SAME. She could then select from an apple, a banana, and an orange, the single object that completed the analogy.

Non-language-trained chimpanzees were tested with a slightly modified procedure because they did not know how to use the tokens SAME and DIFFERENT. For example, with the pair XX as the standard, they were offered alternative pairs of XY, CD, and BB as choices. X might be an apple, Y an orange, C a pear, D an apricot, and B a peach. BB is the correct choice; the relation between a pair of apples is the same as the relation between a pair of peaches. Sarah chose correctly on this task 12 out of 12 times. Peony and Elizabeth, both language-trained, also performed this task at high levels of accuracy. In contrast, non-language-trained chimpanzees responded at chance levels over 360 trials with different analogies. Similarly, children below about 4 years of age failed to perform correctly with analogies of either the XX-YY or the XY-CD type. (In the latter type, the relation between an apple and an orange is the same as the relation between a pear and an apricot; both pairs have the relationship "different.") By the time children are 4½, however, they can solve the XX-YY type but still have difficulty with the XY-CD type. By the time they are 6, they can solve problems of both types. Extensive training improved the performance of the younger children (Premack, 1983).

Proportions. The comprehension of proportions was trained by using either fruits that were whole, or cut into quarters, halves, or three-quarter pieces, or glass cylinders that are either one quarter, one half, three quarters, or completely full. The tests were again given in matching-to-sample format. For example, the animal might be shown a quarter of an apple as the sample and allowed to choose between one quarter and three quarters of an apple. In later tests, proportions of apples were matched with proportions of cylinders and vice versa. For example, one quarter of an apple might be presented as the sample, and the chimp would be required to choose between two cylinders, one one quarter full, and the other one half full. Sarah passed both of these tests, but the non-language-trained chimps passed only when the sample and the alternatives were portions of the same kind of object—that is, either both fruits or both cylinders. When they were both of the same type, the chimps could presumably make the correct choice on the basis of appearance. Performance when the sample and the choices were of different types, however, presumably required the animal to make an abstract judgment about proportions.

Action and causality.   Another type of "sentence completion" task was used to study the chimpanzees' conception of action, specifically the actions of cutting, marking, and wetting. As Figure 8.9 shows, a typical complete sequence consists of three elements: an initial state (e.g., a whole apple), an instrument (e.g., a knife), and a terminal state (e.g., a cut apple). One could interpret this sequence as a kind of metasentence, "starting with a whole apple, a knife is used to convert it to a portion of an apple." In the tests the animal was given two elements of the sequence and was required to fill in the third. The tests shown in Figure 8.9 present an initial and a terminal state, for example, a whole apple and a cut apple. The animal must then fill in the instrument by correctly choosing a knife from among a knife, a bowl of water, and a pencil.

Figure 8.9. Action tests for cutting, wetting, and marking. This figure shows some of the action tests faced by the chimpanzee, Elizabeth. In (A), the chimp had to replace the question symbol in the middle with the agent that would transform a whole apple into a cut apple. In (B), she had to replace the question symbol with the agent that would transform a dry sponge into a wet sponge. [From Premack & Premack, 1983.]

All of the language-trained chimps were capable of completing those novel sequences in which either the terminal states (e.g., cut apple, wet sponge) or the agents (e.g., knife, water pail) were missing. In contrast, the non-language-trained animals did not pass, even if they practiced with eight replications of the same 12 object-agent pairs.

Tests that do not differentiate between language-trained and non-language-trained chimpanzees

Successive same/different judgments.   As described above, both language-trained and non-language-trained chimps perform well on a successive same/different task, in which the subject must judge whether two successively presented objects are the same or different.

Spatial reasoning.   Many children in the 3½- to 4-year-old range have difficulty performing a task that all the chimpanzees solve easily. In one version of this task the subject is shown two widely separated boxes. Into one box is placed, for example, an apple and into the other a banana. The subject is then removed from the room. On returning, the subject sees an experimenter standing midway between the two boxes, eating one of the two fruits. The subject is then allowed to go to and open one box. The box where the food being eaten by the experimenter was hidden is empty. Only the other box, where the alternative food was hidden, contains food. Children under about 4 years of age go to either box equally often. They do not seem able to integrate the information about the foods hidden in each location with the information about the food being eaten by the experimenter. Somewhat older children and the chimpanzees that Premack tested are able to integrate these two sources of information, and they go reliably to the box containing the remaining fruit.

The effects of language training considered

Premack has discovered that language-trained chimpanzees perform some tasks that non-language-trained chimpanzees do not. He has argued that this difference results because language training enhances the animals' intelligence. Specifically, he claims that language training enables animals to use abstract representations. In contrast, non-language-trained animals are limited to imaginal codes. These codes contain no information about the objects they represent other than records of their sensory properties. Tasks that differentiate between language-trained and non-language-trained animals are those that require the subjects to make judgments about the relations between relations or to use an abstract, nonimaginal code. Tasks that fail to differentiate between the two groups are solvable using concrete or imaginal representations.

Premack proposes using a test of isomorphism as a criterion for determining whether purely imaginal codes are sufficient to perform a task:

> ... since we can evaluate the correspondence between items and representations of items (even if only in principle) for these cases, we consider imaginal representations a possibility. On the other hand, problems that concern the relations between relations (problems that do differentiate between the two groups) are, generally speaking, problems in which the isomorphism criterion [between items and their representations] cannot be applied. (Premack, 1983, pp. 126–127)

For example, language-trained animals judge the relation between a can opener and a can to be the same as that between a key and a lock. This judgment presumably cannot be made by comparing images because an open lock—for example, one with one end of its shackle visible—simply does not "look" sufficiently similar to an open can—for example, one with its lid off and the tunafish visible. The common feature—opening—that makes the analogy appropriate, cannot be represented by an image. Similarly, abstract codes are required to judge membership in functional categories. For example, one cannot decide that a top and a doll are members of the same category (toys) on the basis of similarity between their images. Their similarity derives not from their appearance, but from their use in play.

While Premack's interpretation of these data may be attractive (cf. Chapters 4 and 5), it is not the only sensible interpretation. Among the difficulties with his interpretation are the following:

Abstract versus imaginal codes.   Application of an isomorphism criterion, such as Premack proposes, has proved to be extremely problematical for cognitive scientists. The isomorphism criterion relies on personal intuitions regarding the sufficiency of imaginal representations, but intuitions are a poor substitute for data. The only data Premack has to support his distinction is the observed difference between language-trained and non-language-trained chimpanzees, but these are the data he is trying to explain. According to his intuitions, trees and fish can be represented by images because they "look alike," but "opening" cannot be similarly represented. Although one can imagine many different examples of opening, the common property of all of them (i.e., opening) cannot be represented as an image. The concept of opening is different from any imaginable instance of opening. Premack must somehow explain how different examples of opening do not look alike, whereas different examples of fish or people do. This he has not done.

Not everyone shares Premack's intuitions regarding the simplicity of discriminating fish from nonfish, persons from nonpersons, or trees from nontrees. Careful analysis by Herrnstein and others fails to uncover the sensory features that are shared by all slides of fish and by none of the slides without fish. There is no reason to believe that two pictures of people taken from widely different angles and distances, for example, a part of a person close up versus a crowd of people of different races from far away, are any more similar than are the opening of a lock and the opening of a box. If features can be sufficiently complicated to yield appropriate classification of stimuli as disparate as those used by Herrnstein and his associates (e.g., Herrnstein, Loveland, & Cable, 1976), then they should be sufficient to account for judgments regarding opening (See Block, 1983).

Another important difficulty with Premack's conceptualization of the differences he observed between language-trained and non-language-trained chimpanzees is that no single image could ever suffice to represent all members of even simple categories. For example, consider an image of a triangle (isosceles, right, equilateral, large, small, etc.; cf. Fields, 1932) or a generic image of a dog (e.g., chihuahua, German shepard, great Dane, terrier, St. Bernard). Clearly, any animal that can discriminate open-ended categories must either be able to use propositional codes, or such codes cannot be reliably detected on the basis of presumed isomorphisms between representations and objects. In either case, we cannot use differences of this sort to differentiate between language-trained and non-language-trained animals.

The role of relations beween relations.   Premack argued that those tasks that differentiated between language-trained and non-language-trained chimps were those that required the animals to make judgments about relations between relations. As Block (1983) points out, all of the relations that Premack alleges cannot be solved using imaginal codes are closely associated with *activities.* In principle, they could all be judged on the basis of the similarity of the imagined activity, rather than on the basis of the relation. Conversely, judging the relations between relations is also applicable to simpler kinds of tasks that do not differentiate between language-trained and non-language-trained chimps. For example, location is a relation between an object and its environment. The location of food is a relation, the location of the chimp is another relation, and the vector connecting food to a chimpanzee is a relation between the two relations (Miller, 1983). Therefore, the inability of non-language-trained chimps to solve problems that Premack claims require judgments regarding the relations between relations probably does not result from their inability to represent or process such second-order relations; the differences are more likely caused by some other factor.

Language training makes test-wise chimpanzees.   One possible difference that could account for the difference between language-trained and non-language-trained chimpanzees is their degree of test sophistication. Most of the comparisons between the two types were actually comparisons between Sarah and a group of younger chimps. At the time of Premack's 1983 report, Sarah had been involved in tests of one sort or another for more than 19 years. As he notes, much of this training involved specifically the application of relation judgments to "sentence completion." This is the major format for the tests that differentiated between groups of chimps. Thus, in the experience provided by Premack and his associates, Sarah has had 19 years in which to learn that locks open and boxes open, perhaps by associating the same symbol with both examples of opening.[4] In any event, she certainly has had ample opportunity to become so test-wise that she could rapidly determine which of the very few alternative responses provided by the experimenter would yield reinforcement. By this argument, Sarah's success in analogies represents nothing more than her success in labeling relations and actions. Similarly, the action-sequence completion tasks are very similar in form to the sentence completion tasks with which the language-trained chimpanzees were drilled. All of the apes had abundant experience with the actions themselves, so they presumably were able to represent them. Thus, the only thing the non-language-trained chimpanzees lacked was precisely the experience of completing sequences.

The thrust of this argument is that the data are incomplete. As Premack himself notes, these are tentative conclusions based on work in progress. Moreover, they are largely based on the performance of a single animal. Despite these limitations and caveats, however, they are powerful in suggesting important lines of research. They haunt the very foundations of what we believe about language and about comparative cognition. At issue are questions of whether chimpanzees can learn language, what kind of language they can learn, and what it does to them to learn language. More generally, we are led to ask about the effects of language learning on the representational and thinking processes of humans and the relationship between those cognitive skills underlying language and those more generally used. These will turn out to be exciting questions in the future of comparative cognition.

CONCLUSION

The relationship between language and cognition is one of the central issues in cognitive science. It is also likely to be an important issue in comparative cognition because, by working with animals, we can dissociate features of general experience from specific features of language training. There is little doubt that language-trained animals perform differently from non-language-trained animals, but it remains unclear what aspects of the language-training experience are influential in producing this difference.

Understanding the relation between language training and cognition requires that we understand both the process of language training and the cognitive features, skills, and processes that animals have or are capable of acquiring. These issues are at the heart of all biological approaches to cognition, including questions of its evolution and physiology. Undoubtedly, these issues will remain important in the coming years.

SUMMARY

We can study the evolution of language capacities in two ways. The first is to study the fossil and artifact remains of our ancestors. The second is to study currently existing species for evidence of the precursors of language. This second approach has led to two lines of research. One pursues the natural behaviors of animals to see what features of language they naturally possess in their communication system. The other tries to see what capacities animals might have for learning language skills based on their preexisting, but not necessarily demonstrated, capacities.

Five features appear to be characteristic of language. These include reference, grammar, productivity, situational freedom, and communication of new information. Traditional views of animal communication held that it was merely a byproduct of the animal's physiological state. More recent views emphasize the information in animal communication.

Attempts to teach chimpanzees to speak have failed, perhaps because chimps do not have an adequate vocal apparatus. Visual languages have proved more successful in training apes, dolphins, and sea lions. These studies are all suggestive of the presence of linguistic skills in animals, but they are not yet conclusive.

Many animals have been found capable of forming open-ended conceptual categories that cannot be reduced to simple feature discriminations. Language training appears to affect how animals perform on tasks that involve conceptual categories, but it remains unclear what aspects of language training are responsible for these differences.

RECOMMENDED READINGS

Herrnstein, R. J., & de Villiers, P. A. (1980) Fish as a natural category for people and pigeons. *The Psychology of Learning and Motivation, 14,* 59–95.

Premack, D. (1983) The codes of man and beasts. *The Behavioral and Brain Sciences, 6,* 125–167.

Premack, D., & Premack, A. J. (1983) *The mind of an ape.* New York: W. W. Norton.

Ristau, C. A., & Robbins, D. (1982) Language in the great apes: A critical review. *Advances in the Study of Behavior, 12,* 141–255.

Sebeok, T. A. (Ed.)(1977) *How animals communicate.* Bloomington, Ind.: Indiana University Press.

Seidenberg, M. S., & Petitto, L. A. (1979) Signing behavior in apes: A critical review. *Cognition, 7,* 177–215.

Terrace, H. S. (1979) *Nim.* New York: Knopf.

Notes

CHAPTER 1

1. I am here using the term *animal* in its colloquial sense, meaning, more precisely, nonhuman animal. Of course, it is true that humans are also animals, and that the comparison of human and nonhuman animals is simply a special case of interspecies comparison.

2. Comparative cognition adopts a monist position on the relation between mind and brain. They are one and the same thing. According to this position, mind is a functional property of brain activity. The nature of the mind derives from the organization of neural elements and activity.

3. Operant, or Skinnerian, psychologists—also known as behavioral analysists—came part of the way from a purely physicalist perspective. Operant conditioning emphasizes the function of the behavior rather than its form or topography. For example, a typical operant is bar pressing. A rat could press with its right paw, its left paw, its nose, and so forth. Each of these behaviors is an equivalent operant so long as it has the same physically defined effect in a

physically defined situation—for example, producing a force of 0.1 newtons on a particular bar. The issue is not whether the environments and behaviors are physical; it is whether they are physically or informationally defined. An informational definition recognizes that objects with different physical characteristics can be equivalent under defined circumstances.

4. The earliest modern developments of general purpose computers used the reverse analogy (see Hodges, 1983). The developers sought to create machines that would be like human minds. Actual construction of these machines, however, resulted in concrete developments in computers and computing that were not derived from the machine-as-mind metaphor and that supplied content to the later development of the mind-as-machine metaphor.

5. For practical reasons (e.g., finite memory), any actual machine can only approximate a truly universal Turing machine.

6. A related distinction is the difference between knowing how to perform some skill, such as typewriting or riding a bicycle, versus knowing how to describe it.

7. For example, consider the string: 7573656C657373. This string could represent any number of things. It could be a serial number for a television or a driver's license number. It could also be the coded representation of the word *useless*. The appropriate encoding process would be able to "translate" this string into its appropriate form. Cryptography and cryptanalysis are fields concerned with the relation between codes and objects.

8. It is unclear whether the people tested by Kroll and his associates refrained from acoustic recoding because they chose a more efficient code or because the shadowing task prevented them from recoding.

CHAPTER 2

1. During the Dark Ages (500–1200) and the Middle Ages (1200–1500) western intellectual life was dominated by a concern with theological issues and an acceptance of authority as the source of knowledge. In contrast, Descartes's Renaissance was characterized by a new skepticism, in which philosophers questioned all of their basic premises. Descartes attempted to begin with the position of doubting everything and then to see what could be proved. He recognized that even if he were deceived in everything he believed, he would still have to exist in order to be deceived (*cogito ergo sum*). From this foundation based on doubt, Descartes inferred that the mind had an immediately self-evident existence as a thing. He then came to grips with the world around him by assuming the existence of a physical world that paralleled his self-evident mental world.

2. By Darwin's time the soul was generally distinguished from the mind. Thus, scientific discussion turned to consideration of the mind, rather than the soul.

3. Evolutionary continuity does not imply that all species have identical properties or faculties varying only in degree. Instead, it claims that the characteristics of all organisms have developed from the characteristics of their ancestors. Mutation is the only source for new genes and, therefore, of heritable characteristics. Continuity recognizes that species can have unique characteristics, but these are the result of selection from a gene pool, modified by mutation, not the result of special, unique, or purposeful creation. (See Dawkins, 1976.)

4. It is not entirely clear that consciousness means the same thing to every comparative psychologist. Sometimes the term seems to be used as a general alternative to mechanical, reflex-based explanations of behavior. At other times, it seems to refer to something similar to memory, as in the claim that events cannot affect later behavior unless consciously experienced.

5. Kohler recognized that experience was important but that the role of experience was not to provide opportunities for blind trial and error. Instead, experience was to provide knowledge that the animals could later use in a novel and insightful manner (see Birch, 1945; Epstein, Krishnit, Lanza, & Rubin, 1984).

6. Watson recognized that these claims went beyond his available facts; nevertheless, they clearly indicate his radical environmental aspirations for behaviorist psychology.

7. Although Tolman argued that animals behave purposively, he did not suggest that conscious awareness was necessary or even suggested. Animals behave as if they have a purpose, not according to some conscious purpose.

8. The slogan of the Gestalt movement was, "the whole is greater than the sum of its parts," meaning that whole things have the properties of their elements as well as unique or emergent properties that derive from the organization of the elements. The emergent properties of a whole are lost when it is analyzed into its component elements, just as the meaning of a word is lost when its separate letters are scrambled. Tolman was attracted by many features of the Gestalt movement.

9. For more information and significantly different views, one could consult recent issues of the journal *Behaviorism*, books by Rachlin (1970) or Reynolds (1975), or the special issue on Skinner's canonical papers in *The behavioral and brain sciences* (Skinner, 1984).

10. Skinner is a little more elaborate in accounting for species differences. For Skinner, the behavior of an organism is shaped by "(1) the selective action of that environment during the evolution of the species, (2) its effect in shaping and maintaining the repertoire of behavior which converts each member of a species

into a person, and (3) its role as the occasion upon which behavior occurs" (Skinner, 1978, p. 97). Nevertheless, the ways in which each of these factors affects behavior are always the same.

CHAPTER 3

1. The direction of attention can occur at many levels. For example, one way to select visual information is to control the orientation of your eyes. If is difficult to read a book while your eyes are directed toward a television set. This kind of selectivity has generally been uninteresting to psychologists. Instead, they have been more concerned with the kinds of selectivity that are not accompanied by overt receptor orientation. The principles that govern selectivity—what the organism selects and what it neglects—at peripheral and central level are likely to be similar, however, even if the mechanisms are not.

2. A dimension is an attribute that can take on one of several mutually exclusive values. For example, one ball may differ from another along such dimensions as color—if it is red, it cannot also be blue; size—if it is 5 inches across, it cannot also be 7 inches across; or weight—if it weighs 1 kg, it cannot also weigh 2 kg. The stimuli used in psychological experiments often differ along such dimensions as color, brightness, position, and so forth. The term *dimension* is also used to refer to the independent ways in which something can vary. For example, one learning model proposes that learning consists of only one kind of change—that of response potential—ranging from extreme negative (inhibition) to extreme positive (excitation). Other models include more dimensions. One such model asserts that learning consists of changes along two independent dimensions—the organism's response potential and its attentional selectivity. These models are described later in the chapter. An organism can learn to pay attention or to ignore a stimulus without changing its response potential connected to that stimulus.

3. An alternative explanation for these findings is even more damaging to the continuity hypothesis. According to this hypothesis, overtraining makes the animals "test-wise" or more sensitive to contingencies of reinforcement. This is problematical for the continuity position because it argues that animals learn about features of a discrimination that cannot be attributed either to learning about stimuli or about dimensions. Such a hypothesis receives support from learning-set experiments, in which subjects are trained on many discrimination problems in succession. After many problems they are eventually able to respond with near-perfect accuracy on the second trial of a new problem (Harlow, 1949; Kamil, Lougee, & Schulman, 1973).

4. Blough did not, however, test this assumption explicitly.

CHAPTER 4

1. There is some ambiguity about the term *reflex* (see Fearing, 1930). Sometimes it refers to a neural structure involved in the organism's production of behavior in response to stimulation. At other times it refers to a functionally uniform type of behavior. At still others, it refers to a correlation between a stimulus and a response (Skinner, 1938).

2. S-R theorists rarely refer to changes in S-R connections as changes in knowledge. Alternatively, Skinner places learning in contingencies. "Behavior changes because contingencies change, not because a mental entity called a concept develops" (Skinner, 1978, p. 100).

3. The operant behaviorists distinguish the obligatory/automatic kind of reflex characteristic of Pavlov, Sechenov, and others from the idea of a stochastic correlation kind of reflex.

4. In passive avoidance the animal prevents the presentation of an aversive event so long as it refrains from making a particular response. In typical passive avoidance experiments, rats are shocked when they step off of a safety platform onto an electric grid floor. Memory is indexed by the rat's latency to leave the platform. Long latencies indicate good retention from a learning trial.

5. In Pavlov's time, psychology meant introspective structuralism (see Chapter 2).

6. Skinner's account was later found to be incomplete (Staddon & Simmelhag, 1971).

7. See Mackintosh, 1983, p. 31, for more examples of persistent responding despite reinforcer omission.

8. Pecks to the key associated with food were sharp, the birds' beak opening slightly on contact and the eyes closing. Pecks to the key associated with water were soft and of longer duration with the birds' eyes open.

9. Holland and Straub trained a "learned taste aversion" by pairing the food with lithium chloride. A related experiment increased the preference for the US. Injections with the chemical formalin induce a salt-deficiency in rats. Animals that are initially trained to associate one flavor with salt and another flavor with sugar prefer the sugar-associated flavor. Their preferences reverse, however, when they are injected with formalin and given a choice between the two flavors, now without either the sugar or the salt. Rats with an induced salt-deficiency prefer the flavor formerly associated with salt over that formerly associated with sugar (Fudim, 1978).

10. An atom of sodium consists of lower-level units, such as protons and neutrons. The defining characteristic of a chemical element is the number of protons

in its nucleus. If the number changes, the chemical and its properties change. Individual protons do not have the properties of the chemicals that they constitute. Thus, individual protons cannot be understood as sodium; they are sodium only by being in company with a certain number of other protons (the protons themselves even have a substructure). Similarly, an elementary unit of behavior consists of lower-level units such as muscle fibers. The defining characteristic of an elementary behavioral unit is the pattern of action of the muscle fibers and the source of the signal originating the action. Individual muscle fibers cannot meaningfully be understood as an action. Although each fiber can serve as part of a large number of different elementary units, the muscle fiber by itself does not define any particular behavioral unit.

CHAPTER 5

1. This explanation is analogous to the explanation for the effect of surprising changes in chamber illumination during the retention interval. The animal allocates processing capacity to the added stimulus and, as a result, is less able to rehearse the sample.

CHAPTER 6

1. All cognitive activity is the result of the action of the various parts of the brain. Time is represented in the animal's neural pacemaker. Other information is presumably represented in other parts of the animal's brain.

2. The nictitating membrane is a translucent third eyelid present in many animals.

CHAPTER 7

1. This is something of an oversimplification. Readers who are interested in a more adequate description of the assumptions and work in behavioral ecology can consult Dawkins, 1976; Krebs & Davies, 1978, 1981; Wilson, 1976.

2. The evolutionary concept of fitness does not refer to how big and tough the organism is. It refers to the organism's relative success in propagating copies of its genes. Survival of the fittest means that differential reproduction is the mechanism of evolution.

3. Chance was estimated by measuring the area the bird could search with one probe.

4. This is not true for certain plants, such as those that disperse their seeds in edible fruits or for certain parasites.

CHAPTER 8

1. Abstract categories, such as toys or tools, contain physical objects, each of which can be described by a set of physical features, but we cannot point to any specific set of features that is sufficient to define the category members as instances of the category.

2. Notice how the memory demands of serial probe recognition (SPR) are different from those of DMTS. Many more stimuli are used in SPR than in DMTS, and, therefore, the subject performing SPR must apparently maintain information about the physical characteristics of the stimuli. At this point no investigations have been made (so far as I am aware) into how much or what information is maintained about the list items. For example, would the animal respond SAME if a different photo of the same object—perhaps from a different viewpoint—were used as the probe? The impact of SPR performance on theories of working memory (see Chapter 5) relies on these investigations and is currently unclear.

3. To be sure, they all "looked" like white oak leaves. The question is: What makes a white oak leaf look like a white oak leaf? What is the process by which that judgment is made? This point is discussed more fully later in the text.

4. Would similar results be obtained if animals were trained to make one response to members of one artificial class and to make another response to members of another class? Would they then be able to make "functional" categorizations among objects on the basis of the associated response?

References

Adams, C. D. (1982) Variations in the sensitivity of instrumental responding to reinforcer devaluation. *Quarterly Journal of Experimental Psychology, 34B,* 77–98.

Adams, C., & Dickinson, A. (1981) Actions and habits: Variations in associative representations during instrumental learning. In N. E. Spear & R. R. Miller (Eds.), *Information processing in animals: Memory mechanisms.* Hillsdale, N.J.: Erlbaum, 143–166.

Amsel, A., & Rashotte, M. E. (Eds.) (1984) *Mechanisms of adaptive behavior: Clark L. Hull's theoretical papers, with commentary.* New York: Columbia University Press.

Anderson, J. R. (1978) Arguments concerning representations for mental imagery. *Psychological Review, 85,* 249–277.

Anderson, J. R., & Bower, G. H. (1973) *Human associative memory.* Washington, D.C.: Winston.

325

Aschoff, J. (1984) Circadian Timing. In J. Gibbon & L. Allan (Eds.), *Timing and time perception*. New York: Annals of the New York Academy of Sciences, vol. 423, 442–468.

Atkinson, R. C., & Shiffrin, R. M. (1968) Human memory: A proposed system and its control processes. *The Psychology of Learning and Motivation: Advances in Research and Theory, 2,* 89–196.

Baker, A. G., & Mackintosh, N. J. (1979) Preexposure to the CS alone, US alone, or CS and US uncorrelated: Latent inhibition, blocking by context, or learned irrelevance? *Learning and Motivation, 10,* 278–294.

Balda, R. P., & Turek, F. J. (1984) Memory in Birds. In H. L. Roitblat, T. G. Bever, & H. S. Terrace (Eds.), *Animal Cognition*. Hillsdale, N.J.: Erlbaum, 513–532.

Barker, L. M., Best, M., & Domjan, M. (1977) *Learning mechanisms in food selection*. Waco, Texas: Baylor University Press.

Barlow, G. W. (1977) Modal action patterns. In T. A. Sebeok (Ed.), *How animals communicate*. Bloomington, Ind.: Indiana University Press, 98–134.

Baum, W. M. (1981) Matching, undermatching, and overmatching in studies of choice. *Journal of the Experimental Analysis of Behavior, 32,* 269–281.

Beatty, W. W., & Shavalia, D. A. (1980) Spatial memory in rats: Time course of working memory and effect of anesthetics. *Behavioral Biology, 28,* 454–462.

Beer, T., Bethe, A., & von Uexkull, J. (1899) Vorschlage zu einer objektivirender Nomenklatur in der Physiologie der Nervensystems. *Zeitschrift fur Physiologie, 13,* 137–141.

Belovsky, G. E. (1978) Diet optimization in a generalist herbivore, the moose. *Theoretical Population Biology, 14,* 105–134.

Bever, T. G. (1984) The road from behaviorism to rationalism. In H. L. Roitblat, T. G. Bever, & H. S. Terrace (Eds.), *Animal cognition*. Hillsdale, N.J.: Erlbaum, 61–75.

Bever, T. G., Straub, R. O., Terrace, H. S., & Townsend, D. J. (1980) Study of serial behavior in humans and nonhumans. In P. Jucsyk & D. Klein (Eds.), *The nature of thought: Essays in honor of D. O. Hebb*. Hillsdale, N.J.: Erlbaum.

Birch, H. G. (1945) The relation of previous experience to insightful problem solving. *Journal of Comparative and Physiological Psychology, 38,* 367–383.

Bitterman, M. E. (1964) Classical conditioning in the goldfish as a function of the CS-US interval. *Journal of Comparative and Physiological Psychology, 58,* 359–366.

Block, N. (1983) Resemblance and imaginal representation. *The Behavioral and Brain Sciences, 6,* 142–143.

Blough, D. S. (1958) A method for obtaining psychophysical thresholds from the pigeon. *Journal of the Experimental Analysis of Behavior, 1,* 31–43.

Blough, D. S. (1959) Delayed matching in the pigeon. *Journal of the Experimental Analysis of Behavior, 2,* 151–160.

Blough, D. S. (1969) Attention shifts in a maintained discrimination. *Science, 166,* 125–126.

Bolles, R. C. (1975) Learning, motivation and cognition. In W. K. Estes (Ed.), *Handbook of learning and cognition,* vol. 1. Hillsdale, N.J.: Erlbaum, 249–280.

Boring, E. G. (1950) *A history of experimental psychology.* New York: Appleton-Century-Crofts.

Branch, M. N. (1982) Misrepresenting behaviorism. *The Behavioral and Brain Sciences, 5,* 372–373.

Breland, K., & Breland, M. (1961) The misbehavior of organisms. *American Psychologist, 16,* 661–664.

Breland, K., & Breland, M. (1966) *Animal behavior.* New York: Macmillan.

Bridgman, P. W. (1927) *The logic of modern physics.* New York: Macmillan.

Broadbent, D. E. (1958) *Perception and communication.* London: Pergamon.

Brogden, W. J. (1939a) Unconditional stimulus-substitution in the conditioning process. *American Journal of Psychology, 52,* 46–55.

Brogden, W. J. (1939b) The effect of frequency of reinforcement upon the level of conditioning. *Journal of Experimental Psychology, 24,* 419–431.

Brower, L. P. (1971) Prey coloration and predator behavior. In V. G. Dethier (Ed.), *Topics in the study of life: The BIO source book,* section 6. New York: Harper and Row.

Brown, P. L., & Jenkins, H. M. (1968) Auto-shaping of the pigeon's key peck. *Journal of the Experimental Analysis of Behavior, 11,* 1–8.

Brown, T. G. (1914) On the nature of the fundamental activity of the nervous centers; together with an analysis of the conditioning and rhythmic activity in progression, and a theory of evolution of function in the nervous system. *Journal of Physiology, 48,* 18–46.

Bruner, J. S. (1969) Modalities of memory. In G. A. Talland & N. C. Waugh (Eds.), *The pathology of memory.* New York: Academic Press.

Bullock, D. H., & Smith, W. C. (1953) An effect of repeated conditioning-extinction upon operant strength. *Journal of Experimental Psychology, 46,* 349–352.

Cabe, P. A. (1976) Discrimination of stereometric and planometric displays by pigeons. *Perceptual and Motor Skills, 42,* 1243–1250.

Capaldi, E. J., Verry, D. R., & Davidson, T. L. (1980) Memory, serial anticipation pattern learning and transfer in rats. *Animal Learning and Behavior, 8,* 575–585.

Carter, D. E. (1971) *Acquisition of a conditional discrimination: A comparison of matching to sample and symbolic matching.* Ph.D thesis. New York: Columbia University.

Carter, D. E., & Eckerman, D. A. (1975) Symbolic matching by pigeons: Rate of learning complex discriminations predicted from simple discriminations. *Science, 187,* 662–664.

Carter, D. E., & Werner, T. J. (1978) Complex learning and information processing by pigeons: A critical analysis. *Journal of the Experimental Analysis of Behavior, 29,* 565–601.

Catania, A. C. (1963) Concurrent performance: A baseline for the study of reinforcement magnitude. *Journal of the Experimental Analysis of Behavior, 6,* 299–300.

Cerella, J. (1979) Visual classes and natural categories in the pigeon. *Journal of Experimental Psychology: Human Perception and Performance, 5,* 68–77.

Chen, J. S., & Amsel, A. (1980) Recall (versus recognition) immunization against aversive taste anticipations based on illness. *Science, 209,* 851–853.

Cheney, D. L., & Seyfarth, R. M. (1980) Vocal recognition in free-ranging vervet monkeys. *Animal Behaviour, 28,* 362–367.

Cheng, K., & Gallistel, C. R. (1984) Testing the geometric power of an animal's spatial representation. In H. L. Roitblat, T. G. Bever, & H. S. Terrace (Eds.), *Animal cognition.* Hillsdale, N.J.: Erlbaum, 409–423.

Chomsky, N. (1972) *Language and mind.* New York: Harcourt, Brace, Jovanovich.

Church, R. M., & Deluty, M. Z. (1977) Bisection of temporal intervals. *Journal of Experimental Psychology: Animal Behavior Processes, 3,* 216–228.

Church, R. M. (1978) The internal clock. In S. H. Hulse, H. Fowler, & W. K. Honig (Eds.), *Cognitive processes in animal behavior.* Hillsdale, N.J.: Erlbaum, 277–310.

Church, R. M. (1984) Properties of the internal clock. In J. Gibbon & L. Allan (Eds.), *Timing and time perception*. New York: Annals of the New York Academy of Sciences, vol. 423, 566–582.

Church, R. M., & Gibbon, J. (1982) Temporal generalization. *Journal of Experimental Psychology: Animal Behavior Processes, 8,* 165–186.

Cohen, L. R., Looney, T. A., Brady, J. H., & Acuella, A. F. (1976) Differential sample response schedules in the acquisition of conditional discriminations by pigeons. *Journal of the Experimental Analysis of Behavior, 26,* 301–314.

Cohen, N. J., & Squire, L. R. (1981) Retrograde amnesia and remote memory impairment. *Neuropsychologia, 19,* 337–356.

Conrad, R. (1964) Acoustic confusions in immediate memory. *British Journal of Psychology, 55,* 75–84.

Cook, R. G. (1980) Retroactive interference in pigeon short-term memory by a reduction in ambient illumination. *Journal of Experimental Psychology: Animal Behavior Processes, 6,* 326–338.

Cook, R. G., Brown, M. F., & Riley, D. A. (1985) Flexible memory processing by rats: Use of prospective and retrospective information in the radial maze. *Journal of Experimental Psychology: Animal Behavior Processes, 11,* 453–469.

Cowie, R. J., Krebs, J. R., & Sherry, D. F. (1981) Food storing by marsh tits. *Animal Behaviour, 29,* 1252–1259.

Craik, F. I. M., & Lockhart, R. S. (1972) Levels of processing: A framework for memory research. *Journal of Verbal Learning and Verbal Behavior, 11,* 671–684.

Crespi, L. P. (1942) Quantitative variation of incentive and performance in the white rat. *American Journal of Psychology, 55,* 467–517.

Croze, H. J. (1970) Searching image in carrion crows. *Zeitschrift fur Tierpsychologie,* supplement 5, 1–85.

Cumming, W. W., & Berryman, R. R. (1965) Stimulus generalization. In D. I. Mostofsky (Ed.), *Stimulus generalization*. Stanford: Stanford University Press, 284–330.

Curio, E. (1976) *The ethology of predation*. New York: Springer-Verlag.

D'Amato, M. R. (1973) Delayed matching and short-term memory in monkeys. *The Psychology of Learning and Motivation: Advances in Research and Theory, 7,* 227–269.

D'Amato, M. R., & Cox, J. K. (1976) Delay of consequences and short-term memory in monkeys. In D. L. Medin, W. A. Roberts, & R. T. Davis (Eds.),

Processes in animal memory. Hillsdale, N.J.: Erlbaum, 49–78.

D'Amato, M. R., & Fazzaro, J. (1966) Discriminated bar press avoidance maintenance and extinction in rats as a function of shock intensity. *Journal of Comparative and Physiological Psychology, 61,* 313–315.

D'Amato, M. R., Salmon, D. P., & Colombo, M. (1985) Extent and limits of the matching concept in monkeys *(cebus apella). Journal of Experimental Psychology: Animal Behavior Processes, 11,* 35–51.

Darwin, C. R. (1874) *The descent of man, and selection in relation to sex.* New York: Lovell, Coryell, & Co.

Davies, N. B. (1977) Prey selection and social behaviour in wagtails (Aves: Motacillidae). *Journal of Animal Ecology, 46,* 37–57.

Dawkins, M. (1971) Perceptual changes in chicks: Another look at the "search image" concept. *Animal Behavior, 19,* 566–574.

Dawkins, R. (1976) *The selfish gene.* Oxford: Oxford University Press.

Dennett, D. C. (1978) *Brainstorms: Philosophical essays on mind and psychology.* Montgomery, VT.: Bradford.

Dennett, D. C. (1983) Intentional systems in cognitive ecology: "The panglossian paradigm" defended. *The Behavioral and Brain Sciences, 6,* 343–355.

De Ruiter, L. (1952) Some experiments on the camouflage of stick caterpillars. *Behaviour, 4,* 222–232.

Descartes, R. (1637/1960) Discourse on method, and meditations. Translated by L. J. Lafleur. New York: Liberal Arts Press. Originally published 1637.

Descartes, R. (1662) *Traité de l'homme.*

DeValois, R. L., & Jacobs, G. H. (1968) Primate color vision. *Science, 162,* 533–540.

Devine, J. D., Burke, M. W., & Rohack, J. J. (1979) Stimulus similarity and order as factors in visual short-term memory in nonhuman primates. *Journal of Experimental Psychology: Animal Behavior Processes, 5,* 335–354.

Dews, P. B. (1962) The effect of multiple S^{Δ} periods on responding on a fixed-interval schedule. *Journal of the Experimental Analysis of Behavior, 5,* 369–374.

Dews, P. B. (1970) The theory of fixed-interval responding. In W. N. Schoenfeld (Ed.), *The theory of reinforcement schedules.* New York: Appleton-Century-Crofts, 43–61.

Dickinson, A. (1980) *Contemporary animal learning theory.* London: Cambridge University Press.

Dickinson, A., Hall, G., & Mackintosh, N. J. (1976) Surprise and the attenuation of blocking. *Journal of Experimental Psychology: Animal Behavior Processes, 2,* 313–322.

Dickinson, A., Nicholas, D. J., & Adams, C. D. (1983) The effect of the instrumental training contingency on susceptibility to reinforcer devaluation. *Quarterly Journal of Experimental Psychology, 35B,* 35–51.

Duncan, C. P. (1949) The retroactive effect of electroconvulsive shock on learning. *Journal of Comparative and Physiological Psychology, 42,* 32–44.

Edmunds (1974) *Defence in animals: A summary of anti-predator defences.* Burnt Hills, England: Longman.

Ehrenfreund, D. (1948) An experimental test of the continuity theory of discrimination learning with pattern vision. *Journal of Comparative and Physiological Psychology, 41,* 408–422.

Elliott, M. H. (1928) The effect of change of reward on the maze performance of rats. *University of California Publications in Psychology, 4,* 19–30.

Epstein, R., Krishnit, C. E., Lanza, R. P., & Rubin, L. C. (1984) "Insight" in the pigeon: Antecedants and determinants of an intelligent performance. *Nature, 308,* 61–62.

Estes, W. K. (1975) *Handbook of learning and cognitive processes,* vol. 2. Hillsdale, N.J.: Erlbaum.

Estes, W. K., Koch, S., MacCorquodale, K., Meehl, P. E., Mueller, C. G., Jr., Schoenfeld, W. N., & Verplank, W. S. (1954) *Modern learning theory.* New York: Appleton-Century-Crofts.

Fearing, F. (1930) *Reflex action: A study in the history of physiological psychology.* Baltimore: Williams & Wilkins.

Ferster, C. B., & Skinner, B. F. (1957) *Schedules of reinforcement.* New York: Appleton-Century-Crofts.

Fields, P. E. (1932) Studies in concept formation: I. The development of the concept of triangularity by the white rat. *Comparative Psychology Monographs, 9,* 1–70.

Finke, R. A. (1980) Levels of equivalence in imagery and perception. *Psychological Review, 86,* 113–132.

Flaherty, C. F., & Largen, J. (1975) Within subjects positive and negative contrast effects in rats. *Journal of Comparative and Physiological Psychology, 88,* 653–664.

Forbes, S. M., Taylor, M. M., & Lindsay, P. H. (1967) Cue timing in a multi-dimensional detection task. *Perceptual and Motor Skills, 25,* 113–120.

Fouts, R. S. (1974) Capacities for languages in great apes. *Proceedings of the 18th International Congress of Anthropological and Ethnological Sciences.* The Hague: Mouton, 1–20.

Fouts, R. S., & Rigby, R. L. (1977) Man-chimpanzee communication. In T. A. Sebeok (Ed.), *How animals communicate.* Bloomington, Ind.: Indiana University Press, 1034–1054.

Fraenkel, G. (1927) Beitrage zur Geotaxis und Phototaxis von Littorina. *Zeitschrift fur vergleichende Physiologie, 5,* 585–597. Translated and reprinted in C. R. Gallistel (Tr., Ed., 1980), *The organization of action: A new synthesis.* Hillsdale, N.J.: Erlbaum, 149–161.

Frisch, K. von. (1967) *The dance language and orientation of bees.* Translated by L. Chadwick. Cambridge, Mass.: Harvard University Press.

Fudim, O. K. (1978) Sensory preconditioning of flavors with a formalin-produced sodium need. *Journal of Experimental Psychology: Animal Behavior Processes, 4,* 276–285.

Gaffan, D. (1983) Animal amnesia: Some disconnection syndromes? In W. Seifert (Ed.), *Neurobiology of the hippocampus.* New York: Academic Press, 335–373.

Gallistel, C. R. (1980) *The organization of action: A new synthesis.* Hillsdale, N.J.: Erlbaum.

Garcia, J., Ervin, F. R., & Koelling, R. A. (1966) Learning with prolonged delay of reinforcement. *Psychonomic Science, 5,* 121–122.

Garcia, J., & Koelling, R. A. (1966) Relation of cue to consequence in avoidance learning. *Psychonomic Science, 4,* 123–124.

Gardner, R. A., & Gardner, B. T. (1969) Teaching sign language to a chimpanzee. *Science, 165,* 664–672.

Gardner, R. A., & Gardner, B. T. (1975) Early signs of language in child and chimpanzee. *Science, 187,* 752–753.

Garner, W. R. (1974) *The processing of information and structure.* Hillsdale, N.J.: Erlbaum.

Garner, W. R. (1976) Interaction of stimulus dimensions in concept and choice processes. *Cognitive Psychology, 8,* 98–123.

Gatling, F. P. (1952) A study of the continuity of the learning process as measured by habit reversal in the rat. In *Ohio State University Abstracts of doctoral dissertations, 1948–1949,* vol. 60. Columbus, Ohio: 117–121.

Gibbon, J. (1977) Scalar expectancy theory and Weber's law in animal timing. *Psychological Review, 84,* 279–325.

Gibbon, J., & Allan, L. (Eds.) (1984) *Timing and time perception.* New York: Annals of the New York Academy of Sciences, vol. 423.

Gibbon, J., & Church, R. M. (1981) Time left: Linear vs logarithmic subjective time. *Journal of Experimental Psychology: Animal Behavior Processes, 7,* 87–107.

Gibbon, J., & Church, R. M. (1984) Sources of variance in an information processing theory of timing. In H. L. Roitblat, T. G. Bever, & H. S. Terrace (Eds.), *Animal cognition.* Hillsdale, N.J.: Erlbaum, 465–488.

Gibbon, J., Church, R. M., & Meck, W. H. (1984) Scalar timing in memory. In J. Gibbon & L. Allan (Eds.), *Timing and time perception.* New York: Annals of the New York Academy of Sciences, vol. 423, 52–77.

Gibson, J. J. (1966) *The senses considered as perceptual system.* Boston: Houghton-Mifflin.

Giuntoli, M., & Mewaldt, L. R. (1978) Stomach contents of Clark's nutcrackers in western Montana. *Auk, 95,* 595–598.

Gormezano, I. (1972) Investigations of defense and reward conditioning in the rabbit. In A. H. Black & W. F. Prokasy (Eds.), *Classical conditioning II: Current research and theory.* New York: Appleton-Century-Crofts, 151–181.

Gould, J. L. (1975) Honeybee recruitment: The dance-language controversy. *Science, 189,* 685–693.

Gould, J. L. (1976) The dance-language controversy. *Quarterly Review of Biology, 51,* 211–244.

Grant, D. S. (1975) Proactive interference in pigeon short-term memory. *Journal of Experimental Psychology: Animal Behavior Processes, 1,* 207–220.

Grant, D. S. (1981) Short-term memory in the pigeon. In N. E. Spear & R. Miller (Eds.), *Information processing in animals: Memory mechanisms.* Hillsdale, N.J.: Erlbaum, 227–256.

Grant, D. S. (1982) Intratrial proactive interference in pigeon short-term memory: manipulation of stimulus dimension and dimensional similarity. *Learning and Motivation, 13,* 417–433.

Griffin, D. R. (1984) *Animal thinking.* Cambridge, Mass.: Harvard University Press.

Guthrie, E. R. (1935) *The psychology of learning.* New York: Harper & Row.

Hall, G. (1974) Strategies of simultaneous discrimination learning in the pigeon. *Quarterly Journal of Experimental Psychology, 26,* 520–529.

Harlow, H. F. (1949) The formation of learning sets. *Psychological Review, 56,* 51–65.

Hayes, C. (1951) *The ape in our house.* New York: Macmillan.

Hayes-Roth, F., Waterman, D. A., & Lenat, D. B. (1978) Principles of pattern-directed inference systems. In D. A. Waterman & F. Hayes-Roth (Eds.), *Pattern-directed inference systems.* New York: Academic Press, 577–601.

Hearst, E., & Jenkins, H. M. (1974) *Sign tracking: The stimulus-reinforcer relation and directed action.* Austin, Tex.: Psychonomic Society Monographs.

Herman, L. M., & Gordon, J. A. (1974) Auditory delayed matching in the bottlenosed dolphin. *Journal of the Experimental Analysis of Behavior, 21,* 19–26.

Herman, L. M. (1975) Interference and auditory short-term memory in the bottlenosed dolphin. *Animal Learning and Behavior, 3,* 43–48.

Herman, L. M., Richards, D. G., & Wolz, J. P. (1984) Comprehension of sentences by bottlenosed dolphins. *Cognition, 16,* 1–90.

Herrnstein, R. J. (1970) On the law of effect. *Journal of the Experimental Analysis of Behavior, 13,* 243–266.

Herrnstein, R. J. (1984) Objects, categories, and discriminative stimuli. In H. L. Roitblat, T. G. Bever, & H. S. Terrace (Eds.), *Animal Cognition.* Hillsdale, N.J.: Erlbaum, 233–261.

Herrnstein, R. J., & deVilliers, P. A. (1980) Fish as a natural category for people and pigeons. *The Psychology of Learning and Motivation: Advances in Research and Theory, 14,* 60–95.

Herrnstein, R. J., Loveland, D. H., & Cable, C. (1976) Natural concepts in pigeons. *Journal of Experimental Psychology: Animal Behavior Processes, 2,* 285–302.

Hinson, J. M., & Staddon, J. E. R. (1981) Maximizing on interval schedules. In C. M. Bradshaw, C. F. Lowe, & E. Szabad (Eds.), *Recent developments in the quantification of steady-state operant behavior.* Amsterdam: Elsevier/North Holland.

Hinton, G., & Anderson, J. (Eds.) (1981) *Parallel models of associative memory.* Hillsdale, N.J.: Erlbaum.

Hockett, C. F. (1958) *A course in modern linguistics.* New York: Macmillan.

Hockett, C. F., & Altmann, S. A. (1968) A note on design features. In T. A. Sebeok (Ed.), *Animal communication.* Bloomington, Ind.: Indiana University Press, 574–575.

Hodges, A. (1983) *Alan Turing: The enigma.* New York: Simon & Schuster.

Holland, P. C., & Straub, J. J. (1979) Differential effects of two ways of devaluing the unconditioned stimulus after Pavlovian appetitive conditioning. *Journal of Experimental Psychology: Animal Behavior Processes, 5,* 65–68.

Hollard, V. D., & Delius, J. D. (1982) Rotational invariance in visual pattern recognition in pigeons and humans. *Science, 218,* 804–806.

Honig, W. K. (1978) Studies of working memory in the pigeon. In S. H. Hulse, H. Fowler, & W. K. Honig (Eds.), *Cognitive processes in animal behavior,* Hillsdale, N.J.: Erlbaum, 211–248.

Honig, W. K. (1981) Working memory and the temporal map. In N. E. Spear & R. R. Miller (Eds.), *Information processing in animals: Memory mechanisms.* Hillsdale, N.J.: Erlbaum, 167–197.

Honig, W. K. (1984) Contributions of animal memory to the interpretation of animal learning. In H. L. Roitblat, T. G. Bever, & H. S. Terrace (Eds.), *Animal cognition.* Hillsdale, N.J.: Erlbaum, 29–44.

Honig, W. K., & Wasserman, E. A. (1981) Performance of pigeons on delayed simple and conditional discriminations under equivalent training procedures. *Learning and Motivation, 12,* 149–170.

Horn, H. S. (1978) Optimal tactics of reproduction and life-history. In J. R. Krebs & N. B. Davies (Eds.), *Behavioural ecology.* Oxford: Blackwell, 411–430.

Houston, A. I., Kacelnik, A., & McNamara, J. (1982) Some learning rules for acquiring information. In D. J. McFarland (Ed.), *Functional ontogeny.* London: Plenum, 140–191.

Hubbard, S. F., & Cook, R. M. (1978) Optimal foraging by parasitoid wasps. *Journal of Animal Ecology, 47,* 593–604.

Hull, C. L. (1930) Knowledge and purpose as habit mechanism. *Psychological Review, 37,* 511–522.

Hull, C. L. (1931) Goal attraction and directing ideas conceived as habit phenomena. *Psychological Review, 38,* 487–506.

Hull, C. L. (1943) *Principles of Behavior.* New York: Appleton-Century-Crofts.

Hulse, S. H. (1978) Cognitive structure and serial pattern learning by animals. In S. H. Hulse, H. Fowler, & W. K. Honig (Eds.), *Cognitive processes in animal behavior.* Hillsdale, N.J.: Erlbaum, 311–340.

Hulse, S. H., & Campbell, C. E. (1975) "Thinking ahead" in rat discrimination learning. *Animal Learning and Behavior, 3,* 305–311.

Hulse, S. H., & Dorsky, N. P. (1977) Structural complexity as a determinant of serial pattern learning. *Learning and Motivation, 8,* 488–506.

Hulse, S. H., & Dorsky, N. P. (1979) Serial pattern learning by rats: Transfer of a formally defined stimulus relationship and the significance of nonreinforcement. *Animal Learning and Behavior, 7,* 211–220.

Hunter, W. S. (1913) The delayed reaction in animals. *Behavior Monographs, 2,* 21–30.

Hunter, W. S. (1920) The temporal maze and kinaesthetic sensory processes in the white rat. *Psychobiology, 2,* 1–17.

Isaac, D., & Marler, P. (1963) Ordering of sequences of singing behavior of mistle thrush in relation to timing. *Animal Behavior, 11,* 179–188.

James, W. (1892) *The principles of psychology,* 2 volumes. New York: Henry Holt.

Janetos, A. C., & Cole, B. J. (1981) Imperfectly optimal animals. *Behavioral Ecology and Sociobiology, 9,* 203–210.

Jarrard, L. E., & Moise, S. L. (1971) Short-term memory in the monkey. In L. E. Jarrard (Ed.), *Cognitive processes of nonhuman primates.* New York: Academic Press, 1–24.

Jaynes, J. (1973) The problem of animate motion in the seventeenth century. In M. Henry, J. Jaynes, & J. J. Sullivan (Eds.), *Historical conceptions of psychology.* New York: Springer, 166–179.

Jenkins, H. M., & Moore, B. R. (1973) The form of the auto-shaped response with food or water reinforcers. *Journal of the Experimental Analysis of Behavior, 20,* 163–181.

Jennings, H. S. (1906/1923) *Behavior of the lower organisms.* New York: Columbia University Press.

Kahneman, D. (1973) *Attention and effort.* Englewood Cliffs, N.J.: Prentice Hall.

Kamil, A. C. (1978) Systematic foraging by a nectar-feeding bird, the Amakihi (*Loxops virens*). *Journal of Comparative and Physiological Psychology, 92,* 388–396.

Kamil, A. C., & Balda, R. C. (1985) Cache recovery and spatial memory in Clark's Nutcracker (*Nucifraga columbiana*). *Journal of Experimental Psychology: Animal Behavior Processes, 11,* 95–111.

Kamil, A. C., Lougee, M., & Schulman, R. J. (1973) Learning-set behavior in the learning-set experienced bluejay (*Cyanocitta cristata*). *Journal of Comparative and Physiological Psychology, 82,* 394–405.

Kamil, A. C., & Roitblat, H. L. (1985) Foraging theory: Implications for animal learning and cognition. *Annual Review of Psychology, 36,* 141–169.

Kamil, A. C., & Sargent, T. D. (1981) *Foraging behavior: Ecological, ethological, and psychological approaches.* New York: Garland Press.

Kamil, A. C., & Yoerg, S. J. (1982) Learning and foraging behavior. In P. P. G. Bateson & P. H. Klopfer (Eds.), *Perspectives in ethology,* vol. 5. New York: Plenum, 325–364.

Kamin, L. J. (1968) 'Attention-like' processes in classical conditioning. In M. R. Jones (Ed.), *Miami symposium on the prediction of behavior: Aversive stimulation.* Miami: University of Miami Press, 9–33.

Kamin, L. J. (1969) Predictability, surprise, attention and conditioning. In B. A. Campbell & R. M. Church (Eds.), *Punishment and aversive behavior.* New York: Appleton-Century-Crofts, 279–296.

Kellogg, W. N., & Kellogg, L. A. (1933) *The ape and the child: A study of environmental influence on early behavior.* New York: Whittlesey House.

Kendrick, D. F. (1980) Trace superordinate stimulus control of delayed matching-to-sample performance. Unpublished master's thesis, Michigan State University.

Kendrick, D. F., Tranberg, D. K., & Rilling, M. (1981) The effects of illumination on the acquisition of delayed matching-to-sample. *Animal Learning and Behavior, 9,* 202–208.

Kimble, G. A. (1961) *Hilgard and Marquis' conditioning and learning* (2d ed.). New York: Appleton-Century-Crofts.

Kohler, W. (1927/1976) *The mentality of apes.* London: Routledge & Kegan Paul. Reprinted 1976, New York: Liveright.

Konorski, J., & Miller, S. (1937) On two types of conditioned reflex. *Journal of General Psychology, 16,* 264–272.

Konorski, J., & Szwejkowska, G. (1956) Reciprocal transformations of heterogeneous and conditioned reflexes. *Acta Biologica Experimentala, 17,* 141–165.

Kosslyn, S. M. (1983) *Ghosts in the mind's machine.* New York: Norton.

Kramer, T. J., & Rilling, M. (1970) Differential reinforcement of low rates: A selective critique. *Psychological Bulletin, 74,* 224–254.

Kraemer, P. J., & Roberts, W. A. (1984) Short-term memory for visual and auditory stimuli in pigeons. *Animal Learning and Behavior, 12,* 275–284.

Krebs, J. R., & Davies, N. B. (Eds.) (1978) *Behavioral ecology.* Oxford: Blackwell.

Krebs, J. R., Stephens, D. W., & Sutherland, W. J. (1983) Perspectives in optimal foraging. A. H. Brush & G. A. Clark, Jr. (Eds.), *Perspectives in ornithology*. Cambridge: Cambridge University Press, 165–215.

Krechevsky, I. (1932) Hypotheses in rats. *Psychological Review, 39*, 516–532.

Krechevsky, I. (1938) A study of the continuity of the problem-solving process. *Psychological Review, 45*, 107–133.

Kroodsma, D. E. (1980) Winter wren singing behavior: A pinnacle of song complexity. *Condor, 82*, 357–365.

Kruuk, H. (1964) Predators and antipredator behaviour of the black headed gull (*Larus ridibundus*). *Behaviour Supplements, 11*, 1–129.

Kuhn, T. S. (1970) *The structure of scientific revolutions*. Chicago: University of Chicago Press.

LaBarbera, J. D., & Church, R. M. (1974) Magnitude of fear as a function of expected time to an aversive event. *Animal Learning and Behavior, 2*, 199–202.

Lachman, R., Lachman, J. L., & Butterfield, E. R. (1979) *Cognitive psychology and information processing*. Hillsdale, N.J.: Erlbaum.

Lakatos, I. (1970) Falsification and the methodology of scientific research programs. In I. Lakatos & A. Musgrave (Eds.), *Criticism and the growth of knowledge*. London: Cambridge University Press.

Lakatos, I., & Musgrave, A. (1970) *Criticism and the growth of knowledge*. London: Cambridge University Press.

Lamb, M. R. (1972) *Selective attention in pigeons: Effects of cueing on the processing of different types of compound stimuli*. Ph.D. dissertation, University of California, Berkeley.

Lamb, M. R., & Riley, D. A. (1981) Effects of element arrangement on the processing of compound stimuli in pigeons (*Columbia livia*). *Journal of Experimental Psychology: Animal Behavior Processes, 7*, 45–58.

Landwehr, K. (1983) On taking Skinner on his own terms: Comments on Wessell's critique of Skinner's view of cognitive theories. *Behaviorism, 11*, 187–192.

Lashley, K. S. (1929) *Brain mechanisms and intelligence: A quantitative study of injuries to the brain*. Chicago: University of Chicago Press.

Lashley, K. S. (1942) An examination of the continuity theory as applied to discriminative learning. *Journal of General Psychology, 26*, 241–265.

Lashley, K. S. (1951) The problem of serial order in behavior. In L. A. Jeffress (Ed.), *Cerebral mechanisms in behavior*. New York: Wiley, 112–136.

Lashley, K. S., & Ball, J. (1929) Spinal conduction and kinesthetic sensitization in the maze habit. *Journal of Comparative Psychology, 9,* 71–105.

Lawrence, D. H. (1949) Acquired distinctiveness of cues: I. Transfer between discriminations on the basis of familiarity with the stimulus. *Journal of Experimental Psychology, 39,* 770–784.

Lawrence, D. H. (1950) Acquired distinctiveness of cues: II. Selective association in a constant stimulus situation. *Journal of Experimental Psychology, 40,* 175–188.

Lawrence, D. H. (1952) The transfer of a discrimination along a continuum. *Journal of Comparative and Physiological Psychology, 45,* 511–516.

Leith, C. R., and Maki, W. S. (1975) Attention shifts during matching-to-sample performance in pigeons. *Animal Learning and Behavior, 3,* 85–89.

Lenneberg, E. H. (1967) *Biological foundations of language.* New York: Wiley.

Leuin, T. C. (1976) *Selective information processing in pigeons.* Ph.D. dissertation, University of California, Berkeley.

Levine, M. (1970) Human discrimination learning: The subset-sampling assumption. *Psychological Bulletin, 74,* 397–404.

Lieberman, P. (1975) The evolution of speech and language. In J. Kavanaugh & J. Cutting (Eds.), *The role of speech in language.* Cambridge: MIT Press, 83–106.

Lindauer, M. (1955) Schwarmbienen auf Wohnungssuche. *Zeitschrift fur Vergleichende Physiologie, 37,* 263–324.

Lindsay, P. H., Taylor, M. M., & Forbes, S. M. (1968) Attention and multidimensional discrimination. *Perception and Psychophysics, 4,* 113–117.

Locke, J. (1690) *An essay concerning humane understanding.* In four books. London: Thomas Basset.

Loeb, J. (1900) *Comparative physiology of the brain and comparative psychology.* New York: G. P. Putnam's Sons.

Logue, A. W. (1978) Behaviorist John B. Watson and the continuity of species. *Behaviorism, 6,* 71–79.

Logue, A. W. (1979) Taste aversion and the generality of the laws of learning. *Psychological Bulletin, 86,* 276–296.

Looney, T. A., & Cohen, P. S. (1974) Pictorial target control of schedule-induced attack in white Carneaux pigeons. *Journal of the Experimental Analysis of Behavior, 21,* 571–584.

Lovejoy, E. (1966) Analysis of the overlearning reversal effect. *Psychological Review, 73,* 87–103.

Lovejoy, E., & Russell, D. G. (1967) Suppression of learning about a hard cue by the presence of an easy cue. *Psychonomic Science, 8,* 365–366.

Lubow, R. E. (1965) Latent inhibition: Effects of frequency of nonreinforcement preexposure of the CS. *Journal of Comparative and Physiological Psychology, 60,* 454–459.

Lubow, R. E. (1973) Latent inhibition. *Psychological Bulletin, 79,* 398–407.

Lubow, R. E., & Moore, A. V. (1959) Latent inhibition: The effects of nonre-inforced preexposure to the conditioned stimulus. *Journal of Comparative and Physiological Psychology, 52,* 415–419.

MacArthur, R. H., & Pianka, E. R. (1966) On optimal use of a patchy environment. *American Naturalist, 100,* 603–609.

MacFarlane, D. A. (1930) The role of kinesthesis in maze learning. *University of California Publications in Psychology, 4,* 277–305.

Mackintosh, N. J. (1963) The effect of irrelevant cues on reversal learning in the rat. *British Journal of Psychology, 54,* 127–134.

Mackintosh, N. J. (1974) *The psychology of animal learning.* London: Academic Press.

Mackintosh, N. J. (1975) A theory of attention: Variations in the associability of stimuli with reinforcement. *Psychological Review, 82,* 276–298.

Mackintosh, N. J. (1983) *Conditioning and associative learning.* Oxford: Oxford University Press.

Mackintosh, N. J., & Little, L. (1969) Intradimensional and extradimensional shift learning by pigeons. *Psychonomic Science, 14,* 5–6.

Mackintosh, N. J., & Turner, C. (1971) Blocking as a function of novelty of CS and predictability of UCS. *Quarterly Journal of Experimental Psychology, 23,* 359–366.

Macphail, E. M. (1982) *Brain and intelligence in vertebrates.* Oxford: Oxford University Press.

Maki, W. S. (1979a) Discrimination learning without short-term memory: Dissociation of memory processes in pigeons. *Science, 204,* 83–85.

Maki, W. S. (1979b) Pigeon's short-term memories for surprising vs. expected reinforcement and nonreinforcement. *Animal Learning and Behavior, 7,* 31–37.

Maki, W. S. (1981) Directed forgetting in pigeons. In N. E. Spear & R. R.

Miller (Eds.), *Information processing in animals: Memory mechanisms*. Hillsdale, N.J.: Erlbaum, 199–225.

Maki, W. S. (1984) Some problems for a theory of working memory. In H. L. Roitblat, T. G. Bever, & H. S. Terrace (Eds.), *Animal cognition*. Hillsdale, N.J.: Erlbaum, 117–133.

Maki, W. S. (1985) Differential effects of electroconvulsive shock on concurrent spatial memories: "Old" memories are impaired while "new" memories are spared. *Behavioral and Neural Biology, 43*, 162–177.

Maki, W. S., & Hegvik, D. K. (1980) Directed forgetting in pigeons. *Animal Learning and Behavior, 8*, 567–574.

Maki, W. S., Brokofsky, S., & Berg, B. (1979) Spatial memory in rats: Resistance to retroactive interference. *Animal Learning and Behavior, 7*, 25–30.

Maki, W. S., Gillund, G., Hauge, G., & Siders, W. A. (1977) Matching to sample after extinction of observing responses. *Journal of Experimental Psychology: Animal Behavior Processes, 3*, 285–296.

Maki, W. S., & Leith, C. R. (1973) Shared attention in pigeons. *Journal of the Experimental Analysis of Behavior, 19*, 345–349.

Maki, W. S., Moe, J. C., & Bierly, C. M. (1977) Short-term memory for stimuli, responses, and reinforcers. *Journal of Experimental Psychology: Animal Behavior Processes, 3*, 156–217.

Maki, W. S., Olson, D., & Rego, S. (1981) Directed forgetting in pigeons: Analysis of cue functions. *Animal Learning and Behavior, 9*, 189–195.

Mallot, R. W., & Siddall, J. W. (1972) Acquisition of the people concept in pigeons. *Psychological Reports, 31*, 3–13.

Malthus, T. R. (1798) *An essay on the improvement of population, as it affects the future improvement of society. With remarks on the speculations of Mr. Goodwin, M. Condorcet, and other writers*. London: J. Johnson.

Marchant, R. G., III, Mis, F. W., & Moore, J. W. (1972) Conditioned inhibition of the rabbit's nictitating membrane response. *Journal of Experimental Psychology, 95*, 408–411.

Maricq, A. V., Roberts, S., & Church, R. M. (1981) Methamphetamine and time estimation. *Journal of Experimental Psychology: Animal Behavior Processes, 7*, 18–30.

Marshack, A. (1984) The ecology and brain of two-handed bipedalism: An analytic, cognitive, and evolutionary assessment. In H. L. Roitblat, T. G. Bever, & H. S. Terrace (Eds.), *Animal cognition*. Hillsdale, N.J.: Erlbaum, 491–511.

Marshall, J. C. (1971) Can humans talk? In J. Morton (Ed.), *Biological and social factors in linguistics*. London: Logos, 24–52.

Marshall, J. C. (1979) Disorders of language and memory. In M. Gruneberg & P. Morris (Eds.), *Applied problems in memory*. London: Academic Press, 149–267.

Maynard Smith, J. (1978) Optimization theory in evolution. *Annual Review of Ecology and Systematics, 9*, 31–56.

McCulloch, T. L., & Pratt, J. G. (1934) A study of the pre-solution period in weight discrimination by white rats. *Journal of Comparative Psychology, 18*, 271–290.

McGaugh, J. L. (1966) Time-dependent processes in memory storage. *Science, 153*, 1351–1358.

McGaugh, J. L., & Herz, M. J. (1972) *Memory consolidation*. San Francisco: Albion.

Meck, W. H. (1984) Attentional bias between modalities: Effect of the internal clock, memory, and decision stages used in animal time discrimination. In J. Gibbon & L. Allen (Eds.), *Timing and time perception*. New York: Annals of the New York Academy of Sciences, vol. 423, 528–541.

Meck, W. H., Church, R. M., & Olton, D. S. (1984) Hippocampus, time, and memory. *Behavioral Neuroscience, 98*, 3–22.

Mewaldt, R. L. (1956) Nesting behavior of the Clark's nutcracker. *Condor, 58*, 3–23.

Miles, C. G., & Jenkins, H. M. (1973) Overshadowing in operant conditioning as a function of discriminability. *Learning and Motivation, 4*, 11–27.

Miles, H. L. (1983) Apes and language: The search for communicative competence. In J. de Luce & H. T. Wilder (Eds.), *Language in primates: Perspectives and implications*. New York: Springer-Verlag, 43–61.

Miller, G. A. (1956) The magical number seven, plus or minus two. *Psychological Review, 63*, 81–97.

Miller, G. A. (1981) *Language and Speech*. New York: W. H. Freeman.

Miller, G. A. (1983) Cognition and comparative psychology. *The Behavioral and Brain Sciences, 6*, 152–153.

Miller, G. A., Galanter, E., & Pribram, K. H. (1960) *Plans and the structure of behavior*. New York: Henry Holt & Co.

Mishkin, M., & Delacour, J. (1975) An analysis of short-term visual memory in the monkey. *Journal of Experimental Psychology: Animal Behavior Processes, 1*, 326–334.

Moise, S. L. (1976) Proactive effects of stimuli, delays, and response position during delayed matching from sample. *Animal Learning and Behavior, 4,* 37–40.

Moore, E. F. (1956) Gedanken experiments and sequential machines. In C. E. Shannon & J. McCarthy (Eds.), *Automata studies.* Princeton: Princeton University Press, 129–153.

Morgan, C. L. (1894) *An introduction to comparative psychology.* London: Walter Scott.

Morgan, C. T., & Morgan, J. D. (1939) Auditory induction of an abnormal pattern of behavior in rats. *Journal of Comparative Psychology, 27,* 505–508.

Mumma, R., & Warren, J. M. (1968) Two-cue discriminatory learning by cats. *Journal of Comparative and Physiological Psychology, 66,* 116–122.

Neimark, E. D., & Estes, W. K. (1967) *Stimulus sampling theory.* San Francisco: Holden Day.

Neisser, U. (1967) *Cognitive psychology.* New York: Appleton-Century-Crofts.

Nelson, K. (1973) Structure and strategy in learning to talk. *Monographs in Social Research and Child Development, 38,* 1–137.

Newell, A., Shaw, J. C., & Simon, H. A. (1958) Elements of a theory of human problem solving. *Psychological Review, 65,* 151–166.

Norman, D. A. (1973) What have animal experiments taught us about human memory? In J. A. Deutsch (Ed.), *The physiological basis of memory.* New York: Academic, 397–414.

O'Keefe, J., & Nadel, L. (1978) *The hippocampus as a cognitive map.* Oxford: Clarendon Press.

Olton, D. S. (1978) Characteristics of spatial memory. In S. H. Hulse, H. Fowler, & W. K. Honig (Eds.), *Cognitive processes in animal behavior.* Hillsdale, N.J.: Erlbaum, 341–373.

Olton, D. S. (1979) Mazes, maps, and memory. *American Psychologist, 34,* 588–596.

Olton, D. S. (1983) Memory functions and the hippocampus. In W. Seifert (Ed.), *Neurobiology of the hippocampus.* New York: Academic Press, 335–373.

Olton, D. S., & Collison, C. (1979) Intramaze cues and "odor trails" fail to direct choice behavior on an elevated maze. *Animal Learning and Behavior, 7,* 221–223.

Olton, D. S., Collison, C., & Werz, W. A. (1977) Spatial memory and radial arm maze performance by rats. *Learning and Motivation, 8,* 289–314.

Olton, D. S., & Samuelson, R. J. (1976) Remembrance of places past: Spatial memory in rats. *Journal of Experimental Psychology: Animal Behavior Processes, 2,* 97–116.

Orians, G. H. (1981) Foraging behavior and the evolution of discriminatory abilities. In A. C. Kamil & T. D. Sargent (Eds.), *Foraging behavior: Ecological, ethological, and psychological approaches.* New York: Garland, 389–405.

Parker, G. A. (1978) Searching for mates. In J. R. Krebs & N. B. Davies (Eds.), *Behavioural ecology: An evolutionary approach.* Oxford: Blackwell, 214–244.

Parks, T. E., Kroll, N. E., Salzberg, P. M., & Parkinson, S. R. (1972) Persistence of visual memory as indicated by decision time in a matching task. *Journal of Experimental Psychology, 92,* 437–438.

Pate, J. L., & Rumbaugh, D. M. (1983) The language-like behavior of Lana chimpanzee: Is it merely discrimination and paired-associate learning? *Animal Learning and Behavior, 11,* 134–138.

Patten, R. L., & Rudy, J. W. (1967) The Sheffield omission training procedure applied to the conditioning of the licking response in rats. *Psychonomic Science, 8,* 463–464.

Patterson, F. G. (1978) Linguistic capabilities of a young lowland gorilla. In F. C. C. Peng (Ed.), *Sign language and language acquisition in man and ape.* Boulder: Westview, 161–201.

Patterson, F. G. (1978) The gestures of a gorilla: Language acquisition in another pongid. *Brain and Language, 5,* 72–97.

Pavlov, I. P. (1927) *Conditioned reflexes.* Oxford: Oxford University Press. Reprinted 1960. New York: Dover.

Pepperberg, I. M. (1981) Functional vocalizations by an African grey parrot (*Psittacus erithacus*). *Zeitschrift fur Tiepsychologie, 5,* 139–160.

Pepperberg, I. M. (1983) Cognition in the African grey parrot: Preliminary evidence for auditory/vocal comprehension of a class concept. *Animal Learning and Behavior, 11,* 179–185.

Peterson, G. B. (1984) How expectancies guide behavior. In H. L. Roitblat, T. G. Bever, & H. S. Terrace (Eds.), *Animal cognition.* Hillsdale, N.J.: Erlbaum, 135–148.

Peterson, G. B., & Trapold, M. A. (1980) Effects of altering outcome expectancies in pigeons' delayed conditional discrimination performance. *Learning and Motivation, 11,* 267–288.

Peterson, G. B., Wheeler, R. L., & Trapold, M. A. (1980) Enhancement of pigeons' conditional discrimination performance by expectancies of reinforcement and nonreinforcement. *Animal Learning and Behavior, 8,* 22–30.

Pietrewicz, A. T., & Kamil, A. C. (1979) Search image formation in the blue jay (*Cyanocitta cristata*). *Science, 204,* 1332–1333.

Pietrewicz, A. T., & Kamil, A. C. (1981) Search images and the detection of cryptic prey: An operant approach. In A. C. Kamil & T. D. Sargent (Eds.), *Foraging behavior: Ecological, ethological, and psychological approaches.* New York: Garland, 311–332.

Platt, J. R. (1964) Strong inference. *Science, 146,* 347–353.

Platt, J. R., Kuch, D. O., & Bitgood, S. C. (1973) Rats' lever-press duration as psychophysical judgments of time. *Journal of the Experimental Analysis of Behavior, 19,* 239–250.

Poole, J., & Lander, D. G. (1971) The pigeon's concept of pigeon. *Psychonomic Science, 25,* 157–158.

Premack, D. (1971) On the assessment of language competence in the chimpanzee. In A. Schrier & F. Stollnitz (Eds.), *Behavior of nonhuman primates,* vol. 4. New York: Academic Press, 186–228.

Premack, D. (1976) *Intelligence in ape and man.* Hillsdale, N.J.: Erlbaum.

Premack, D. (1983) The codes of man and beasts. *The Behavioral and Brain Sciences, 6,* 125–167.

Premack, D., & Premack, A. J. (1983) *The mind of an ape.* New York: Norton.

Purdy, J. E., & Cross, H. A. (1979) The role of R-S expectancy in discrimination and discrimination reversal learning. *Learning and Motivation, 10,* 211–227.

Pyke, G. H. (1979) The economics of territory size and time budget in the golden-winged sunbirds. *American Naturalist, 114,* 131–145.

Pyke, G. H., Pulliam, H. R., & Charnov, E. L. (1977) Optimal foraging: A selective review of theory and tests. *Quarterly Review of Biology, 52,* 137–154.

Pylyshyn, Z. (1973) What the mind's eye tells the mind's brain: A critique of mental imagery. *Psychological Bulletin, 80,* 1–24.

Rachlin, H. (1970) *About behaviorism.* San Francisco: W. H. Freeman.

Radnitzky, G., & Anderson, G. (1978) *Progress and rationality in science. Boston studies in the philosophy of science, 58,* Dordrecht: D. Reidel.

Reid, L. S. (1953) The development of noncontinuity behavior through continuity learning. *Journal of Experimental Psychology, 46,* 107–112.

Renner, M. (1960) The contribution of the honeybees to the study of time-sense and astronomical orientation. *Cold Spring Harbor Symposium on Quantitative Biology, 25,* 361–367.

Rescorla, R. A., & Wagner, A. R. (1972) A theory of Pavlovian conditioning: Variations in the effectiveness of reinforcement and nonreinforcement. In A. H. Black & W. F. Prokasy (Eds.), *Classical conditioning II.* New York: Appleton-Century-Crofts, 64–99.

Rescorla, R. A. (1967) Pavlovian conditioning and its proper control procedures. *Psychological Review, 74,* 71–80.

Rescorla, R. A. (1969) Pavlovian conditioned inhibition. *Psychological Bulletin, 72,* 77–94.

Reynolds, G. S. (1961) Attention in the pigeon. *Journal of the Experimental Analysis of Behavior, 4,* 179–184.

Reynolds, G. S. (1975) *A primer of operant conditioning.* Glenview, Ill.: Scott-Foresman.

Riccio, D. C., & Ebner, D. L. (1981) Postacquisition modifications of memory. In N. E. Spear & R. R. Miller (Eds.), *Information processing in animals: Memory mechanisms.* Hillsdale, N.J.: Erlbaum, 291–317.

Richardson, K. W., & Warzak, W. J. (1981) Stimulus stringing by pigeons. *Journal of the Experimental Analysis of Behavior, 36,* 267–276.

Richelle, M., & Lejeune, H. (1980) *Time in animal behavior.* London: Pergamon.

Riley, D. A. (1968) *Discrimination learning.* Boston: Allyn and Bacon.

Riley, D. A. (1984) Do pigeons decompose stimulus compounds? In H. L. Roitblat, T. G. Bever, & H. S. Terrace (Eds.), *Animal cognition:* Hillsdale, N.J.: Erlbaum, 330–350.

Riley, D. A., & Roitblat, H. L. (1978) Selective attention and related cognitive processes in pigeons. In S. H. Hulse, H. Fowler, & W. K. Honig (Eds.), *Cognitive processes in animal behavior.* Hillsdale, N.J.: Erlbaum, 249–276.

Ristau, C. A., & Robbins, D. (1982) Language in the great apes: A critical review. *Advances in the Study of Behavior, 12,* 141–255.

Ritchie, B. F., Ebeling, E., & Roth, W. (1950) Evidence for continuity in the discrimination of vertical and horizontal patterns. *Journal of Comparative and Physiological Psychology, 43,* 168–180.

Roberts, S. (1981) Isolation of an internal clock. *Journal of Experimental Psychology: Animal Behavior Processes, 7,* 242–268.

Roberts, S. (1982) Cross modal use of an internal clock. *Journal of Experimental Psychology: Animal Behavior Processes, 8,* 2–22.

Roberts, S. (1983) Properties and function of an internal clock. In R. L. Mellgren (Ed.), *Animal Cognition and Behavior.* Amsterdam: North-Holland, 345–398.

Roberts, W. A. (1972) Short-term memory in the pigeon: Effects of repetition and spacing. *Journal of Experimental Psychology: Animal Behavior Processes, 6,* 217–237.

Roberts, W. A. (1980) Distribution of trials and intertrial retention in delayed matching to sample with pigeons. *Journal of Experimental Psychology: Animal Behavior Processes, 6,* 217–237.

Roberts, W. A. (1981) Retroactive inhibition in rat spatial memory. *Animal Learning and Behavior, 9,* 566–574.

Roberts, W. A. (1984) Some issues in animal spatial memory. In H. L. Roitblat, T. G. Bever, & H. S. Terrace (Eds.), *Animal cognition.* Hillsdale, N.J.: Erlbaum, 425–443.

Roberts, W. A., & Grant, D. S. (1974) Short-term memory in the pigeon with the presentation time precisely controlled. *Learning and Motivation, 5,* 393–408.

Roberts, W. A., & Grant, D. S. (1976) Studies of short-term memory in the pigeon using the delayed matching to sample procedure. In D. L. Medin, W. A. Roberts, W. A., & R. T. Davis (Eds.) *Processes of animal memory.* Hillsdale, N.J.: Erlbaum, 79–112.

Roberts, W. A., & Grant, D. S. (1978) An analysis of light-induced retroactive inhibition in pigeon short-term memory. *Journal of Experimental Psychology: Animal Behavior Processes, 4,* 219–236.

Roberts, W. A., & Kraemer, P. J. (1984) Temporal variables in delayed matching to sample. In J. Gibbon & L. Allan (Eds.), *Timing and time perception.* New York: Annals of the New York Academy of Sciences, vol. 423, 335–345.

Roberts, W. A., & Smythe, W. E. (1979) Memory lists for spatial events in the rat. *Learning and Motivation, 10,* 313–336.

Roitblat, H. L. (1980) Codes and coding processes in pigeon short-term memory. *Animal Learning and Behavior, 8,* 341–351.

Roitblat, H. L. (1982a) The meaning of representation in animal memory. *The Behavioral and Brain Sciences, 5,* 353–406.

Roitblat, H. L. (1982b) Decision making, evolution, and cognition. In H. D. Schmidt & G. Tembrock (Eds.), *Evolution and determination of animal and human behavior.* Berlin, GDR: VEB Deutscher Verlag der Wissenschaften, 108–116.

Roitblat, H. L. (1984a) Representations in pigeon working memory. In H. L. Roitblat, T. G. Bever, & H. S. Terrace (Eds.), *Animal cognition.* Hillsdale, N.J.: Erlbaum, 79–97.

Roitblat, H. L. (1984b) Pigeon working memory: Models for delayed matching-to-sample performance. In M. L. Commons, A. R. Wagner, & R. J. Herrnstein (Eds.), *Quantitative analyses of behavior: Discrimination processes,* vol. 4. Cambridge, Mass.: Ballinger, 161–181.

Roitblat, H. L., Bever, T. G., & Terrace, H. S. (1984) *Animal cognition.* Hillsdale, N.J.: Erlbaum.

Roitblat, H. L., Pologe, B., & Scopatz, R. A. (1983) The representation of items in serial position. *Animal Learning and Behavior, 11,* 489–498.

Roitblat, H. L., & Scopatz, R. A. (1983) Directed forgetting in pigeon delayed matching-to-sample (DMTS) performance. Paper presented at the meeting of the Eastern Psychological Association, Philadelphia.

Roitblat, H. L., & Scopatz, R. A. (1983b) Sequential effects in pigeon delayed matching-to-sample performance. *Journal of Experimental Psychology: Animal Behavior Processes, 9,* 202–221.

Roitblat, H. L., Scopatz, R. A., & Bever, T. G. (1985) *The discrimination of three-item sequences by pigeons.* Submitted for publication.

Roitblat, H. L., Tham, W., & Golub, L. (1982) Performance of *Betta splendens* in a radial arm maze. *Animal Learning and Behavior, 10,* 108–114.

Romanes, G. J. (1882) *Animal intelligence.* London: Kegan Paul.

Romanes, G. J. (1883/1977) *Animal intelligence.* Washington, D.C.: University Publications of America.

Romanes, G. J. (1884/1969) *Animal intelligence.* New York: Appleton.

Rothblat, L. A., & Wilson, W. A., Jr. (1968) Intradimensional shifts in the monkey within and across sensory modalities. *Journal of Comparative and Physiological Psychology, 66,* 549–553.

Rozin, P. (1969) Central or peripheral mediation of learning with long CS-UCS intervals in the feeding system. *Journal of Comparative and Physiological Psychology, 77,* 476–481.

Rumbaugh, D. M. (Ed., 1977) *Language learning by a chimpanzee: The Lana project.* New York: Academic Press.

Rumbaugh, D. M., & Gill, T. (1976) The mastery of language-type skills by the chimpanzee (*Pan*). In S. R. Harnad, H. D. Steklis, & J. Lancaster (Eds.), *Origins and evolution of language and speech*. New York: Annals of the New York Academy of Sciences, vol. 280.

Rumbaugh, D. M., & Gill, T. V. (1977) Lana's acquisition of language skills. In D. M. Rumbaugh, (Ed.), *Language learning by a chimpanzee: The Lana project*. New York: Academic Press, 165–192.

Rusak, B., & Zucker, I. (1975) Biological rhythms and animal behavior. *Annual Review of Psychology, 26*, 137–171.

Sands, S. F., Urcuioli, P. J., Wright, A. A., & Santiago, H. C. (1984) Serial position effects and rehearsal in primates. In H. L. Roitblat, T. G. Bever, & H. S. Terrace (Eds.), *Animal cognition*. Hillsdale, N.J.: Erlbaum, 375–388.

Saunders, D. S. (1977) *An introduction to biological rhythms*. Glasgow: Blackie.

Savage-Rumbaugh, E. S. (1984) Acquisition of functional symbol usage in apes and children. In H. L. Roitblat, T. G. Bever, & H. S. Terrace (Eds.), *Animal cognition*. Hillsdale, N.J.: Erlbaum, 291–310.

Savage-Rumbaugh, E. S., Pate, J. L., Lawson, J., Smith, S. T., & Rosenbaum, S. (1983) Can a chimpanzee make a statement? *Journal of Experimental Psychology: General, 112*, 457–492.

Savage-Rumbaugh, E. S., & Rumbaugh, D. M. (1978) Symbolization, language and chimpanzees: A theoretical reevaluation based on initial language acquisition processes in four young *Pan Troglodytes*. *Brain and Language, 6*, 265–300.

Savage-Rumbaugh, E. S., Wilkerson, B. J., & Bakeman, R. (1977) Spontaneous gestural communication among conspecifics in the pygmy chimpanzee. In G. H. Bourne (Ed.), *Progress in Ape Research*. New York: Academic Press, 97–116.

Scharff, J. L. (1982) Skinner's concept of the operant: From necessitarian to probabilistic causality. *Behaviorism, 10*, 45–54.

Schoener, T. W. (1971) Theory of feeding strategies. *Annual Review of Ecology and Systematics, 2*, 369–404.

Schusterman, R. J., & Krieger, K. (1984) California sea lions are capable of semantic comprehension. *The Psychological Record, 34*, 3–23.

Schusterman, R. J. (1962) Transfer effects of successive discrimination reversal training in chimpanzees. *Science, 137*, 422–423.

Schwartz, R. M., Schwartz, M., & Tees, R. C. (1971) Optional intradimensional and extradimensional shifts in the rat. *Journal of Comparative and Physiological Psychology, 77*, 470–475.

Sebeok, T. A. (Ed.) (1977) *How animals communicate.* Bloomington, Ind.: Indiana University Press.

Sechenov, I. M. (1863/1965) Refleksy Golovnogo Mozga. St. Petersburg. Translated: *Reflexes of the Brain.* Originally published, 1863, Cambridge: MIT Press.

Seidenberg, M. S., and Petitto, L. A. (1979) Signing behavior in apes: A critical view. *Cognition, 7,* 177–215.

Seyfarth, R. M., & Cheney, D. L. (1980) The ontogeny of vervet monkey alarm calling behavior: A preliminary report. *Zeitschrift fur Tierpsychologie, 54,* 37–56.

Seyfarth, R. M., Cheney, D. L., & Marler, P. (1980) Vervet monkey responses to three different alarm calls. Evidence of predator classification and semantic communication. *Science, 210,* 801–803.

Shannon, C. E. (1948) A mathematical theory of communication. *Bell System Technical Journal, 27,* 379–423.

Shavalia, D. A., Dodge, A. A., & Beatty, W. W. (1981) Time-dependent effects of ECS on spatial memory in rats. *Behavioral and Neural Biology, 31,* 261–273.

Sheffield, F. D. (1965) Relation between classical conditioning and instrumental learning. In W. F. Prokasy (Ed.), *Classical conditioning: A Symposium.* New York: Appleton-Century-Crofts, 302–322.

Shepard, R. N., & Metzler, J. (1971). Mental rotation of 3–D objects. *Science, 171,* 701–703.

Shepp, B. E., & Eimas, P. D. (1964) Intradimensional and extradimensional shifts in the rat. *Journal of Comparative and Physiological Psychology, 57,* 357–361.

Shepp, B. E., & Schrier, A. M. (1969) Consecutive intradimensional and extradimensional shifts in monkeys. *Journal of Comparative and Physiological Psychology, 67,* 199–203.

Sherman, P. W. (1979) Nepotism and the evolution of alarm calls. *Science, 197,* 1246–1253.

Sherry, D. F., Krebs, J. R., & Cowie, R. J. (1981) Memory for the location of stored food in marsh tits. *Animal Behavior, 29,* 1260–1266.

Shettleworth, S. J. (1973) Food reinforcement and the organization of behaviour in golden hamsters. In R. A. Hinde & J. Stevenson-Hinde (Eds.), *Constraints on learning.* London: Academic Press, 243–263.

Shettleworth, S. J. (1975) Reinforcement and the organization of behaviour in golden hamsters: Hunger, environment, and food reinforcement. *Journal of Experimental Psychology: Animal Behavior Processes, 104,* 56–87.

Shettleworth, S. J. (1983) Memory in food hoarding birds. *Scientific American, 248,* (3), 102–111.

Shettleworth, S. J., & Krebs, J. R. (1982) How marsh tits find their hoards: The roles of site preference and spatial memory. *Journal of Experimental Psychology: Animal Behavior Processes, 8,* 354–375.

Shimp, C. P. (1976) Short-term memory in the pigeon: Relative recency. *Journal of the Experimental Analysis of Behavior, 25,* 55–61.

Silver, R., & Bittman, E. L. (1984) *Reproductive mechanisms: Interaction of circadian and interval timing.* In J. Gibbon & L. Allan (Eds.), *Timing and time perception.* New York: Annals of the New York Academy of Sciences, vol. 423, 488–514.

Skinner, B. F. (1931) The concept of the reflex in the description of behavior. *Journal of General Psychology, 5,* 427–458.

Skinner, B. F. (1934) The extinction of chained reflexes. *Proceedings of the National Academy of Science, 20,* 234–237.

Skinner, B. F. (1935) Two types of conditioned reflex and a pseudotype. *Journal of General Psychology, 12,* 66–77.

Skinner, B. F. (1938) *The Behavior of organisms.* New York: Appleton-Century-Crofts.

Skinner, B. F. (1948) "Superstition" in the pigeon. *Journal of Experimental Psychology, 38,* 168–172.

Skinner, B. F. (1950) Are theories of learning necessary? *Psychological Review, 57,* 193–216.

Skinner, B. F. (1956) A case history in scientific method. *American Psychologist, 11,* 221–233.

Skinner, B. F. (1957) *Verbal behavior.* New York: Appleton-Century-Crofts.

Skinner, B. F. (1961) *Cumulative record.* New York: Appleton-Century-Crofts.

Skinner, B. F. (1974) *About behaviorism.* New York: Knopf.

Skinner, B. F. (1978) Why I am not a cognitive psychologist. In B. F. Skinner, *Reflections on behaviorism and society.* Englewood Cliffs, N.J.: Prentice Hall, 97–112.

Skinner, B. F. (1984) Canonical papers of B. F. Skinner. *The Behavioral and Brain Sciences, 7,* 473–724.

Small, W. S. (1901) Experimental study of the mental processes of the rat. *American Journal of Psychology, 12,* 206–239.

Smith, J. C., & Roll, D. L. (1967) Trace conditioning with X-rays as the aversive stimulus. *Psychonomic Science, 9,* 11–12.

Smith, M. C. (1968) CS-US interval and US intensity in classical conditioning of the rabbit's nictitating membrane response. *Journal of Comparative and Physiological Psychology, 66,* 679–687.

Smith, W. J. (1977) *The Behavior of communicating.* Cambridge, Mass.: Harvard University Press.

Solomon, R. L., & Turner, L. H. (1962) Discriminative classical conditioning in dogs paralyzed by curare can later control discriminative avoidance response in the normal state. *Psychological Review, 69,* 202–219.

Spear, N. E. (1973) Retrieval of memory in animals. *Psychological Review, 80,* 163–194.

Spear, N. E. (1976) Retrieval of memories. In W. K. Estes (Ed.), *Handbook of learning and cognitive processes, vol. 4: Attention and memory.* Hillsdale, N.J.: Erlbaum, 17–90.

Spence, K. W. (1936) The nature of discrimination learning in animals. *Psychological Review, 43,* 427–449.

Spence, K. W. (1937) The differential response in animals to stimuli varying within a single dimension. *Psychological Review, 44,* 430–444.

Spence, K. W. (1945) An experimental test of continuity and non-continuity theories of discrimination learning. *Journal of Experimental Psychology, 35,* 253–266.

Spence, K. W. (1952) The nature of the response in discrimination learning. *Psychological Review, 59,* 89–93.

Squire, L. R. (1983) Memory and the brain. In S. Friedman, K. Klivington, & R. Peterson (Eds.), *Brain, cognition and education.* New York: Academic Press.

Staddon, J. E. R. (1983) *Adaptive behavior and learning.* New York: Oxford University Press.

Staddon, J. E. R. (1984) Time and memory. In J. Gibbon & L. Allan (Eds.), *Timing and time perception.* New York: Annals of the New York Academy of Sciences, vol. 423, 322–334.

Staddon, J. E. R., & Simmelhag, V. L. (1971) The "superstition" experiment: A reexamination of its implications for the principles of reinforcement. *Psychological Review, 78*, 3–43.

Straub, R. O., & Terrace, H. S. (1981) Generalization of serial learning in the pigeon. *Animal Learning and Behavior, 9*, 454–468.

Straub, R. O. (1979) *Serial learning and representation of a sequence in the pigeon.* Ph.D. dissertation, New York: Columbia University.

Straub, R. O., Seidenberg, M. S., Bever, T. G., & Terrace, H. S. (1979) Serial learning in the pigeon. *Journal of the Experimental Analysis of Behavior, 32,* 137–148.

Stubbs, A. (1968) The discrimination of stimulus duration by pigeons. *Journal of the Experimental Analysis of Behavior, 11,* 223–238.

Stubbs, A. (1969) Contiguity of briefly presented stimuli with food reinforcement. *Journal of the Experimental Analysis of Behavior, 12,* 271–278.

Stubbs, A. (1976) Response bias and the discrimination of stimulus duration. *Journal of the Experimental Analysis of Behavior, 25,* 243–250.

Stubbs, D. A., Dreyfus, L. R., & Fetterman, J. G. (1984) The perception of temporal events. In J. Gibbon & L. Allan (Eds.), *Timing and time perception.* New York: Annals of the New York Academy of Sciences, vol. 423, 30–42.

Sutherland, N. S., & Mackintosh, N. J. (1971) *Mechanisms of animal discrimination learning.* New York: Academic Press.

Suzuki, S., Augerinos, G., & Black, A. H. (1980) Stimulus control of spatial behavior on the eight-arm maze in rats. *Learning and Motivation, 11,* 1–18.

Terman, M., Gibbon, J., Fairhurst, S., & Waring, A. (1984) Daily meal anticipation: Interaction of circadian and interval timing. In J. Gibbon & L. Allan (Eds.), *Timing and time perception.* New York: Annals of the New York Academy of Sciences, vol. 423, 470–487.

Terrace, H. S. (1979) *Nim.* New York: Knopf.

Terrace, H. S. (1981) Animal versus human minds. *The Behavioral and Brain Sciences, 5,* 391–392.

Terrace, H. S. (1982) Can animals think? *New Society,* 1982, 4 March, 339–343.

Terrace, H. S. (1984) Animal cognition. In H. L. Roitblat, T. G. Bever, & H. S. Terrace (Eds.), *Animal cognition.* Hillsdale, N.J.: Erlbaum, 7–28.

Terrace, H. S., Petitto, L. A., Sanders, R. J., & Bever, T. G. (1979) Can an ape create a sentence? *Science, 206*, 891–902.

Thompson, C. R., & Church, R. M. (1980) An explanation of the language of a chimpanzee. *Science, 208*, 313–314.

Thompson, R. K. R., & Herman, L. M. (1977) Memory for lists of sounds by bottle-nosed dolphins: Convergence of memory process with humans? *Science, 195*, 501–503.

Thorndike, E. L. (1898) Animal intelligence: An experimental study of the associative processes in animals. *Psychological Review Monograph Supplements, 2*(8), 1–109.

Thorndike, E. L. (1901) The intelligence of monkeys. *Popular Science Monthly, 59*(3), 273–279.

Thorndike, E. L. (1911) *Animal intelligence: Experimental studies.* New York: Macmillan.

Thorpe, W. H. (1974) *Animal nature and human nature.* Garden City, N.Y.: Anchor.

Tinbergen, L. (1960) The natural control of insects in a pinewoods. I. Factors influencing the intensity of predation. *Archives Neerlandaises de Zoologie, 13*, 265–343.

Tinbergen, N. (1951) *The study of instinct.* Oxford: Oxford University Press.

Tinklepaugh, O. L. (1928) An experimental study of representative factors in monkeys. *Journal of Comparative Psychology, 8*, 197–236.

Tolman, E. C., & Honzik, C. H. (1930a) Degrees of hunger, reward and non-reward, and maze learning in rats. *University of California Publications in Psychology, 4*, 241–256.

Tolman, E. C., & Honzik, C. H. (1930b) Introduction and removal of reward and maze performance in rats. *University of California Publications in Psychology, 4*, 257–275.

Tolman, E. C. (1932) *Purposive behavior in animals and men.* New York: Century.

Tolman, E. C. (1936) Connectionism; Wants, interests, and attitudes. *Character and Personality, 4*, 245–253.

Tolman, E. C. (1938) The determiners of behavior at a choice point. *Psychological Review, 45*, 1–41.

Tolman, E. C. (1948) Cognitive maps in rats and men. *Psychological Review, 55*, 189–208.

Tolman, E. C. (1959) Principles of purposive behavior. In S. Koch (Ed.), *Psychology: A study of science*. New York: McGraw-Hill, 92–157.

Tolman, E. C., Ritchie, B. F., & Kalish, D. (1946) Studies in spatial learning I. Orientation and the short-cut. *Journal of Experimental Psychology, 36*, 13–24.

Tomback, D. F. (1977) Foraging strategies of Clark's nutcrackers. *Living Bird, 18*, 123–161.

Tomback, D. F. (1980) How nutcrackers find their seed stores. *Condor, 32*, 10–19.

Tomback, D. F. (1983) Nutcrackers and pines: Coevolution or coadaptation? In H. Nitecki (Ed.), *Coevolution*. Chicago: University of Chicago Press, 179–223.

Tranberg, D. K., & Rilling, M. (1980) Delay-interval illumination changes interfere with pigeon short-term memory. *Journal of the Experimental Analysis of Behavior, 33*, 39–49.

Trapold, M. A. (1970) Are expectancies based upon different positive reinforcing events discriminably different? *Learning and Motivation, 1*, 129–140.

Tulving, E. (1972) Episodic and semantic memory. In E. Tulving & W. Donaldson (Eds.), *Organization of memory*. New York: Academic, 381–403.

Turing, A. M. (1936). On computable numbers, with an application to the Entscheidungs problem. *Proceedings of the London Mathematics Society (Series 2) 42*, 230–265.

Turrisi, F. D., Shepp, B. E., & Eimas, P. D. (1969) Intra- and extra-dimensional shifts with constant- and variable-irrelevant dimensions in the rat. *Psychonomic Science, 14*, 19–20.

Uexkull, J. von (1934) Streifzuge durch die Umwelten von Tieren un Menshcen. Translated in C. H. Schiller (Ed.), *Instinctive Behaviour*. London: Methuen.

Underwood, B. J. (1969) Attributes of memory. *Psychological Review, 76*, 559–573.

Van Iersal, J. J., & Van den Assem, J. (1965) Aspects of orientation in the diggerwasp *Bembix rostrata*. *Animal Behavior Supplements, 1*.

Vander Wall, S. B. (1982) An experimental analysis of cache recovery in Clark's nutcracker. *Animal Behavior, 30*, 84–94.

Vander Wall, S. B., & Balda, R. P. (1977) Coadaptations of the Clark's nutcracker and the piñon pine for efficient seed harvest and dispersal. *Ecological Monographs, 47*, 89–111.

Vandercar, D. H., & Schneiderman, N. (1967) Interstimulus interval functions in different response systems during classical discrimination conditioning of rabbits. *Psychonomic Science, 9*, 9–10.

Voeks, V. W. (1950) Formalization and clarification of a theory of learning. *Journal of Psychology, 30,* 341–363.

Waage, J. K. (1979) Foraging for patchily distributed hosts by the parisitoid, *Nemeritis canescens. Journal of Animal Ecology, 48,* 353–371.

Wagner, A. R. (1981) SOP: A model of automatic memory processing in animal behavior. In N. E. Spear & R. R. Miller (Eds.), *Information processing in animals: Memory mechanisms.* Hillsdale, N.J.: Erlbaum.

Walker, J. A., & Olton, D. S. (1979) The role of response and reward in spatial memory. *Learning and Motivation, 10,* 73–84.

Walker, S. (1983) *Animal thought.* London: Routledge & Kegan Paul.

Wasserman, E. A. (1984) Animal intelligence: Understanding the minds of animals through their behavioral ambassadors. In H. L. Roitblat, T. G. Bever, & H. S. Terrace (Eds.), *Animal cognition.* Hillsdale, N.J.: Erlbaum.

Waterman, D. A., & Hayes-Roth, F. (Eds.) (1978) *Pattern directed inference systems.* New York: Academic Press.

Watson, J. B. (1907) Kinaesthetic and organic sensations: Their role in the reactions of the white rat to the maze. *Psychological Monographs, 8* (2, whole number 33).

Watson, J. B. (1925) *Behaviorism.* New York: Norton.

Watson, J. B. (1914) *Behavior: An Introduction to Comparative Psychology.* New York: Holt, Rinehart & Winston.

Watson, R. I. (1965) The historical background of national trends in psychology. *Journal of the History of the Behavioral Sciences, 1,* 130–138.

Weimer, W. B. (1979) *Notes on the Methodology of Scientific Research.* Hillsdale, N.J.: Erlbaum.

Weisman, R. G., Wasserman, E. A., Dodd, P. W., & Larew, M. B. (1980) Representation and retention of two-event sequences in pigeons. *Journal of Experimental Psychology: Animal Behavior Processes, 6,* 312–325.

Weiss, P. (1941) Self-differentiation of the basic patterns of coordination. *Comparative Psychology Monographs, 17*(4).

Werner, G. E., & Hall, D. J. (1974) Optimal foraging and size selection of prey by the bluegill sunfish (*Lepomis macrochirus*). *Ecology, 55,* 1042–1052.

Wessells, M. G. (1973) Errorless discrimination, autoshaping, and conditioned inhibition. *Science, 182,* 941–943.

Wessells, M. G. (1982) A critique of Skinner's views on the obstructive character of cognitive theories. *Behaviorism, 10,* 65–84.

Wessells, M. G. (1984) Unusual terminology or unusual metatheory: A reply to Professor Landwehr. *Behaviorism, 11,* 193–198.

Wickens, D. D. (1938) The transference of conditioned excitation and conditioned inhibition from one muscle group to the antagonistic group. *Journal of Experimental Psychology, 22,* 101–123.

Williams, D. R. (1965) Classical conditioning and incentive motivation. In W. F. Prokasy (Ed.), *Classical conditioning: A symposium.* New York: Appleton-Century-Crofts, 340–357.

Williams, D. R., & Williams, H. (1969) Auto-maintenance in the pigeon: Sustained pecking despite contingent non-reinforcement. *Journal of the Experimental Analysis of Behavior, 12,* 511–520.

Wilson, E. O. (1976) *Sociobiology.* Cambridge, Mass.: Harvard University Press.

Winefield, A. H., & Jeeves, M. A. (1971) The effect of overtraining on transfer between tasks involving the same stimulus dimension. *Quarterly Journal of Experimental Psychology, 23,* 234–242.

Wolff, J. L. (1967) Concept-shift and discrimination-reversal learning in humans. *Psychological Bulletin, 68,* 369–408.

Woodard, W. T., Schoel, W. M., & Bitterman, M. E. (1971) Reversal learning with singly presented stimuli in pigeons and goldfish. *Journal of Comparative and Physiological Psychology, 76,* 460–467.

Woodruff, G., & Premack, D. (1979) Intentional communication in the chimpanzee: The development of deception, *Cognition, 7,* 333–362.

Worsham, R. W. (1975) Temporal discrimination factors in the delayed matching-to-sample task in monkeys. *Animal Learning and Behavior, 3,* 93–97.

Wright, A. A., Santiago, H. C., Sands, S. F., & Urcuioli, P. J. (1982) Pigeon and monkey serial probe recognition: Acquisition, strategies, and serial position effects. In H. L. Roitblat, T. G. Bever, & H. S. Terrace (Eds.), *Animal cognition.* Hillsdale, N.J.: Erlbaum, 353–373.

Yerkes, R. M. (1925) *Chimpanzee intelligence and its vocal expression.* Baltimore: Williams & Wilkins.

Yerkes, R. M., & Yerkes, A. (1929) *The great apes: A study of anthropoid life.* New Haven, Conn.: Yale University Press.

Zach, R. (1978) Selection and dropping of whelks by northwestern crows. *Behaviour, 67,* 134–148.

Zach, R. (1979) Shell dropping: Decision making and optimal foraging in northwestern crows. *Behaviour, 68,* 106–117.

Zach, R., & Smith, J. N. M. (1981) Optimal foraging in wild birds? In A. C. Kamil & T. D. Sargent (Eds.), *Foraging behavior: Ecological, ethological, and psychological approaches*. New York: Garland, 95–109.

Zach, R., & Falls, J. B. (1979) Foraging and territoriality of male ovenbirds (*Aves: Parulidae*) in a heterogeneous habitat. *Journal of Animal Ecology, 48,* 32–52.

Zahorik, D. M., & Houpt, K. A. (1981) Species differences in feeding strategies, food hazards, and the ability to learn food aversions. In A. C. Kamil & T. D. Sargent (Eds.), *Foraging behavior: Ecological, ethological, and psychological approaches*. New York: Garland, 289–310.

Zamble, E. (1967) Classical conditioning of excitement anticipatory to food reward. *Journal of Comparative and Physiological Psychology, 63,* 526–529.

Zeaman, D., & House, B. J. (1963) The role of attention in retardate discrimination learning. In N. R. Ellis (Ed.), *Handbook of mental deficiency: Psychological theory and research*. New York: McGraw-Hill, 159–223.

Zentall, T. R. (1973) Memory in the pigeon: Retroactive inhibition in a delayed matching task. *Bulletin of the Psychonomic Society, 1,* 126–128.

Zentall, T. R., Edwards, C. A., Moore, B. S., & Hogan, D. E. (1981) Identity: The basis for both matching and oddity learning in pigeons. *Journal of Experimental Psychology: Animal Behavior Processes, 7,* 70–86.

Zentall, T. R., & Hogan, D. E. (1974) Abstract concept learning in the pigeon. *Journal of Experimental Psychology, 102,* 393–398.

Zentall, T. R., & Hogan, D. E. (1976) Pigeons can learn identity or difference, or both. *Science, 191,* 408–409.

Zentall, T. R., & Hogan, D. E. (1978) Same/different concept learning in the pigeon: The effect of negative instances and prior adaptation to the transfer stimuli. *Journal of Experimental Analysis of Behavior, 30,* 177–186.

Zentall, T. R., Hogan, D. E., & Edwards, C. A. (1984) Cognitive factors in conditional learning by pigeons. In H. L. Roitblat, T. G. Bever, & H. S. Terrace (Eds.), *Animal cognition*. Hillsdale, N.J.: Erlbaum, 389–405.

Illustration Credits

Figure 1.2
From Shepard, R. N., & Metzler, J. (1971) Mental rotation of 3-D objects. *Science, 171,* 701–703. © 1971 by the AAAS.

Figure 2.2
From Tolman, E. C., & Honzik, C. H. (1930) Introduction and removal of reward and maze performance in rats. *University of California Publications in Psychology, 4,* 257–275.

Figure 3.1
From Woodard, W. T., Schoel, W. M., & Bitterman, M. E. (1971) Reversal learning with singly presented stimuli in pi-geons and goldfish. *Journal of Comparative and Physiological Psychology, 76,* 460–467. Copyright 1976 by the American Psychological Association. Reprinted by permission of the author.

Figure 3.2
From Levine, M. (1970) Human discrimination learning: The subset-sampling assumption. *Psychological Bulletin, 74,* 397–404. Copyright 1974 by the American Psychological Association. Reprinted by permission of the author.

Figure 3.3
From Sutherland, N. S., & Mackintosh, N. J. (1971) *Mechanisms of animal dis-*

crimination learning. New York: Academic Press. Adapted from Sutherland, N. S. (1964) The learning of discrimination by animals, *Endeavor, 23,* 69–78.

Figure 3.4
From Lindsay, P. H., Taylor, M. M., & Forbes, S. M. (1968) Attention and multidimensional discrimination. *Perception and Psychophysics, 4,* 113–117. Courtesy of the Psychonomic Society.

Figure 3.5
After Blough, D. S. (1969) Attention shifts in maintained discrimination. *Science, 166,* 125–126. © 1969 by the AAAS.

Figure 3.7
From Riley, D. A., Roitblat, H. L. (1978) Selective attention and related cognitive processes in pigeons. In S. H. Hulse, H. Fowler, & W. K. Honig (Eds.), *Cognitive processes in animal behavior.* Hillsdale, N.J.: Erlbaum, 249–276. Copyright 1978 by Lawrence Erlbaum Associates, Inc. Reprinted with permission.

Figure 3.8
From Lamb, M. R., & Riley, D. A. (1981) Effects of element arrangement of the processing of compound stimuli in pigeons (*Columba livia*). *Journal of Experimental Psychology: Animal Behavior Processes, 7,* 45–58. Copyright 1981 by the American Psychological Association. Reprinted by permission of the author.

Figure 5.2A
From Roitblat, H. L., Tham, W., Golub, L. (1982) Performance of *Betta splendens* in a radial arm maze. *Animal Learning and Behavior, 10,* 108–104. Courtesy of the Psychonomic Society.

Figure 5.2B
From Olton, D. S., Collison, C., & Werz, W. A. (1977) Spatial memory and radial arm maze performance by rats. *Learning and Motivation, 8,* 289–314.

Figures 5.7 and 5.8
From Roitblat, H. L. (1982) The meaning of representation in animal memory. *The Behavioral and Brain Sciences, 5,* 353–406. Courtesy of Cambridge University Press.

Figure 5.9
From Roitblat, H. L. (1980) Codes and coding processes in pigeon short-term memory. *Animal Learning and Behavior, 8,* 341–351. Courtesy of the Psychonomic Society.

Figure 5.10
From Roitblat, H. L., & Scopatz, R. A. (1983) Sequential effects in pigeon delayed matching-to-sample performance. *Journal of Experimental Psychology: Animal Behavior Processes, 9,* 202–221. Copyright 1983 by the American Psychological Association. Reprinted by permission of the author.

Figure 6.1
After Dews, P. B. (1962) The effect of multiple SΔ periods on responding on a fixed-interval schedule. *Journal of the Experimental Analysis of Behavior, 5,* 369–374. Copyright 1962 by the Society of the Experimental Analysis of Behavior, Inc.

Figure 6.2
From Stubbs, A. (1968) The discrimination of stimulus duration by pigeons. *Journal of the Experimental Analysis of Behavior, 11,* 223–238. Copyright 1968 by the Society for the Experimental Analysis of Behavior, Inc.

Figure 6.3
From Church, R. M., & Gibbon, J. (1982) Temporal generalization. *Journal of Experimental Psychology: Animal Behavior Processes, 8,* 165–186. Copyright 1982 by the American Psychological Association. Reprinted by permission of the author.

Figure 6.4
From Roberts, S. (1981) Isolation of an internal clock. *Journal of Experimental Psychology: Animal Behavior Processes, 7,* 242–268. Copyright 1981 by the American Psychological Association. Reprinted by permission of the author.

Figure 6.5
From Church, R. M. (1984) Properties of the internal clock. In J. Gibbon & L. Allan (Eds.), *Timing and time perception.* New York: Annals of the New York Academy of Sciences, vol. 423, 566–582.

Figure 6.6
From Roberts, S. (1981) Isolation of an internal clock. *Journal of Experimental Psychology: Animal Behavior Processes, 7,* 242–268. Copyright 1981 by the American Psychological Association. Reprinted by permission of the author.

Figure 6.8
From Hulse, S. H., & Campbell, C. E. (1975) "Thinking ahead" in rat discrimination learning. *Animal Learning and Behavior, 3,* 305–311. Courtesy of the Psychonomic Society.

Figure 7.1A
From Zach, R. (1978) Selection and dropping of whelks by northwestern crows. *Behaviour, 67,* 134–148. Courtesy of E. J. Brill, Leiden.

Figure 7.1B
From Zach, R. (1979) Shell dropping: Decision making and optimal foraging in northwestern crows. *Behaviour, 68,* 106–117. Courtesy of E. J. Brill, Leiden.

Figure 7.2
From Davies, N. B. (1977) Prey selection and social behaviour in wagtails (Aves: Motacillidae). *Journal of Animal Ecology, 46,* 37–57. Courtesy of Blackwell Scientific Publications Limited.

Figure 7.3
From Roitblat, H. L. (1982) Decision making, evolution, and cognition. In H. D. Schmidt & G. Tembrock (Eds.), *Evolution and determination of animal and human behavior.* Berlin, GDR: VEB Deutscher Verlag der Wissenschaften, 108–116. Courtesy of North-Holland Publishing Company, Amsterdam.

Figures 7.4A, 7.4B, and 7.5
From Shettleworth, S. J. (1983) Memory in food hoarding birds. *Scientific American, 248*(3), 102–111. Copyright © 1983 by Scientific American, Inc. All rights reserved. Photograph in Figure 7.4 by S. Vander Wall.

Figure 7.6
From Pietrewicz, A. T., & Kamil, A. C. (1981) Search images and the detection of cryptic prey: An operant approach. In A. C. Kamil & T. D. Sargent (Eds.), *Foraging behavior: Ecological, ethological, and psychological approaches.* New York: Garland, 311–332.

Figure 7.8
From Seyfarth, R. M., & Cheney, D. L. (1980) The ontogeny of vervet monkey alarm calling behavior: A preliminary report. *Zeitschrift fur Tierpsychologie, 54,* 37–56.

Figure 8.3
From Savage-Rumbaugh, E. S., Pate, J. L., Lawson, J., Smith, S. T., & Rosenbaum, S. (1983) Can a chimpanzee make a statement? *Journal of Experimental Psychology: General, 112,* 457–492. Copyright 1983 by the American Psychological Association. Reprinted by permission of the author.

Figures 8.4 and 8.5
From Herman, L. M., Richards, D. G., & Wolz, J. P. (1984) Comprehension of sentences by bottlenosed dolphins. *Cognition,*

16, 129–219. Courtesy of North-Holland Publishing Company, Amsterdam.

Figure 8.6
From Cerella, J. (1979) Visual classes and natural categories in the pigeon: *Journal of Experimental Psychology: Human Perception and Performance, 5,* 68–77. Copyright 1979 by the American Psychological Association. Reprinted by permission of the author.

Figure 8.7
Based on drawings in Keeton, *Biological Science,* 2d ed. New York: Norton.

Figures 8.8 and 8.9
Adapted from Premack, D., & Premack, A. J. (1983) *The mind of an ape.* New York: Norton.

Name Index

Subject Index